Teaching Italian American Literature, Film, and Popular Culture

Modern Language Association of America
Options for Teaching

For a complete listing of titles,
see the last pages of this book.

Teaching Italian American Literature, Film, and Popular Culture

Edited by
Edvige Giunta
and
Kathleen Zamboni McCormick

The Modern Language Association of America
New York   2010

MLA and the MODERN LANGUAGE ASSOCIATION are trademarks
owned by the Modern Language Association of America. For information about
obtaining permission to reprint material from MLA book publications, send
your request by mail (see address below), e-mail (permissions@mla.org), or fax
(646 458-0030).

Library of Congress Cataloging-in-Publication Data

Teaching Italian American literature, film, and popular culture / edited by
Edvige Giunta and Kathleen Zamboni McCormick.
    p. cm.—(Options for teaching, ISSN 1079-2562 ; 28)
  Includes bibliographical references and index.
  ISBN 978-1-60329-066-1 (hardcover : alk. paper)
  ISBN 978-1-60329-067-8 (pbk. : alk. paper)
  1. American literature—Italian American authors—Study and teaching.
2. Italian Americans in literature—Study and teaching. 3. Italian Americans
in motion pictures—Study and teaching. 4. Italian Americans—Intellectual
life—Study and teaching. I. Giunta, Edvige. II. McCormick, Kathleen.
  PS153.I8T43 2010
  810.9'8510730711—dc22   2009051332

Options for Teaching 28
ISSN 1079-2562

Cover illustration of the paperback edition: Photograph from the collection of
Maria and Manfredo DiCesare.

Printed on recycled paper

Published by The Modern Language Association of America
26 Broadway, New York, NY 10004-1789
www.mla.org

This book is dedicated to Cettina Minasola Giunta and Edith Ruth Zamboni. We are grateful for our mothers' teaching and their love.

Contents

Acknowledgments

Since its inception in 2003, this project has undergone many changes. It has grown and finally come to its completion thanks to the work, support, and inspiration provided by many people.

First and foremost, we would like to express our gratitude to Joseph Gibaldi, former director of Book Acquisitions and Development at the Modern Language Association, who believed in this project and whose enthusiasm, faith, and invaluable insights have shaped this book in major ways. We are especially grateful to Nancy Carnevale for her detailed reading of drafts of the introduction and extensive bibliographic suggestions on the history of Italian emigration. We also want to acknowledge Jacqueline Ellis, coeditor of *Transformations: The Journal of Inclusive Scholarship and Pedagogy*, for her helpful comments on the introduction. Kathleen McCormick thanks Mary Saracino for the gift of her wonderful book *The Singing of Swans*, which came at just the right time to provide the motivation for that final push to complete the manuscript.

The contributors to the volume have been incredibly gracious and patient through several years of work that have required countless revisions. Extensive work lies behind the many short gems of essays in this volume. Our contributors' knowledge of and dedication to the field of Italian American studies and their faith that the process of teaching can truly change minds have motivated them to commit to a project that at times seemed daunting and never-ending. We want to thank them for their fine work.

We—and all the contributors—want to thank our students. It is in our classrooms that we have seen what powerful results the numerous pedagogies we offer in this book are capable of producing and have witnessed firsthand the importance and relevance of Italian American studies to students of all backgrounds.

During the process of our conceptualizing and writing this book, many other babies have been born. We want to acknowledge and welcome into this world Andrew Coello, Chiara Di Nardo Di Maio, Adrian Galletta, Maia Galletta, Zoe Galletta, Michaelangelo Gardaphé, Maddalena Romeo Lehmann, Gianna Fortuna Limongello, Gabriele Julian Pettener, Maria Pettener, and Luca Poldi. We have also lost many family members, often some of the people who have most motivated us to engage in Italian American studies. We recognize and thank Alberto Del Giudice, Giovanni Labate, Edith Ruth

Zamboni McCormick, Nunziatina Nuncibello Minasola, Peppina Morabito, Andrea Ossip, Natalina Sollazzo, and Helen Fowler Tuttle.

We would like to thank Sonia Kane, assistant director of publications at the MLA. Although she came late into the project, she took it on with the commitment necessary to bring it to publication. We are grateful to the outside readers of the manuscript and to the MLA Publications Committee members who offered numerous suggestions in the drafting stages of the book. Special thanks also go to Sara Pastel for her excellent copyediting and to Hannah Wolfson for indexing the book in such a timely fashion.

Finally, we would like to thank our families, especially our husbands. Edvige Giunta would like to thank Joshua Fausty, life companion and intellectual partner, for being her greatest source of support. He was the first to believe in this project, even when it was a barely formed idea. Throughout its several stages, he has been a patient and inspiring listener, whose ideas and comments have made this book better. Kathleen McCormick thanks Gary Waller for his endless patience, love, and suggestions and for his willingness to cook wonderful meals while she kept on writing and editing. Gary, you nourish the soul as well as the mind and the body. Our children, Emily, Matteo, and Philip, have graciously shared their mothers with the demands that a book brings and have motivated us to edit a collection that may influence a class they take in college.

**Edvige Giunta and
Kathleen Zamboni McCormick**

Introduction

*There is a sense in which Italian Americans do not know who they
are, either as Italians or Americans.... [A] recovery of historical
memory [must be] an attempt to do justice to the experience of multiple identity under unjust circumstances hostile to self-respecting
assertions of identity.*

—David A. J. Richards,
Italian American: The Racializing of an Ethnic Identity

"Where Is Italian American Literature?"

In 1993, the *New York Times* published the now notorious article by Gay
Talese "Where Are the Italian-American Novelists?" in which Talese la-
mented the scarcity of great works of Italian American literature. The article prompted a strong reaction by many Italian American scholars and
writers, who accused Talese of being uninformed, some arguing that the
question he should have asked was not "where are the novelists?" but
"why are the novelists ignored?" (Tamburri, "Beyond 'Pizza'" 155). The
journal *Italian Americana* invited Italian American intellectuals to offer
their responses in "a candid exchange with Talese's essay" (Gioia, "Low

1

Visibility" 10). Dana Gioia, then the poetry editor of the journal, participated in this exchange and disagreed with many of Talese's points, especially his description of "*static* attributes" that defined Italian Americans, such as his claim that "the solitary nature of writing has made it less attractive to Italian Americans," whom he regarded as "essentially . . . village dwellers" (Gioia, "Low Visibility" 10). Yet Gioia also reluctantly agreed with Talese's "carefully worded" argument that "[t]here is no *widely-recognized* body of literature dealing with Italian American immigration" (8). Italian American literature, Gioia argued, "is nearly invisible in terms of cultural presence. . . . [T]hese books [are] not read by the general public; most of them aren't read within the Italian American community" (8).

Over a century of Italian American writing existed before Talese asked his question, and extensive scholarly work on Italian American history, literature, film, and popular culture has been produced since he posed it (see in this volume Aleandri; Bona; Covino; Del Giudice; Gabaccia; Romeo; Sciorra; Taviano; Tamburri; Viscusi). Nevertheless, the question of recognition raised by Talese remains. Italian American literature has only recently begun to attain recognition, especially in comparison with other ethnic and emerging American literatures, an instructive comparison for those considering Italian American literature as a key strand among them (Giunta, *Writing* 1–7).

In the explosion of Italian American scholarly, creative, and archival work since 1980, scholars and writers have still found it necessary to foreground questions of recognition, visibility, and recovery in their critical assessment of Italian American literature (Barolini, *Dream Book*; Bona, *Claiming*; Gardaphé, *Italian Signs*; Giunta, *Writing*; Guida, *Peasant*; Mannino and Vitiello; Tamburri, *Semiotic*; Viscusi, *Buried Caesars*). What scholars have been recovering—and what we hope will enter American cultural history, particularly in our classrooms—is over one hundred years of Italian American history and literary production, events and works that often played a significant role in their particular cultural moment but have been largely forgotten. Not only does their recovery provide us with a rich literature, but it also helps create a more complex understanding of American history and culture.

Italian American authors have achieved national or international recognition when their novels have been adapted for the screen, as in Tom Perrotta's *Election*, made into a film by Alexander Payne, or Beverly Donofrio's *Riding in Cars with Boys*, adapted by the Italian American director

Penny Marshall. Others have become known through their involvement with literary groups, like the beat poets Lawrence Ferlinghetti, Gregory Corso, and Diane di Prima (Quinn). Some are known for their experimental writing, like Carole Maso (Gardaphé, *Italian Signs* 141–49), Cris Mazza, Mary Caponegro (Gardaphé, *Italian Signs* 192–98), and Leslie Scalapino. Don DeLillo is a well-known Italian American writer, but his work is not easily classified as Italian American: Daniel Aaron argues that in DeLillo's novels "hardly a vibration betrays an ethnic consciousness" (68), though scholars such as Fred Gardaphé and John Paul Russo have written extensively about DeLillo as an Italian American author (Gardaphé, *Italian Signs* 172–92; see Russo's essay in this volume). For too many readers, however, Mario Puzo remains *the* Italian American author best known by a wide academic and nonacademic readership, though the iconic status of Francis Ford Coppola's three-part film adaptation of *The Godfather* remains largely responsible for Puzo's international recognition.

There has also been a significant growth in the number of Italian American studies programs and courses on Italian American culture in colleges and universities in the United States; at the same time, many nonspecialists have become increasingly interested in incorporating Italian American texts into their courses both in the United States and in Italy. Nevertheless, many educators—teaching courses in American literature, American history, ethnic literature, women's literature, memoir, working-class literature, and other subjects—can be heard asking a variation of the question Talese asked over fifteen years ago: Where is Italian American literature?

This volume gathers the perspectives and pedagogical experiences of over thirty scholars and teachers of Italian American studies who offer answers to that question. The contributors propose innovative ways of teaching Italian American texts and integrating them with other texts in a wide array of courses. For novices to the field, the volume also serves as an introduction to historically and culturally informed ways of reading Italian America and to many types of Italian American texts, including fiction, poetry, memoir, theater, performance, film, oral histories, and television. If these texts are introduced into classrooms, if students find them compelling and helpful in constructing a new narrative of American life, and if students leave the class wanting to read more, then the process of recovering an intellectual and ethnic past is fully under way. This book aims to facilitate such a process for Italian American literature and culture.

The Italian American Immigrant Experience

> *The most difficult thing to get hold of, in studying any past period,*
> *is th[e] felt sense of the quality of life at a particular place and time:*
> *a sense of the ways in which the particular activities combined into*
> *a way of thinking and living. . . . [W]e are most conscious of such*
> *contact in the arts of a period.*
>
> —Raymond Williams, *The Long Revolution*

The Early Immigrants

The material conditions of a group dramatically affect its cultural productions—its self-representations as well as its representations by others. Literature and the arts make it possible to recover and critically understand a forgotten, even repressed, historical past. Historical narratives alone, while vital, cannot provide the kind of creative revision necessary for an ethnic group to achieve cultural legitimacy and dignity, as African American writers have learned—and taught other American ethnic groups. Italian American literature, too, helps create a cultural tradition and a sense of a collective identity and shared past. The recovery of many forgotten moments in Italian American history promotes a better understanding of Italian American literature; conversely, the literature promotes a recovery and a better understanding of the history.

We provide here three historical snapshots, that is, three examples of recovered Italian American history: the 1891 lynching of eleven Italian Americans, which presents a starkly clear picture of the entanglement of Italian Americans in American racial issues; the Triangle Shirtwaist Factory fire of 1911, which brings into focus the place of Italian Americans in the hierarchies of social class; and the Sacco and Vanzetti case of the 1920s, an important moment for exploring Italian traditions of political radicalism and their position in the larger American political landscape. The initial recovery of an event leads to further work, both historical and creative, in the present, with broader ramifications and greater awareness of the links between Italian Americans and other Americans. We emphasize the interconnectedness between the creation of literary texts and historical recovery. In our discussions of these snapshots, we suggest connections to other related events or issues—such as the murder of Yusuf Hawkins in Bensonhurst in 1989 and the debate over Columbus Day—that in different ways have become the catalysts for a more active and clearly articulated Italian American progressive and antiracist political vision.

Fourteen million Italians left Italy between 1876 and 1914. According to the 1850 census, there were 3,545 Italians living in the United States. In 1910, that number rose to 1,345,125 (Russo, "From Italophilia" 69). The 2005–07 American Community Survey indicated that Italian Americans made up over 17,760,000—approximately 6%—of the United States population (2,800,000 in New York State alone, where they constitute the state's largest ethnic group). "Who are the Italian Americans?" "What is Italian American literature?" Answering these questions necessitates a brief reconstruction of the stories of the Italians who first entered the United States and the expectations about Italy and Italians that preceded and, in a sense, greeted them there.

Most Italians who left Italy for America did not think of themselves as Italians. Their cultural identities were tied to the villages and towns from which they came. Italy was a new nation, but the annexation of the south had not fulfilled the promise of better living conditions for the majority of its population. The unification of Italy in 1861 had paradoxically resulted in further political and social fragmentation, which directly affected the Italians who would come to America. The Risorgimento enabled northern Italy to more easily exploit southern Italy. In the introduction to his translation of Antonio Gramsci's *The Southern Question* Pasquale Verdicchio writes that in 1860, after Giuseppe Garibaldi's so-called liberation of Sicily and the south from Bourbon rule,

> [i]t soon became obvious to the Southern masses that the effort was to benefit them much less than they had been led to believe. The collaboration of Northern "liberators" with Southern landowners further rooted the imbalances that had been established by the Bourbons. (4)

This collaboration intensified the problems of the destitute population of the rural south. The agrarian crisis that hit Europe in 1880, mainly due to the import of cheap Russian and American grain, caused a dramatic surge in migration from the Italian south (Astarita 288–89).

Environmental disasters and the scarcity of water, together with the brutal oppression of a still feudal agricultural economy, propelled great numbers of southern Italians to leave, at first temporarily, as migrants and later, in greater numbers, as settlers (Cinel; Gabaccia, *From Sicily*; La Sorte;

Mangione and Morreale; Von Drehle 108; Yans-McLaughlin). In the late nineteenth century, in works such as *I malavoglia* (*The House by the Medlar Tree*), the Sicilian verist writer Giovanni Verga powerfully depicted the abject living conditions of the poor of the Italian south that led to the massive migration (De Vito; Guida, *Peasant*). At the beginning of the twenty-first century, the Italian American author Louise DeSalvo wrote of the droughts that turned the Italian south into a wasteland and propelled so many to leave, including her grandfather, who

> lived in Puglia when whatever potable water was available was sold to the poor at exorbitant prices; when much of the water of Puglia was tainted and undrinkable; when much of the water of Puglia was standing water, which bred mosquitoes, which gave the people of Puglia malaria, which killed the people of Puglia in astonishing numbers. ("'Mbriago" 5)

For the poor of the south, "America beckoned" (4). Economically and politically disenfranchised—literacy and land ownership requirements made about 70% of Sicilian men ineligible to vote as late as 1912 (Astarita 287)—people left Italy to rescue themselves from the brutality and hopelessness of their lives in their native country.

Leaving was not painless, and America did not simply represent a place of hope. Men were frequently the first to emigrate, often leaving wives and children behind. In her story "La Merica," the Sicilian writer Maria Messina offers an eloquent description of what America represented in southern Italy, where so many experienced the traumatic separation, often permanent, not only from their place of birth but also from their immediate family: "*La Merica* is a woodworm that eats away at things, a sickness that attacks, and when the time comes for a man to buy a suitcase, there's nothing that can hold him back" (34). Repeatedly, in Italian American literature, we find characters, male and female, described as suffering from physical and mental illnesses and even the mutilation of limbs (Bryant; Cappello; De Rosa, *Paper Fish*; DeSalvo, *Vertigo*; Hendin, *Right Thing*; Ragusa, "Baked Ziti"; the films *Baggage* [Lloyd], *Fuori/Outside* [Ragusa], and *Household Saints* [Savoca]). Often, these characters are not the immigrants themselves but their children and descendants.

> The illnesses—physical and social—that affect the characters and narrators in these texts foreground the trauma of emigration as an injury, and the ethnic subject as the inarticulate storyteller who must learn how to develop a language to tell her stories. (Giunta, "They")

Over a century after the mass migration, Italian American women writers depict the irrevocable sense of loss and disconnection that their female ancestors experienced and passed on to the later generations (Barolini, *Umbertina*; DeSalvo, *Crazy*; Giunta, "Persephone's Daughters"; Ragusa, *Skin*).

In the early stages of their immigration to the United States, Italians faced harsh work conditions, prejudice, and discrimination. As Donna R. Gabaccia writes in the opening essay of this book, "By the time Ellis Island opened to guard the gates of the United States in 1892, few middle-class Americans viewed the Italians passing through its halls as representatives of a superior European civilization." In 1888, the United States consul in Naples wrote:

> [T]he persons emigrated from this country to the United States during the last two years belong to the poorest and most ignorant classes; they are without any school education and with few exceptions are unable to write their names; they have no conception of our institutions and form of Government. . . . Of the persons emigrating to the United States from here 85 or 90 per cent are farm hands.
> (qtd. in Astarita 289–90)

The first Italian immigrants were neither the makers of high culture—the imagined descendants of Dante, Boccaccio, or Petrarch, Italians revered by Americans such as Henry James, Washington Irving, and Nathaniel Hawthorne (see Kvidera in this volume)—nor the barbarians they were made out to be by the northern Italian scientific positivists such as Alfredo Niceforo and Giuseppe Sergi, the criminologist Cesare Lombroso, or the American Edward C. Banfield and his theory of amoral familism (Banfield; P. D'Agostino; see Gabaccia, in this volume and "Race" 52, 54; Gibson; T. Guglielmo, *White on Arrival* 22–23 and "No Color Barrier" 30–35; Guida, *Peasant*; Verdicchio, *Bound*). Early representations of Italian immigrants in postbellum America illustrate, as John Paul Russo explains, a shift "from italophilia to italophobia." Russo calls attention to the oblique but significant comparison William Dean Howells draws between the Italians and the African Americans who moved into the Boston area in the late nineteenth century ("From Italophilia" 55) and points out that the benevolent attitudes Americans had held toward Italian immigrants before the 1880s dramatically changed once Italian immigrants began to settle en masse in the United States and became "Americanized aliens" (59; Richards 181–87).

While northern Italians were regarded as Europeans (though not all those who emigrated from the north were educated or skilled laborers), southern Italian immigrants were considered among the ignorant masses meant for menial labor. By 1899, the United States Bureau of Immigration had classified northern and southern Italians as "distinctive races": northern Italians were recorded as "Keltic" and southern Italians as "Iberic" (T. Guglielmo, "No Color Barrier" 34). In 1911, the United States Commission on Immigration report included the "Dictionary of Races and Peoples," which cataloged northern and southern Italians separately (Jacobson, *Whiteness* 78–80; Roediger, *Working* 4, 16). Southern Italians were also stigmatized as violent criminals and as overly focused on bodily pleasure (see Gabaccia in this volume). Although records on the subject are mixed (La Sorte 45), for many the screening to which the newly arrived were subjected at Ellis Island could be characterized as dehumanizing (Kraut). The film *The Golden Door*, directed by Emanuele Crialese, depicts the culturally biased screening process as embodying a cold professionalism utterly foreign to the immigrants. Psychological testing was also devised to create discriminatory classifications that placed southern Italians at the bottom of the labor hierarchy (E. Messina, "Stereotyping"). Discussing Margaret Mead's research on the use of intelligence tests "to reinforce contemporary notions of racial hierarchy," Nancy Carnevale points out:

> Italians held a decidedly low place in that hierarchy. . . . [Mead] writes that intelligence testing had "allocate[d] to the Italian a place below the negro." But intelligence tests were not only used to justify racialist public policies such as Jim Crow and immigration laws. As Mead noted, average citizens drew upon them to justify popular notions of race. Mead's main concern, however, was with the practice of placing children in the public schools according to their performance on tests which she believed put the children of immigrants at a disadvantage. (57)

Having to choose among limited options, because of their lack of skills and preference for outdoor work, Italian immigrants usually ended up in low-wage, seasonal pick-and-shovel jobs. Immigrant women became homeworkers in the garment industry, took in boarders, and ran family businesses (Vecchio; Soyer). While there were greater opportunities for work in the United States than in Italy, most immigrants continued to find themselves politically and socially disenfranchised.

The 1891 New Orleans Lynching

In New Orleans in 1891, "perceptions of Italians' racial distinctness became deadly" (Jacobson, *Whiteness* 56): eleven Italian Americans were lynched for the alleged murder of the city police superintendent David Hennessey. This is, according to the National Italian American Foundation ("1891"), the largest mass lynching in American history. The lynching was carried out by the White League (a Reconstruction-era version of the KKK) on the grounds of Italian Americans' "*innate* criminality" rather than on any actual evidence (Jacobson, *Whiteness* 56). The bodies of the men were displayed outside the prison and hung on lampposts. In the racial discourse in which this and other events were "comprehended and narrated," the lynching was used as evidence of the eleven men's guilt and was accorded instant approbation by the popular press (56–61).

The day after the lynching, the *New York Times* represented the eleven Italian Americans as follows:

> These sneaking and cowardly Sicilians who have transplanted to this country their lawless passions, the cutthroat practices, and the oath-bound societies of their native country, are to us a pest without mitigation. Our own rattlesnakes are as good citizens as they are.
> (qtd. in Jacobson, *Whiteness* 56)

A lynching that was committed in the American South by a dangerous racist group at the end of the nineteenth century was thus justified in the North by a reputable newspaper within merely a day—a rapid transfer of news that reinforced stereotypes about the dangers that southern Italians posed to the nation. In his essay "Lynch Law and Unrestricted Immigration," published in the *North American Review* soon after the lynching, Congressman Henry Cabot Lodge blamed this and other lynchings on the "dangerous societies" of many immigrant groups against whom law-abiding Americans were trying to protect themselves (Richards 174). Although there was no more evidence connecting the eleven Sicilians to organized crime than there was to link them to Hennessey's murder, Lodge implied that the men lynched in New Orleans were members of the Mafia as well as murderers (Jacobson, *Whiteness* 60). While the Black Hand, an organized Italian crime group, did exist in some Little Italys (T. Guglielmo, *White on Arrival* 78–86), the criminality of an organization composed of a small percentage of Italians was generalized to a whole people. Through this process, Italians came to be known as violent, lower-class criminals—and an invented ethnicity took shape.

There are other issues, of course, to consider—primarily those of race and class. In the late nineteenth century and the early twentieth century, Italian immigrants worked on the plantations of the South alongside African Americans (Scarpaci; Roediger, *Towards the Abolition*). Mary Bucci Bush's novella *Drowning*, inspired by her family history, centers on an Italian immigrant family working on a plantation of the South alongside African Americans at the turn of the century—an example of what David R. Roediger would call "in-among" (*Working* 50). Italians fraternized with local blacks and even intermarried: "From being 'like Negroes' to being 'as bad as Negroes' was but a trifling step in dominant Southern thinking," where Italians could be lynched simply for "violating local racial codes by 'fraternizing' with blacks" (Jacobson, *Whiteness* 57). Such violations may have gotten the eleven Sicilian men lynched in New Orleans.

Roediger argues that "racial categorization and consciousness of race among new immigrants"—including but hardly confined to Italians—in the late nineteenth and early twentieth centuries were "dauntingly complicated." His terms "inbetweenness" and "in-among" attempt to give language to racial categorizations that intermingled biological and cultural attributes (*Working* 50–51): almost anything, from brain size to the capacity to sweat to where one lived and what one ate, could become an index of one's inferior racial status. Roediger's discussion of the New Orleans lynching and its justification at the time on the basis of southern Italians' "biology and habits"—their "low, receding foreheads, repulsive countenances and slovenly attire" (52)—highlights the virulence and mutability of American racism during the period when Italians were entering the country in their largest numbers.

The historical amnesia that many Italian Americans maintained about their past—an amnesia clearly encouraged by conventional American history and by a desire to assimilate—meant that for many years the memory of this lynching was repressed. But with this memory's recovery has come a significant reexamination of the lynching and its implications in numerous critical contexts, including the historical debates about whiteness discussed below. In addition, the lynching has spawned many creative endeavors in which it is juxtaposed to contemporary, sometimes personal, events and to the experience of other ethnic groups, particularly African Americans. The lynching is the subject of a poem by Rose Romano, "Dago Street," in which the poet reconstructs the events leading to the lynching and the lynching itself, interweaving the historical narrative with her own experiences as an Italian American of prejudice and discrimination and of the "pain" of "cultural suicide" (22). *Vendetta: A True Story of the Worst Lynching in America, the Mass Murder of Italian-Americans in New Orleans in 1891, the Vicious Motivations behind It, and the Tragic Repercussions That Linger to This Day* (original title), by Richard Gambino, was the first book-length examination of the lynching, and it was adapted for the screen in 1999. In his discussion of the film, Peter Bondanella notes that "the connection between Italians and the Mafia so indelibly etched in the American imagination was born in the aftermath of the event dramatized in this film" (19).

Kym Ragusa presents an insightful and evocative exploration of racial issues between Italian Americans and African Americans in the documentary *Fuori/Outside* and the memoir *The Skin between Us*. Revisiting the complicated relationship between her African American maternal family and her Italian American paternal family, Ragusa "straddles personal and collective experience" and interrogates the question of race and color (Perez 94). She retraces the stages of her problematic entrance into her Italian American family. After rejecting her at first because she is African American, they later embrace her but forget both her blackness and their own family's immigrant history. In a voice-over to *Fuori/Outside*, Ragusa notes that the Italian American grandmother—the same one who displayed racist attitudes toward her "black" grandchild—grew up in a time in which Italian immigrants were lynched just as African Americans were. Louise DeSalvo, in her memoiristic essay "Color: White / Complexion: Dark," reads her southern Italian grandmother's naturalization papers as a document of the racialization of Italian Americans. Hiram Perez calls this essay a "model for writing about culture and memory," even outside Italian American contexts (90). The work of all these authors is about connections and disconnections in Italian American history and the necessary role of memory in uncovering and exploring them.

The Triangle Shirtwaist Factory Fire

In the early twentieth century, daughters of immigrants and second-generation women immigrants were a major part of the industrial labor force, especially in the garment industry. Many became victims of workplace accidents, such as the infamous Triangle Shirtwaist Factory fire of 25 March 1911. The fire was caused by inadequate safety measures. Most of the 146 workers—20 men and 126 women—who died in the fire were Jewish and Italian girls and women. Their average age was nineteen (Orleck; Stein; Zandy, "Fire Poetry").

The fire occurred after the strike of the garment workers—primarily immigrant women—of 1909–10, which had started at the Triangle Factory: despite their determination, by the end of the strike the workers had only achieved small victories (Stein; Von Drehle). During working hours doors had been locked by the factory owners for fear that the workers would steal fabric. Without adequate fire escapes and open doors from the factories to the street, the workers were trapped. Most of those who did not die in the fire jumped to their death from the ninth and tenth floors of the Asch Building.

Writing about some of the poetry inspired by the Triangle fire, Janet Zandy notes that the fire represents "a site of subjugated historical memory, . . . a source of inspiration, and . . . a symbolic link to the tragedies of lives lost and stunted because of unsafe working conditions and economic oppression." She contends that the memory of the Triangle fire was "nearly lost" to the popular culture and that what kept it alive was at least in part its use "as a subject for literary expression." The production of the literary from the trauma of historical memory, Zandy suggests, exemplifies what Gramsci recognized as "culture produced *within and out of* the circumstances of lived experience" rather than culture "imposed *on* [subjects] from sites of power" ("Fire Poetry" 34).

This chapter of United States history has long been seen as a key event of women's, labor, and Jewish history, but not Italian American history—yet another forgotten moment that has until recently deprived Italian Americans of knowledge of their history and understanding of their culture. The Triangle fire—whose anniversary is marked in Italy on 8 March, International Women's Day—has only of late been recovered as part of Italian American history. The contemporary study of Italian American history through the critical lens of working-class studies has now made such historical reclamation possible and has prompted creative responses by writers such as Maria Terrone, Paola Corso, and Phyllis Capello and artists such as Nancy Azara. Since 2004, the filmmaker Roy Campolongo has been working on *The Triangle Fire: A Documentary*, which

> chronicles those remarkable times, when the rising forces of industry converged with the greatest mass migration in history . . . [and]

explore[s] the dramatic events of the late 19th, and early 20th century labor movement, that reached a crescendo with the Triangle shirt-waist factory fire of 1911. (*Triangle Fire*)

For many, the class politics and solidarity that the Triangle fire embodies have the power to inspire politically important cross-cultural alliances. Thus the restored memory of the fire offers Italian Americans an oppor-tunity to learn about and recover their forgotten working-class history. In her compelling poem "Girl Talk," Corso addresses both the Triangle fire "girls" and the "girls" who continue to be victimized in the sweatshops of today:

> And the Triangle girls say
> to the Chinese girls, the Indonesian girls,
> the Vietnamese, the Taiwanese
>   girls girls,
>
> take the chopsticks you can't hold
> at lunch because your fingers are too numb
> and glue them to the Velcro of the shoe
>
> take the vertigo, the headache, the vomiting,
> the memory loss, shortness of breath, the cancer
> and glue it to the glue of the shoe
>
> take the glue glue toxic glue
> and put it under his nose, a Nike nose,
> an anything-goes nose and make him sniff.
>
>   (617)

A poem like Corso's can be written in a cultural context that encourages a collective intellectual engagement to recover Italian American history. In turn, such a poem can contribute to a politicized and culturally in-formed Italian American and American consciousness.

The Sacco and Vanzetti Case

Prejudice against southern and eastern Europeans, including Italians, led to the discriminatory imposition of racial quotas on immigration. After the Immigration Act of 1924—the Johnson-Reed Act—immigration was lim-ited to 150,000 a year, and each country was allotted a certain quota. The Italian quota was set at fewer than 4,000, something that could perhaps have been predicted from the spirit of Henry Cabot Lodge's article. During this time, the prejudice toward Italian immigrants was exacerbated by the climate of fear and persecution created by the Red Scare.

In 1920, two Italian anarchists without any criminal record, Nicola Sacco and Bartolomeo Vanzetti, were accused of murder and robbery in South Braintree, Massachusetts. Their political radicalism attracted the suspicions of the police, who initially meant to arrest someone else. The arrest, the trial, and eventually the execution of the men in 1927 occurred in a climate of great tension, in which the two accused became symbols of alleged social justice and the epitome of foreign danger that immigrants represented. Scholarly texts, documentaries, and conferences have reexamined the Sacco and Vanzetti case, especially its representation by the media (Delamater and Trasciatti), and connected it with a broader understanding of the social and political atmosphere of the 1920s.

Italian immigrants had been actively involved in socialist and anarchist circles since the early 1900s (Cannistraro and Meyer; see Guglielmo in this volume). But that Italian Americans had fought for workers' rights and social justice in the early part of the century was forgotten as, years later, Italian Americans became too often identified with racism and bigotry. In 1989, a seventeen-year-old African American, Yusuf Hawkins, was shot to death in the Italian American neighborhood of Bensonhurst, in Brooklyn. Hawkins had gone to Bensonhurst with three friends to buy a used car, when a group of men, mostly Italian Americans, approached him. His death was the result of a hate crime. Italian American intellectuals and artists condemned the violence in the Italian neighborhood and began to explore the complex causes that triggered the violence, causes that can be fully understood only by reconstructing and analyzing the history of Italian American immigration and assimilation into whiteness (De Stefano; *Fuori/Outside*; Sciorra, "Italians"; Torgovnick, "On Being"; Viscusi, "Breaking"). For Joseph Sciorra, the murder led Italian Americans to develop "a more expansive, self-reflective, and socially engaged sense of identity" ("Italians" 206). Sciorra argues that "the tragedy of Yusuf Hawkins' death engendered an examination of conscience and values among Italian Americans in ways that simply did not exist before" (209). He believes that such an examination can result in the development of a "new ethnicity," though he cautions that this new ethnicity cannot be achieved "without struggle" and that it "remains a continuous and dynamic process." Out of the tragedy of Hawkins's death, Sciorra contends, "a network of self-identified and articulate Italian Americans who stand against racism and other forms of exploitation has been established" (209).

This same network identified by Sciorra has interrogated the status of a problematic Italian American icon, Christopher Columbus. The heated debate over the status of Columbus as either celebrated explorer or brutal colonizer has created tensions among Italian Americans; many activists and intellectuals support coalitions for transforming Columbus Day into Native American Day, and many angrily reject the critique of Columbus as anachronistic. The debate prompted Robert Viscusi to compose in 1992 the now classic *An Oration upon the Most Recent Death of Christopher Columbus*, in which he neither embraces nor renounces Columbus but offers an ironical, layered perspective on the origin and evolution of the Columbus myth.

At the turn of the twenty-first century, it became clear that Italian America was increasingly interested in reexamining its historical past—whether in terms of the racialization of southern Italian immigrants, the working-class origins of most Italian Americans, or the rich and complex inheritance of political radicalism, the memory of which has been obscured by disturbing manifestations of racism in Italian American communities such as Bensonhurst or the uncritical devotion to a fifteenth-century man whose life and actions have little, if anything, to do with the history of the Sicilian men lynched in New Orleans, the Triangle workers, or Sacco and Vanzetti.

Relative Prosperity and Ambiguous Acceptance in the 1930s

The 1930s was a time of relative economic, social, and cultural prosperity for Italian American communities and their representatives: writers such as Pietro di Donato, John Fante, and Jerre Mangione published works that were well received by readers and critics. Di Donato's *Christ in Concrete* won acclaim from many sources, including the *New York Times*, *Time Magazine*, and *Il progresso italo-americano*, and was chosen over John Steinbeck's *The Grapes of Wrath* as a selection of the 1939 Book of the Month Club (M. Esposito 47). But praise for the book tended to focus on its language and style rather than its polemical nature. As one reads the book today and feels the power of its prose and the pathos of its images of an exploited immigrant group—knowing that it was not the worker but the outlaw who would be cast in the role of cultural icon for Italian Americans—one can interrogate the web of political, religious, and ideological forces that affects the reception and distribution of texts and that allows *Christ in Concrete* and a film like *Scarface*, both of which came out in the 1930s, to represent such different versions of cultural capital for Italian Americans.

In the 1930s, Italian Americans were also entering and succeeding in other areas. Rudolph Valentino's popularity had exploded in the 1920s, and other Italians in cinema were acquiring recognition, such as the directors Frank Borzage and Frank Capra. In politics, the mayors of both New York and San Francisco were Italian American (Di Stasi, "How" 169–70). Italian Americans also gained significant recognition in sports— though not without some racial ambivalence, particularly in media coverage—with such "Dashing Dagos" and "Walloping Wops" (Baldassaro) as the eventual Hall of Famers Joe DiMaggio, Ernie Lombardi, and Rinaldo Angelo Paolinelli, who changed his name and is remembered as Babe Pinelli. As Phil (formerly Fiero) Rizzuto said about the common practice of anglicizing Italian names, "A ball player has to be as American as the Statue of Liberty" (qtd. in Baldassaro 98).

World War II Internment of "Enemy Aliens"

With the outbreak of World War II, Italians in the United States became suspect, even though some historians point out that the war marked a time of greater inclusiveness for American ethnic minorities, including Italians (Gerstle; T. Guglielmo, *White on Arrival*; Jacobson, *Whiteness*). During the war, 600,000 Italian immigrants were categorized, like Japanese Americans, as enemy aliens and were subject to discriminatory treatment (Di Stasi, "How" 170 and *Una Storia*). About 1,500 people, many of whom were involved in activities such as teaching Italian or radio broadcasting, were arrested and put in internment camps (Carnevale 162). Although the arrests often had a primarily symbolic function, the imperative not to speak "the enemy language" was acutely felt in Italian American households and communities all over the United States (161). As Nancy Carnevale observes:

> The message conveyed to Italian Americans through the actions of the FBI and the pervasive attitudes that informed them was clear: the use of the Italian language was incompatible with being or becoming a loyal American during the war years. (167)

For many children of immigrants and their descendants, the silencing of the language of their origins resulted from much more than a generic pressure or desire to assimilate into Anglo America. To speak Italian meant, during World War II, to be anti-American, to be an enemy.

Race, Ethnicity, and Shades of Whiteness

Following World War II, Italian Americans became increasingly assimilated into mainstream American society. Discussions of race became modified in academic and, to some extent, popular discourse. The term *ethnicity* became widely used in the United States "to describe those who had been formerly discussed as members of a less-than-white race, nation, or people" (Brodkin 144). As Karen Brodkin points out in her study *How Jews Became White Folks and What That Says about Race in America*, the hope for a pluralist and democratic society that erased social and racial inequalities would not soon become fully realized, but "[e]thnic pluralism gave rise to a new construction of a specifically Jewish whiteness . . . [that contrasted] Jews as a model minority with African Americans as culturally deficient" (144). This pernicious comparative strategy, which only perpetuated racism, can be helpful in understanding the construction of Italian American ethnicity along a continuum of whiteness, in which whiteness carries the privilege of legitimate, full American identity.

The discussion of Italian ethnicity in relation to the question of whiteness has emerged in the wake of the scholarly debate on how people become racialized in the United States, illustrated by studies like Brodkin's, Noel Ignatiev's *How the Irish Became White*, and the first comprehensive synthesis of the topic, Paul Spickard's *Almost All Aliens: Immigration, Race, and Colonialism in American History and Identity*. It is in the context of a discussion that considers the "lesser whiteness" of early Italian immigrants that we must consider the repercussions of a historical amnesia about the material conditions of the assimilation of Italian Americans in the United States. The recovery of key episodes in Italian American history and culture that bear a complex relation to these conditions—such as the Sacco and Vanzetti case, the rapid rise to fame and then the equally rapid descent into obscurity of novels like *Christ in Concrete*, the internment of Italian Americans in World War II, and even the racially inflected media coverage of Italian American baseball players—is essential to our understanding not only of Italian American literature of the past and present but also of the complexities of the so-called American melting pot.

The attempt to develop a detailed historical understanding of an Italian American past has enabled many discussions to emerge in which scholars can locate Italian Americans in a more intricate social web and analyze how issues such as whiteness implicated Italian Americans as well as other immigrant groups. Contemporary historians, as we saw in the first snapshot, now generally recognize that Italian immigrants were deeply affected by issues of color and race, even though Thomas Guglielmo argues that, regardless of the ethnic and racial prejudices that Italians endured during the time of highest immigration (1880–1920) and for many years after, they were regarded in America as "white on arrival" ("No Color Barrier"; *White on Arrival* 3–13). Most historians disagree. Matthew Frye Jacobson, like Guglielmo, recognizes a distinction between race and color but does not find that this distinction gave Italians as many advantages as Guglielmo seems to contend. Jacobson argues that some significant prejudice against Italians arose from their social actions, such as taking jobs that were conventionally thought to be "black" jobs or living with ease in neighborhoods with blacks, and for this, Italians were called "dago" and "guinea," commonly understood to mean "white nigger" (57).

Broadening the social context of Jacobson's argument, David A. J. Richards notes that between 1880 and 1920, quite apart from Italian immigration, the United States was experiencing a period of particularly virulent racism; he goes so far as to contend that racism was one form of social glue that held "Americans" together (158–81). While the United States was never unified in its support of slavery, after abolition the country did unify, especially in the South, in its firmly racist beliefs (Richards 158–61). One problem, Richards argues, that early Italian immigrants caused for Americans was that they did not enter the country with a prejudice against African Americans or Jews and were willing to do business with them and live with them; the Italians' behavior called into question the justification of American racism and inadvertently threatened dominant American patterns of oppression. For a time, he suggests, this type of behavior led to increasing suppression of Italians (173–76), but ultimately, after World War II, Italians were actively recruited in a "crusade for Americanization" that invited them to "indulge [in] . . .

racist assumptions" against others (177), what Richards calls the "Faustian bargain" (193).

Historical debates, films, and literature that analyze issues such as degrees of whiteness are emerging thanks to a strong commitment to recovering as much as possible of the lived experiences of Italian Americans and other groups in the nineteenth and twentieth centuries. This recovery potentially involves everything from naturalization papers to restaurant and theater policies to newspapers, music, legislation, oral history, and literature (see in this volume Aleandri; Del Giudice; Guglielmo).

Italian Americans Today

While the mass migration of Italians to the Americas dramatically diminished throughout the twentieth century, immigration has continued, though its demographics have changed. The history of Italian Americans' conflicted assimilation into white America has complicated their position in the multicultural United States arena. Instead of peasant and unskilled laborers who had little awareness or attachment to their newly created Italian national identity, more recently, trained professionals have been migrating to the United States, reflecting the Italian phenomenon of intellectual unemployment and brain drain as well as American immigration laws that discourage the entrance of untrained laborers. In 1992, however, the Italian citizenship legislation conferred the right to vote on many third-generation Italian Americans, thus changing the relationship that Italian Americans maintain with the country of their ancestors, a country in which they may be paradoxically in the position to exercise greater political agency than their Italian-born ancestors ever could.

Since the 1980s, the aspiration to a homogeneous Italian cultural identity has been unsettled by large migratory movements into Italy from Africa, eastern Europe, and Asia, and many of these immigrants are now producing their own brand of Italian literature (Parati, *Migration Italy*; see Pietralunga in this volume). Just as scholars in the United States are defining the canons of Italian American literature as a strand of American literature, Italian writers such as Tiziana Rinaldi, who live and write in the United States but write and publish in Italian, compel us to ponder the ways in which nation and language continually redefine and challenge the boundaries of Italian American literature.

Stereotypical Images of Italian Americans:
The "Invented Tradition"

I saw clearly that students felt comfortable using descriptive words [about Italian Americans] that ranged from simple stereotype to ethnic slur—perhaps, not surprisingly, because they often interpreted these designations as positive.

—Roseanne Giannini Quinn, in this volume

The Mafia as Big Business in American Entertainment

When most Americans think about Italian Americans today, the first images that come to mind are not those we have discussed above. Rather, they are usually mafiosi from *The Godfather* films or *The Sopranos*, fantastic figures who have more in common with the American gangster hero than with the flesh-and-blood mafiosi that Italian politicians, intellectuals, and writers have so forcefully and courageously denounced (Cutrufelli; Falcone; La Spina). While both *The Godfather* films and *The Sopranos* have been criticized by many for their stereotypical treatment of Italian Americans, they are also praised by others for their writing, acting, filming, directing and even, by some, for their contribution to Italian American culture (Barreca, *Sitdown*; Lavery, *This Thing* and *Reading*; Viscusi, *Buried Caesars* 189–217; Yacowar). Virtually every poll about America's favorite films lists *The Godfather* films, particularly the first and second, in the top five, if not at number one (Russo, "Hidden Godfather"). And David Chase's successful HBO series, *The Sopranos*, in which the romanticizing of the American gangster perhaps reached its apex, has won awards from over twenty-five different organizations, including Emmys, Golden Globes, Screen Actors Guild, and Banff Television Festival, and has been nominated for awards by countless other organizations ("Awards"). The Mafia is big business in the American entertainment industry. But the business comes at a cost: the invented mafioso of American film and television—while having little relation to most Italians or Italian Americans—has had significant detrimental effects on the emergence and recognition of an extensive body of literature that could call itself Italian American, and it has impeded and still impedes the development of a readership for a fuller and more complex view of Italian America.

The "Invented Tradition"

Some Italian American scholars—including many of the contributors to this volume—are concerned that, despite the rich work of historical recovery being done in Italian American studies, portrayals of Italian Americans are still frequently overshadowed by stereotypes and in particular that the stereotype of the Mafia figure is seen as a quintessential manifestation of the Italian American. In themselves, these stereotypes serve as evidence of the amnesia surrounding Italian American history, and they have a potent effect on the way Americans conceptualize Italian Americans. Thus many essays in this volume—and, to a certain extent, even this introduction—provide practical strategies to help students use their knowledge of stereotypes to develop more nuanced readings of Italian American texts in which Mafia and gangster images are either absent or challenged (see in this volume Bondanella; Centineo; Del Principe; Quinn; Ruffner; Tamburri, "Contested"), texts that seek to recover and understand the realities of an Italian American past and present.

The Mafia of American film and television drama bears little resemblance to the real Mafia. In *La mafia spiegata ai miei figli (e anche ai figli degli altri)* ("How to Explain the Mafia to My Children [and Other People's Children]"), the Sicilian writer Silvana La Spina writes that "the Mafia is not merely an organization, but a state of mind—fear, cowardice, indolence, and, of course, mistrust" (100; trans. Giunta). While La Spina urges young people to "fight" for their survival against the Sicilian Mafia, Americans of all ethnic backgrounds have become enamored with iconic mafiosi. Exceptions, of course, exist. George De Stefano is one of the few American scholars who has refocused the discussion of the Mafia in historical, political, and nonglamorous terms. The Italian American filmmaker Anthony Fragola completed in 2008 the documentary *Un bellissimo ricordo / A Beautiful Memory: A Mother and Her Sons against the Mafia*, on the Sicilian activist Peppino Impastato, killed by the Mafia in Sicily in 1978.

Eric Hobsbawm and Terence Ranger's influential concept of the "invented tradition"—"a set of practices, which seek to inculcate certain values and norms of behavior . . . which automatically [imply] continuity with the past" (1)—can help us develop a further perspective on the distinctive path that dominant stereotypical representations of Italian American immigration and assimilation have followed and how those stereotypes have, for many, obscured genuine historical inquiry and understanding (on "invented ethnicity," see also Sollors, *Invention*; Conzen, Gerber, Morawska, Pozzetta, and Vecoli). Invented traditions symbolize collective identities, legitimize social hierarchies, and enable people to enter particular social contexts, even though the connection of the invented tradition with the actual past may be tenuous or fictitious (Hobsbawm and Ranger 9).

The stereotypes of Italian Americans as working class, overly eroticized, anti-intellectual, naturally violent, and yet at the same time glamorous (see Tamburri, "Contested Place," in this volume) provide a striking example of Hobsbawm and Ranger's concept. In film, and somewhat later in television, beginning in the twentieth century and continuing in the present, a new invented tradition of Italian Americans took hold: it retained traces of the violent and criminal attributes that followed Italians from southern Italy to Ellis Island but softened them into a gangster figure who became significantly less threatening and more romanticized. Starting with films such as *At the Altar, The Avenging Conscience, Little Caesar, Scarface, Kiss of Death*, then *The Godfather* trilogy, *Goodfellas*, and *The Sopranos* (Messenger; De Stefano; Gardaphé, *From Wiseguys*; see in this volume Bondanella; Tamburri, "Contested Place"), the Italian American gangster quickly became and has remained the most powerful and influential representation of Italian Americans in the United States. This representation appealed both to non-Italian Americans, who could plug it into the larger tradition of the American gangster, and to many Italian Americans, who recognized on some level that, if one had to be labeled a criminal, it was better to be romanticized than persecuted.

The invented tradition of the American gangster represented Italian Americans on the silver screen as relatively sympathetic figures; it helped develop a strong Italian American presence in the entertainment industry and may even have aided in the assimilation of Italians into white America. David Pattie argues that in *The Godfather* films the Mafia stands up for the little guy in America: the films portray "a rogue police force for the poor . . . in a country whose justice system was biased in favor of the Anglo-Saxon Rich" (139). Peter Biskind contends that "*The Godfather* looked forward to the conservative family values of the Reagan era . . . in its emphasis on generational reconciliation" (164). And Bondanella, always careful to emphasize the difference between Hollywood Italians and real Italian Americans, nonetheless argues that whatever stereotype Italians play—from gangster to Romeo to Dago—the awards that Hollywood Italian films and Italian American actors have won "stand as a recognition of the vital role Italian Americans have played in the creation of

America's identity" (91). Coppola himself stated that *The Godfather* was "about power" and that he saw the Mafia in the movies "as a metaphor for America" (qtd. in Bondanella 242).

Russo observes that many in Italian America believe that they have not yet "found the poet, novelist, dramatist, composer, or director to present the story of its great migration, one of the largest in modern history, in an artistic form equal to its significance for them." And he asks whether *The Godfather* films might "fill, at least partially, this void in the Italian American consciousness" ("Hidden Godfather"). While Russo clearly disagrees with such an assessment, he recognizes that this is exactly how the films function in the hearts and minds of many Italian Americans. He notes that Pellegrino D'Acierno argues, with many others, not only that *The Godfather* trilogy has "raised [the gangster film] to the level of art film" but also that it may well be the "most central, cultural text of the Italian American experience" (D'Acierno, "Cinema" 568–69). Such a statement indicates the symbolized collective identities that the invented tradition can create. Talese's question—"Where are the Italian-American novelists?"—points to another powerful aspect of the invented tradition: the capacity to obscure a more complex, pluralistic, and at times contradictory set of cultural productions.

Some Consequences of an Invented Tradition

For many Italian Americans, the cost of becoming American was actually forgetting the processes by which their Americanization had occurred. Such a disconnection with their cultural past could explain a delay either in creating texts outside the invented tradition—texts that would attempt to recover the actual lived historical and contemporary experiences of the group and that also complicate the recovery by not creating the kind of cohesive image of the invented tradition—or in recognizing that such works did already exist and were continuing to be produced. The second is, in fact, what happened for many Italian Americans. As this volume and so many scholarly books of the last two decades record, powerful Italian American texts were being produced, but they were not being circulated. The dominance of the invented tradition of the Italian American gangster, combined with other stereotypes, particularly of the Italian American as anti-intellectual (Covello), as well as the pressure of the "crusade for Americanization" (Richards 193), slowed the establishment of a recognized Italian American literary tradition.

This process also shows that, to be successful, an invented tradition has to be filtered through the lens of the dominant culture, to ensure that it will create powerful but palatable images, stories, and representations of the stereotyped group that legitimate their position in the society at large. But when that work of legitimization is completed—and the group begins to both recover and record its lived historical and contemporary experiences—the dominant group may not be receptive to stories, images, histories, or any representations of the group that do not conform to the existing representations. And this scenario exactly reflects the dominant group's reception of Italian American literature. For the most part, it isn't read. Often, its existence isn't even recognized.

Today, students in our classes are still more likely to read Mario Puzo's *The Godfather* than his *The Fortunate Pilgrim*. In comparing these two novels, Richards argues that *The Fortunate Pilgrim* presents an "intimate" and complexly rendered portrait of actual Italian American family life, which, he contends, is of "ultimate value" to real Italian Americans. Russo calls *The Fortunate Pilgrim* Puzo's "smaller, finer novel" ("Hidden Godfather"). As Richards points out, however, even for an author with Puzo's reputation, "such stories, subverting stereotypes, will not be popular" (205). Comparing the reception of Puzo's family novel with that of his mob novel gives us a glimpse into the difficulty of gaining recognition for work that subverts stereotypes—even when written by the most well-known Italian American author. And there are further consequences still. If *The Godfather* and other such films and television shows are perceived by Italian Americans as filling a void in the representation of their immigrant experiences, it surely opens another: if Italian Americans embrace an invented tradition, they will have no motivation to recover the historically real tradition discussed above.

Authors in this volume who analyzed *The Sopranos* note regretfully that it is the primary source of information about Italian Americans for many of their students. Given the results of studies done since 1998 regarding the dominant perception of Italian America's relation to organized crime, the stereotypes in *The Sopranos* may suggest that Italian Americans are less assimilated into mainstream American than they might appear. In a 1996 survey commissioned by the Sons of Italy, approximately seventy-five percent of Americans were found to think that "most Italian Americans are associated in some way with organized crime" (Dabbene). And there is no reason to think that these numbers are decreasing. The findings are, in relation to Italian Americans, perhaps the most telling example of the power of an invented tradition.

Russo argues that the epic nature of *The Godfather* trilogy—which Coppola encouraged by calling it a saga ("Hidden Godfather")—helps move it out of the real and into the mythical. If *The Godfather* films function for many as *the* story of Italian American immigration, then *The Sopranos* represents *the* story of Italian American assimilation. In discussing the place of *The Sopranos* in Italian American life, Bondanella observes:

> [M]ost audiences . . . enthusiastically followed the lives of a group of Italian Americans who were so completely assimilated into American society that they became universal representations of us all, even if some of their activities took place outside the law. (221 in this volume)

If Bondanella's reading presents an accurate depiction of American viewers, then where might they stand on the question of cultural amnesia? Will they think that the ground has been cleared for an embrace of nonstereotypical Italian American literature or that the time has simply passed?

Organization of This Volume

This volume introduces several Italian American texts with which many readers may not be familiar. The strategies presented here for teaching Italian American fiction, poetry, memoir, political writings, oral histories, art, film, television, and dramatic texts offer exciting opportunities, for both teachers and students. The book is divided into five parts: "Mapping Italian American Studies," "Considering Italian American Literature," "Revisiting Italian American Film and Popular Culture," "Historical and Interdisciplinary Intersections," and "Resources."

Part I: Mapping Italian American Studies

Moving systematically from history to literature, film, and popular culture and from the United States to Italy, part 1 introduces readers to Italian American studies. In the opening essay, Donna R. Gabaccia presents the historical contexts of Italian immigration to the United States. The following two essays—on the history of Italian American literary studies, by Robert Viscusi, and the history of Italian American film and television studies, by Anthony Julian Tamburri—trace the development of these areas. While this volume focuses on the United States, we have sought to recognize changing political conditions and the necessity to view Italian American culture in a global context. Mark Pietralunga offers an overview of Italian American studies in Italy, where this field has been receiving much attention. The section ends with a case study by Fred Gardaphé focused on the creation of a program in Italian American studies.

Part 2: Considering Italian American Literature

In this section, readers can dip into any genre—fiction, poetry, memoir, oral history, and theater and performance—and gain a sense of the field and pedagogical insights. Some of the essays present historical as well as cultural information that can contextualize each genre and extend arguments made about the history of literary studies by Viscusi in part 1. Other essays demonstrate successful approaches to teaching a range of texts in diverse courses and contexts.

Mary Jo Bona's overview of the "rich harvest" of Italian American fiction traces the history of the genre from the turn of the twentieth century to the present through several key texts; it also examines the way in which Italian American literature both works within and breaks away from literary traditions and conventions. Peter Covino's survey of Italian American poetry outlines the existence of a rich and diverse tradition and builds evocative connections between Italian American poets and a classical European past. The other essays in this section focus on multigenerational gender analysis (De Angelis), Catholicism (Russo), and avant-garde fiction (Hendin). Rose De Angelis demonstrates an approach by which a teacher's juxtaposition of historical texts with fiction helps students "strip down" and "de-essentialize" conventional notions of gender, which in turn shapes the analyses of the characters and the texts. Josephine Gattuso Hendin explains how her students read avant-garde authors such as Gilbert Sorrentino and Giose Rimanelli by using reading and writing techniques that spring from her theory of "experiential experimentalism."

Caterina Romeo's essay introduces autobiography and memoir and analyzes the function of memory in immigrant culture. Romeo historicizes Italian American autobiographical narratives and examines different manifestations of the genre. The other essays on autobiography and memoir demonstrate how many of the issues raised by Romeo can be used productively in the classroom. They focus on family (Del Principe), cross-cultural identification (Luciano), and memoir-writing strategies (DeSalvo).

Oral history, as well, involves personal and collective remembering. The essays on oral history introduce readers to the major methodologies of the field, particularly in relation to Italian American oral history (Del Giudice), and traces the stages of a specific oral history class project (Trubiano).

Very little teaching of early Italian American theater and drama exists because few texts are in print. The essays addressing this field provide readers with extensive overviews of early playwrights (Aleandri) and later performance artists (Sciorra). The essay on teaching performance art (Taviano) maps out pedagogical activities that bring to life the study of performance artists.

Part 3: Revisiting Italian American Film and Popular Culture

Part 3 addresses the area of Italian American work that is best known by academic and popular audiences alike: film and television. While some essays reference *The Godfather* films and *The Sopranos*, others expose readers to lesser-known examples of commercial and independent film.

Two essays focus on an overview of Italian American film and television (Tamburri; Bondanella). The other two are more pedagogical and focus on specific artists. Courtney Judith Ruffner discusses teaching *Happy Days* and *The Sopranos* and describes how she instructs students to think critically about the construction of gendered ethnic identity. Of particular interest to language teachers—and to anyone wishing to engage in cross-cultural comparisons—is the study of Italian dubbing of Italian American films (Centineo).

Part 4: Historical and Interdisciplinary Approaches

All the essays in part 4 are pedagogical and cross-disciplinary; most are presented in the context of a particular course. This part is divided into three sections: "Race and Gender Politics," "Work and Social Class," and "Historical Intersections." Part 4 will appeal to readers who are looking for a more issue-based approach to teaching; it considers strategies for the integration of Italian American texts into existing courses, such as those in American literature and history, ethnic studies, composition, and women's studies. Kimberly A. Costino revisits ways of teaching freshman composition by looking at questions of race and racial formation in Italian American literacy narratives. Literacy narratives are rich biographical or autobiographical accounts of the many contexts in which people use reading and writing and of their multiple social purposes. Jennifer Guglielmo, Roseanne Giannini Quinn, and Clarissa Clò are aware that students need to be prepared for materials that they will find intellectually or ideologically challenging, and they present exciting pedagogical strategies that can be easily transferred from Italian American courses to many other teaching situations and texts. Guglielmo has brought to light political texts by early-twentieth-century Italian immigrant women who were involved in the labor movement as well as international anarchist and socialist circles: these texts may constitute some of the earliest examples of Italian American women's literature. Guglielmo demonstrates how she motivates her students to read them from a deeply analytical position. Quinn asks students to analyze gender issues raised—in what appears to be a straightforward manner—in Italian American pop culture, to think critically and take active stances on these issues before they go on to read more complex literature and theory. Clò helps students explore the significance of the multiethnic cross-cultural encounters figured in Italian American women's texts and asks how these "marginal" stories contribute to understanding and shaping the core of American, European, and world history.

In the section "Work and Social Class," Teresa Fiore demonstrates how she draws from a variety of topics, "ranging from food and family to religion and sexuality," and texts from multiple disciplines that analyze social class, language, and immigrant identity to support students' reading of *Christ in Concrete*. Elvira G. Di Fabio and Carol Bonomo Albright adopt an interdisciplinary approach to teaching a course on the Italian American experience, richly juxtaposing paintings, photography, fiction, and nonfiction.

In "Historical Intersections," Peter Kvidera provides key examples from canonical American texts by Margaret Fuller, Nathaniel Hawthorne, and Henry James to help students examine the ambivalence underlying American descriptions of the grandeur of Italy, an ambivalence that would play directly into stereotypes of Italians during the mass migration. Ilaria Serra, in focusing on travel to and from Italy and the United States, develops strategies to encourage students to compare and contrast the myths about the two countries.

Part 5: Resources

This part includes a review of anthologies that can be used in teaching Italian American studies and an extensive bibliography that is drawn from the sources cited in all the essays in this volume.

Developing Connections across the Book

The essays in this volume cover a wide range of subjects: the politics of whiteness, cross-cultural communities, interethnic or interracial connections, multiple ethnic belonging, and the allegiances one may establish with members of other ethnic communities through marriage, migration, politics, sexuality, friendship, and work. The issue of multiethnic relations and identities is central to this volume, and we believe it is a historically important and pedagogically productive point of entrance into a study of Italian American culture. How creative works relate to Italy is another important issue addressed by several contributors: the history of Italian American studies in Italy (Pietralunga), viewing Italy through canonical American literary texts (Kvidera), and travel literature (Serra). The north-south dichotomy (Gabaccia); peasant culture (Russo); literacy (Costino); as well as language acquisition, loss, and transformation (Centineo) are addressed from different angles: these include immigrant literature (Di Fabio and Albright), working-class studies (Fiore), oral history (Trubiano and Del Giudice), and theater and performance (Aleandri; Sciorra; Taviano). Themes and issues as well as authors and texts discussed in one section are referenced again in other parts of the book, with different inflections. We think this echoing, which will allow readers to link essays across sections, helps convey the sense of Italian American literature, film, and popular culture as a body of work that, while diverse, also reflects shared assumptions—if not about all the answers, then at least about some of the key questions. This book presents a set of texts that at once establishes and challenges canons, conventions, themes, and expectations. Italian American studies has for a long time been in conversation with American culture at large. We hope that this book will foster a deeper and more complex appreciation of its role in the culture of the United States.

Part I

Mapping Italian American Studies

Donna R. Gabaccia

The History of Italians in the United States

Today's Italian Americans are the demographic legacy of one of the largest migrations of laborers in recent world history. A sizable group (roughly sixteen million or about six percent of the United States population), Italian Americans include only a small number (about half a million) actually born in Italy; most are children, grandchildren, and great-grandchildren of the five million immigrants who arrived between 1880 and 1920. Although still concentrated in the urban northeast and in California, Italian Americans no longer differ significantly in education or socioeconomic status from other urban Americans of European descent. But, like other "white ethnics" (a term still applied to those with roots in Catholic and Orthodox Christian southern and eastern Europe, along with Jewish Americans), they carry the burden of their immigration history.

The historical memory of most Italian Americans includes decades of virulent nativist hostility and immigration restriction. It often includes family stories of economic struggle; low-wage, low-status manual or blue-collar work; and class resentments. It includes as well social habits that may still reflect working-class strategies to ensure family and community security; while rooted in rural Italy, such cultural tool kits have been transformed by urban, industrial life, by pressures to Americanize, and by belated but significant economic mobility. Even as Americans of Italian descent became cultural producers, popular American culture continued to associate the group with violent criminality and familism; with premodern attitudes toward sex, gender, child rearing, and race; and with the bodily pleasures of food and heterosexual eroticism.

Making "Italians": Culture and Class during the Proletarian Mass Migrations

The few Italian immigrants who arrived in the United States before the 1880s did little to disrupt long-standing American and European associations of Italy with art and music. Long before there was an Italian national state (formed in 1860), both Italian nationalists and intellectuals accepted Roman classicism, Renaissance humanist culture, and baroque art and music as distinctly Italian expressions of creativity. Gilded Age and Progressive Era North Americans still looked to Europe for leadership in the cultural arena. Throughout the nineteenth century, small numbers of Italian musicians, artists, architects, chefs, and performers immigrated to the United States. Wealthy Americans also traveled to Italy, hoping to learn to appreciate the high culture produced by an older civilization.

Already in the years after the French Revolution, however, radical republican exiles, chimney sweeps, and street performers had slowly begun to replace artisans and artists as the most visible of Italy's migrants. By the time Ellis Island opened to guard the gates of the United States in 1892, few middle-class Americans viewed the Italians passing through its halls as representatives of a superior European civilization. Most of Italy's migrants were illiterate and semiliterate peasants; they were predominantly men looking for temporary jobs as pick-and-shovel workers. Although artisans, skilled masons, petty entrepreneurs, and even some professionals numbered among them, poorer migrants exemplified the vast and worldwide population movement that has rightfully been called the proletarian mass migrations. Whether southern Italians (the majority of migrants) or rural northern Italians, few spoke the language of Dante. Ambitious, hardworking, and shrewd, the mass migrants introduced Americans to an Italy that few tourists or intellectuals had ever encountered.

As growing numbers of humble immigrant men called over wives and Italian settlements grew (and were labeled Little Italys by Americans), fears of "racial suicide" quickly developed among longtime Americans.

According to the immigration historian Roger Daniels, Americans decided that the newest immigrants were "not like us." Scientific racism provided an explanation for their differences. To understand the new immigrants, Americans turned to Italy's intellectuals, who were busy drawing negative portraits of an Italy—rural, poor, and southern—they had discovered in the course of Italian unification. (Following Edward Said, the anthropologist and historian Jane Schneider has termed northern Italians' racialization of southerners as "orientalism in one country.") Italy's elites disparaged southern Italians—notably Neapolitans, Calabrians, and Sicilians—as primitive and backward races, closer in their levels of civilization to Africans than to Lombards or Venetians and characterized by high rates of criminality.

Many of Italy's most influential racial theorists of the era of the mass migrations were—like Cesare Lombroso—not only positivists but founders and updaters of the scholarly field of criminology. The influence and translation of their works cemented among foreign readers an association of Italians with crime that would persist over the decades. On the basis of their publications, federal agents at Ellis Island began counting northern and southern Italian immigrants as two distinct races in 1899. American nativists demanded the exclusion of Europe's racially inferior immigrants, along with Asians.

While American nativists worked to exclude the uncivilized, immigrants from Italy quietly created their own working-class cultures of everyday life in the United States. Americans sometimes viewed settlements of immigrants as transplanted Italian villages, but only rarely were urban enclaves homogeneous. Clusters of Sicilians, Neapolitans, Piedmontese, and Calabrians could be identified, of course. But most urban neighborhoods and rural settlements of Italian agriculturalists in California and Louisiana were multiregional and sometimes even multinational mixes of immigrants. Such enclaves functioned as melting pots that "made Italians" of millions of migrants possessing only family-, village-, and region-based identities. New linguistic pidgins mixed Italian regional grammars with American vocabularies, and, by the 1920s and 1930s, the foodways, folk devotions, saints' cults, proverbs, and marriage and family customs of the many and strikingly diverse regions of Italy were also blending. The result was a new folk culture that seemed Italian (especially to Americans) but was also made in America.

The residents of American Little Italys were the most sedentary half of Italy's migrants—the other half returned to Italy or circulated repeatedly in and out of home villages and their offshoots in Argentina, North America, Brazil, northern Europe, and around the Mediterranean. Even so, Little Italys' single men and married men living without families remained surprisingly mobile: many moved in and out of urban neighborhoods following seasonal bouts of labor at distant construction sites. Reunified families moved about frequently, changing their housing as relatives and friends arrived and left and as children entered the labor force or left to form households of their own. Most social histories of Italian immigrant neighborhoods in the United States rightly emphasize the families' intent focus on achieving family stability and financial security in the midst of kaleidoscopic urban and economic change. The pursuit of cash through wage earning, homework, and the keeping of boarders dominated everyday existence. Immigrants viewed early work experience as children's best preparation for life; at most, they might select a single child, usually a boy, for education beyond a few years of elementary school.

But work was not all. Catholic parishes, mutual aid societies, local unions, and Italian-language newspapers representing a wide range of political perspectives provided institutional nodes for immigrant community formation. Even for such hardworking people, moments of leisure and of creativity proved possible. Italian-language theater, opera, comic reviews, puppet shows, and eventually films—many of them produced in Italy or by peripatetic performers from Italy—all drew audiences in the largest Little Italys: New York, Boston, Philadelphia, and San Francisco. Women continued to make lace and to decorate altars and small shrines to chosen saints; men employed in construction used their skills to build and to renovate domestic spaces. Even in tenement districts, immigrants raised small animals; in less densely populated enclaves, gardening in small backyard plots was almost universal, as was the fermenting of homemade wines and the preservation of tomatoes and other vegetables.

Backyard gardens, domestic rituals, and family meals were not typically the key elements American observers identified as Italian immigrant culture in the twentieth century. Few Americans had either the language skills or the personal sympathies that gave them access to the lived, everyday folk cultures of Little Italy. American commentators focused, instead, on what they saw in public. Americans viewed Little Italy as distressingly dirty and noisy but also colorful: men, women, and children alike participated in a bustling street life that included street play, marketing, and casual socializing. Elementary school teachers and romantic observers such as Jacob Riis sometimes did claim to uncover artistic predilections even among Italian street urchins, youthful speakers of New York slang, and "swarthy" Italian men or women with colorful scarves who sang as they worked outside on stoops, sidewalks, streets, and parks on sunny days.

Like other racializations, Americans' association of Little Italy with dirt, public street life, food, noise, and large swarms of children mixed pleasure and attraction with fear. American intellectuals were hard-pressed to reconcile cultural stereotypes of Italy emerging from tours to Roman ruins, Renaissance art museums, or Catholic cathedrals or from visits to the Metropolitan Museum of Art or to occasional opera performances with the folk culture of Little Italy. Beginning in the first decade of the twentieth century, Americans instead focused negative attention on the Black Hand criminal gangs in Little Italys that extorted money from local businessmen with threats of violence. Fears of Italian-speaking anarchist bomb throwers soon blended with popular newspaper (and later filmed) images of Mafia plotters and of passionate but also knife-wielding and vengeful husbands and gamblers—similar to the images that had emerged from the pens of Italy's positivist scientists.

Even the longtime Americans who abandoned scientific racism, who called themselves Americanizers or progressive reformers, and who imagined immigrants abandoning Little Italys' folk cultures were distressed to recognize that the latest wave of immigration from poor countries such as Italy coincided with a profound crisis at the heart of American culture. How could Americans transmit to the newcomers the culture of the country's nineteenth-century Protestant elite when Americans themselves seemed increasingly to reject that culture? Signs of cultural crisis were everywhere in the late nineteenth century as Americans came to terms with westward expansion, the Civil War, the abolition of slavery, and rapid industrialization. Since the 1870s, American robber barons and new captains of industry had jettisoned the modest mores of New England to adopt and then to transform aristocratic European patterns of consumption. Immigrants poured into the United States just as national marketplaces brought the products of corporate capitalism to the masses and just as production of new market-oriented and nationally available forms of commercial culture (symbolized by dime novels, Crackerjacks, nickelodeons, and dance halls) captured American imaginations. Young generations of intellectual bohemians seemed eager to experiment with the culinary and artistic hedonism they found in the "Dago red" (wine) and ash cans of immigrant neighborhoods on the East and West coasts, while the

social settlement-house movement also claimed to discover more respectable cultural gifts that immigrants might contribute to the making of a
new American culture.

Those who worked most closely with immigrants—notably social
workers and public school teachers—recognized the temptation to newly
arrived immigrants of the newly commercialized mass forms of American
culture. Settlement workers hoped to preserve old-world dances, music,
and handicrafts in part because immigrants' children found these European folk practices less attractive than places such as Coney Island. Like
many immigrant parents, settlement workers seemed destined to lose their
battles against the pleasures of mass consumerism. Despite their efforts to
teach immigrant girls the parsimony of the New England household decor
and the culinary benefits of codfish and cream sauce, teachers of home economics classes regularly bemoaned girls' preferences for cheap finery, gilt,
and the foods of the corner "poison shop" (Gabaccia, "Italian-American
Cookbooks"). Italian immigrant parents, meanwhile, complained that the
young wanted only to play and, when they worked, to control enough of
their own wages to indulge in the entertainment of cheap commercial
novelties.

Americans' complex response to the crises of American culture took
a wide variety of forms, from Protestant religious revivals to campaigns
against alcohol consumption to fears about the moral dangers posed by
urban growth. Collectively, this backlash helped nativists achieve their
goal of reducing immigration. In the 1920s, Congress excluded Asian
immigrants on racial grounds while institutionalizing the racial inferior-
ity of Italians and other southern and eastern Europeans by establishing
highly restrictive national origins quotas, thus ending the proletarian
mass migrations.

Ethnic and National Cultures in the
Era of Restriction, 1924–65

Millions of second- and third-generation Italian Americans came of age
during the era of restriction. Restriction, the Great Depression, and World
War II sharply diminished both the influx and influence of immigrant
newcomers, causing Italian American folk culture to diverge still further
from the regional peasant cultures of Italy. Worldwide battles between
fascist and antifascist activists nevertheless managed to influence Italian

Americans' complex transition from immigrants to ethnics in the United States in the 1920s and 1930s. While American intellectuals increasingly viewed Italian immigrants as white Europeans en route to complete assimilation—a point seemingly confirmed by Italian Americans' enthusiastic participation in the American, not the Italian, army during World War II—American commercial culture perpetuated older stereotypes. Even under continued restriction, Italian migration to the United States increased temporarily between 1950 and 1965, but the newcomers represented a small minority among the much larger migration of seven million Italians who traveled instead to northern Europe, Canada, Australia, and Latin America.

As the children and grandchildren of immigrants sought to create American identities for themselves, the era of restriction generated sharply contradictory messages about Italy and about the place of Italian Americans in American society. The execution of Nicola Sacco and Bartolomeo Vanzetti seemed to mark the death of proletarian Italian American radicalism even as the number of Italian American union activists continued to rise with the organization of the Congress of Industrial Organizations (CIO) in the 1930s. The class-conscious early novels of Italian American writers and the reworking of mainstream American cultural and political themes by persons such as the Italian American filmmaker Frank Capra or the Italian American politician Fiorello LaGuardia did not stop the rapid popularization and spread of mass media images of Italian American gangsters. These stereotypes drew on the long traditions of Italian and American scientific racism. But their most immediate roots were in the simultaneous rise of the Hollywood culture industry and the Prohibition-related illicit businesses that fell increasingly into Italian American hands in the 1920s and 1930s. More benignly, Americans in the era of restriction came to accept Italian American folk foodways, even learning to cook and to prepare the cuisine at home. Dishes such as spaghetti and meatballs and (somewhat later) pizza increasingly symbolized not only the intimacy and pleasures but also the conservatism of large Italian American families; yet they also focused Americans' attention on the stereotype of the limiting and exclusively domestic concerns of the Italian American women who served the violent, patriarchal men of their communities.

The rise of fascism and the worldwide conflicts between supporters and opponents of Benito Mussolini deeply shaped identities among Italian Americans. Many admired Mussolini for the pride he encouraged in what he called the "Italian race." It may seem ironic that nationalism and pride in the Italian race soared along with the Americanization of immigrants and their children. (Rates of naturalization picked up notably in the late 1930s.) The temporary enthusiasm for Mussolini that the scholar Rudolph J. Vecoli has labeled the "fascisticization" of Italian Americans encouraged ethnic pride, even if expressed in distinctly American ways. The University of Chicago sociologists who popularized American use of the term *ethnicity* in the 1920s and 1930s generally linked it to the inexorable progress European immigrants were making toward full assimilation into American life. During the 1940s, Italian American men proclaimed their nationalism and love of their adopted country through high rates of military enrollment, even as the United States went to war with Italy. Hollywood celebrated this process, too, although the countless multiethnic (but resolutely white) "buddy" movies of the World War II era failed to displace the gangster as the most common symbol of Italian American masculinity. Ethnic identities, love of the United States, assimilation, and negative stereotypes coexisted by war's end.

While sociologist theorists of the era of restriction focused on ethnicity and assimilation, more recent scholarship describes instead how the children and grandchildren of Italian immigrants became white in the interwar years. Mussolini and his war in Ethiopia in 1935 insisted that Italians were an expansive race, capable of ruling a new empire governed from Rome. Restricted at Ellis Island but nevertheless free to naturalize and, as native-born citizens of the second generation, to exercise the full rights of United States citizens, Italian Americans embraced whiteness also in part as a response to the great African American migration—itself a population movement sparked by the sharp restrictions placed on international migrations. Unlike their more upwardly mobile Jewish immigrant counterparts, whose higher levels of high school and college education facilitated earlier moves to middle-class districts and suburbs, blue-collar Italian Americans were more likely to remain in cities as newcomers from the black South replaced older immigrants (Kessner). Competition for housing and urban resources, the usual turf battles that accompanied urban ethnic transitions, and the association of Americanization with white-skin privilege often resulted in sharp conflicts between Italian American and African American or Puerto Rican neighbors. But those same neighbors could sometimes also become collaborators, as many did, for example, in the political following of the East Harlem legislator Vito Marcantonio. Increasingly, too, politically active Italian Americans urged their legislators and unions to oppose the race-based restrictions imposed on them.

Since 1965: New Italians and New Italian Americans in a Globalizing World

By the time the United States eliminated its discriminatory national origins quotas in 1965, Italy had begun to experience its own economic miracle. Over the next forty years this country emblematic of emigration attracted immigrants from Africa, Eastern Europe, and Asia. The small numbers of Italians who migrated to the United States in the late years of the twentieth century more often left with cultural capital—education, professional experience and ambitions, secularism, and linguistic facility (in Italian, English, and other languages)—than with close family ties to their working-class predecessors.

The cultural distance between Italian Americans and the new arrivals from Italy often seemed as great or even greater than between Italian Americans and other Americans. Italy—once the exporter of pick-and-shovel men—had again become an important cultural producer and exporter worldwide of style, taste, and consumer design. Now numbering among the most prosperous nations of the world and a site visited by millions of American tourists each year, Italy had become a country Americans looked to for definitions of the good life (sometimes even called *la dolce vita*) at the end of the millennium.

The grandchildren of Italian immigrants could not easily claim these new cultural associations for themselves. Although educational levels (especially among Italian American women) gradually rose to the national norm, most Italian Americans were still relative newcomers to middle-class life. And by the 1970s, a prideful sense of white ethnicity among Italian Americans and other descendants of eastern and southern European immigrants often struck American intellectuals as an expression more of backlash against the increasingly assertive claims to equality by African Americans than of claims to legitimacy in a multicultural America. Those Italian voters who moved into the Republican Party to vote for culturally conservative candidates such as Richard Nixon in the 1970s or Ronald Reagan in the 1980s seemed to provide additional evidence that it was whiteness that sustained Italian American ethnicity. Even those who in the 1970s and 1980s proudly acknowledged their Italian origins to census takers were often the products of one or more generations of mixed marriages among white Catholics of recent foreign origins. Few Italian Americans spoke Italian; few claimed Italian citizenship when Italy opened this option in the 1990s.

As they joined the American middle classes, Italian Americans contributed more widely to American cultural production. Writers and filmmakers such as Martin Scorsese and Mario Puzo attracted negative attention for appearing to feed the continuing American obsession with Italian criminality with their tales of urban violence, Mafia, and criminal life. Some particularly angry Italian American ethnic activists even claimed improbably that popular culture Italian bashing lingered in an otherwise multicultural or politically correct America as the only socially acceptable expression of ethnic stereotyping. At the same time, however, poets, artists, and writers of Italian origin revisited the working-class communities and beliefs of their grandparents, providing new glimpses of divisions of race, class, gender, and sexuality simmering behind the facade of family solidarity and Catholic conformity. For the largest group of Italian Americans, memories or experience of Little Italy were of little relevance; these mattered only occasionally during quiet, private moments of family or religious celebrations or in family memory and domestic memorabilia. According to some scholars, Italian American ethnicity had entered its twilight, shrinking to purely symbolic value.

While Italian American academics struggled to create Italian American studies curricula to reinterpret the once-disparaged life of immigrant proletarians, a much larger group of newly prosperous and solidly middle-class Italian Americans revisited even older cultural stereotypes. For many Italian Americans today, the most important sense of connection to an Italian past is to some of the same forms of Italian culture that attracted America's middle-class culture seekers in the nineteenth century—classical Rome, the Renaissance, and the baroque Catholic Counter-Reformation. Whether such historical identifications can erase the millions of family histories rooted in Italy's rural and peasant poverty, in the proletarian strivings of the mass migrants, in the mid-century battles of fascists and antifascists, or in the acquisition of whiteness and mainstream middle-class status is a question to be answered only in the twenty-first century.

Robert Viscusi

The History
of Italian American
Literary Studies

Italian American literary studies, which scarcely existed in the 1960s, has since developed into a large and flourishing field. While the inner concerns of this discursive arena have seemed to drive its growth, almost everything that happens in a diaspora culture responds to larger and wider forces than may be visible on a local scene narrowly observed. We have now arrived at a point where earlier preoccupations take on new clarity thanks to their place in an intensifying critical awareness of the connection between local matters such as immigration and assimilation and the global dynamics of cultural flow and undertow. In the field of Italian American literary studies, this critical point of clarity has been reached by the reversal of polarity that has changed Italy from a point of origin for migrants to a point of arrival. For literary and cultural studies, this reversal amounts to a Copernican turn.

It is now possible, according to Graziella Parati, a leading student of this shift, "to articulate the concept of a destination culture that soars over national borders and linguistic separations" (*Migration Italy* 89). Parati uses this concept as a way of talking about the writings of contemporary immigrants to Italy from Africa and eastern Europe. One may extend her already ample articulation of the concept. Diaspora literatures inevitably question national borders and linguistic separations. At any point in their history, studies of such literatures will reflect concerns that reach far beyond the local. Our understanding of these concerns now places us in a position to consider the history of Italian American literary studies along a single line of development, falling into three large periods. The first we may call colonial (1820–1941), the second postcolonial (1941–91), and the third global (1991–present). I use the terms *colonial* and *postcolonial* differently from the ways they are used conventionally in literary theory, though there are traces of those distinctions in my definitions as well. By *colonial*, I mean that while Italians are entering the United States, they are entering it not as colonizers (in the manner, say, of the British who colonized India) but as people who will live in a colonized relationship both to this new sovereignty and to the one they have left behind. Their status in the United States at this point echoes that of a conventionally colonized group because they do not gain positions of power in the mainstream society and can even be seen as resisting American attempts to force them to learn the dominant language and to adopt the values of the dominant culture; their status in relation to Italy is that of "colonials" who have little power to define their own culture without deferring to metropolitan canons of cultural authenticity—*italianità*, in this case, as defined in Italy and only in Italy. By using *postcolonial* to refer to Italian American writing in the period 1941–91, I am suggesting that Italians have stayed in America and assimilated to some extent but also that they have been "colonized" by it. Further, their work reflects much of the cultural and political agenda that metropolitan Italy deployed in dealing with Italian emigrants who lived in places that Italy called its *colonie*. The familiar expressions *immigration* and *assimilation*, useful as they are, focus on destination, as if travel moved in one direction and did not affect or reflect relations in larger circles. This narrow focus does not suit diaspora literary studies, which needs to chart forces of cultural hegemony. Such forces do not follow simple patterns of population movement so much as they respond to tensions that accompany the appearance of transnational political, economic, and cultural spaces.

We can think of these spaces in terms of linguistic polarities. In the Italian American colonial period, the dominant literary language of Italian America is Italian: in this context, the metropolitan culture of Italy and of its national language exercises enormous gravitational pull. Italy is present in spaces where it is not necessarily visible. Thus when Italian Americans in this period do write in English, they are always working against the background of a massively italophone literature. In the post-colonial period, the dominant literary language of Italian America is English: in this context, the metropolitan culture of the United States exercises an enormous hegemonic presence. Anglo-American space, with its huge capacity for expansion, surrounds every act of language. Thus when Italian Americans in this period do write in Italian, they are always working against the background of an extensively anglophone literature. In the global period, Italian American writers begin to rediscover and revalue Italian speech, including dialect, alongside their predominantly Anglo-American speech. In sum, the languages that writers use need to be considered against the background of the geographies that affect their use.

Colonial Italian America

When Italian Americans lived in Italian, they called their settlements *colonie* ("colonies"). It made sense. These settlements were entrepôts in the international circuit of Italian American trade. Such colonies were lively markets in food, money, and, above all, cheap labor. There were banks where workers might send money back to Italy. There were daily and weekly newspapers that kept the immigrants informed of political, cultural, and economic events in Italy. While these settlements were not formal colonies, they belonged to the long history of trading empires that had been an important part of Italy's presence in the world since the time of the Crusades. Thus it comes as no surprise that these were places where the major concerns of life referred to their points of origin in Italy. The cultures, high and low, of the *colonie* displayed an indelibly imitative and secondary quality, typical of life in provinces far from the metropolis, that visitors from Italy rarely failed to note.

Americans did not think of these settlements as colonies of Italy but took to calling them Little Italys, a spatial designation with an American colonial map built into it, implying that these neighborhoods functioned as liminal arenas where Americans might go to taste forbidden "Italian" pleasures: everything from white slavery in the 1890s to imported gin in the 1920s, all delivered in a carnival atmosphere of singing waiters serving spicy food in the *pizzerie* and tommy gun diplomats slaughtering one another in the wet streets outside. The Italian Americans were usually recent immigrants, and many of them lived as *uccelli di passaggio* ("birds of passage"), traveling frequently between Italy and the United States. A large number of them remained subjects of the Italian crown.

In its Italian colonial period (1820–1941), Italian American literary history was written in the language of the colony. Italian American literary studies begin in Italian. *Le memorie di Lorenzo Da Ponte* (1823) connects the beginnings of Italian American literature with the glories of European high culture. Later on, during the flood tide of immigration (1880–1924), many Italian-language newspapers and other periodicals published journalists, poets, and novelists whose works form the basis for an understanding of Italian American literary history. In New York City in the 1850s, Giovanni Francesco Secchi di Casale began to publish the poetry and fiction of Italian American writers in *L'eco d'Italia* (a weekly paper that eventually became a daily). In 1881, Carlo Barsotti began publication of *Il progresso italo-americano*, a daily paper that published many writers who became leading voices of the Italian colony, chief among them Bernardino Ciambelli. In 1893, the Sisca family began publication of *La follia di New York*, a journal that became a central organ of literary life in the Italian colony. Throughout the history of this and other *colonie* in the United States, there were always writers who wrote only or largely in Italian—that is, in some recognizable form of the national language of Italy (for accounts of Italian American literary work composed principally in Italian, see Prezzolini, *Trapiantati*; Massara; Martelli; Durante, *Figli* and *Italoamericani*; Marazzi, *Little America*; Maffi; and Fontanella, *Parola*). Some writers wrote either in Italian dialect or in some regionally inflected form of national Italian (see Haller, *Lingua*; Marazzi, *Little America*; Massara). Since this work's chief organs were Italian-language newspapers like *Il progresso italo-americano* and *L'eco d'Italia*, its chief critics were journalists, though the occasional metropolitan Italian, either in exile or on tour, had something memorable to offer. Of these the most famous was Giuseppe Prezzolini, an ex-futurist and a longtime professor of Italian at Columbia University, whose collection of essays *I trapiantati* ("The Transplanted") surveys the literary productions of the colonials with a keen and not totally unsympathetic eye (Betocchi). A frequent feature of colonial literary production was an unquestioning reliance on the aesthetic standards and ideology of the homeland. Thus it was that visiting intellectuals often found little to admire in a culture that appeared to them slavishly imitative and grotesquely syncretic.

When Italian Americans did work in English in this period, it was in the context of a large Italian cultural and linguistic agenda, reflected in their work. John Fante's fiction of the 1930s, seen from this angle, is an unremitting critique of Italian familial and cultural expectations. Pietro di Donato's masterwork *Christ in Concrete* is written to suggest to the anglophone reader as much as possible of the texture and rhythm of Italian speech and thought, thus providing a privileged insider's view of the "real" life of the Italian quarter. A little later, John Ciardi made his reputation as an academic poet with his classic translation of Dante Alighieri's *Comedia*. These pioneers have been the first Italian American writers to inspire full-scale monographs (Cooper; Collins; Paoletti; Napolitano; Ciefelli).

The Italian Americans who best escaped the enclosure of the Italian colony were singers and songwriters, who entered English through the side door of jazz, where Italian political agendas were distinctly irrelevant, even unwelcome. Thus Louis Prima sang with the hybrid authority of New Orleans jazz and Jimmy Durante with the wit of the ragtime barroom, while Frank Sinatra achieved a dominant position among popular singers with his studied use of Louis Armstrong's breath control, Billie Holiday's phrasing, and Count Basie's orchestrations. This ability to enter the hegemonic language through the path of a nonhegemonic poetics gave these popular singers the cultural authority that might, according to Gay Talese, more plausibly have been expected from great novelists ("Where"). Still, it is worth noting that the carnival atmosphere of Little Italy followed these singers throughout their careers, Prima playing the sexualized Italian, Durante the singing waiter, and Sinatra the friend of friends. Italian Americans were as colonized in English as they were in Italian.

Bourgeois Italians in the United States have steadily resisted the shadow of Little Italy, while Italian academics in the United States have long promoted the literary authority of the national standard dialect. There were Italians teaching polite conversational Italian and canonical literature even in prerevolutionary North America. In the 1820s, Lorenzo Da Ponte was the first professor of Italian at Columbia College, later Columbia University. Since that time, the academic profession of Italian has often acted as a colonial office of Italian literary culture, reminding well-to-do Americans that the culture of Italian Americans needed always to be subordinated to a more rigorous, more elegant, more aristocratic, and generally superior standard. To this day, there are many professors of Italian who resist the suggestion that their field might sensibly study the writings of Italians in the United States, particularly when those writers address their readers in English, as if there were between them a deep tribal divide (Valesio 271).

Postcolonial Italian America

Postcolonial Italian America began abruptly. Benito Mussolini declared war on the United States on 11 December 1941, and posters almost instantly appeared in the Italian neighborhoods enjoining the Italian Americans, "Don't Speak the Enemy's Language. Speak American!" And speak American they did. And, as best they could, they would dress American and think American too. The price of Italian identity for many in 1942 was internment; many others, the more than 600,000 Italian Americans who had yet to take United States citizenship were required to visit the post offices and register themselves as "Enemy Aliens" (DiStasi, *Storia*). This was when the majority of the Italian colony decided to accept aspirations to American identity. For a long time afterward, most Italian Americans wanted to obscure and forget much of their visible Italianness and instead to imitate American fashions, think American thoughts, and speak the American dialect of English.

In a postcolonial culture, things do not always progress along a readily detectable line of development. There are ancient stars whose light first reaches earth long after they have collapsed into black holes millions of light-years distant and died. Similarly, some postcolonial phenomena spring to life out of the darkness of deep oblivion.

During the early years of this period, Italian Americans did not so much abandon their colonial status as feel that it had abandoned them. The status of enemy alien was enough to place the entire question under interdict. It did not even begin to feel like a postcolonial condition until the issue of what it might mean to call oneself Italian American started to inspire public discussion. Thus it was only with the ethnic revival of the late 1960s and early 1970s that a new wave of thinkers and writers began to read the traces of the lost Italian colonies. At the same time, these readers started to treat the Americanizing ambitions of Italian Americans as dubious and insubstantial. Many such investigators were among the founders of the American Italian Historical Association (AIHA) in 1967. When these intellectuals began to explore the specific history and culture of Italian America, they discovered that even after decades of energetic Americanization, much of the colonial culture of Italian America continued to reveal itself. Italian American literary studies in English had begun modestly enough during this period, with the publication of Olga Pera-gallo's bibliography in 1949. When AIHA's volume *The Italian American Novel*, edited by John Cammett, was published in 1969, it was clear that a new agenda was being announced.

Literary studies, since its beginnings, has configured the field in several ways that reflect its complex phenomenology. Many critical texts display a supple attention that accommodates more than one concern and that may show awareness of more than one kind of unfolding. Nonetheless, it is useful to make some cartographic distinctions to understand the task of Italian American literary studies during the critical years when postcolonial questions first began to arise: we can usefully point to four kinds of postcolonial space—transcolonial, archaeological, differential, and discursive—each a new arena and a fresh investigation.

Transcolonial Space

During much of the period in question, Italian Americans found themselves choosing to migrate from one colonial position to another. I call transcolonial space the arena where one changes cultural allegiance without losing one's marginality. "Transcolonial subjectivity," according to Françoise Lionnet, "exists in tension with multiple epistemological locations, including traditional centers of power" (29). This space stands on the material basis that stubbornly supports any account of Italian American phenomenology—whether literary or political, social, psychological, economic, or historical—during the postwar period. In literary history, this material basis takes the form of hegemonic structures. Every critic who approaches Italian American writing must take into account the two spatial hegemonies that constitute its field of production, each one offering the Italian American population its own form of cultural marginality.

Many critics frame their accounts with the populous geographical displacements that give meaning to the term *migration*. Such works as Giuseppe Prezzolini's *I trapiantati* ("The Transplanted"), Giuseppe Massara's *Americani*, Emilio Franzina's *Dall'Arcadia in America*, Peter Carravetta's "Con/Texts before the Journeys: Migration, Narration, and Historical Identitites," and Luigi Fontanella's *La parola transfuga* ("Renegade Speech") are built on the elusive phenomenalism of displacement, a condition of living metaphor wherein every space becomes the shadow of some other space, a situation in which borders give way to discontinuities.

Accounts of Italian American writing in English give less attention to this oscillating geography and more to the intricate architecture of emotional and ideological spaces. Rose Basile Green's *The Italian-American Novel: A Document of the Interaction of Two Cultures* is a kind of endless tour of the ideological contact zone. Green's Italian America resembles an Italian neighborhood in which ambitious young people escape to the other side of town, where whiter folks play golf and send their children to college. In this zone, every bedroom has a window that opens on a conversation taking place in another language. The more earnestly people try to raise their offspring as Italians, the more irresistibly they tend to produce children who act like Americans, marry Americans, or, at the very minimum, think about Americans all the time. And later, when those children attempt to replicate these aspirations in their own offspring, those children are dreaming of Italy, or at least of Italian food.

Transcolonial space, though it is the earliest form of postcolonial space in Italian America, continues to attract the attention of writers who treat Italian American literature within the parameters of positivist geography and clear class divisions. Seen in an Italian national perspective, the transcoloniality of Italian American writing is its most distinguishing characteristic. Seen in almost any conceivable Italian American perspective, transcoloniality is a set of critical obligations: names written in Italian are pronounced in American English; Italian American stories that take place in California can never completely free themselves from points on the other side of the world, points that may appear as origins or destinations or both. The system of transcolonial space for a long time functioned as a way of keeping certain structures of meaning firmly in place: the order of families and the order of national boundaries reinforced each other, so that the social and personal meanings of the expression *Italian American* acquired a formidable stability, facilitating the construction and maintenance of stereotyped characters and characteristics that for a long time seemed plausible, natural, and permanently fixed. This ideological effect has been the engine of a continuing discomfort among Italian American critical thinkers, and it has helped fuel many efforts to denaturalize the boundaries—personal, social, and national—that characterize the Italian American transcolonial space (see Ciongoli and Parini, Preface xiii). The problems of transcolonial social agendas gave life in 1974 to Richard Gambino's *Blood of My Blood* and to the journal *Italian Americana*, which Gambino and Ernest Falbo founded that same year (they were later joined by Bruno Arcudi). Eventually, the topics that had given the journal its salience began to lose their dramatic appeal, and *Italian Americana* suspended publication in 1986.

Archaeological Space

An early effort to interrupt the transcolonial order took place in the late 1970s, when Luigi Ballerini and Fiorenza Weinapple at New York University conducted a series of seminars on Italian and Italian American languages. Linguists, literary historians, psychoanalysts, sociologists, anthropologists, and poets all took part in these discussions, which had as their premise the existence of an Italian American common language, or koine. The organizers took this premise to imply that one could trace the varieties of Italian American language using methods similar to those that scholars had employed in producing the massive linguistic atlas of all the varieties of Italian spoken in Italy. The workability of this premise was never demonstrated, and no atlas was written. Yet simply opening the inquiry produced a new way of looking at Italian American writing, which could now be seen in the light of *la questione della lingua* ("the debate about language"), the spinal column of Italian literary history. It now became possible to consider Italian American literary space in a vertical rather than topological extension. Hermann Haller produced his major study of the Italian language as it had evolved in the columns of *Il progresso italo-americano* (*Lingua*). I began a project that considered Italian American writing in relation to its long Italian antecedence (Viscusi, "*De Vulgari*," "*Caso*," "Semiology"). Posing the archaeological question disturbed the apparently foursquare stability of transcolonial geography and proved to be one step in a critical movement that was destined to grow rapidly in range and power.

Differential Space

The question of how Italian American literature differentiated itself in a world of discrete postcolonialities quickly became pressing and eventually formed the focus for a large critical literature that examined the semiotics of Italian American narrative. William Boelhower in 1982 first addressed the question of immigrant narrative and ethnic semiosis in Italian American writing (*Immigrant Autobiography*), a theme he returned to in a major theoretical statement a few years later, *Through a Glass Darkly: Ethnic*

Semiosis in American Literature. Making a sharp turn away from the positivist social history that had dominated thinking in Italian American studies, Boelhower moved this discussion into a phenomenological arena where the questions were different and the answers unimaginable. What did it mean to construct an Italian American self through the lens of, say, the late works of Henry James? One of Boelhower's more notorious riddles, it subtended a telescoping of transcolonial space into the narrow confines of the differential gaze. It meant transforming an identity through the introduction of a determined positionality. In retrospect, this definition of differential space seems the last necessary preparation for what has turned out to be the decisive moment in the history of Italian American literary studies. Boelhower's work has had a major impact in subsequent decades.

Discursive Space

Before anything else could happen, however, it was necessary to open a forum that belonged specifically to Italian American writing. In 1985, Helen Barolini published her precedent-setting collection, *The Dream Book: An Anthology of Writings by Italian American Women.* Barolini aimed to clear a discursive space for women's writing, where the agenda is first and foremost *écriture féminine,* where questions of dominance, empire, ethnicity, race, and class all first must answer to the questions posed by the inherited division of the sexes and the ongoing social construction of gender roles and their intricate equipments of licenses and prohibitions, their codes of what can and cannot be thought or said or done. This intervention became critical for the entire field of Italian American literary studies. The promotion of Barolini's anthology inspired large-scale group readings, and writers saw that they themselves formed an audience. *The Dream Book* had opened an Italian American literary public space.

In 1989, the murder of Yusuf Hawkins in Bensonhurst led to significant protest and public analysis of Italian American social pathology, almost none of it delivered by Italian American intellectuals. This striking absence inspired me to deliver the essay "Breaking the Silence: Strategic Imperatives for Italian American Culture" at the AIHA Conference in San Francisco in November 1989 (Viscusi). This paper's call for "authoritative discourse" (3), the right of Italian Americans to claim a public forum to address issues that affected their communities, had a strong appeal for many scholars and writers who at that moment were beginning to speak out in new ways. In 1990, Anthony Julian Tamburri, Paolo A. Giordano, and Fred L. Gardaphé introduced the journal *VIA: Voices in Italian Americana*, and Carol Bonomo Albright revived the journal *Italian Americana*. In 1991, the editors of *VIA* published *From the Margin: Writings in Italian Americana*, a major collection of contemporary Italian American writing that presented rich offerings in poetry, fiction, and nonfiction. In 1994, Mary Jo Bona edited *The Voices We Carry: Recent Italian/American Women's Fiction*. All these publications were greeted with similar enthusiasm in the new public space that Barolini's work had called forth from the mist. In this new discursive space, it was possible to explore much more freely and expansively the postcolonial territories that had already been opened. In spring 1991, a group of writers in New York City responded to "Breaking the Silence" by forming the Italian American Writers Association (IAWA), which aimed to promote Italian American writing. IAWA has done many things, always focusing on keeping an open forum for the reading and discussing of Italian American works. The concept of opening new spaces has continued to bear fruit: in fall 2001, a group of cultural workers formed the Malìa Collective, dedicated to promoting the creative work of Italian American women.

Global Italian America

In the years since the early 1990s, Italian American literary studies have explored a world with a different dimensionality. The logic of postcolonialism has led to an awareness of new kinds of commonality and an understanding that cultural forces may flow in many directions simultaneously. As early as 1985, the sociologist Richard D. Alba had suggested that Italian Americans were becoming European Americans, a prescient notion that grew in resonance as the European Union made its reality felt in Italy, transforming it from a metropolitan center of *italianità* into a series of intersections in contintental, transcontinental, and global networks. By the early 1990s, the rise of the Lega Lombarda, with its program of regional secession, and the collapse of the First Republic in Italy underlined the instability of the colonial and postcolonial maps alike. At the same time in the United States, the debates surrounding the quincentenary of Columbus's arrival in the Caribbean removed this figure from his position in Italian American mythology and placed him at the center of a global controversy. Since that time, Italian American literary studies has been coming to terms with a series of rapidly evolving cultural challenges. Here I distinguish four kinds of global space—semiotic, transnational, cosmopolitan, and virtual—but the possible number is much larger, now when new cultural maps are proliferating.

Semiotic Space

The cumulative effect of postcolonial investigations and liberations in this field has been to open many conversations that had long been kept closed and to begin questioning and reconfiguring the very bases of Italian American studies. The construction of *Italian American* as a figure of speech came under unforgettable observation in Tamburri's *To Hyphenate or Not to Hyphenate? The Italian/American Writer as* Other *American.* Tamburri followed this work with *A Semiotic of Ethnicity: In (Re)Cognition of the Italian/American Writer,* a work whose title places the entire enterprise of Italian American writing within diacritical marks. Tamburri has consistently queried the theoretical and philological rigor of Italian American literary studies. A questioning of stable narratives of literary construction also characterizes Gardaphé's key text *Italian Signs, American Streets: The Evolution of Italian American Narrative,* which offers a thorough Viconian theory of literary typologies. A wide-ranging semiotic curiosity runs through the essays in Pellegrino D'Acierno's *Italian American Heritage.* A similar sensibility shapes Gardaphé's more recent works, *Leaving Little Italy* and *From Wiseguys to Wise Men.* The latter work is a significant entry in the growing bibliography of Italian American gender studies, as is George Guida's *The Peasant and the Pen.* Basic in this arena is Bona's *Claiming a Tradition,* which lays down an archaeological claim within the discursive space already opened up by Barolini. Mary Ann Mannino's *Revisionary Identities: Strategies of Empowerment in the Writings of Italian/American Women* makes a similar gesture, placing even more emphasis on political issues. Edvige Giunta's *Writing with an Accent: Contemporary Italian American Women Authors* doubly displaces the master narrative of Italian American colonialism and postcolonialism by reconstructing both authorial gender and linguistic authority. Tommi Avicolli Mecca and Tamburri's collection *Fuori: Essays by Italian/American Lesbians and Gays* provides another radical challenge to the authority of gender construction. Josephine Gattuso Hendin argues that Italian American literature has by now recoded itself and belongs to the history of American literature ("New World"), a position much in line with the recent work of Marc Shell and of Werner Sollors (*Multilingual America*).

All this activity has given a new tone to Italian American studies. Since the late 1990s, creative writers and literary critics have often dominated meetings of the AIHA, founded in 1967 by social scientists and immigration historians. Many of the writers have been influenced by the theories of memoir developed by Louise DeSalvo and Edvige Giunta in *The Milk of Almonds* and by the anthologies edited by Maria Mazziotti Gillan and Jennifer Gillan and by Carol Bonomo Albright and Joanna Clapps Herman. These works have in common a steady attention to the production of new forms of meaning, new signs of difference, and a reliance on the semiotic indeterminacy of origins that flows from the work of Boelhower, Tamburri, and Gardaphé.

Transnational Space

An especially important innovation in this period was Lawrence Di Stasi's *Una Storia Segreta: The Secret History of Italian American Evacuation and Internment during World War II.* By establishing the conditions under which Italian Americans stopped speaking their own language and knowing their own history, Di Stasi underlined the necessity to construct a new Italian American narrative, one that would revisit the transnational spaces that continue to affect the possibilities of Italian American writing. In this connection, works by Francesco Durante (*Italoamericana*, vols. 1 and 2), Giunta (*Writing*), and Martino Marazzi (*Voices*) have all made important contributions, as have the critical narratives of Pasquale Verdicchio (*Bound*). One can follow much of this theoretical advance in essay collections: Jennifer Burns and Loredana Polezzi have addressed these issues directly in their groundbreaking *Borderlines: Migrazioni e identità nel Novecento,* as have Beverly Allen and Mary Russo in *Revisioning Italy: National Identity and Global Culture* and Boelhower and Rocco Pallone in *Adjusting Sites: New Essays in Italian American Studies.* Many of the basic theoretical questions have been surveyed in David Forgacs and Robert Lumley's *Italian Cultural Studies.* Parati, in *Migration Italy*, has not only opened, but also richly explored critical perspectives for making a transnational narrative genuinely global. Her attention to the nonce words and improvised creoles of migrant writers in Italy makes good company for another important element in the new transnationality: the linguistic freedom that arises when regional languages grow in strength as national boundaries weaken. There has been a formidable interest in Italian regional writing. Haller has published widely in this field, including two anthologies of dialect literature, *The Hidden Italy* and *The Other Italy*. Luigi Bonaffini has edited two large trilingual anthologies (dialect poetry translated into both Italian and English [*Dialect*; Bonaffini and Serrao]) and has begun work on the *Journal of Italian Translation*, which gives equal attention to all the languages of Italy. Gaetano Cipolla continues to build a major library of translations of Sicilian writing, especially poetry.

In the transnational context, projects originally conceived within the archaeological space of the 1980s take on a different valence. Robert Casillo and John Paul Russo have begun to publish their major books, long in development, on the representation of Italy and of Italian America in both American and European canonical texts. Originally focused on the genealogy of stereotypes, these works now have the effect of expanding the geographic and historical range of the sources of Italian American realities. Something similar happened to my project, which began long ago with *la questione della lingua* and finally emerged as *Buried Caesars*, an investigation of how nationalist ideologies, including the fetish of a standard language, appear in a transnational age as elements in a large cultural symptomatology much in need of fresh examination.

Cosmopolitan Space

The novels of Don DeLillo, in particular *Mao II*, *Underworld*, and *Cosmopolis*, have been in dialogue with the criticism of Frank Lentricchia (*Introducing*) to construct a vision of cosmopolis with the range and particularity one associates with full-blown paranoia or the fiction of Thomas Pynchon. Both DeLillo and Lentricchia have been at pains to place in this universal apocalypse the framed photograph of Italian America circa 1950, when the old colonial certitudes were already dissolving into the acid liquid of anticommunism and baseball, the beginnings of a nonspecific Americanism that by the 1990s had become the prototype front window of a global marketplace where you can buy the same cup of coffee in the same container anywhere in the world, from the Forbidden City to the *banlieux* of Montréal.

A similar extension has grown out of the new field of diaspora studies. In 1991, Jean-Jacques Marchand published *La letteratura dell'emigrazione. Gli scrittori di lingua italiana nel mondo* ("The Literature of Emigration:

Italian-Language Writers in the World"), the proceedings of a major conference at the Université de Lausanne that considered for the first time writings in Italian from all over the Italian diaspora, from Berlin to Buenos Aires to Melbourne to Vancouver. This work mobilized as an analytic tool the concept of Italian as a world language, one spoken, written, and studied in many parts of the literate world. In this arena, as in so many others, the global space reveals itself as the inevitable next step in a process that began in the nineteenth century with the mass movements of peasants to the cities, within the nation and across its borders, wherever the factories were humming. The work of historians like Emilio Franzina (*Dall 'Arcadia*), Donna R. Gabaccia (*Italy's Many Diasporas*), and Mark I. Choate has tracked the historical changes. The growth of Italian Canadian, Italian German, Italian British, Italian Australian, Italian Brazilian, Italian Argentine, and Italian American literatures now seems to be part of a single phenomenon, each literature sharing many common elements with the others as well as displaying many signs of its distinct ecology. And most recently, the elements naming these binational literary formations have been reversed, so that we are studying Arab Italian, Albanian Italian, Somali Italian, and many other new versions of what has come to be a global literary phenomenon. At the same time, in the United States, such scholars as Jennifer Guglielmo and Salvatore Salerno, Joseph Cosco, and Steven Belluscio began to write new maps of Italian American space that included a great deal of attention to African and African American cultural inheritances and direction of development.

Virtual Space

No history of literary studies now can ignore the growth of virtual space since the 1990s. The library of Italian American writing, like the library of everything else, grows universally available even as it no longer exists in one place or another. The State University of New York, Stony Brook, is now teaching Italian American literature as a virtual course. The Web will tell you what courses are being offered in hundreds of places, and it will often provide the syllabi and other course materials too, as well as the e-mail addresses of the instructors, so that it is not unusual for active professionals in the field to receive e-mail inquiries from graduate students and researchers on the other side of the ocean or the other side of town. The Web is simultaneously global and intimate. *H-ItAm*, a bulletin board dedicated to discussions of Italian American studies, advertises itself as a "virtual piazza." IAWA maintains an online bibliography of Italian American books. As the universal digital library takes form, the narrow enclosures of a colonial literature and the impassioned rediscoveries of a postcolonial criticism become parts of a past that is now constantly rearranging. The Italian Ministry of Labor has recently launched *E.USIC: Empowerment of US-Italy Community* as a "bilingual virtual community," with the object of stimulating research and discussion across linguistic and geographic borders on the Italian and American *i-Italy* sites. New formulas of identity construction and new maps of influence appear on the Web every day.

The Web site has become an important scene of genealogy, where anyone can trace family history on vast sites organized by the Mormon Church or follow the passage of ancestors on the Ellis Island site, which gives photos of the ships and registers of the names of the people who sailed in them, complete with towns of origin. These towns often maintain Web sites, especially in Italy, now a wealthy country and, as always, interested in commerce with its transnationals everywhere. Some sites are scenes of literary study, like Daniela Gioseffi's anthology *ItalianAmericanWriters.com* or the bibliography sites that allow access to endless quantities of printed matter. Joseph Sciorra's *Italian Rap* promotes and provides an introduction to a continually creolizing vision of *italianità* (there is a page entitled "Contamination"). There are interactive bulletin boards where people can discuss *The Sopranos* or the works of Diane di Prima, sites where they can write about how Little Italy has returned to earth, this time as a new kind of shopping mall, appearing along the highways here and there, as chapters in further narratives of desire and displacement.

Anthony Julian Tamburri

The History of Italian American Film and Television Studies

If one revisits the history of Italians and Italian Americans in the major media forms, it becomes apparent that there has been a consistently strong Italian and Italian American presence in cinema, music, television, theater, and other media. Be it Rudolph Valentino, Frank Sinatra, Anne Bancroft, or Ezio Pinza, Italian Americans have been present in the popular media, even though the status of that presence has been debatable at times. Indeed, the debate rages on today. The studies discussed here convey the sense of an ongoing discussion but also collectively reveal the need for further investigation.

Cinema

Essays on Italian American cinema are numerous, though single-authored book-length studies that pay attention to individual filmmakers instead of Italian American cinema as a whole seem to prevail. I focus here on surveying scholarship that looks broadly at Italian American cinema and therefore do not discuss books on particular directors, which rarely consider the filmmaker's ethnicity. The broader studies presented in this essay are more relevant to an understanding of Italian American cinema as a culturally inflected phenomenon.

Lee Lourdeaux's *Italian and Irish Filmmakers in America: Ford, Capra, Coppola, and Scorsese* analyzes three Italian American directors and one Irish American director. The book focuses on a range of topics: Hollywood's stereotypes of the Irish and Italians as police, priests, politicians, and gangsters in movies in the 1920s; John Ford's portrayal of Irish America; Frank Capra's comedies as social commentaries about the Anglo-American ethic; Francis Ford Coppola's themes of conflict between Italian America and Anglo-America; and Martin Scorsese's articulation of Catholic Italian America and mainstream culture. Throughout, Lourdeaux underscores the importance of the directors' ethnic heritage and their Catholicism and provides an excellent comparison of the Irish and the Italians, especially in his positioning of Capra as a bridge between the two ethnic groups.

The films by Coppola and Scorsese, however, fit Lordeaux's interpretive scheme somewhat better than the westerns by Ford and the comedies by Capra. Unfortunately, the book does not give a detailed analysis of every film by these directors. Capra's *A Hole in the Head*, for example, receives only a brief mention. John Paul Russo's essay "An Unacknowledged Masterpiece: Capra's Italian-American Film" provides an astute analysis of this film, paying attention to its historical and artistic significance, not only in the history of Capra's movies but also in a general discourse of Italian American and American cinema.

Paola Casella's *Hollywood Italian* is a film encyclopedia of sorts and could serve as an introduction to orient a reader unfamiliar with Italian American cinema. The book is divided into sections that consist of chapters and subchapters dedicated to many films; each section is introduced by a short chapter on cultural history as well as the specific film history pertinent to that section. The bibliography lists more popular than academic sources. While the book is useful for finding quick, general information, I do not recommend it for scholarly research.

Pellegrino D'Acierno's "Cinema Paradiso: The Italian American Presence in American Cinema" offers a detailed and theoretically sophisticated history of the genre yet is still accessible to the theoretically uninitiated. D'Acierno's readings of films by Coppola, Scorsese, and Capra invite the reader to reconsider these films. His analysis of Coppola's *The Godfather*, for example, underscores the filmmaker's skill at romanticizing the outlaw figure—the film "trap[s] the spectator in an imaginary identification with the outlaw" (573)—and simultaneously critiquing that same figure by portraying Vito Corleone as a monster at the end of his life.

The collection *Screening Ethnicity*, edited by Anna Camaiti Hostert and Anthony Julian Tamburri, includes essays by scholars from the United States, Italy, and France. The book gathers an array of critical voices from various theoretical perspectives. Organized in three sections—"Specific Themes, Multiple Voices"; "The 'Bad Boys' of Italian/American Cinema"; and "Different Voices, Different Tones"—the essays explore issues such as gender, race, structural narrative, and Mafia as an Italian American theme and, in addition to the so-called masters, cover such filmmakers as Abel Ferrara, Nancy Savoca, Quentin Tarantino, and Stanley Tucci. The collection closes with an essay on three shorts (fiction, music video, documentary) and a conversation with Annabella Sciorra, an actor of the post-boomer generation.

My closing essay in this volume developed into a larger project, my book *Italian/American Short Films and Videos: A Semiotic Reading*, dedicated to the short film (under sixty minutes). Divided into three sections, the book examines two fictional films, two narrative music videos, and two documentaries. In each case, one film articulates the director's Italian American heritage, while the other constitutes a more implicit expression of the director's ethnicity. The study demonstrates how it becomes the reader's task to invest the films' physical signs with Italian American meaning.

Giuliana Muscio's *Piccole Italie, grandi schermi* ("Little Italys, Big Screens"), a study of the first fifty years of American cinema, examines the representation of Italians and Italian Americans. Muscio traces both the activities of the cinematic world and their sociopolitical contexts. Her first chapter discusses the roots of this cinema—from the stage to the screen. The second chapter focuses on the figure of the Italian and the Italian American in film from 1895 to 1940, analyzing various types of "Italian" characters represented, culminating in the gangster figure. The remaining three chapters deal with the development of representations of the Italian and Italian American in film in both the United States and Italy. The result is an original bilingual and bicultural analysis.

Peter Bondanella's *Hollywood Italians: Dagos, Palookas, Romeos, Wise Guys, and Sopranos* juxtaposes stereotypical roles of Italian Americans in American society with their portrayals in American cinema. As his subtitle signals, these portrayals include primarily immigrants, boxers, Latin lovers, and mafiosi. Bondanella insists that these classifications demonstrate the Italian and Italian American dedication to admirable values such as the preservation of family and hard work. Much of his book centers on the gangster figure, a representation that, while indeed ubiquitous, may be doing more harm than good for an informed understanding of the history and place of Italian Americans in American culture. Bondanella would like to see the Italian American favorably ensconced in American society, despite negative portrayals. In fact, he points to *The Sopranos* as a prime example of how Italian Americans have moved into mainstream society. Furthermore, Bondanella sees in *The Sopranos* a more satisfactory representation of Italian Americans insofar as the characters portray a plethora of individuals: mobsters, psychotherapists, teachers, lawyers, and, of course, local, regional, and national law enforcement agents.

To demystify the Mafia as represented in various films and television programs, one must go beyond the diachronic and thematic and examine audience response. George De Stefano's *An Offer We Can't Refuse* provides a detailed analytic history of representations of Mafia in film and television. His end point is that, regardless of the various successes of the Italian American, the Mafia myth remains the Italian American icon par excellence. Fred Gardaphé's *From Wiseguys to Wise Men* examines the Mafia in literature and film, grounding his readings in the figure of the trickster. Gardaphé demonstrates how such a figure can be manipulated in various ways: held up as a model (*The Godfather*); exemplified as a stunted stage (*Mean Streets*); or ridiculed, as Italian Americans themselves have done (Giose Rimanelli's novel *Benedetta in Guysterland*). Both De Stefano and Gardaphé provide the springboard from which to build a reader-response or semiotic analysis of the evolution and implications of representations of the Italian American gangster. They offer a one-two punch for a reexamination and a new discussion of this figure, a discussion that does not fall back on steadfast determinism (read, outright condemnation) but allows for a more constructive conversation that could lead to a greater understanding of the phenomenon.

There are significantly more essays than books on Italian American film, though few existed before the 1970s, when some fundamental essays first brought to light basic yet significant issues. Mirella Jona Affron's "The Italian-American in American Films, 1918–1971" provides an inventory of films accompanied by the list of cast and characters and a brief plot line. A companion piece is Karen Szczepanski's "The Scalding Pot: Stereotyping of Italian American Males in Hollywood Films," which examines negative portrayals of Italian American men in Hollywood film. These two essays set a tone that solidifies into a denunciation of everyone and every articulation related to the gangster stereotype.

Four brief but significant essays appeared in 1978 in a collection edited by Randall M. Miller, *Ethnic Images in American Film and Television*. Joseph Papaleo's "Ethnic Pictures and Ethnic Fate: The Media Image of Italian-Americans" discusses the Italian stereotype built on excess and its possible effect on Italian Americans. Richard N. Juliani's "The Image of the Italian in American Film and Television" addresses, in a comparative mode, ethnic stereotypes in films and television, lamenting the absence of greater diversity in the representation of Italian Americans. Michael Parenti's "The Italian-American and the Mass Media" outlines six aspects of the dilemma of the Italian American: "the invisible man," "minor stock characters," "the grateful immigrant," "the mafia gangster," "the 'respectables,'" and "the jivy delinquent." These six categories could each become the basis of larger studies. Finally, Joseph Monte's "Correcting the Image of the Italian in American Film and Television" calls for a campaign to confront media stereotyping head-on. A short article, to be sure, it calls for outright criticism and, if possible, censure of those who engage in the continued figuration of the gangster figure.

In 1980, Miller edited another volume, *The Kaleidoscopic Lens: How Hollywood Views Ethnic Groups*, which includes Daniel Golden's "The Fate of *La Famiglia*: Italian Images in American Film." Golden offers a history of the development of Italian images in American cinema, showing how this imagery has its roots in other cultural productions, such as the "serious and popular literatures of England" (75), nineteenth-century cartoons, and even the *New York Times* (77). He also underscores how the dominant imagery of the Italian is not static; rather, it seems to transform itself with subsequent generations.

During the 1980s, several important essays on single films were published. Ben Lawton's "*Taxi Driver*: 'New Hybrid Film' or 'Liberated Cinema'?" is one of the first rigorous analyses of a film by an Italian American director. This groundbreaking essay adapts Pier Paolo Pasolini's theoretical notions of liberated cinema to an Italian American genre and artist not yet recognized by the dominant culture. Following Pasolini's concept of art as revolutionary only when the artist is breaking the rules of the system in which he operates (Lawton, "*Taxi Driver*" 239), Scorsese's *Taxi Driver* engages in such aesthetics by demystifying the "heroes of old" while criticizing "the media's transformation of seriously disturbed individuals into heroes, up to and including the Bronson revenge films" (244). Robert Casillo's and John Paul Russo's essays on Scorsese and Coppola, respectively, contribute to the rigorous analysis of Italian American cinema during that period. Casillo's 1985 essay, "Catholicism and Violence in the Films of Martin Scorsese," examines the seemingly contradictory themes in Scorsese's early cinema. The article marks the beginning of a larger study that culminated in his *Gangster Priest*. Russo deconstructs Coppola's *Godfather* series in his 1986 essay, "The Hidden Godfather: Plenitude and Absence in Francis Ford Coppola's *Godfather I* and *II*," which demonstrates how such films have insinuated themselves into the collective imaginary of the United States. Russo examines the *coincidentia oppositorum* of the Mafia conquering the family, belying to a certain degree the notion of Mafia as metaphor for American life.

In addition to these significant essays, Carlos Cortes's "Italian-Americans in Film: From Immigrants to Icons" offers an initial integral view of the presence of Italian Americans in United States cinema. Beginning with the silent era, Cortes divides his history of Italian American cinema into periods (1900–28, 1928–45, 1945–70, 1970–) and offers a critical panorama of the presence of Italian Americans in cinema as both actors and directors.

In the 1990s, Lawton published the essay "America through Italian/American Eyes: Dream or Nightmare?," in which he interrogates the intention behind films by the likes of Coppola, Scorsese, and Michael Cimino. Lawton's 1995 essay, "What Is 'ItalianAmerican' Cinema?," underscores the inherent problematics of the field at this time—Why such a field? How do Italian Americans feel about such a category regarding their self-identity as "American"? Where are the cultural critics of Italian American studies? Relying on the term "ItalianAmerican," Lawton briefly rehearses its history in a skeptical mode, challenging the reader to take up some of the questions the essay raises. Finally, in an early issue of *VIA: Voices in Italian Americana*, Jacqueline Reich addresses the teaching of Italian American visual culture, from course conception to classroom praxis.

More recent essays on Italian American film look back to the first half of the twentieth century and revisit the narrative challenges of representing Italians and Italian Americans in film. Jonathan Cavallero examines the rhetorical strategies behind the use of the Italian in early American cinema in his "Gangsters, Fessos, Tricksters, and Sopranos: The Historical Roots of Italian American Stereotype Anxiety." Thomas Ferraro looks at Italian American cinema as one of several cultural "artifacts" of Italian American culture in *Feeling Italian* (2), a book organized around "ten case studies at the intersection of culture, idiom, and artifact" (6; among them, Maria Barbella, Joseph Stella, and Madonna). Considering the media "integral to the persistence and dissemination, transformation and recovery, of Italianate sensibilities," Ferraro proposes that, today, only through cultural "artifacts" can we understand what it means "to feel Italian" in the United States (2). Robert Casillo rethinks dominant Italian American stereotypes in his "Reflections on Italian American Cinema," in which he discusses the pros and cons of some recent studies on the topic. He also addresses the issue of what constitutes Italian American cinema, concluding:

> Ideally, nothing should prevent the ethnic artist from treating his own ethnic background; yet the artist should have the equal right of ignoring his ethnicity when his or her creative interests and necessities dictate otherwise, without having to undergo the imputation of cultural betrayal, crime, or even symbolic murder. (26–27)

In "Women of the Shadows: Italian American Women, Ethnicity and Racism in American Cinema," Francesca Canadé Sautman takes up gender issues, considering how film may underscore gender stereotypes. In "Grey Shades, Black Tones: Italian Americans, Race and Racism in American Film," she concentrates on race, demonstrating how

> film participates and is complicit in the play between reinvention and reaffirmation of tradition, between creativity and repetition, between self-affirming cultural strategies and subservient ones, that generate complex discursive and visual narratives on the screen. (4)

Dawn Esposito's "The Italian Mother: The Wild Woman Within" examines the representation of the mother, underscoring "her point of entry into the space of femininity" (32), juxtaposing it with the patriarchal space that dominates Italian American cinema, and thus revealing cinema's current "parameters of ideology" (32). Esposito then turns to spectatorship in her essay "Gloria, Maerose, Irene, and Me: Mafia Women and Abject Spectatorship." Discussing gender issues in films by Nancy Savoca and Marylou Tibaldo-Bongiorno, Anna Camaiti Hostert likewise shows how women directors work in a state of "*in-between-ness*," a "privileged location from where to observe and describe the conflicts which arise from the conflagrating experiences of different ethnic worlds" (61).

Despite the paucity of work on the gender issue and the notably small number of female Italian American directors, several critics have singled out Savoca as one of the most original figures in contemporary Italian American cinema. In addition to appearing in several broadly focused essays, she is the subject of a few single-subject essays. In "The Quest for True Love: Ethnicity in Nancy Savoca's Domestic Film Comedy," Edvige Giunta addresses large gender issues and considers how the domestic setting—the space of female discourse—often functions in film as a metaphor for the ambivalence Italian American women feel toward their ethnicity. The essay considers Savoca's questioning of "the most elemental constructions of ethnicity and gender in Italian/American culture" in her first film, *True Love* (259). Gloria Nardini's "Is It True Love? or Not? Patterns of Ethnicity and Gender in Nancy Savoca" follows a similar line of thinking. Nardini sees *True Love* as an "intimate and ironic view of marriage" from a female perspective, in which ethnicity and gender serve as the foundation for producing meaning (9). Aaron Baker and Juliann Vitullo's "Mysticism and the Household Saints of Everyday Life" discusses Savoca's second explicitly Italian American film, *Household Saints*. Here, the authors analyze how ethnicity and religion contribute to "constructions of domesticity and femininity" in a post–World War II Italian American community (57).

Essays on short films made by Italian Americans are few in number and seem to concentrate on a single subject. Giunta ("Figuring Race") and Hiram Perez focus on Kym Ragusa's short film on biraciality *Fuori/Outside*. My essay "Spectacular Imagery in Italian/American Short Films: Race as Stage-Display Pageantry" examines the representation of race in a fiction piece, a music video, and a documentary; my "Italian/American Briefs: Re-visiting the Short Subject" analyzes three short fictional films. Italian American short films have generally succeeded in offering their viewers a new way of seeing Italian America and its many facets; they tend to uncover viewers' relation to the internal and external dynamics of all the Little Italys as notions of race, gender, sexuality, companionship, and family, among others, come to the fore. *Newness* becomes the operative word as these filmmakers have succeeded in maintaining an artistic freedom that has allowed them to engage in different forms of a sui generis creativity. They have, therefore, avoided at all costs falling victim to the shackles of both a thematic and formalistic tradition, instead appropriating a more liberating and expansive discourse.

Television

In the history of television, as in that of the silver screen, Italian Americans have been a presence both in front of and behind the camera. Scholarship on the subject, though, is still scant. In addition to John A. Lent's entry in *The Italian American Experience*, two other specific studies exist: Robert Lichter and Linda Lichter's hard-to-find *Italian American Characters in Television Entertainment* and Andrew Brizzolara's "The Image of Italian Americans on U.S. Television." Finally, the Web site "Italian (Includes Sicilians)" lists the various shows in which "Italian" characters have appeared since the onset of television in the United States.

The absence of studies of Italian Americans on television emphasizes two general issues: the continued problem of minimal scholarly attention paid to Italian Americans and a lack of interest about representations of Italian Americans on television that seems to exist even among scholars in Italian American studies. Many cultural critics, journalistic and academic, whose ethnic heritage is Italian do not pay as much attention to developing analyses of representations of their own ethnicities as other "ethnic" cultural critics seem to do. The question of self-identity may contribute to the situation: Italian Americans tend to self-identify as Americans and to avoid ethnic self-identification.

The high number of creative cultural productions of Italian Americans is contrasted by the paucity of critical studies, especially books. We are left with a dearth of sustained studies of Italians on television. What we find instead is a series of books on management, life style, philosophy, and cooking based on the HBO series *The Sopranos*. Some include *Leadership Sopranos Style: How to Become a More Effective Boss* (Himsel); *Tony Soprano on Management: Leadership Lessons Inspired by America's Favorite Mobster* (A. Schneider); *The Sopranos: The Book*; *The Sopranos Family Cookbook: As Compiled by Artie Bucco* (Rucker and Scicolone); or even *The Soprano State: New Jersey's Culture of Corruption* (Ingle and McClure), a book that has virtually nothing to do with the television program but takes its title from it. Even the very few that are serious in intent, such as Regina Barreca's *A Sitdown with the Sopranos*, raise a host of questions. Why, for instance, just *The Sopranos*? Cannot, indeed, should not this show provoke more general questions about the overall representation of Italians and Italian Americans on television? The risk of books such as Barreca's, even in their seriousness, is that they willy-nilly reinforce old stereotypes, especially when they open with sentences like the following:

> A signature phrase of *The Godfather*, the gun/cannoli line is emblematic of what Tony and his family are fitfully trying to accomplish in *The Sopranos*: they want to seize what is best of Italian American culture—the appetites, the passions, the affections, the humor—while leaving behind on the table the bitterness, the alienation, the crime, and the violence. (1)

I would submit that the best of Italian American culture includes more than "the appetites, the passions, the affections, the humor." More work clearly lies ahead.

Lent's contribution is an encyclopedic entry that offers both a history and an analysis of the presence of the many Italian Americans on television. Lichter and Lichter's analysis studies Italians on television through 1982, demonstrating how the medium has continued to perpetuate conventional Italian American stereotypes. Brizzolara's article enumerates the Italian American stereotypes perpetuated by television and also analyzes how they might have a negative impact on viewers, particularly Italian American youth. Brizzolara uses two essays from Miller's *Ethnic Images in American Film and Television* to provide further evidence of the continued negative depiction of Italian Americans on television. He also cites the New York state senator John D. Calandra, who argued that young Italian Americans run the risk of suffering the "emotional handicap of a negative self-conduct" (4), having been assailed by the plethora of negative stereotypes.

The Web site "Italian (Includes Sicilians)"—which claims to be approximately ninety percent complete—consists of short descriptions of the many television programs that have dealt with, directly and indirectly, the figure of the Italian and Italian American since the advent of television. The basic information the reader is able to cull from it offers a relatively representative snapshot of what was being aired on television, especially during its early years.

Allen L. Woll and Miller's "The Italians" both rehearses a history of the representation of Italians and Italian Americans and provides an in-depth bibliography through the mid-1980s. Looking at film and television, the authors offer a sensitive, rigorous reading of the history of representations of Italian Americans. They cover the literature on the movies as well as analyze the more popular films about Italian Americans.

In the United States mainstream, Italian Americans have enjoyed success, be it in business, education, the scientific community, or politics. The issue we still need to revisit is the seemingly inexplicable disconnect between such success and the limited body of intellectual work that provides a critical examination of the Italian American presence in film and on television. The need for more book-length studies is especially pressing for the figure of the Italian and Italian American on television. A variety of images have, throughout the years, been considered positive only because they do not underwrite the Mafia figure. Nevertheless, some of these portrayals might prove just as damaging. One ignored Italian American on television is George Costanza from *Seinfeld*; a more cumbersome figure would be difficult to create. He is socially awkward, self-loathing, stingy, neurotic, and dominated by his parents, characteristics readily associated with the Italian *mammone* ("mamma's boy"). Such buffoonery, simplicity of thought, and, to some extent, goofiness proved part and parcel of the Italian family of *Everybody Loves Raymond*. The question then becomes one of choice, measure, and comprehension: What do we choose to accept or reject? How do we critique what we choose to reject? And how do we deal with those who decide to depict and embrace such figures on either the large or small screen? These issues, for the most part, have not yet been explored in a rigorous, dispassionate manner; it is precisely such serious scholarly analysis that we need to develop as part of our interpretive range.

Mark Pietralunga

Italian American Studies in Italy

A long neglected dimension of Italian historiography, the study of Italian emigration has become a recognized area of research, though still largely marginalized in the Italian university system. A global debate on the migration question has encouraged Italian scholars to expand their methods of inquiry and to adopt an interdisciplinary approach to examine the Italian emigration of the last two hundred years. With the emergence of Italy as a country of immigration, some have called for a redefinition of the traditional concept of Italian national literature into a transnational one, thus promoting the reappraisal of the literature and culture of emigration (Gnisci 99). The political debate surrounding the approval in 2001 of a law granting Italian citizens living abroad the right to vote in Italian elections and the initiatives at the local, regional, and national levels to champion Italians in the world as an important resource for Italy as well as the country of settlement have further contributed to the cultural legitimatization of Italian American studies in Italy.

In his essay "Emigrazione transoceanica e ricerca storica in Italia: Gli ultimi anni (1978–1988)" ("Transoceanic Emigration and Historical Research in Italy: Recent Years 1978–1988") Emilio Franzina offers an indispensable overview of the studies on Italian emigration in Italy, noting that Italian interest in the question of emigration moved from a slow awakening in the late 1970s to a significant scientific output during the 1980s. Suggesting that Italian historians should open themselves to comparative and collaborative inquiries such as those promoted by scholars of transnational studies abroad, Franzina argues in favor of a regional or local approach that privileges the origins of migration and suggests that the history of the transoceanic emigration be understood also through novels, short stories, songs, and autobiographies of immigrants.

In 1990, the Giovanni Agnelli Foundation, a major Italian cultural institution for the study of emigration, co-organized with the University of Lausanne a conference on literature and emigration and writers of the Italian language in the world. The conference proceedings, edited by Jean-Jacques Marchand, appeared the following year in the Agnelli Foundation's newly created publication series, Popolazioni e culture italiane nel mondo ("Italian Populations and Cultures in the World"). What emerged from this conference was the awareness that the writings by Italian emigrants ought not be relegated to the marginal, accessory position ascribed to them by the cultural elite and traditional literary criticism. One finds, for example, a perceived negative bias toward Italian American emigrants and their literature in the writings of influential critics like Emilio Cecchi and Giuseppe Prezzolini. The conference articulated a need for the literary sphere to redefine its criteria on the basis of studies by historians, sociologists, and linguists to provide a more inclusive panorama of Italian cultural history.

Franzina's groundbreaking study *Dall'Arcadia in America: Attività letteraria ed emigrazione transoceanica in Italia (1850–1940)* ("From Arcadia to America: Literary Activity and Transoceanic Emigration in Italy, 1850–1940") examines the reluctance and lack of interest that the academic culture has shown toward studying the nearly one hundred years of literary activity produced by Italian emigrant writers, many of whom have come from the subaltern classes of the peninsula. Up to that moment, only a handful of literary critics in Italy had analyzed the literary and paraliterary writings that emigration had inspired. Franzina's interdisciplinary approach was evident in the exploration of such topics as emigration and the myth of America between autobiography and the serial novel, the mass exodus in verse and in music, emigration and cinema, emigrant novels at the turn of the century, and the America of the immigrants between literary *meridionalismo* ("meridionalism") and propaganda of the fascist regime. In the closing essay to the edited collection of conference proceedings on Italian American literature and culture, *Il sogno italo-americano: Realtà e immaginario dell'emigrazione negli Stati Uniti* ("The Italian American Dream: Reality and Imagination of Emigration to the United States"), Sebastiano Martelli echoes Franzina's comments concerning the deficiencies of Italian literary criticism's treatment of emigration literature while also reconfirming the need for a multidisciplinary and global approach to a literature that presents a peculiar mixture of literary forms and models. Refering to the depiction of emigrants' arrival at Ellis Island in Henry Roth's 1934 novel *Call It Sleep*, Martelli signals the absence of a major Italian novel on emigration and underlines the long-standing unease of the Italian intellectual regarding a social phenomenon of such vast dimensions.

The publication in 2001 of the first volume of the anthology *Italoamericana: Storia e letteratura degli italiani negli Stati Uniti, 1776–1880* ("Italoamericana: History and Literature of Italians in the United States"), edited by Francesco Durante, introduced a territory that was largely unknown to a nonspecialist public. In his historical and literary panorama of Italian American immigration to the United States that covers the earliest period of Italian American literary activity (1776–1880), Durante adopts a comparative approach that expands the canon beyond literary parameters. In doing so, he circumvents an exclusive, aesthetic standard, which has often relegated these texts to the sphere of social and historical commentaries. Durante suggests that the negative judgment of Italian American culture, especially that produced in the Italian *colonie* ("colonies") beginning in the 1880s, by prestigious cultural mediators between Italy and America explains the neglect suffered by Italian American culture. In 2005, Durante published the second volume of the *Italoamericana* anthology (1880–1943), which focuses on the great migration and the Little Italys. In this 950-page volume, he presents more than eighty authors with their practically unknown texts, taken largely from rare collections of Italian American newspapers and books. Durante also edited *Figli di due mondi* ("Children of Two Worlds"), the first anthology of Italian American writers of the 1930s and 1940s.

Martino Marazzi's study *Misteri di Little Italy: Storie e testi della letteratura italoamericana* ("Mysteries of Little Italy: Stories and Memoirs from Italian American Literature"), with its multidisciplinary transatlantic approach to Italian American literature, has contributed to introducing Italian American literature and culture to a wide Italian audience and to helping overcome stereotypes of Italian Americans. In the expanded,

English edition of this study, *Voices of Italian America: A History of Early Italian Literature with a Critical Anthology*, Marazzi notes the role of Italian research centers in promoting a better understanding of immigration. In addition to the Giovanni Agnelli Foundation—which also sponsors the *Italiani nel Mondo* Web site with links to the online international scholarly journal *Altreitalie*—the Centro Studi Emigrazione (CSER), established in 1963 in Rome by the General Administration of the Scalabrinian Missionaries to study the sociological, historical, political, theological, and pastoral aspects of national and international migration movements, promotes research on Italian communities abroad. The CSER publishes the international journal *Studi emigrazione*, on migration and ethnic groups.

In the field of Italian American cinema, there has been a rich production of studies on Italian American filmmakers and actors and on the question of ethnicity and American identity. A large part of the research has been limited to scholarly articles on topics ranging from the first generation of Italian Americans in Hollywood to more contemporary figures such as Martin Scorsese, Robert De Niro, Abel Ferrara, and John Turturro. On the other hand, there have been very few panoramic book-length studies on Italian American cinema. To date, three volumes stand out: *Hollywood Italian: Gli italiani nell'America di celluloide* ("Hollywood Italians: The Italians in Celluloid America"), by Paola Casella; *Scene italoamericane. Rappresentazioni cinematografiche degli italiani d'America* (*Screening Ethnicity: Cinematographic Representations of Italian Americans in the United States*), edited by Anna Camaiti Hostert and Anthony Julian Tamburri; and *Piccole Italie, grandi schermi. Scambi cinematografici tra Italia e gli Stati Uniti, 1895–1945* ("Little Italys, Big Screens: Cinematographic Exchanges between Italy and the United States, 1895–1945"), by Giuliana Muscio.

The good fortune of emigration studies in recent years is reflected by the numerous conferences, exhibits, Web sites, associations, museums, and books dedicated to Italian American culture. Italy has witnessed the development of regional and local institutes and associations, which have become pillars of the bounty of activities related to emigration. The various regional branches of the Italiani nel Mondo association have been especially active in bringing a consciousness of Italians abroad through the organization of conferences, libraries, and Web sites. Local emigration studies centers serve as repositories for archival sources and memorabilia about migrants from small subnational and subregional areas and have sponsored the publication of Italian American writings. The Ecoistituto della Valle del Ticino in Cuggiano (Milan) published in 2003 the Italian translation of *Rosa: The Life of an Italian Immigrant* (*Rosa: Vita di una emigrante italiana*), edited by Marie Hall Ets, with a new introduction by Maddalenna Tirabassi. Many publishing houses have been active in promoting Italian American literature. Il Grappolo, thanks to the efforts of its editor, Antonio Corbusiero, has published the works of Pascal D'Angelo, Joe Pagano, Pietro di Donato, Arturo Giovannitti, and Joseph Tusiani and sponsored the Pascal D'Angelo Research Institute for Emigration Literature in San Severino (Salerno). Avagliano inaugurated the series Transatlantico, directed by Francesco Durante and focused on the theme of multiethnicity from the perspective of the departure and return between Europe and the two Americas, and has published an anthology of the writings of John Fante, Hilda Perini, and Anthony Turano as well as novels by Pagano, Robert Viscusi, and Michele Fiaschetti. Marcos y Marcos and Fazi are both publishers of Fante. Cosmo Iannone has three series on emigration—Quaderni sull'emigrazione, Reti, and I Memoriali ("Notebooks on Emigration," "Networks," and "Memoirs"), directed by Norberto Lombardi—and has published works by Giose Rimanelli and by Govannitti, as well as the interdisciplinary collection edited by Nick Ceramella and Giuseppe Massara, *Merica. Forme della cultura italoamericana* ("Merica: Forms of Italian American Culture"). Donzelli's output is highlighted by the definitive two-volume history of Italian emigration, *Storia dell'emigrazione italiana* (Bevilacqua, De Clementi, and Franzina). This monumental collaborative venture—which includes contributions of some seventy scholars on such topics as return migration, women in migration, the cultural aspects and representations of migration (popular literature, letters, songs, theater, films, radio, television, and food), Little Italys, anti-Italian racism, Italians and "others," and Italians on the Web—not only serves as testimony to the maturity of Italian scholarship in the field of Italian American studies but also marks the political and national prominence that such a topic has garnered in Italy today as a result of the project's sponsorship by the National Committee of Celebration of the Ministry of Cultural Properties and Activities.

There has been an increasing interest in Italian American studies by such leading commercial presses as Einaudi, Feltrinelli, Mondadori, and Rizzoli, whose titles are not merely restricted to best-selling authors like Don DeLillo or David Balducci. Most notably, the works of Fante have attracted the attention of Italy's major commercial presses. Einaudi has published several of his novels and short stories, with introductions by some of Italy's leading writers and filmmakers; Mondadori, on the other hand, has published the writings of Fante in its prestigious I Meridiani series on the twentieth anniversary of his death. Gian Antonio Stella's bestseller *L'orda: Quando gli albanesi eravamo noi* ("The Horde: When We Were the Albanians"), published by Rizzoli, presents a highly accessible portrait of the unwelcoming attitudes and intolerance of western Europe, northern Africa, and the Americas in the nineteenth and twentieth centuries toward Italian American emigrants that, as the subtitle suggests, bears many similarities to the racial and ethnic prejudices concerning the recent influx of immigrants to Italy. In 2003, Rizzoli published Melania G. Mazzucco's best-selling and critically acclaimed novel *Vita* (*Vita: A Novel*), considered by many the first novel by an Italian author on the Italian emigration. The translation of this novel into English in 2005 marked an important step in bringing the Italian perspective on the Italian American experience into mainstream American culture. In 2006, Elena Gianini Belotti published the novel *Pane amaro* ("Bitter Bread"), which narrates the true story of an Italian emigrant in America. Each of these novels is based in part on the author's family history, and each promotes a reflection of Italy's past and present, as the country has become a type of America for hundreds of thousands of men and women coming from other world shores. In his introduction to the Italian translation of *Are Italians White? How Race Is Made in America* (*Gli italiani sono bianchi? Come l'America ha costruito la razza*), Gian Antonio Stella, like Mazzucco and Gianini Bellotti, views the experience of Italian emigrants in America as an integral part of Italian history. For Stella, a full understanding of the hardships and racism that plagued the daily life of the Italian emigrants both in the country of origin and settlement "può solo aiutarci a crescere" 'can only help us [Italians] grow' (15; my trans.).

There has been a concerted effort to introduce the literature by Italian American women writers to an Italian readership to create a relationship of continuity between Italian women emigrants and their land of origin and between Italian women of America and Italian women of Italy (Romeo 32). In 2001, the renowned Italian feminist writer Maria Rosa Cutrufelli enlisted Edvige Giunta and Caterina Romeo to edit a special issue of *Tuttestorie* devoted to Italian American women that included translations of scholarly and creative works by Italian American women as well as contributions by Italian women. In 2004, another key Italian feminist publication, *Leggendaria*, edited by Anna Maria Crispino, devoted a special issue to the same subject: in her editorial, Crispino suggested that the work of the "daughters of two worlds" interrogates Italian identity on both sides of the Atlantic (3). Tirabassi's edited collection of the writings on Italian migrations by Amy Allemand Bernardy, *Ripensare la patria grande* ("Thinking Back to the Great Homeland"), offers a sociologically oriented analysis of the life conditions of the emigrants in the United States during the most fervent years of the migration (1900–30). In her preface, Tirabassi notes that Bernardy stands out in the universe of writers on emigration for her comprehensive treatment of the phenomenon of the Italian migration in the years of its development (15).

The translation of texts is, of course, key in this growing awareness in Italy of women's contribution to Italian American literature and culture. Among the autobiographies and memoirs that have appeared in recent years are Blandina Segale's *Suor Blandina: Una suora italiana nel West* (*At the End of the Santa Fe Trail*), considered a "small classic in the category of eyewitness accounts" (Simmons xiii); the life story of Rosa Cavalleri (Ets); Louise DeSalvo's family memoir *Vertigo*; and Kym Ragusa's *La pelle che ci separa* (*The Skin between Us*). In 2007, Nutrimenti, the publisher of DeSalvo's and Ragusa's memoirs, also published Tina De Rosa's *Pesci di carta* (*Paper Fish*). In 2002, the University of Siena published a translation of Edvige Giunta's essays on the memoir, *Dire l'indicibile. Il memoir delle autrici italo americane* (*To Say the Unspeakable: The Memoirs of Italian American Women Writers*) in its series Quaderni di studi sulle donne ("Notebooks of Women's Studies"). In 2005, the first Italian full-length study of the literature of Italian American women was published: Romeo's *Narrative tra due sponde: Memoir di italiane d'America* ("Narratives between Two Shores: The Memoir of Italian American Women"). Romeo explains how the memoirs of Italian American women depart from the conventions of autobiography in their emphasis on collective as opposed to individual memory. According to Romeo, a key element of these memoirs is the complicated relationship that the women entertain with their families and with the patriarchal community to which they belong. While she focuses on the work of memorists DeSalvo and Mary Cappello, in an early chapter Romeo recognizes the impact of Helen Barolini's *The Dream Book* on the recovery of Italian American cultural memory and the discovery of a literary tradition of Italian American women, which paved the way for the Italian American memoirs published in the 1990s.

In 2001, Barolini's multigenerational immigrant women's saga, *Umbertina*, appeared in the Translatlantic series of Avagliano Press. In 2003, the same series published Barolini's novel *Passaggio in Italia* (*Crossing the Alps*), which treats a young Italian American woman's search for identity in the midst of the ruins of postwar Italy. The following year Barolini's collection of essays, *Chiaroscuro: Saggi sull'identità* ("Chiaroscuro: Essays on Identity"), was published by Guerini e Associati with an insightful introduction by Antonia Arslan. Other translated works of fiction that have contributed toward legitimizing Italian American women's literature are Agnes Rossi's portrayal of marginal figures in *Gonna a spacco* (*Split Skirt*), Mary Caponegro's collection of short stories *Materia prima* ("Raw Material"), and Gioia Timpanelli's modern-day retelling of Sicilian fairy tales, *De anima sicula* (*Sometimes the Soul: Two Novellas of Sicily*). A prolific generation of Italian women authors and feminist intellectuals must be given some credit for paving the way for the growing visibility of Italian American women in Italy today.

Though the rich scholarly production on Italian emigration and its culture has not been matched by academic recognition, the subject of Italian American migration has been taught in Italian universities since the 1960s. The Associazione Italiana di Studi Nord-Americani (AISNA) has played an important role in bringing an awareness of Italian American studies to universities in Italy. In 1983, AISNA organized a conference at the University of Catania on Italy and Italians in America. The conference proceedings were published in the *RSA Journal–Rivista di Studi Nord Americani*, sponsored by AISNA (Rizzardi). The association has subsequently included workshops dedicated to Italian Americans at its biennial international meetings. In addition, the prominent journal *Àcoma: Rivista internazionale di studi nordamericani* is published under the aegis of the University of Bergamo and the University of Rome, La Sapienza. While few Italian institutions offer courses, much less formal degree programs, devoted to Italian American studies, topics related to the Italian American migration have been taught at the universities of Sassari, Rome, Florence, Siena, Turin, and Padua. These courses, however, are offered under the titles of more conventional or traditional disciplines, like English literature, Anglo-American literature, or history of North America. While there are no doctoral programs in Italian American studies, a few interdisciplinary programs, such as the doctorate in the history of women writings within the Department of Philological, Linguistic, and Literary

Studies at the University of Rome, La Sapienza, have granted degrees in the discipline.

The active dialogue among Italian Americanists at an international level, such as the 2004 conference sponsored by the journal *Altreitalie* in Turin, Emigrazione italiana: Percorsi interpretativi tra diaspora, transnationalism e generazioni (Rethinking Italian Migrations: Diaspora, Transnationalism, and Generations), bodes well for the continued growth of Italian American studies in Italy. In her introduction to the proceedings of this conference, Tirabassi mentions the great strides that Italian migration studies has made in Italy in recent years. Yet she is quick to point out that the discipline's emergence from the margins does require some caution. She argues that although emigration studies has become an unexpectedly popular field, scholars must maintain a high level of rigor so that their work will not become merely fashionable but will be the means by which genuine growth of the discipline can occur (*Itinera* 8). To continue its upward trajectory, Italian American studies in Italy needs to remain receptive to developing critical concepts of ethnic identity, displacement, and diaspora, and the question of emigration needs to speak to the collective history of the nation.

Fred Gardaphé

Creating a Program in Italian American Studies

The beneficiary of earlier social protest movements that produced such academic programs as African American and women's studies, Italian American studies developed in earnest only recently. Unlike many other ethnic and gender studies programs, programs in Italian American studies did not result from direct, popular political actions. Discrete and individualized work was conducted to create the earliest efforts in the new field, and political activity has only become a recent strategy for those advocating its development.

The most celebrated case of political action surrounded the evolution of the John D. Calandra Institute of the City University of New York system. After years of operating as a research and career counseling center, the Calandra Institute, fortified by a study conducted by Richard Gambino, received permanent funding when it won the 1992 Scelsa v. City University of New York lawsuit. A settlement reached in 1994 granted the institute research status, provided permanent funding to foster higher education for Italian Americans, and attached a Distinguished Professorship to the institute through Queens College—first occupied by Philip Cannistraro from 1995 until his death in 2005.

During the 1990s, Mario B. Mignone, then chairperson of the Department of French and Italian at the State University of New York, Stony Brook, and director of the Center for Italian Studies, began to realize that the work being presented at conferences of organizations such as the American Italian Historical Association, the American Association of Italian Studies, and the American Association of Teachers of Italian should speak to the growing community of Italian Americans who populated Long Island. Aware that Italian Americans had moved from urban to suburban areas, especially to the Nassau and Suffolk counties of Long Island, Mignone organized events, such as conferences on Italian American women and on Italians on Long Island, that drew the surrounding community to the academy.

As the Italian American presence in the state legislature increased, Mignone tapped into this growing political power to gain state funds to support Italian American studies. A key figure in this effort was the New York State senator Kenneth P. LaValle, chair of the Higher Education Committee of the Senate. Through the Center for Italian Studies, Mignone applied for state grants available to educational institutions and raised monies from private sources. These funds went to produce academic conferences, community events, and visits from professors and artists. In fall 1990, Mignone developed the first course in Italian American studies, which was such a success that he decided to propose a minor in the subject and subsequently pursued additional state funding for the center. In 1993, a minor in Italian American studies was approved by the university's curriculum committee, and for the fiscal year 1993–94 the center was awarded $200,000 in state funds.

Increased funding enabled Mignone to bring in Gambino as a visiting professor in spring 1994. Gambino took a leave from his position at Queens College, where he had developed the earliest Italian American studies courses in the social sciences in the 1970s and 1980s. Gambino taught humanities and social sciences at Stony Brook until 1997. Mignone used state funding to create a new departmental line in Italian American studies. In 1998, I was hired as Stony Brook's first director of Italian American studies. A year later, Stony Brook also hired Mary Jo Bona. The Stony Brook team created a plan that would solidify the program through the establishment of an endowed professorship, the development of library resources, and student scholarships.

UNICO National (the largest Italian American service organization) joined the Center for Italian Studies in a 2006 fund-raising campaign to raise $1.5 million to create the Alphonse M. D'Amato Professorship, the first privately funded endowed professorship in Italian American studies in the State University of New York system. (Peter Carravetta was appointed the first Alphonse M. D'Amato Professor.) UNICO had previously assisted in the fund-raising of endowed professorships in Italian studies at the University of Connecticut, Storrs; Seton Hall University; and California State University, Long Beach, and is currently involved in similar campaigns at Montclair State University and Hofstra University, where Pellegrino D'Acierno was appointed to the professorship. Stony Brook's Melville Library dedicated significant monies to expand its holdings in the field, making Stony Brook's one of the best Italian American collections in the United States, and, despite tight budget constraints, the library continues to keep up with the growing scholarship in the field. The library's special collection has initiated an Italian American archives project that has acquired Edward Cifelli's papers on John Ciardi; papers from the author and artist Valenti Angelo; the immigrant journals of Agosto Lentricchia, the grandfather of the Duke University scholar and writer, Frank Lentricchia; the papers of the playwright Richard Vetere; and the papers of Pietro di Donato. The next project will be the creation of graduate and undergraduate scholarships.

Because of the 9/11 terrorist attacks, the New York State budget for higher education faced a crisis. As a result, the Center for Italian Studies has not enjoyed its earlier levels of funding and has needed to rely more on private funding. Nevertheless, the academic program has continued to grow and has come to serve over two thousand students a year. The minor in Italian American studies has since grown into the leading undergraduate Italian American studies program in the United States.

The key to the success of Italian American studies at Stony Brook is the high concentration of Italian Americans in the Long Island population (conservative estimates figure that Italian Americans make up close to twenty-eight percent of the population). The program, which exists only as a minor, is housed in the Department of European Languages, Literatures, and Cultures. Because some of the courses were approved by the university to fulfill general education requirements, the program attracted students of all backgrounds.

The gateway course of the program is The Italian American Scene, an introductory, lecture-based interdisciplinary course that surveys historical as well as artistic highlights of the Italian presence in American history and culture. The upper-level film course, Images of Italian Americans in

Film, fills to maximum enrollment each semester largely because it is part of a thriving major in cinema and cultural studies. These courses were designed with those general requirements in mind and continue to serve the needs of humanities and social science programs that have suffered from rigorous budget slashing since 2003. Italian American materials have also been integrated into existing courses in cultural studies and humanities, in such departments as English and women's studies. In addition, some new courses were created, such as an undergraduate comparative course on Italian American and African American women writers and a graduate course in Italian American literature. Faculty members in traditional Italian studies areas have contributed to the program through courses in contemporary Italy, autobiography, poetry, and the origins of Italian culture. This array of courses gives students the opportunity to study Italian American culture in multiple contexts—from American minorities to the Italian diaspora, though the emphasis of the Stony Brook program is primarily on the Italian immigration to the United States.

Students are encouraged to link their work in Italian American studies with other fields. Combined with a major in political science, history, science, or psychology, Italian American studies provides students with an in-depth exploration of the role of ethnicity in the United States and throughout the world. A student majoring in sociology might find that a focus on how Italian Americans assimilated into American society will shed light on theoretical approaches to the study of urban and suburban cultures. Students majoring in American studies might use this program to study the culture of a specific ethnic group. A student pursuing a pre-med or prelaw major might use Italian American studies to establish an understanding of a community that she or he might serve. In essence, the program has been designed to add to the general education of the Stony Brook undergraduate and to offer a chance for comprehensive study for those interested in Italian American culture.

The completion of the minor in Italian American studies requires twenty-one credits. All courses offered to fulfill the requirements of the minor must be passed with a grade of C or higher. The required courses include, in addition to two Italian language courses, The Italian American Scene; Images of Italian American Women (which covers literature, film, politics, and music), cross-listed with women's studies; The Italian American Experience in Literature (built around a canon of classic and contemporary authors such as Pietro di Donato, Mari Tomasi, John Fante, Helen Barolini, Tina De Rosa, Tony Ardizzone, and Carole Maso), which fulfills an English and comparative studies major requirement; Italian Americans and Ethnic Relations (a historical and sociological examination, from colonial America to the present, of the experiences of ethnic minorities in the United States); Images of Italian Americans in Film (covers mainstream and independent American cinema from the silent era to the present); Topics on Italian American Studies: The Gangster in Literature (draws on Greek mythology, historical and sociological studies of American masculinity and violence, and popular culture studies to provide a context for the reading and understanding of the gangster); and The Emigrant Experience in Italian Literature (featuring accounts of such Italian authors as Ignazio Silone and Primo Levi). Other undergraduate courses on Italian and Italian American art, literature, and culture (all taught in English) that contribute to the Italian American studies minor include Italian Civilization through the Ages; Sex and Politics in Italian Cinema; Twentieth-Century Italian Theater; Sex, Love, and Tragedy in Early Italian Literature: Dante, Petrarch, and Boccaccio; Modern Italy; The Early Renaissance in Italy; The Age of Michelangelo in Central Italy; Splendor of Renaissance Art in Italy; Special Topics in Italian Studies; and Italian American Studies in Social and Behavioral Sciences. The range and availability of these courses are one reason that the Italian language program continues to thrive at a time when language programs in French, German, and Russian are struggling to survive.

The future of Italian American culture will rely on the continued relation between the academy and ethnic communities of the United States. Italian American studies at Stony Brook is the result of a unique partnership created between the academic and local communities with the purpose of improving educational opportunities for all students. The partnership thrives because both communities benefit from mutual respect and support and because both work to identify problems and to create the opportunities for resolving them. This dynamic has successfully combined the resources of the university and the surrounding Italian American population to support the research and development of scholarly work and instructional strategies that have shed light on this important aspect of American history and culture.

Part II

Considering Italian American Literature

Fiction and Poetry

Mary Jo Bona

Rich Harvest: An Overview of Italian American Fiction

The great exodus of the 1880s through the 1920s, halted by the passage of the 1924 Johnson Act, brought southern Italian and Sicilian emigrants to the United States, bearing a collective sense of uprooting. Despite a trauma of loss, what emerges from the great migration for Italians in nineteenth-century America is a vibrant literary life produced by scores of immigrant newspapers and their writers, from New York to San Francisco. In fact, the first writers of Italian America were journalists—often for both Italian and Italian American periodicals. A rich and layered literary culture existed in the pages of such papers as *Corriere d'America* and *Il progresso italo-americano*, which published works by immigrant writers whose fictions were often serialized in such volumes.

An Italian American aesthetic can be seen in such early works, which introduce themes that became basic to the second generation of Italian American writers in the 1930s and 1940s. From the social realism of end-of-century Italian American writers to an enhanced and revivified literary realism of second-generation sons and daughters, the locus that homogenizes the response to migration is the urban enclave, often referred to as a Little Italy. Serving as a cultural buffer for immigrants, such locales were prototypical settings of immigrant journalists, whose papers were avidly devoured by communities of migrants. While crowded tenement living made life difficult for immigrants, the enclave—and its periodicals, radical politics, parodic vaudevillian performers, and sacred *feste*—provided displaced Italians with a cultural space that recognized their struggles to survive American discrimination and the rebukes of their more assimilated children. Work, education, Americanization, loss of cultural ideals (including dialectal languages), struggles between the first and second generations, and the demands and exploitations of a market economy represent recurring themes of immigrant newspapers, re-created with vigor and flamboyance in nineteenth-century Italian American fiction.

Ventura and Ciambelli: Early Practitioners of Street-Corner Fictions

Two fin de siècle writers, Luigi Donato Ventura and Bernardino Ciambelli, possibly the earliest Italian American fiction writers, explore themes such as the trauma of migration and the difficult adjustment of immigrants and their children in ethnic ghettos. Paving a path for writers of the next generation, Ventura and Ciambelli introduce a theme that has become an archetype in Italian American fiction: the recurring conflict with institutional authorities, in particular the police and the judicial system. Ventura's 1885 novella, *Peppino*, offers an early version of the father-son plot so arrestingly featured in the subsequent generation of Italian American writers such as Louis Forgione, John Fante, and Pietro di Donato. Likewise, the sprawling, detective-like fictions of Ciambelli's *I misteri di Mulberry Street* blaze a trail for Garibaldi M. Lapolla, Guido D'Agostino, and Mario Puzo, each of whom re-creates the lures and traps of *campanilismo* ("village-mindedness").

Perhaps aware of the native-born American prejudice against the Italian language, Ventura, an adult émigré, first wrote *Peppino* in French, a language considered vastly superior to the dialects of Italian immigrants (*Peppino* was translated into English a year later). Featuring an Abruzzese immigrant boy, a bootblack on the Lower East Side of New York, *Peppino* introduces a father figure for the twelve-year-old child laborer, who immigrated with older brothers to America. As folksy in voice as Washington Irving and as precise in sociological detail as the urban photographer and social worker Jacob Riis, the narrator of *Peppino* functions as a cultural mediator who sympathetically represents the ordeals of impoverished immigrant children. Throughout successive conflicts for both the narrator (a penniless journalist) and Peppino (who is eventually run over by a peddler's cart), Ventura portrays the Italian colony as a multiethnic space and urban life as a nightmare for new immigrants, especially those bereft of paternal protection.

Displaying a journalistic style of reportage, Ciambelli, like Ventura before him, reached a readership well beyond the Italian colony to which he remained indebted for his depiction of the seamier side of tenement living in *I misteri di Mulberry Street.* Reflecting an awareness of the punitive characteristics of the American police force and judiciary, Ciambelli examines with great melodrama and force the machinations of Italians and Americans, good and bad detectives and policemen, and a host of other characters (including wanton women and rogues). Despite his excess, Ciambelli's focus on the metropolitan terrain offers a vision of late-nineteenth-century malaise, exposing the physical and social problems of urban America. The generation of writers following Ventura and Ciambelli examines with more literary acuity the telling effects of cultural uprooting, writing in a language—English—that their parents could not even read.

Di Donato, Fante, and Tomasi: Exemplars of Literary Realism

The pain of assimilation, the formidable struggle between Italian and American cultural values, including an extension of a critique of American capitalism, inform the works of the second-generation Italian American writers Pietro di Donato (*Christ in Concrete*), John Fante (*Wait until Spring, Bandini*), Mari Tomasi (*Like Lesser Gods*), Garibaldi M. Lapolla (*The Grand Gennaro*), Guido D'Agostino (*Olives on the Apple Tree*), George Panetta (*We Ride a White Donkey*), and Jerre Mangione (*The Ship and the Flame*).

Autobiographical fiction of the 1930s and 1940s was written by authors who migrated to America as children or who were born shortly after their parents made the transatlantic crossing. The first and arguably the most significant work of Italian American literature of this era is di Donato's *Christ in Concrete*, also the first Italian American literary work to achieve enormous recognition in literary circles. Di Donato reached a national audience in 1937 when *Esquire* published his short story "Christ in Concrete," which portrays the untimely death of the author's father in an avoidable construction accident. Di Donato expanded the story into a novel of the same name, and it became the main selection of the Book-of-the-Month Club, chosen over John Steinbeck's *The Grapes of Wrath.* Employing a vernacular English that simulates the dialectal languages of

Italian immigrant laborers, di Donato re-creates the poetic voices of a semiliterate ethnic group to which American society had turned a deaf ear. Extending the topics promulgated by the earlier writers, di Donato documents the destruction of the Italian family in America, beginning with the father's death, which is caused by the competitive greed and indifference of American capitalism.

The idiomatic style of di Donato is replaced with the deceptively simple styles of Fante and Tomasi, who portray Italian families negotiating with the American dream through education and upward mobility but also, at times, through a rejection of Italian cultural codes of *l'ordine della famiglia* ("regulations governing family life"). A bildungsroman, *Wait until Spring, Bandini* is Fante's exploration of generational differences between Italian parents and American children, who have imbibed native-born hostility toward their ethnic group. In this novel, the father's anger stems from the peripheral work of stonemasonry and bricklaying in the building trades in Denver, Colorado. Praised by James T. Farrell, *Wait until Spring, Bandini* also enjoyed the support of H. L. Mencken, who earlier published many of Fante's short stories (Moreau). Like di Donato, Fante examines the tension between a devout mother (whose Catholicism is rejected by the protagonist son) and a philandering father (whose poverty overshadows his artisanship). As does the oldest son of di Donato's *Christ in Concrete*, Fante's boy protagonist rejects his heritage, but this rejection emerges from a deep sense of ethnic self-hatred.

What may be best described as a communal bildungsroman focusing on the development of an Italian family and community in America, Tomasi's *Like Lesser Gods* is the first major novel written by an Italian American woman. Receiving fine reviews (including one in the *New York Times*), *Like Lesser Gods* fictionalizes the stonecutting industry of Barre, Vermont, and the town's Italian immigrant community. While Tomasi portrays stoneworkers who die from noxious dust particles inhaled from the granite they work, she suppresses a discussion of the radical origins of anarchism within this Italian community and instead maximizes the lyrical quality of the enclave, commemorating an entire generation of skilled laborers.

Puzo, Barolini, and Bryant: Ethnic Redeemers of Italian America

Often considered a repressive and censorious decade, the 1950s in America nonetheless produced daring literature by second-generation Italian

American women writers, the most noteworthy being Julia Savarese's *The Weak and the Strong*, Antonia Pola's *Who Can Buy the Stars?*, Octavia Waldo's *A Cup of the Sun*, Diana Cavallo's *A Bridge of Leaves*, and Marion Benasutti's *No Steady Job for Papa*. Pola's *Who Can Buy the Stars?* provides an unusual portrait of a first-generation woman bootlegger, who continues selling liquor despite aspersions cast against her by her Indiana community. Savarese's naturalistic *The Weak and the Strong* focuses on the ruinous effects of the Great Depression on an Italian American family in New York City tenements. Unlike di Donato's tragic mother figure, Annunziata, Savarese's ironically named protagonist, Fortuna, although impoverished and ultimately widowed, does not succumb to death. Anger fuels her determination to survive, anger comparable with the mother's rage in Benasutti's *No Steady Job for Papa*. Waldo's *A Cup of the Sun* and Cavallo's *A Bridge of Leaves* demonstrate the influences of modernism in structure and character, whether the novel is set in a traditional Little Italy (Waldo) or is a psychological exploration of ethnic duality (Cavallo).

With increased education in American schools, the dismantling of Italian enclaves followed by migration to outlying suburbs, and ethnic revivals emerging out of protest movements of the 1960s and 1970s, many writers came to celebrate and mythologize Italian cultural identity. Three of the most influential and prolific of those writers are Mario Puzo, Helen Barolini, and Dorothy Bryant. Like their forebears, these authors published early autobiographical novels based on the experience of their ancestors' migration and adjustment in America. Puzo received critical acclaim for his autobiographical novel, *The Fortunate Pilgrim*, which recreates the Italian colony in the New York tenements of Hell's Kitchen of the 1920s and 1930s and features one of the most remarkable female figures in all Italian American literature, Lucia Santa (named after the Sicilian saint who plucked out her eyes). Negotiating cleverly between family-centered Italian values and new-world ways, Lucia Santa demonstrates the *furberia* ("wiliness") needed to survive as an unvalued immigrant in America. Puzo explores how Lucia Santa manipulates, to her family's advantage, the police force and the public school, institutions that threatened to decrease parental authority in America. After she enlists the help of the police to escort her insane husband to an asylum, Lucia Santa assumes complete maternal control of her brood of children. Puzo thus carefully extends an exploration of how immigrant families adjusted to the demands of institutional authorities in America.

In his acclaimed third novel, *The Godfather*, Puzo examined *onore* ("honor"), *fare bella figura* ("creating a beautiful figure in public"), and family solidarity, which he fictionalized in Vito Corleone, the novel's patriarch. A "genuinely mythic" work of fiction, as Puzo wrote in *The Godfather Papers* (33), this best-selling novel catapulted its author into the national limelight, exceeding in critical acclaim all previous works of Italian American fiction, including di Donato's popular *Christ in Concrete*. One of the most widely read novels of the twentieth century, *The Godfather* spent sixty-seven weeks on the *New York Times* best-seller list. Puzo thereafter collaborated with Francis Ford Coppola on the equally successful film adaptations (*The Godfather*, *The Godfather II*, and *The Godfather III*). While antidefamation groups decried the author's resurrection of the criminal element, Puzo's artistic intention in *The Godfather* was to present a mythical portrayal of an enclosed world of Sicilian Americans protected by a familial system of *comparatico* ("godparenthood") and a benevolent despot who fights righteously against corrupt American institutions of business and government. Puzo, like Ciambelli, di Donato, and Fante before him, critiques American capitalism, suggesting that American businessmen and politicians are not unlike the members of the organized crime they overtly fight against but with whom they are covertly in collusion. Puzo's achievement, however, remains his ability to seduce readers into accepting the Corleone family justice as righteous and rejecting the faceless style of American corporatism.

Ethnic revivals emerging from movements for social change celebrated not only cultural identity but also the capacity for self-determination of individuals. Italian American women writers, capitalizing on ethnic revivalism and feminism, produced works that make individual women's development central, often through sexual and educational exploration. In this way, their works offer a variegated ethnic consciousness that is partly influenced by the social realism of the 1930s and 1940s and directly contrasts Puzo's nostalgic mythologizing of the Italian family and, especially, of brutal males as devoted fathers.

Helen Barolini's realist novel *Umbertina* provides an antidote to Puzo's romance. While it did not receive the accolades of other generational novels (such as Alex Haley's *Roots*), *Umbertina* is one of the most important epics of Italian America. In the novel, which spans four generations and two centuries of Italian and Italian American womanhood and traverses two continents, Barolini gives voice to the titular character, Umbertina, whose immigrant story resonates throughout, spiritually influencing successive generations of women. Feminizing the immigrant experience, *Umbertina* extends depictions of the female quest for autonomy earlier portrayed in Michael De Capite's *Maria* and Waldo's *A Cup of the Sun.*

A prolific and award-winning author, Bryant (née Calvetti) established her own press in 1978 to ensure that her body of work remained in print. Similar to Fante in her unsparing realist style and her regional focus on the American West, Bryant fictionalizes the history of the serial migration that her grandfathers experienced in relocating to San Francisco—which by 1924 had the sixth largest Italian community in the United States. Her third novel, *Miss Giardino*, focuses on the retired English teacher Anna Giardino, the youngest child of northern Italian immigrants, whose American dreams were destroyed by unhealthy mining conditions and unethical corporate practices. Anna's conflicting position as second-generation Italian daughter and highly educated American teacher enables her to reflect intellectually on culture and social class. Moreover, Bryant's experimental narrative style in *Miss Giardino*, which parallels the complicated movements of the protagonist's mind, anticipates the shift toward modernist techniques by Italian American writers in the 1980s and beyond.

De Rosa and Ardizzone, Maso and DeLillo: Modern and Postmodern Stylists

A renaissance of third-generation (and beyond) Italian American writers has produced a cornucopia of work in all genres since the 1980s. Although influenced by the experiments of modernism and postmodernism, many authors return to themes germane to earlier works—Italian codes of behavior, Little Italy settings, generational conflict, and an ongoing critique (implicit and explicit) of American institutions. Central to recent works and truly an Italian American archetype is the frequently mythologized ancestor who represents fine moral character, as in Tina De Rosa's *Paper Fish* and Tony Ardizzone's *In the Garden of Papa Santuzzu*. Nominated for a Carl Sandburg award and extolled by Louise DeSalvo on the front cover as "the best Italian-American novel by a woman of this century," *Paper Fish* combines the story of immigration with poetic narrative experimentation to eulogize a dying Little Italy on Chicago's West Side. Though different from *Christ in Concrete* in technique and style, De Rosa's *Paper Fish* employs dreamlike states and an agonistic weltanschauung that recalls di Donato's classic. Like her literary forebears, De Rosa tells a story of immigration and generational struggle within an ethnic locale, but she diverges from literary realism in her nonlinear narrative, focusing on how memory and imagination reinterpret familial loss. Through the dialectal voice of the paternal grandmother, De Rosa reimagines nineteenth-century southern Italian culture, conflating generations and places and building a narrative space for Carmolina, the artist-protagonist, who records the dissolution of her Italian community in America with the searing detail of a lone eyewitness.

Donning several literary hats, including historian, folklorist, and magical realist, Ardizzone, in his *In the Garden of Papa Santuzzu*, reimagines through the voices of twelve speakers the arduous journey from Sicily to America during the great migration. At the heart of the stories—based in Sicily and America—is a belief in a cultural community whose familial rules support an anticlerical and antigovernmental ethos. With exquisite timing and ribald humor, Ardizzone holds a mirror up to the new-world garden of America and finds it lacking. Communal family identity and social justice for minorities—topics treated as sacrosanct by Ventura, di Donato, Tomasi, and Fante—allow Ardizzone to praise the cultural elements of Italian identity in its religion, cuisine, language, and storytelling. Similarly, Josephine Gattuso Hendin (*The Right Thing to Do*) and Adria Bernardi (*In the Gathering Woods*) infuse their works with features of Italian folklore, reinforcing the continuing importance of vernacular Italian culture on American writing.

Two prolific writers of distinctive innovation are Carole Maso and Don DeLillo. As Italian American ethnicity continues to be a source and subject of American literature, these writers (and others such as Felice Picano and Mary Caponegro) increasingly write out of several contexts, ethnicity serving only as a strand, sometimes a mere filament, within the complex weaving of a narrative. Maso's debut novel, *Ghost Dance*, explores the development of the multiethnic Vanessa Turin, whose psychological fragmentation reflects her parents' loss of ancestral traditions. Vanessa weaves into narrative her close ties with her paternal Italian grandparents. Maso's return to the archetypal figures of the grandparents demonstrates an allegiance to cultural traditions as sources of sustenance to searching third-generation grandchildren. Through imaginative reconstruction, Vanessa pieces together her Italian American father's past, resisting his silence through storytelling. As Maso says of *Ghost Dance*, one must speak against silence "to live next to silence, but to speak" ("Interview" 34). Stylistically and thematically, Maso enlarges her fictional canvas, employing conventions of lyrical poetry within the novel genre, dramatizing the multitextured quality of the imaginative mind. Moreover, Maso extends a critique of capitalism highlighted in many novels of Italian America in her indictment of corporate America's greed in the name of industrial progress. Throughout *Ghost Dance*, Maso examines the costs of injustice not only for European-descended cultural groups such as Italian Americans but also for blacks and Native Americans, who suffered forced assimilation and successive migrations imposed by the United States government. Maso's multidimensional novel embraces America as its subject, inflecting postmodernity with ethnic identities.

One of the most prolific and lauded writers of Italian American background is Don DeLillo, whose monumental *Underworld*, incorporates features of *italianità* while examining a post–World War II America, from its waste management to its avant-garde artists. Like Maso, DeLillo embraces the multicultural dimensions of America and employs multiple perspectives to examine the effects of ethnic heritage on a country buoyed and threatened by nuclear power. Through the principal perspective of Nick Costanza Shay, DeLillo examines the shift in America from a rather parochial and self-protected country to a world power of overwhelming proportions, deftly paralleling Nick's own journey from his Bronx Italian ghetto to the affluent suburbs of Arizona.

Since the nineteenth century, writers of Italian America have closely examined the cultural—religious, culinary, linguistic—shifts that occur when immigrants and their progeny are compelled to migrate to a country with different values. DeLillo enlarges this scope by probing into the lives of many Americans confronted by America's shift from thriving industrial power to postmodern superpower whose competitions are global, secretive, and deadly. Nick's ultimate migration west indeed parallels the secondary migrations so many Italian immigrants made in their effort to thrive, but his move also emphasizes the changes in America in the second half of the twentieth century.

DeLillo, like many Italian American writers before him, introduces a figure of intellectual prominence, who functions both as a necessary recursion to Italian American cultural codes and a beloved community leader. DeLillo's Albert Bronzini, like Tomasi's Italian teacher, Michele Tiffone, in *Like Lesser Gods*, offers a vision, however nostalgic and atavistic in the cyberspace of postmodern culture that *Underworld* represents, of a mentor for confused youth and a benevolent model of patriarchal warmth and comfort.

Ethnic characters must invent ways to understand themselves in the face of American multiculturalism and multiplicity. Such a requirement began for Italian Americans in the nineteenth century, when they made the courageous crossing to another world, learning how to communicate with other immigrants from equally different lands. With the deftness of experimentation, fiction writers of Italian America continue to refine the meanings of ethnicity, American identity, and literary writing as they negotiate ethnic codes with radical but deeply human creativity.

Peter Covino

Innovation, Interdisciplinarity, and Cultural Exchange in Italian American Poetry

[D]e brises riches, sont ouvertes à l'esprit des voyageurs et des nobles—
qui permettent, aux heures du jour, à toutes les tarentelles des côtes.
> —Arthur Rimbaud, *"Promontoire"*

[B]reezes, open to the spirit of the travellers and the nobility—and
they allow, during daylight hours, every tarantella of the coasts.

Toward a Poetics of Inclusion

Italian American poets have been influenced by a long tradition of tireless struggle against any form of containment, whether emotional, linguistic, or the result of rigid (and often destructive) nationalistic borders. As a logical consequence of mass emigration, even the earliest Italian American poets confronted issues of psychic dislocation, while often reinvigorating accepted poetic forms. The unique language resulting from the Italian diasporas has contributed to a textured and nuanced English, often inflected with dialect words and related linguistic inventions.

Beyond exploring issues of immigration, poverty, and Catholicism, much Italian American poetry integrates a classical, European, and Italian

97

cultural past and present. Yet many Italian Americans who have only had access to higher education for a relatively short time are disconnected from earlier traditions, mostly because of a division they perceive between academic culture and an emerging, "less evolved" Italian American one. In her incisive essay "Neo-Orientalism in Italy (1848–1995)," the historian Jane Schneider explores "the tenacious catalogue of stereotypes" that began in northern Italy—"as formed through the imposition of northern institution and practices"—and accompanied the large majority of southern Italian immigrants to the United States (1, 9). Schneider encourages readers to challenge and deconstruct orientalist discourses that persist in viewing Italian Americans as primitive, ignorant, and corrupt (4).

One of the first anthologies to include Italian American poetry, the *Anthology of Italian and Italo-American Poetry* was compiled in 1955 by the poet and professor of Italian Rodolfo Pucelli. Pucelli's division of the anthology (a slim 113 pages) into sections forces readers to consider the interrelationships among poetries in Italian, Italian dialect, and English. Olga Peragallo's posthumously published *Italian American Authors and Their Contributions to American Literature* offers brief biographical and critical overviews about early writers such as Arturo Giovannitti (124–28), Pascal D'Angelo (66–69), and Emanuel Carnevali (36–40), alongside others who started writing in the 1940s, such as John Ciardi (45–47), Vincent Ferrini (99–100), and Rosa Marinoni (née Zagnoni) (148–51). Peragallo also includes an entry on Lisi Cipriani (50–52), an early Italian American woman novelist-poet whose *The Cry of Defeat* was reviewed in the *New York Times*. The most thorough early history of literary activity by Italian Americans has been compiled by Francesco Durante, a journalist and professor of comparative literature at the University of Naples. His two-volume study, *Italoamericana: Storia e letterature degli Italiani negli Stati Uniti*, covering the periods 1776–1880 and 1880–1940, was written in Italian and published in Italy. These volumes offer meticulous commentary and examples of representative prose, poetry, excerpts of plays, and related literary artifacts from significant writers of earlier eras, who wrote almost exclusively in Italian or Italian dialects. Anthony Julian Tamburri's essay "Poetry" and Dana Gioia's essay "What Is Italian American Poetry?" remain the most concisely informative pieces about the field. Tamburri writes with a keen awareness of Italian influences; Gioia concludes his essay with an impassioned call for critics to begin a comprehensive and critical examination of Italian American poetry, one poet at a time.

Assessing the Early Years: 1805–1940

Lorenzo and Oonalska, a rediscovered epistolary novel by Giuseppe Roc-chietti, recounts the story of an Italian political exile who escaped the oppressive Austrian Hungarian Empire and exemplifies the earliest poetic production by Italians in the United States. Rocchietti, regarded as one of the earliest Italian American writers, emigrated from Italy in 1831 (see Bonomo and DiFabio in this volume). In its attempt to incorporate vari-ous conventions of writing—including original poems written in Italian, diaristic techniques, frequent classical and European poetic allusions, and political discourse—*Lorenzo and Oonalska* is indebted to Ugo Foscolo's *Le ultime lettere di Jacopo Ortis* ("The Final Letters of Jacopo Ortis") and Dante's *Vita Nuova* ("New Life"), in which philosophical prose appears alongside some of the first sonnets and canzones ever written.

From that early era of emigration, perhaps the best-known Italian American poet remains Arturo Giovannitti, even though he published only one book of poetry in his lifetime, *Arrows in the Gale*. *The Collected Poems* was issued in 1975, long after his death, by Arno Press, a division of the *New York Times*. Giovannitti earned a bachelor's degree while study-ing in Pennsylvania, where he first observed the oppressive treatment of immigrant miners. Eventually, he became a celebrated labor activist and newspaper reporter, best known for his role in the strike in Lawrence, Massachusetts, in 1912. Giovannitti wrote some poems in forms, but the bulk of his work is prose driven and overtly political. Today he is remem-bered most for his frequently anthologized Whitmanesque poem, "The Walker," written during his imprisonment for labor activism:

> I hear footsteps over my head all night.
> They come and they go. Again they come and they go all night.
> They come one eternity in four paces and they go one eternity in four
>   paces, and between the coming and the going there is Silence and
>   the Night and the Infinite.
>
> (Mangione and Morreale 289)

The so-called pick-and-shovel poet, Pascal D'Angelo, emigrated from Abruzzo as a teenager and was one of the first well-published Italian American poets. Carl Van Doren included D'Angelo's poems in the *Na-tion*; subsequent publications appeared in the *Literary Review*, the *New York Times*, and the *New York Tribune*. His autobiographical *Son of Italy* contains most of his poems, many of which are written in free verse and characterized by lively imagery, despite some stilted nineteenth-century diction. The poems provide social commentary and linguistic evidence of resistance toward upper-class literary culture, as in this example from "The City":

> Yet the city itself is lifting street-lamps,
> like a million cups filled with light,
> To quench from the upraised eyes their thirst of gloom;
> . . . .
> The factory smoke is unfolding in protesting curves
> Like phantoms of black unappeased desires,
> yearning and struggling and pointing upward.
>
> (149)

Emanuel Carnevali has emerged as an iconic figure in early Italian American poetry, mainly because his work represents a clear, modernist break with earlier examples that tended to be imitative, formally constricted, and influenced by sentimental nineteenth-century models. Florentine by birth, Carnevali was championed by Ezra Pound, William Carlos Williams, and Harriet Monroe, the editor of *Poetry*, where his poems were first published. Although Carnevali only published one book in his lifetime, *A Hurried Man*, his best poems consist of sharp-witted lyrics that are surprisingly contemporary in their fractured exploration of his exile from his native Italy, as this example from "The Return" suggests: "O Italy, O great shoe, do not/Kick me away again!" (Barone 74). He eventually returned to Italy, where he died at a young age of encephalitis. In yet another prescient and quirky poem, "Sorrow's Headquarters," in "5—A Warning from Ages" he writes:

> Through my hair
> the comb
> passes
> quickly
> quickly.
>   (Barone 79)

The writer Kay Boyle was so impressed by Carnevali's work that she compiled his remarkable autobiographical prose-poem sketches and other writings in the posthumous *The Autobiography of Emanuel Carnevali*. A recent edition of his work, *Furnished Rooms*, edited by the well-known experimental Italian American poet–fiction writer–critic Dennis Barone, contains an informative afterword that covers some major thematic issues.

A noteworthy essay about Carnevali's work was written in Italian by the Rutgers University Italian professor Alessandro Vettori and was included in *Binding the Lands: Proceedings of the Third Annual Symposium of the Italian Poetry Society of America* (Carrera and Vettori).

Beside Carnevali, some of the best Italian American poetry of the early period of mass immigration is found in Pietro di Donato's *Christ in Concrete*. The novel's charged poetic language is the result of the author's reliance on an inventive polyglot language—which insists on integrating Italian dialects, Italian, and a rugged phonetic and literal working-class Italian and Italian American English. The emotional breadth and psychic associations are often astonishing, as in this passage, where the loss of a character's leg in a bricklaying accident is suggested through skillful synecdochic riddling:

> And that which wore swaddling, that scampered in olive grove, that bore him on boat to America, that braced back arm and heart into pick and shovel, that footed Job, that would have pressed rude joy between sweet-sweet thighs, and that knelt him to God . . . was expressed down to the basement, hastily wrapped in old newspapers, soaked in kerosene, and dumped into the incinerator. (90)

Recent reassessments of this pre–World War II era of creative production by di Donato and Carnevali, among others, have helped establish an expanded poetic context characterized by such innovative trends as a proliferation of surreal detail and a conscious blurring of poetry and prose, along with unconventional uses of code-switching techniques (moving from one language and cultural system to another).

Formalist Trends and the Rise of a Counterculture: 1940s–1970s

The 1940s and 1950s heralded a new, more educated, second wave of Italian American poets, led by John Ciardi, perhaps the most important Italian American poet, and Joseph Tusiani. Both Tusiani and Ciardi are also well known as translators, Ciardi of Dante and Tusiani of Michelangelo's and Torquato Tasso's poetry. Ciardi's *As If: Poems New and Selected* and *The Collected Poems of John Ciardi* (Ciardi and Ciefelli) have garnered consistent and well-deserved critical attention from scholars such as Louis Untermayer and Miller Williams; his poems are frequently anthologized in mainstream publications. The recent reassessment of Tusiani in *Joseph*

Tusiani: Poet, Translator, Humanist: An International Homage (Giordano) and the latest collection of his poetry, *Ethnicity: Selected Poems*, both edited by Paolo A. Giordano, make a strong argument for his lasting influence as well. Remarkably, Tusiani has also published prize-winning poetry collections in Italian and Latin. Among his poems in English, part 2 of *Gente Mia* ("My People") is especially influential, as this excerpt from "Wishing for a Wrong Number" makes poignantly clear:

> Call me, whoever you are, and tell me
> whatever you please. Speak even
> of wind and heaven to
> a wounded eagle in the grass, of bread and fire
> to a famished beggar in the snow.
> Be cruel and be rude
> but talk to me and let me know
> that I am not alone
> in this human solitude.
> (Giordano 109–10)

Among other scholar-poets, Lewis Turco is a clear heir to Ciardi. *A Book of Fears* is a collection of linked sonnets that are surprisingly relaxed and straightforward yet maintain a formal rigor; *The Shifting Web: New and Selected Poems* likewise contains many often anthologized poems. Turco's recently published *Fearful Pleasures* continues to showcase his strong erudition in poems carefully crafted over an influential career that spans more than forty years. The poet-translator Felix Stefanile's work is indebted to both Ciardi's attention to craft and to Tusiani's easy access to worldliness and strong human emotion. Stefanile's poems treat Italian American themes directly, and his work integrates deep image poetry with a casual, nonaggressive confessionalism: *The Dance at St. Gabriel's* and *The Country of Absence* are among his best books. His restrained lyric-narrative impulse is especially strong in the Petrarchan sonnet "Taking Sides with John Ciardi" and the memorable elegy "The Dance at St. Gabriel's." The latter poem was written for a fellow Italian American who, able to afford an education at New York University—a rarity for Italian Americans of the day—was killed fighting in World War II.

In the 1960s, the gap between a formal academic Italian American poetics and a more interdisciplinary hybridity of experimental poetry that began with modernism widened. The liberal political climate was reflected in the new and looser poetic styles most noticeable in such famous beat writers as Gregory Corso, Lawrence Ferlinghetti, Diane di Prima, John Giorno, and Phillip Lamantia. Original hipsters and freethinkers, Corso and Ferlinghetti (also the famous editor of City Lights Books) remain among the best-known Italian American writers; their work is well anthologized and the subject of a considerable critical literature. Corso's oblique and condensed lyrics often function as powerful challenges to limiting stereotypes. "The Last Gangster" offers a representative example:

> Waiting by the window
> my feet enwrapped with the dead bootleggers of Chicago
> I am the last gangster, safe, at last,
> waiting by a bullet-proof window.
>
> I look down the street and know
> the two torpedoes from St. Louis.
> I've watched them grow old
> . . . guns rusting in their arthritic hands.
>
> (31)

In a country that was experiencing rapid sociocultural change, the beat poets' antiestablishment ethos and wide-ranging, wild poetic styles were especially welcoming to emerging voices, Italian Americans among them.

More recent bibliographic sources for Italian American poets can be found in the American Italian Historical Association's online annotated bibliography of Italian American studies and in Ferdinando Alfonsi's anthology *Poeti italo-americani e italo-canadesi / Italo-American and Italo-Canadian Poets*, which also includes a sampling of poems by poets who write in English and in Italian. Alfonsi's *Dictionary of Italian-American Poets* includes a comprehensive list of Italian American poets, including biographical information when available. Alfonsi also published the collection of essays *Poesia italo-americana: Saggi e testi / Italian American Poetry: Essays and Texts*, which offers helpful assessments of the poets Arthur Clements and Maria Mazziotti Gillan, among others.

Contemporary Italian American Poetry—An Expanded Definition

In *Italian Signs, American Streets*, Fred Gardaphé suggests that recent works by Italian Americans have entered a more self-reflective and philosophical period that incorporate Italian "signs"—references to things

Italian or *italianità*—as semiotic markers that need to be unpacked and explicated in the context of an amplified and diverse cultural experience. An expanded definition of Italian American poetic production continues to be dominated by an academic culture that is also beginning to embrace the contributions of emerging innovators—including those of hybrid or cryptoethnic (hidden) Italian American identities, women writers, and scholars of Italian studies and Italian. The growing field of Italian American poetry continues to be enriched by the works of notable contemporary translator-scholars and poets such as Luigi Bonaffini, Geoffrey Brock, Emanuel Di Pasquale, Luigi Fontanella, Andrew Frisardi, Allen Mandelbaum, Jonathan Galassi, Dana Gioia, Michael Palma, Lawrence Smith, and Paul Vangelisti and also by American poets who write eloquently and have spent considerable time in Italy. Some Italian American poets with established academic reputations—those who have taught in major universities, published several collections, or edited and written significant scholarly books or anthologies—include David Citino, Gerald Costanza, and Jay Parini. Full biographical notes and a sampling of poems by some of these better-known contemporary Italian American poets are readily available online and in recent anthologies published by mainstream presses, such as *The Italian American Reader* (Tonelli).

As the proliferation of recent anthologies of Italian American writing and poetry attest, contemporary Italian American poets engage Italian American culture in their works in increasingly sophisticated and dramatically different ways. Paul Mariani's "The Statue," from his collection *The Great Wheel* (26–27), likely expands readers' conceptions of an Italian American literary aesthetic. The poem chronicles a reverse migration of sorts, a pilgrimage to Sulmona, Abruzzi, the birthplace of Ovid, where the persona is accompanied by Allen Mandelbaum, the great translator of Vergil and Dante. Ironically, Mandelbaum is the only person in the group who speaks Italian

> straining hour
> after hour for three baffled monoglots, so that
> one might eat the bistecca of one's desire
> rather than the tripe & ink squid one's language
> had concocted.
>
> (26)

Mariani's poem is an insightful testimony to cultural reeducation and literary friendship. His relaxed tone throughout this collection is notable, even as other poems confront heart-wrenching subjects of particular relevance to the Italian American narrator, such as his student Frank Serpico's exposure of police corruption and the poet's memories of his father's wartime experience and his mother's death.

In his most recent collection, *Interrogations at Noon*, Dana Gioia offers an equally compelling account of the importance of classical literary models. Gioia gains inspiration from his translations of Seneca in such poems as "Descent into the Underworld" and "Juno Plots Her Revenge." Gioia emphasizes a particular Italian American sensibility by revitalizing classical myth and Roman drama.

W. S. Di Piero, a poet, translator, and scholar, continues to incorporate examples of Italian and Italian American culture in his poetry while also evolving as a poetic stylist. Many of Di Piero's poems from a recent collection, *Brother Fire*, including the title poem—a strange apocalyptic, Browningesque send-up indebted to Saint Francis of Assisi—expand themes familiar from other collections, including physical and emotional displacement, whether from former lovers, Di Piero's south Philadelphia Italian American neighbors, or some imagined psychic, historical past: "To Brother Fire I offer/our endless poor-men's wars/our starved ruined planet" (6). While Di Piero's early poems tend to be more narrative, his recent work impressionistically explores changing demographics, multiculturalism, and the role of working-class consciousness in academia. Di Piero's poetry has assumed a lyrical intensity and incisiveness that make the turns of the poems especially startling. This new work has much in common with that of fellow San Franciscan poet Diane di Prima and second-generation New York school–inspired poets like Joseph Ceravolo; Paul Violi, recent winner of the Ciardi Lifetime Achievement Award; Gerard Malanga; Elaine Equi; and Robert Viscusi, also a respected cultural critic of Italian American literature.

The scholar-poet-essayists Leslie Scalapino and Gilbert Sorrentino pose a special challenge to any categorization as Italian American since the work of both writers is rooted in an experimental language-poetry aesthetic and each professes an idiosyncratic, nonestablishment ethos. John Paul Russo's essay "The Choice of Gilbert Sorrentino," included in the influential anthology *From the Margin: Writings in Italian Americana* (Tamburri, Giordano, and Gardaphé), offers an exemplary close reading of many of the cultural and aesthetic tensions in Sorrentino's work while emphasizing the difficulties of classifying experimental writing. *From the Margin* also includes a fine selection of poems from nineteen poets, perhaps most notable the poet-translator-editor Jonathan Galassi, whose elegiac poems about Montale and San Francesco are especially noteworthy (189–90).

Italian American women continue to be active forces of change and thematic innovation in the development of contemporary Italian American poetry, most notably Sandra Mortola Gilbert, Daniela Gioseffi, Maria Mazziotti Gillan, and especially the influential Diane di Prima. All four frequently write poems that explore Italian American identity, employing a wide variety of styles, from Gilbert's subtle lyricism to Gillan's detailed, confessional narratives to Gioseffi's feminist exhortations. Gilbert's finest poems tend to be confident, stripped-down lyrics. The most frequent themes in her poetry include traveling to the Mediterranean, her Sicilian relatives and heritage, and the tragic, wrongful death of her beloved husband. Many of her poems, such as "Sorrow," "Death," and "2085" (*Kissing*), are characterized by a modernist clarity and a direct but understated sensuality reminiscent of D. H. Lawrence's poems in *Birds, Beasts, and Flowers.*

The writer-activist Gioseffi's best poetry collections include the protofeminist *Eggs in the Lake* and the recent bilingual *Blood Autumn / Autunno di sangue: Poems New and Selected,* in which the poet explores explosive themes related to her family's emigration from Puglia as well as more polemical sociopolitical and environmental issues. Over the last twenty years, Gillan has gained increasing influence in the Italian American literary community and in wider circles thanks, in part, to her work as an anthologist and as the director of the Poetry Center at Passaic County Community College. She is the author of several poetry collections, including *Where I Come From: Selected and New Poems, Italian Women in Black Dresses,* and *All That Lies between Us.* Gillan is especially skilled at moderating a heightened emotionality with a strong sense of intimacy in language that is accessible and beautifully paced. Her poems offer a wellspring of anecdotes about family life and growing up in the ethnically diverse city of Paterson, New Jersey.

Perhaps no contemporary Italian American poet today has been as influential, especially to other Italian American women writers, as di Prima, whose career spans nearly fifty years. Di Prima's eventful life as a social activist, her legendary friendships with other beat poets, and her relationship with Amiri Baraka have contributed a certain literary mystique to her persona. *Pieces of Song,* her selected poems, best illustrates her original, populist, yet rigorous poetic vision. As the references to Arthur

Rimbaud in the first poem of the collection make clear, di Prima's poetics is predicated on a sense of urgency and unconventional narrative strategies. Di Prima's clear-hearted notes and seemingly casual jottings result in innovative prose poems, compressed lyrics, rants, and Charles Olson–influenced projected verses, which are directly linked to a prophetic tradition that harkens back to William Blake and earlier Eastern religious texts. Her unabashed references to working-class Italian American markers are unadorned yet resonant, whether they are as mundane as "salami" or more dispassionate responses to her own family's racism and their reactions to her liberal lifestyle.

A kinship exists between the poems of a newer generation of Italian American women and di Prima's. The direct, feminist, and engaging poems of Kim Addonizio, Donna Masini, Dorothy Barresi, Anne Marie Macari, and others who foreground issues of sexual identity—such as Mary Jo Bona, Rachel Guido De Vries, Rosette Capotorto, and Vittoria Repetto—seem inspired by di Prima's brave energies. Italian American women poets in general are enjoying a much deserved period of recognition, as suggested by the recent successes of Lucia Perillo, winner of the MacArthur Prize and National Book Award, and Addonizio, National Book Award finalist and recipient of the Ciardi Lifetime Achievement Award. Addonizio's conversational language addresses single motherhood and working-class themes directly, while Perillo's textured narratives explore midwestern suburban culture and her battle with multiple sclerosis as well as issues of multiculturalism and inclusiveness in America. The poet and university professor Dorothy Barresi's work remains particularly inventive and aesthetically restless over three impressive collections.

Other emerging poets of Italian descent are Sarah Manguso, a recent American Academy in Rome fellow; Kathleen Ossip, winner of the 2002 *American Poetry Review* First Book Award; Stephen Massimilla, Jane Tassi, and Gerry LaFemina—all Bordighera Prize winners; Christopher Arigo, winner of the 2002 Pavement Saw Press prize; Chris Stroffolino, Jennifer Scappettone, and George Guida—three widely published college professors; and Cynthia Tedesco, Angelo Verga, Carrie Anne Tocci, and Mary Giaimo. These poets are influenced by poetries that value humor, indirection, and, in some cases, mysticism. They extend the experimental tradition not only of Italian American poetry but also of experimental Italian poetry that starts with Filippo Marinetti and the futurist movement and reaches today to such contemporary Italian writers as Andrea Zanzotto and other *neoavanguardisti*. Interestingly enough, a poet such as Michael Palmer (2006 winner of the prestigious Wallace Stevens Award from the Academy of American Poets for proven mastery in the art of poetry), whose poetry values a decentered identity, is nevertheless inspired by Zanzotto and other Italian avant-garde innovators, even though memories of his Italian American family are also a vital element of his poetry.

A newer generation of Italian American poets with unprecedented access to educational opportunities—and the willingness to share work across ever-evolving computerized media—seems entirely comfortable integrating a variety of poetic aesthetics, from traditional and formal schools to poetry that is theoretical, political, feminist, and especially direct in confronting ethnic stereotypes and issues of sexual identity. The immediate future of Italian American poetry seems particularly promising since so much of the skillful experimental work by emerging poets continues to be informed by a complex philosophical commitment to intellectual integrity and cultural exchange. As Italian Americans are appointed to key professorships and editorial positions, Italian American poetry continues to attest to the diversity of our varied and evolving cultural heritages. Many Italian American poets, emboldened by recent innovation and wider acceptance, seem poised to keep poetry "absolument moderne" ("absolutely modern"; Rimbaud 52), or to search for the truly prophetic—so that, no matter how arduous or elusive, the work remains fresh and vibrant.

Rose De Angelis

"Stripping Down" Gender Roles in Italian American Fiction by Women

Marist College has a significant number of Italian American students of either single or double ancestry; most know little about their cultural heritage, and what they do know often reflects the misconceptions they have gleaned from popular culture. Many students, for example, may regard Italian American women as one-dimensional figures defined by the traditional image of the *mater dolorosa* ("sorrowful mother"). Therefore, when I designed Italian American Women Writers—a course that satisfies the English major's requirement in comparative, ethnic, or national literature; the college's cultural diversity requirement; and the core requirement in literature—I had several objectives in mind: to establish the existence of an Italian American women's literary canon; to introduce students to alternative female identities that undermine the domestic ideology; and to help them trace generational transformations. Helen Barolini's *Umbertina*, Mari Tomasi's *Like Lesser Gods*, Antonia Pola's *Who Can Buy the Stars?*, and Louisa Ermelino's *The Sisters Mallone* represent an excellent cluster of texts to achieve my pedagogical goals.

The female characters in these novels challenge, some privately, others publicly, the gender-specific roles of *capo famiglia* ("head of the family") and *mater dolorosa* and thus de-essentialize male and female identities.

They participate in what the anthropologist George M. Foster calls "stripping down," a conscious or unconscious peeling away of the excess and sometimes stultifying layers of cultural paraphernalia (12). They enact change: some gradually, as in *Umbertina* and *Who Can Buy the Stars?*, in which the female protagonists sporadically rebel against their husbands and societal constraints; some more aggressively, as in *Like Lesser Gods* and *The Sisters Mallone*, in which Maria Dalli destroys her husband's stonework and Helen Mallone resorts to violence as retribution.

I use primary and secondary sources to help my students frame their reading of these texts: Sandra Mortola Gilbert's *"Piacere Conoscerla,"* one of the first readings, offers a context for changing gender expectations in Italy and the United States. Jerre Mangione and Ben Morreale's *La Storia* and Betty Boyd Caroli, Robert F. Harney, and Lydio F. Tomasi's edited collection *The Italian Immigrant Woman in North America* serve as reference tools for students to learn about social and cultural conditions in Italy and the United States during the great migration.

As their first assignment, students choose a place or immigrant experience in *Umbertina* and compare the experience of the characters in the novel with those of the historical immigrants. Some students researched Cato, New York (where Umbertina and Serafino settle down), and found that in the late nineteenth century it was an agricultural community and that today eight percent of its constituency claims Italian ancestry. Other students research the changes in the immigrant communities in the Mulberry Street district in New York City (where Umbertina and her family first live on their arrival in the United States) over the last century.

Most students think of Italian American immigrants as huddled on the East Coast, unaware of the Italian American presence in the West, South, and Midwest, and therefore are intrigued by *Who Can Buy the Stars?*, in which the protagonist is a northern Italian woman who, two decades after Umbertina, arrives in the United States, settles in Indiana, and becomes the entrepreneur in her family. Marietta's rags-to-riches tale, with its romantic twist and a dash of unlawful activity, makes the reading highly engaging. Students read two chapters from Richard Gambino's *Blood of My Blood*, "*L'Uomo di Pazienza*—The Ideal of Manliness" and "*La Serietà*—The Ideal of Womanliness," and Helen Barolini's introduction to *The Dream Book*; these readings provide different perspectives on the place of the Italian woman and the changes in the United States as she avails herself of new social, economic, and educational possibilities. I ask students to use the models provided by Gambino and Barolini to consider gender roles in the two novels. Students typically find Gambino's image of the male and female too rigidly crafted. Some comment on how readily Umbertina and Marietta negotiate their power within and outside the family. They point out that both women still equate familial responsibilities with personal fulfillment, but once they arrive in the United States, they replace their husbands as providers, assuming the role of *capo famiglia* and embracing the assertiveness and aggressiveness that go with it. Marietta's no-nonsense business tactics, her independence, and her emotional distance from her family fall far short of Gambino's ideal of the Italian woman who lives, eats, and breathes for her family. Some students note that these women are in the process of stripping down: fewer restrictions and less public scrutiny enable them to shed some of the traditions that limited their agency in Italy.

Like Marietta, Maria Dalli, the first-generation Italian American protagonist of Mari Tomasi's *Like Lesser Gods*, is northern Italian and does not settle in the ethnic neighborhoods of New York; she goes instead to Vermont, among the granite quarriers and stone carvers of Granitetown. A few students note that Maria's *serietà* ("seriousness"), like Umbertina's, is reflected in her dedication to her husband and family: she is attentive to her family's needs, but, like the other two matriarchs, Umbertina and Marietta, she disregards the cultural mandate of subservience that Gambino suggests is pervasive in first-generation Italian women and demonstrates a strength that is as "unflinching as granite" (Tomasi 256). Feeling that granite work compromises not only her husband's health but also the stability of her family, Maria vandalizes Pietro's memorial masterpiece, hoping to change his mind about stone carving, a profession that brought the threat of deathly lung disease to immigrant male workers.

In the ensuing discussion of Maria Dalli, I introduce the subject of female sexuality and the Madonna/whore dichotomy. For the most part, students assume that in Italian culture sexuality is a male prerogative, that good Italian women are not sexual beings, and that most Italian women view sex in religious terms: a sin before marriage and a duty after it. Maria Dalli redefines the Italian woman as a sexual being, albeit within the marital bond. As Mary Jo Bona notes, Maria shares an emotional, spiritual, and physical relationship with her husband, Pietro (*Claiming* 32). Umbertina, Marietta, and Maria—my students determine—both undermine and reinforce gender myths and stereotypes: while they all subscribe to an androcentric view of marriage, they each redefine the boundaries of male and female behavior within and outside marriage as they unpeel the layers of tradition. Most students agree that Umbertina is the most traditional: she fulfills the sexless, self-sacrificial role of dutiful mother even as she is not the obedient wife. Marietta surprises them because of her interest in financial earning rather than domestic life and because she defies the masculine taboo on female sexuality by becoming the aggressor. Finally, they see Maria Dalli as a nurturing and dutiful homemaker with no interests outside her family and yet find her far from subservient. These first-generation women deconstruct Gambino's image by incorporating the aggressiveness and assertiveness usually associated with male subjectivity and by shedding layer by layer the cultural constraints that governed female behavior in Italy.

Further into the semester, students read the other sections of Barolini's novel—"Marguerite, 1927–1973" and "Tina, 1950– "—and *The Sisters Mallone* and examine the changes in third- and fourth-generation Italian American women. As secondary reading, I assign Bona's *"Mater Dolorosa* No More?," Carole A. Clemente's "The Italian-American Woman: Searching for a Sense of Identity through Literature," and Carol Bonomo Albright's "Definitions of Womanhood: Class, Acculturation, and Feminism." These essays help the students understand the image of the suffering and self-sacrificing mother and Italian women's negotiation with traditions. Students note that generational differences and educational and economic possibilities determine how successful each woman is in stripping down the vestiges of the Old World and dressing herself instead with those of the New World in the hopes of self-actualization.

Umbertina's granddaughter, Marguerite, the protagonist of part 2, is a third-generation Italian American woman who reflects the fragmentation of the hyphenated identity. Raised by second-generation Italian Americans intent on distancing themselves from their ethnicity and influenced by the lure of Americanization, Marguerite is caught between the push of conformity and family ties and the pull of unrealized aspirations. In part 3, fourth-generation Tina, Umbertina's great-granddaughter, the offspring of Marguerite and an Italian father, successfully capitalizes on America's social and cultural inventory and her own cultural heritage. Tina manifests what Carol Bonomo Albright refers to as "integrated autonomy" (126). Tina resumes the quest on which her mother had embarked, but she redirects the journey so that she can realize herself personally and professionally. As a paper assignment, I ask students to consider the journey on which each woman in this family embarks and explore connections among the three characters and the historical and cultural moments and modes they represent.

By the time students read *The Sisters Mallone*, a novel that spans more than two decades, 1929–53, they are not surprised by the sexually liberated Mallone sisters, Mary, Helen, and Gracie. The sisters' lust for power and independence has been nurtured by their grandmother, first-generation Anona, who settles in Hell's Kitchen, a predominantly Irish area in New York City, even after the influenza epidemic of 1918 claims the life of all the men in her family—and her daughter—in order to escape the censorious gaze of her Italian compatriots. Students note that, like Umbertina, Anona makes food and the kitchen table the center from which she manages and controls her granddaughters. Yet Anona also undermines traditional gender expectations, and her rebellion becomes a cautionary tale for the three sisters. Students enjoy her antics and say that Anona sets the example for her granddaughters' private and public disregard of male authority.

From reading these novels, my students learn that the dynamics of familial relationships serve as a catalyst for establishing the rules of conduct and power not only within a particular family but also within the broader societal context. As a classroom exercise, I divide my students into groups and ask each group to consider how family dynamics affect the lives of Marguerite in *Umbertina* and Gracie in *The Sisters Mallone*. Some students are critical of Marguerite's desire to realize herself outside the home at the expense of her family. On the other hand, most students like Gracie, who assumes the traditional role of wife and mother without sacrificing her individuality or her agency. Students speculate that Anona's parenting—raising the three girls more like boys—enables Gracie to peel away the layers of cultural garb that Marguerite never truly sheds. The Mallone sisters represent the more extreme variations of female empowerment for my students. Some are shocked by Helen's and Mary's comportment and, for that matter, Anona's drinking and the freedom she allows the girls even at a young age. Yet whenever I teach Ermelino's novel, unfailingly students single it out as their favorite book. Anona and her three granddaughters reflect a vision of female identity in an America free of the cultural constraints of the Old World. These women discard the traditions that may limit their agency, even if it means using force or blurring the lines between right and wrong, and students say that they cannot help rooting for them.

In Barolini's novel, Umbertina says, "The important thing is to find your place. Everything depends on that. You find your place, you work, and like planting seeds, everything grows" (*Umbertina* 133). The female characters in these novels, some more than others, recontextualize the woman's place and the relation of others to it, integrating public and private, family and business, Italian and American. As one of their last assignments, I ask my students to chart the evolution of female identity in the works we have read. Some students note that the first generation of Italian American women arrive in America with cultural baggage foisted on them, and, as one generation gives way to another, they discover what is possible, what needs to be left by the wayside, and what boundaries can be refashioned in America. They strip themselves of those rituals, beliefs, and obligations that no longer serve their purposes and dress themselves instead with the nuances of freedom, afforded to them by education, financial independence, and sometimes an impotent or absent male, selecting and rejecting for themselves those traits that best suit them in the formation of their independent identities. Some comment that the most successful women are those in relationships in which the Italian male is less forceful or nonexistent; most note that each woman is a point on a continuum of change that is affected by time, motivation, and possibility and that some women succeed in redefining themselves as active agents and refuting their role as passive victims of their gender and ethnicity.

John Paul Russo

Religion in Don DeLillo's
White Noise and *Underworld*

Italian Catholicism combines the concept of a single transcendent deity
with the belief in the local presence, accessibility, and immanence of the
divine, often through intercessors, in everyday life. When Italian Catholicism in its regional variants migrated to America, it met new challenges,
confronted an Irish church hierarchy, and took on a life of its own as Italian American Catholicism. What were the principal religious beliefs that
the immigrants brought to America? What would inform their art and
culture? Answering these questions helps lay the groundwork for teaching many works of Italian American fiction.

Irish American Catholicism, which from the 1850s imposed its distinctive doctrinal orientation on the church in America, shared certain
features with northern European and American Protestantism: an emphasis on transcendence, juridical formalism, neo-Puritanism, and a concentration on church attendance and instruction. As a result, the church hierarchy frowned on manifestations of the Italian immigrants' popular religion.
Feste ("saint's day celebrations") were a case in point: they were criticized
for being outdoors (as opposed to within the church's dark interior, symbolic of the inner soul), for being too noisy (as opposed to solemn), too
random and spontaneous (as opposed to ritualized, though processions

follow specific routes), and for being too much fun for such a serious matter as religion (Orsi 55). A *festa* typically includes not only a procession with a raised statue of the Redeemer, Madonna, or patron saint but also a bazaar, food, tournaments, prizes, music and dancing, fireworks, and entertainment. Could there be a better example of immanence in its joyful epiphanic moment than a saint's procession?

The immanent doctrine was perfectly suited to incorporate southern Italian peasant beliefs in the world of magic and witchcraft, often with a highly emotional coloring, such as amulets, the *malocchio* ("evil eye"), and *corno* ("horns"). Cleaving to their popular Catholicism, with front-yard shrines, *feste*, saints' cults, and "strange" devotional practices, Italian immigrants clashed again and again with a hostile church hierarchy. The immigrants were not infrequently told to sit in the back of the church or to conduct their services in the church basement. The "Italian Problem" was how to make Italian immigrants into American Catholics. As it happened, becoming an American Catholic entailed becoming a modern American, which had its measures of pain, testing, and doubt.

As for the Italian American "religione della casa" ("religion of the home"), though the phrase describes Giovanni Verga's novel *I malavoglia* (176), the concept traces to the Romans, for whom religion, with its *lares* ("family ancestors") and *penates* ("protectors of the house and the cupboard"), begins in the home. At the outset of Vergil's *Aeneid*, an epic that seems written for immigrants, Aeneas carries his family gods from Troy to Italy. Having lost one home, he goes in search of another. He has the higher *pietas* ("piety"), the foremost value in the epic. Wherever one's household gods are, there one's home is. *Pietas* begins in the home and extends outward in concentric circles from the family to the community to the state to the universe. The Christian ideal of the Holy Family was one of the most familiar subjects in Italian art, high and popular. For the sacred hearth of the Romans, Italians and Italian Americans substituted the kitchen table (Cinotto 120). The elaborate ritualism of Sunday dinner is or was a common feature in Italian American households (Gambino, *Blood* 16). *Pietas*, the religion of the home, family, and community, is the foundation of Little Italy, which became a byword for a safe, cohesive neighborhood in American culture.

Lastly, differing markedly from American religious notions was the immigrants' approach to death: a condition of familiar, natural acceptance of a universal fate, "half-way between passive resignation and mystical trust," which Philippe Ariès calls "tamed death" (103). As an approach to death, *tame* refers to an emotional tenor that does not deny deep mourning but subsumes it in a larger pattern of patient endurance, ritualism, traditionalism, communal participation, and the "greatest of all death's lessons: life goes on" (Schiavelli 160). In life, people wanted to be near the dead; their cemeteries were close to their churches, in town centers, or within a short walking distance, symbolizing the "coexistence of the living and the dead" (14). Physical death was a kind of sleep, an intermediary state between this life and the Last Judgment. Without an appreciation of tame death, one can misconstrue Italian American religious behavior, as George Steiner does when he argues that "it is Mafia burials that preserve the flamboyant desolation of the romantics" (114). Yet, given its elaborate religious rites, public spectacle, and emphasis on clan survival, the Mafia treatment of death is tame and diametrically opposed to the intense inwardness of the romantic cult of the dead. The baroque ceremoniousness of Italian immigrants and their offspring is much closer to the classical world.

With these basic themes in mind, students will be better equipped to examine such texts as Don DeLillo's *White Noise* and *Underworld*. The latter is the first of his novels to have an Italian American protagonist and the first to have major scenes set in a Little Italy in the Bronx: a bustling Little Italy in its glowing twilight of the late 1940s and early 1950s. DeLillo's concern with immanence and analogical imagery, the family, *festa* and cults, and tame death—typically in his portrayal of consumerism, the media, and technological society—extends through his entire career. The emphasis on divine immanence over dualistic transcendence is fully realized in both novels, providing abundant examples for class discussion and paper assignments.

When, in *Underworld*, Sisters Edgar and Gracie drive into the ruins of the south Bronx to deliver food and medicine, they encounter sickness, drugs, hunger, blindness, epilepsy, AIDS, cocaine babies, and abandoned children. Among the "hardest cases" in tenement corridors, Sister Gracie "believed the proof of God's creativity eddied from the fact that you could not surmise the life, even remotely, of his humblest shut-in" (245–46). Extreme abjection challenges her imaginative empathy beyond the human limit, bordering on the immensity of the sacred. God bestows grace on the nun, true to her name (perhaps too obviously), in the attempt to "surmise" the situation, the recognition of its impossibility, and the willingness to close the distance between herself and the abject. The eddy, a contrary motion in a current, implies the whirling of the spirit against the resisting nonspirit.

Underworld's protagonist, Nick Shay, shares some biographical facts with DeLillo: both are born in 1936, grow up in the Bronx Little Italy, have Catholic (and Jesuit) educations, and work early in their careers at writing advertising copy. Nick, however, has only one Italian parent, his father (from the same province of Molise as DeLillo's); Nick's mother is Irish, and he receives her name after his father abandons her. The novel follows Nick's progress from working-class origins to worldly success. At the close, he is in his sixties, a retired director of a high-tech waste containment company, living in Phoenix, Arizona. DeLillo's method of contrasting the worlds of corporate, technologized America and Little Italy derives from his religious training, enabling him and his narrator to draw on an Aquinian tradition and vocabulary. *Underworld* continually emphasizes immanence over transcendence, as can be seen in such lines as "the Jesuits taught me to examine things for second meanings and deeper connections" (88) and, repeatedly, "everything is connected" (131, 289, 408, 825, 826).

Given this refrain, one world or underworld informs another. The term *underworld* refers initially to Nick's job of finding sites for burying nuclear and other waste. But, on the ethnic side, the underworld is the *malavita* of Nick's father, who disappeared under mysterious circumstances when Nick was eleven; Nick himself flirted with the Mafia in his teens. The Mob may be responsible for the father's disappearance into that other underworld, the classical land of the dead, through which Nick searches for him, like Aeneas for Anchises, though Nick's search is in vain. At sixteen, Nick accidentally shot to death a person trying to get him involved in drugs. Years later, on a business trip to Milan, Nick finds himself on the Via della Spiga, in the fashionable Montenapoleone district, the kind of place where a well-heeled American might stay. Suddenly, an Italian seen from the back recalls the person Nick murdered: "half a second in Milan . . . reminded me of a thousand things at once, long ago" (88). *Via* is "the way," and *spiga*, or "ear of corn," is sacred to Ceres, goddess of the natural cycle of life, death, and rebirth: "Ceres's way." The dead man returns alive to Nick's guilt-ridden consciousness. Finally, underworld is Nick's death-in-life existence in the "unspeakable hanging heat" of his sprawling Phoenix suburb, "a hundred and eight degrees"—DeLillo's version of hell, with little possibility of a phoenixlike rebirth from the ashes (86, 85). These underworlds are linked through loss, waste, and death.

Connectedness is fully realized in the technological environment, from waste containment and recycling down to the tight meshes of electronic communication: "fax machines," "voice mail," "e-mail" (806), and "the web, the net" (808). In Nick's office the "caress of linked grids" "lap around you" (89, 806), imparting a sense of "order," "command," "self-esteem" (89) and the pseudointimacy of contemporary communication through which "everybody is everywhere at once" (805). Though the technological system denies the grounds of the immanent mode, the reverse is not the case. The Christian universe contains the technological system, so that one may analogize every form of man-made apparatus. Global technologism, with its advertised fantasy of human interconnectedness, is the dark other of an objective spiritual order of the mystical community on earth and heaven.

One does not proceed far into *Underworld* without realizing that connectedness as achieved by technology is associated with increasing disconnectedness on the human level (Osteen 216). Thus the Italian American religion of the home is honored more in the breach than in the observance. Nick suspects his wife of having an affair (she is, and he is, too). He communicates poorly with his mother, whom he insists on dislodging from her crumbling neighborhood to live virtually as a prisoner in the back room of his house in Arizona. Nor can he fathom the reason for his father's abandonment; as his brother Matt says, "he did the unthinkable Italian crime. He walked out on his family. They don't even have a name for this" (204). Nick is uncomfortable in his old Bronx neighborhood, which he visits only rarely. But he is farthest from the "distant mystery" of himself (810).

By contraries of analogy, the spirit in its highest exaltation links to the crudest matter: waste in all its forms, from nuclear landfills to the "lowest household trash" and Swiftian "synthetic feces" for the product testing of diapers (88, 805). Location on the hierarchical scale of being imparts a particular valence, even a negative one, so that Nick can actually say, waste is a "religious thing," its management is a "faith to embrace" (282); he lost his other faith. His company builds "pyramids of waste above and below the earth" (106), the sacred tomb monuments of consumer society, the final destination of those staggering displays of expendable goods, as in the supermarket scene in *White Noise* (325–26). Nick's colleagues are "Church Fathers of waste in all its transmutations" (102), the parodic inversion of the real church fathers who consecrate the bread and wine in transubstantiation; "we entomb contaminated waste with a sense of reverence and dread" (88). Through its analogical relation to his own damaged soul, waste intimates the fear of death, loss of transcendence, and despair over civilization's waste masquerading as productivity. Nick's specialization in "hazardous" waste makes ironic the fact that his spiritual life risks nothing (106). In waste he hears a "whisper of mystical contemplation" (281): the solemnity of the dead, the distance of the sacred, the hidden God.

True to the exacting formalism of his religious training, Nick analogizes home waste "according to the guidelines" (803):

> [W]e separated our waste into glass and cans and paper products. Then we did clear glass versus colored glass. . . . Then we did newspapers including glossy inserts but were careful not to tie the bundles in twine, which is always the temptation. (89)

Concern with technique and ritualistic precision, a parodic Last Judgment of garbage expressed in a dry tone and paratactic mode, suggests a parallel spiritual world. With the "solemn aura" of "universal waste" in mind, Nick's viewpoint shifts in the process: "people look at their garbage differently now, seeing every bottle and crushed carton in a planetary context" (88). Not only do these passages on proper bagging satirize American habits, but they also analogize the containment and preservation of spirit in a hierarchical context *sub specie eternitatis*: "planetary."

As for *festa*, Nick's teacher Bronzini recalls a saint's day every summer when the members of the church band played "heart-heavy pieces that brought women's faces to the open windows of the tenements" (736). In this portrait of Little Italy, women are associated with the home. Playing a dirgelike song, the male musicians "slow-step along a certain residential street and stop at a particular private house, a frame structure with a front porch and rose trellis, the home of the olive oil importer" (736). The Mafia boss lives in a more expensive frame house, not a tenement, and fronts as an olive oil importer. Bloodred, the rose on the "shady" house is a flower of death (737). Turning aside from their true mission, the band members in their white shirts and black pants (the dress of priests and altar boys) enter this house of death and, in a satanic inversion of epiphany, pay homage to a hidden godfather by taking a sacrificial "glass of red wine" (737), also the color of blood, which profanes the saint's mass.

DeLillo's espousal of tame death is best exemplified by *White Noise* where he satirizes socially imposed, media-driven attitudes toward death, from panic to morbid curiosity to outright suppression. A chemical spill or, in sanitized technical language, an "airborne toxic event," obsesses Jack Gladney, professor of "Hitler Studies" at a small midwestern college (117). Fearing deadly contamination, he undergoes exhaustive, inconclusive medical tests, an "awesome technology wrested from the gods," which only make him feel "televised so to speak," separated from his body, and "a stranger in [his] own dying" (142). His doctor, a cold technician who brims with health, is "eager to see how [Gladney's] death is progressing" (325). One test called SIMUVAC makes a computer-calculated probability of his own death; according to the computer, Gladney is already dead. "Dylar," a new drug, supposedly takes away the fear of death. From time to time, like Gulliver, Gladney has a moment of understated awareness: "I could easily imagine a perfectly healthy person being made ill just taking these tests" (277). This is Ariès's death untamed, in which an excessive preoccupation with death betrays a fear of life.

In a Catholic hospital, at the end of *White Noise*, Gladney gazes at a picture of John F. Kennedy and Pope John XXIII holding hands "in heaven," which is partly cloudy (a hilarious sign of an imperfect understanding of heaven); "sentimentally refreshed" by this afterlife, Gladney regresses to his childhood (316–17). Looking at the picture, he asks the tough-minded Sister Hermann Marie, who is dressing his wound: " 'What does the Church say about heaven today? Is it still the old heaven, like that, in the sky?' She turned to glance at the picture. 'Do you think we are stupid?' " (317). Repudiating Gladney in the bluntest terms, she urges patience and duty in this world; she believes in poverty, chastity, and obedience but not in "the old heaven and hell" (318), and she concludes by furiously lambasting him in German, which the professor of Hitler studies does not even know. In sum, the sister believes in tame death, the simple acceptance of the ineluctable fact.

DeLillo's most daring use of analogy is through the computer. In *Underworld*, Nick's son, Jeff, finds the Web site "http://blk.www/dd.com/miraculum" (810), on which "the miracles come scrolling down" (806–07). The word *scrolling* puns on medieval religious literature, analogizing the computer to the reception of the sacred. Jeff shies away from discussing religion with his father; for this suburbanized young man of our time, a third-generation Italian American, the "real miracle" is "the web, the net"

(808), and the old Bronx is an "American gulag" with which he cannot associate himself in any way (807). But Nick, yearning for lost spirituality and drawn back to the Bronx of his upbringing, pursues on his own the mysteries of the screen.

Underworld's last seventeen pages are mainly commentaries of reports off the Web, punctuated by keystrokes. From the miracle Web site, one learns that a twelve-year-old homeless girl named Esmeralda, who was found raped and murdered in the south Bronx, has become a cult figure. Her death unleashed a wild outpouring of grief. A graffiti artist paints a large mural of the child that becomes widely known. Then, every eight minutes at night, the beam of a passing train, symbolic of divine light, illuminates a dark section of a billboard advertising Minute Maid orange juice, revealing the maiden Esmeralda to the believers. It is a kind of accidental epiphany, except that there are no accidents in a world where everything connects. Hundreds of people come to pray at the billboard; the frenzied crowds grow larger, like the cult scene in Federico Fellini's *La Dolce Vita* (a possible influence). While Sister Gracie denounces cultism as "tabloid superstition," old Sister Edgar, recalling Pope Gregory the Great, admonishes her: "Don't pray to pictures, pray to saints" (819). She sees Esmeralda's face beneath the "rainbow of bounteous juice" and feels an "animating spirit" (822). Eventually, the advertisement is removed and interest tapers off.

The final pages of *Underworld* form an unveiling, an act of grace. With another keystroke a word appears on the computer screen, "in Sanskrit, Greek, Latin and Arabic, in a thousand languages" (826). What is this word? Before disclosure, three "commands" appear: "Fasten, fit closely, bind together" (827), that is, prepare to bind up the soul as if one were tying up, say, the garbage. Nick, who wanted to teach Latin, knows that religion derives from *re-ligare*, to bind back or fasten, to bond. *Lux sancta* descends in "drenching noon," where mystical noon is symbolic of the spirit "in its fullness" manifesting itself in the natural world (Perella 31, 33); "drenching" recalls *trempé* from Leconte De Lisle's "Midi." As in the mystical writings of Saint Bonaventure (Eco 46), DeLillo treats light as both a physical and metaphysical entity. The light reveals a "monk's candle reflected in the slope of the phone," linking the Catholic Middle Ages with technological modernity (826); light makes the "tissued grain of the deskwood alive" and intensifies the "yellow of the yellow of the pencils," where the hyperrealized grain and brilliant yellow signify a visionary moment (827). The imagery suggests divine inspiration visiting the writer at work. Then the word floats on the "lunar milk of the data stream" (metaphors of nourishment), a word that is more of a prayer uttered pianissimo than a claim fulfilled: "Peace" (827). In the light shed around and in the home, blessing (as it were) the home and illuminating the gathered mysteries of the quotidian, Nick perceives that both the underworld and the divine world may be intimated in the day-to-day world, which is the lasting lesson of Italian American Catholicism.

Josephine Gattuso Hendin

Avant-Garde Italian American Fiction: Experiential Experimentalism

Italian American avant-garde fiction brings something distinctive to courses in postmodernity. Fredric Jameson and Jean Baudrillard characterize postmodernism as the cutting edge of the new information and media technology that expresses the dominance of late capitalism in every aspect of human life. For them, postmodern fiction is peopled by characters whose emotional life is shallow and even schizophrenic. Such characters have little sense of history, lack continuities of feeling or even memory, and are dominated by an all-powerful media controlled by corporate interests. In my courses in postmodernism and experimentalism, I include masters of the artistry encompassed by such theories: Paul Auster, David Foster Wallace, Kathy Acker, Joseph McElroy, Angela Carter, and Thomas Pynchon. But work by such authors as Don DeLillo and Gilbert Sorrentino, who infuse ethnicity into their narratives, transcends those formulations and brings something different to the study of the avant-garde. Italian American writers bring to innovative fiction what I call an experiential experimentalism.

Italian American experiential experimentalism restores to the imaginary of avant-garde fiction the individual's experience of connectedness to both American and Italian American culture and the power of heritage, memory, and emotional depth. It brings a current sense of tumultuous change into the individual's heart, mind, and daily life. In its focus on absorbing broad dislocations of identity and social reality into ordinary life and sensibility, Italian American avant-garde writing restores to experimentalism those models of continuity and emotion that conventional postmodern theory rejects.

Avant-garde Italian American writers whose heritage is one of southern Italian poverty describe living as an experiment in self-formation. Experimentalism, for such writers, is grounded in everyday encounters and can be expressed in depictions of multiethnic urban streets, recognitions of class differences, and the contemporary stressors on the traditional authority and cohesiveness of the family. An avant-garde use of pop culture and media stereotyping can also enable an innovative use of the fluidity of the postmodern human subject. Gilbert Sorrentino's *Little Casino*, Giose Rimanelli's *Benedetta in Guysterland*, and Don DeLillo's masterwork, *Underworld*, are major examples of what makes Italian American experimentalism unique in its capacity to use Italian American life—and even America's love affair with Mafia movies—to open up the force of contemporary experience.

Experiential experimentalism points the way to teaching techniques that work. How best to teach the literary essentials students need to know? Avant-garde techniques such as stream of consciousness, free association, montage, aleatory or chance composition, parody, metafiction, and references to pop culture as a way to universalize themes are complex and often complicated for undergraduate students to grasp. Students, however, can begin to understand how such forms work and affect meaning by using their own writing and lives to try out experimental techniques after they have read a fairly accessible Italian American avant-garde text.

Sorrentino's novel *Little Casino* provides a good teaching opportunity to convey how ordinary experiences can be used for radical experiments in form. In the novel, the real gambling palace is the house of language, and our daily lives are games of chance. The novel consists of fifty-two two-to-six-page anecdotal chapters—one for each week of the year. Each forms a primary text, and Sorrentino ends each with commentary on the anecdote he has just written. This produces a montage of surreal moments in which life seems invaded by the uncanny and then followed by an interpretation of its meanings. In one chapter, "Buddy Mazzolini, The Boy Bus Driver . . . drives down Ocean Parkway." The bus displays "heartbreaking images," photos of the "young, smiling, foolish, and hopeful. Look at the lost people in the pictures!" (71). This snapshot art, instead of the advertisements one normally finds on a bus, helps even despairing passengers see their possible or former selves in the display. The bus moves through Brooklyn streets that anchor characters to place and memory. Sorrentino's following commentary is a prayer for luck on whatever routes life takes (71–72). As a writer, Sorrentino serves as our bus driver whose fictions—as both art and commentary—show that our journeys are all gambles in a casino world governed by chance and the unexpected. *Little Casino* reveals a changing human scene given meaning and made metafictional by all the words, images, reflections, and prayers we use to try to explain what happens. Sorrentino's announced goal is to "open all the doors" in a time when any door can lead to revelation ("Gilbert"). In the open-door house of avant-garde fiction, anything can pop in.

I ask students to write a paragraph describing an ordinary experience—playing a game, attending a family dinner, taking a cab or train. I then ask them to rewrite the same anecdote as if it were a dream or as if they remembered the middle or end before the beginning or to add one other element—for example, a word from a language other than English or a fragment of a pop song or a line from a movie. To conquer any inhibitions over such unusual assignments, students are asked to submit this work anonymously, to omit any specifically identifying information, and to invent episodes and use fictional personae. I let them know that I may use their responses in class or in other venues. Student work is photocopied and distributed for frank class discussion. I use these exercises to help students overcome the strangeness of experimental forms and to underscore how the perspective on or placement of events may affect their meaning. Class discussion can focus on relations between form and meaning, how sequence affects meaning, and on how alogical, dreamlike associations can invigorate, express, or extend the meaning of ordinary events. Just as avant-garde writers open up the strangeness of everyday lives, I ask students in these assignments to open up ordinary experience to the unexpected.

Such assignments perfectly complement Sorrentino's chosen form of short episodes followed by commentaries. One student wrote a realistic initial paragraph about a young woman preparing Easter dinner with her mother and included a recipe for leg of lamb, a traditional Easter dish. The daughter cut cross-shaped slices in the lamb and filled them with fresh garlic and rosemary and, when the lamb was cooked, brought it to a carefully set dinner table while her mother kept pouring red wine for everyone as they enjoyed the lamb. The second paragraph was a dream-like version that focused on the dinner as a feast of communion. It played on the associations of Easter with resurrection and used the leg of lamb as an extended metaphor: "The table was set in white cloth like an altar and we laid the Lamb of God upon it. Blood ran from his cross-cuts. We gathered at the table and drank red wine until the leg rose up and danced." The third paragraph began with the leg of lamb dancing: "It jumped and turned, whirling back into the kitchen and I cried as I pinned it down, cut crosses into it, and wondered at its life."

Another student responded to Sorrentino's gritty urban scenes. He described a young man getting on the subway to go to his part-time job. In his first paragraph he wrote:

> I wasn't in the mood, but I had to go. The platform stank in the heat and there were bright yellow signs that said "WARNING! POISON!" above pictures of rats crossed out. The signs were hung everywhere—even on the wall above the tracks so that people on the platform could read them and know poison had been put down on the tracks. Who were the signs for? There weren't any people walking their dogs on the tracks and the rats couldn't read.

In his dream version, he wrote:

> I was standing on the crowded platform watching for the train. Suddenly, I noticed the crowd was composed of rats standing on two legs, some six feet tall. One was reading a *New York Post* with the headline: "CITY KILLS SUBWAY RIDERS." Another rat turned to me and said: "Watch out for the poison!"

Asked how the dream version commented on the realistic one, a student explained, "It means we are all in the same boat—anything can happen to any of us."

America's love affair with Mafia movies fills pop culture and stereotypes Italian Americans. Rimanelli's *Benedetta in Guysterland*, winner of an American Book Award, is a tour de force of postmodern parody, an inquiry into the Mob genre as one of the multiple fictions through which we understand ourselves and explore issues of power, submission, and perception. Its title uses the name Benedetta ("blessed") and guysterland ("land of the guys") to suggest a media-driven version of the Sicilian mobster and his American mistress. Through these characters, the novel contrasts

America, as an "innocent" young country importing its knowledge of transgression from Europe, with Sicily, as an ancient land long familiar with evil. Framed around pop culture's fascination with sex and violence and Rimanelli's infatuation with modern writing, the novel exploits stereotypes, reaffirming their hold on the American consciousness while undermining them. Written as the love letter by Benedetta Ashfield from Appalachia to Joe Adonis, "guyster" head of the Mamma Mia Importing Company, the novel explodes the pop roles of mobster and mistress onto the stage of literature and culture. Adonis is the voice of Sicilian wisdom, and Benedetta is America as a young, seductive, Lolita-style nymphet. Benedetta declares, "Sicilians are . . . older than the Romans . . . while my people came here on the Mayflower. . . . My first memories are Nabokov County memories" (68). Rimanelli mixes pop culture and belles lettres by a highly developed use of citation and allusion, bringing Vladimir Nabokov, James Joyce, Theodore Roethke, and others into the tale of mobster and mistress. Just as dialogue from *The Godfather* films has entered ordinary speech ("I'll make him an offer he can't refuse"), so Rimanelli's citatory parodies import Nabokov and his nymphet into the world of the guysters to exploit analogies between high and pop culture, to underscore how multiple fictions color the lenses we use to see ourselves, and to suggest that America's passion for the Mob genre is love as obsession. I ask students to focus on how a name, word, or phrase from a film or popular song can help define an important theme or turning point, a climax of action, meaning, or perception.

DeLillo's *Underworld* (discussed at length elsewhere in this volume) illustrates how the use of single words and phrases can sum up a central concept or symbol. DeLillo uses Nick (Constanza) Shay's ethnic journey from poverty in a Bronx Little Italy to an upscale life in the American Southwest as a waste management executive to define the arc of American progress, achievement, and prosperity in the postwar years. Nick's ethnic perspective is expressed in his use of an Italian word to define his awareness of the unintended consequences and losses that shadow his progress and his life. As Nick says, "There's a word in Italian. *Dietrologia*. It means the science of what is behind something. A suspicious event. The science of what is behind an event. . . . The science of dark forces" (280). Those "dark forces" reveal the underworld of feelings, consequences, and interpretations that are the downside of progress. The novel is an exercise in *dietrologia*, in interpretation of public and personal achievement in terms of the toxins and pain that can accompany both.

The phrase "waste management" is central to the "imaginary science" of *dietrologia* and also illustrates the suggestive power of a single phrase. Waste management is both a familiar underworld enterprise and a metaphor for seeking redemption from all that pollutes one's life. Literal and figurative fallout drives Nick to the calling of waste management that can counter the toxins produced by America's success in industry, by nuclear arms and power, and even by the poisoning of private life in an America of unraveling families and disillusionment with authority. Nick's father "did the unthinkable Italian crime. He walked out on his family. They don't even have a name for this" (204). Nick's ethnic identity was literally impaired when his mother changed his name from his father's, Constanza, to her own, Shay, in retaliation, relegating Nick's name to the garbage heap and leaving him fixated on his heritage and determined to reclaim it.

Given his belief that his father did not run out but was killed, or "wasted," Nick's career in waste management involves the effort to retrieve his father as a figure of value, as a usable heritage of love and authority. DeLillo sees forms of waste in public and private life as mirror images of each other, the world and underworld we live in simultaneously. *Underworld* shows that experiential experimentalism can shape the novel into an art of recycling, an art tasked with building meaning and value out of losses as well as achievements and affirming the lives we have. *Dietrologia* is the "imaginary science" of an experimental novel that finds heroism in redeeming loss from waste.

While I do not expect students to write like DeLillo, they can pull words from lived, popular culture and experience the pleasure of experimenting with them. After reading DeLillo, students are asked to select a key word or phrase that is experiential but with which they can also experiment from a pop film or song. The most moving student response to this assignment came two years after 9/11 and involved a powerful use of the simple phrase "falling in love." The speaker in the response is a young woman who saw people jump from the World Trade Center on September 11 and writes:

> They were falling in love—two people holding hands, being pulled apart in the wind and heat, but hanging on to each other. They were falling fast, but the faster they fell, the longer it seemed to take. They would not let go of each other.

Language play can capture an immigrant ancestry of migration and reverse migration that makes the transatlantic provenance of Italian

American writers central to fiction and memoir. Plays on Italian and English words capture two cultures. Robert Viscusi's American Book Award–winning novel, *Astoria*, depicts an American-born hero traveling through Europe looking for the meaning of his heritage in the upheavals sparked by the Napoleonic wars. In a novel that serves as an imaginative history, family memories and world history intersect. Punning on his birthplace, Astoria, New York, as "l'Astoria" and *la storia* (translatable as both "history" and "story"), the narrator conflates fantasy and fact through wordplay. Viscusi writes, "So l'Astoria for me . . . has become *la storia*, the situation of some powerful cloud of dream romances" encompassing personal and social history (37).

Collisions between Italian traditions and American modernity can be inscribed in narrative form. In *The Right Thing to Do*, also a winner of an American Book Award, Josephine Gattuso Hendin explodes the Italian folktale and storytelling tradition into postmodern uncertainty. Hendin uses the spellbinding relation between teller and tale and the certitudes conveyed by the folk form to convey the conflict between a Sicilian father and his American daughter. The father's retelling of a gripping story from his Sicilian past reflects his effort to hold his daughter enthralled by the traditional woman's life he has scripted for her, even as she embraces all the changes he fears. By replacing closure, the traditional denouement of the folktale, with multiple possible endings and opposing interpretations of the story's events, the father expresses his recognition, if not his acceptance, of her unruly American life. This innovative use of postmodern uncertainty functions as a tool for reconciliation.

Frank Lentricchia's *The Edge of Night* poses the problem of self-discovery and self-definition in an experimental autobiography in which literacy, language, and reading play a central role. A childhood in a working-class family that reads little and an adulthood as a distinguished literary scholar pin Lentricchia's identity between reality and poetics. In his metafictional memoir, he emerges as part literary invention and part real figure. Mary Caponegro's *Tales from the Next Village* lyrically provides slices of Italian American experience that play off the importance of *campanilismo*—life circumscribed by village culture—against America's sense of open roads. Fred Gardaphé's *Moustache Pete Is Dead!* is a dramatic monologue that exploits his mastery of accented or broken English to reveal the ongoing hold of the immigrant voice. All these writers use the potential larger meanings contained in familiar forms and ordinary names, phrases, and experiences to convey the doubleness of even assimilated lives.

Italian American writers ground avant-garde fiction in the lived experience of uncertainty and changing times, forging a remarkable, experiential experimentalism that records how the dislocations of our time and the impact of popular culture play into our imagination and experience of the current moment. They bring the depth of life to our appreciation of postmodernity, creating a distinctive writing style and reading experience.

Caterina Romeo

Remembering, Misremembering, and Forgetting the Motherland

The process of remembering, of elaborating the past, and of rewriting the present from often unconventional perspectives is instrumental to understanding the history of migration and what prompted it. Remembering can be painful, however, especially when memories highlight conflicts between the cultures of origin and adoption and, even more, when they expose contradictions within one's culture of origin.

The literary production of Italian immigrants in the United States begins in the nineteenth century, mostly as an account of the experience of migration and particularly of the immigrants' sense of uprooting and displacement. This production also centers on the immigrants' longing for an idealized, even imaginary home that, as Salman Rushdie suggests in his essay "Imaginary Homelands," survives—or is created—only in the memory of migrants. Early Italian American autobiographies include frontier narratives, immigrant stories of success, travel memoirs, intellectual autobiographies, and memoirs that question the relationship between the "ethnic" community and its members. The first recognized Italian American autobiographers, Lorenzo Da Ponte and Blandina Segale, are exceptional characters in Italian American literature: unlike most Italian American writers (and their families), they both arrived in the United

States before the great migration of the 1880s, and their migration was motivated by personal or political reasons.[1] Da Ponte, Mozart's famous librettist and an Italian poet, gives an account of his turbulent and adventurous life in his *Memorie di Lorenzo Da Ponte*, written in Italian in 1823 and later translated into English (*Memoirs of Lorenzo Da Ponte*) in 1929. Da Ponte, who can be considered more an expatriate than an immigrant, fled to the United States in 1805 to escape his creditors and later founded a school of Italian in New York, promoting Italian language, opera, and culture. Segale's *At the End of the Santa Fe Trail*, written between 1872 and 1893 but published in 1932, is the first autobiography in English by an author of Italian origins. This epistolary travel autobiography is an extraordinary account from the frontier territories of the Southwest, where Segale had been sent by the Order of the Sisters of Charity to do mission work among the Native Americans and to found schools and hospitals. Segale's text questions the stereotypes of female passivity and resignation that later are so often associated with Italian American women.

The autobiography of Rosa Cassettari, as told to Marie Hall Ets, foregrounds the centrality of storytelling and the oral tradition in immigrant narratives. Rosa's stories were collected between 1918 and 1931, but *Rosa: The Life of an Italian Immigrant* was published in 1970. One of the few accounts of the life of a first-generation Italian immigrant at the turn of the twentieth century, *Rosa* recounts Rosa's experiences in northern Italy and the United States. Unlike many traditional immigrant stories of success or hardship in the new country, Rosa's story focuses on how migration can prompt personal and artistic growth.

In the 1920s and in the following decades, Italian American autobiographies turned to migration and assimilation, often telling stories of deprivation and scrutinizing the process of becoming an American, as in Constantine Panunzio's *The Soul of an Immigrant* (1921) and Edward Corsi's *In the Shadow of Liberty: The Chronicle of Ellis Island* (1935). These autobiographies can often be read as stories of success, in which the immigrants find access to financial comfort through their own and their families' hard work and sacrifice and assimilate—to some extent—into American society. Pascal D'Angelo's *Son of Italy* (1924) recounts a different kind of success: not interested in the material success that America can offer, D'Angelo abandons his job as a worker to become a poet. Jerre Mangione's *Mount Allegro: A Memoir of Italian American Life* (1943) celebrates the land of origin, familiar to the writer only through the stories of his parents and grandparents, while recognizing the necessity to abandon a world that hinders his development and keeps him from becoming an American. Later on, after visiting Sicily, Mangione strengthens his ties with his family's land of origin in autobiographical texts that blend personal and political issues (*Reunion in Sicily* [1950], *A Passion for Sicilians: The World around Danilo Dolci* [1968]).

The end of the 1960s saw the publication of another groundbreaking autobiographical text, Diane di Prima's 1969 *Memoirs of a Beatnik*. Written as autobiographical fiction, this text recounts the transgressive experiences of the most influential woman artist of the beat generation. In the 1970s, new autobiographical tendencies emerged. Authors like Richard Gambino (*Blood of My Blood* [1974]), Barbara Grizzuti Harrison (*Off Center* [1980]), and Helen Barolini ("A Circular Journey" [1978], "Becoming a Literary Person out of Context" [1986], and other essays later collected in *Chiaroscuro*) write autobiographical essays in which they combine their personal experience as "ethnic" immigrants with cultural and critical analysis.

The last decade of the millennium is characterized by the flourishing of the memoir, which shifts the focus of personal narratives from one's life to one's memory and its discontinuities, from the factual truth to the authenticity of the process of remembering. The memoir acquires a simultaneously personal and political meaning. Italian American writers, especially women, have contributed significantly to this genre, exploring the relation between migration and memory and between their position as outsiders in the mainstream culture and their roles in patriarchal Italian American culture, which privileges family and community. Thus female creativity, desire, and sexuality become central to their narratives. In one of the most extraordinary Italian American memoirs, *Vertigo* (1996), Louise DeSalvo examines the marginalization of her working-class family, but she also exposes the positions of Italian American women in their own communities. Connecting her vertigo with other space-related problems and with the depression experienced by the women in her family, DeSalvo recounts her struggle to become a critic and a writer in a community that felt—and at times still feels—more comfortable with women who embrace domestic roles and in American society, where the notion of Italian American is not associated with intellectual accomplishments. In the 1990 memoir *Riding in Cars with Boys: Confessions of a Bad Girl Who Makes Good* (which was made into a movie in 2001), Beverly Donofrio writes of the practical and emotional difficulties of being a teenage mother and then a single mother, of her deep but conflicted relationship with her son, and of her determination to become a writer despite many adversities.

The conventional role of motherhood is also at the core of Carole Maso's 2000 journal *The Room Lit by Roses: A Journal of Pregnancy and Birth*. Maso situates her pregnancy and maternal experience within her lesbian relationship, thus implicitly questioning the traditional structure of the family and the conventional rules of acceptable sexuality.

If Maso presents the space that she and her partner have created for their daughter as safe and harmonious, other women writers often denounce unhealthy relationships in traditional heterosexual families. The safety of the domestic space is questioned in many of the memoirs in the 2002 anthology *The Milk of Almonds: Italian American Women Writers on Food and Culture* (DeSalvo and Giunta), in which the articulations of power and the positions of women in the family are explored through the relationship between women and food. In Nancy Caronia's "Go to Hell," the nurturing power of food is demystified and its function reversed to cover painful stories of incest and abuse. In Loryn Lipari's "Cracked," memories of Sunday dinners at her grandmother's house blend with recipes for the preparation of the crack the author smokes, and the healing power of food is contrasted with the destructive effect of her drug addiction. Anorexia often appears in texts written by Italian American women and strongly contrasts with the traditional image of food's communal consumption as a way of reinforcing a sense of family and community, as in Cheryl Burke's "Bone, Veins, and Fat." The author's working-class family resorts to food consumption to solve—or better, to avoid—conflicts and to construct a false sense of familial harmony.

Many Italian American writers have questioned the role of Catholicism in their communities while uncovering its hypocrisy and complicity with patriarchy. In memoirs such as Flavia Alaya's *Under the Rose: A Confession* (1999), religion does not constitute a source of hope or salvation. The author tells the story of her life as the companion of a Catholic priest with whom she has two children. In other texts, the connection of Catholicism to more ancient forms of religion and rituals is combined with journeys of personal discovery and reconnection with one's origins. Susan Caperna Lloyd explores rituals and traditions of the black Madonna in Sicily in her 1992 *No Pictures in My Grave: A Spiritual Journey in Sicily*. The author uncovers connections between the Catholic cult of the Madonna and the myth of Demeter and Persephone, while reconnecting this central female figure of Catholicism with pagan goddesses and ancient divinities and analyzing their social function to better understand the condition of contemporary women in Sicily. In *Looking for Mary; or, The*

Blessed Mother and Me (2000), Beverly Donofrio describes her spiritual transformation from a nonbeliever—who had rejected the excesses of Catholicism to which her Italian American family had exposed her—to a fervent if unconventional devotee of the Madonna.

Lloyd's and Donofrio's texts can also be read as travel memoirs. In the 1990s, this genre assumed different connotations from Segale's account of her discovery of the Wild West: authors undertake a journey in search of their past to re-create a connection with their origins. In Maria Laurino's *Were You Always an Italian? Ancestors and Other Icons of Italian America* (2000), for example, the author initially identifies with the urban people of Rome and Milan whom she met during her travels to Italy. Only later does she venture to the little village in the southern region of Campania, where her family had originated. Far from being nostalgic, the text is an account of what the author perceives as a rather primitive society still suffering from poverty and deprivation. In *Stolen Figs: And Other Adventures in Calabria* (2003), Mark Rotella blends his personal account with a sociological and historical analysis of the southern region of Calabria. Visiting with his father the land from which their family originated, Rotella discovers a part of Italy that has little in common with popular and touristy Tuscany and Umbria. Calabria soon becomes the real protagonist of the book. Paul Paolicelli recounts his three-year-long exploration of Italy, especially of southern Italy, in his 2000 memoir, *Dances with Luigi: A Grandson's Search for His Italian Roots*, and in his 2003 travelogue, *Under the Southern Sun: Stories of the Real Italy and the Americans It Created*. Prompted by his curiosity about his grandfather, the author connects not only with a past that was almost completely unknown to him but also with his present as an Italian American. In *Mattanza: Love and Death in the Sea of Sicily* and *The Stone Boudoir: Travels through the Hidden Villages of Sicily* (2002), Theresa Maggio explores ancient rituals and their connections with contemporary life. Whether she observes and records the fishing of the bluefin tuna in the little island of Favignana or ventures to discover the hidden beauty of small Sicilian villages, the author gives a realistic portrait of hard and precarious lives, devoid of nostalgia.

Many Italian American writers refuse to reduce Italy to a romanticized "imaginary homeland." If guilt for having abandoned the motherland is often present in immigrant literature, some writers also express anger and resentment at the land of origin for not being able to provide them or their ancestors with what they needed to survive. In Louise DeSalvo's 2004 *Crazy in the Kitchen: Food, Feuds, and Forgiveness in an Italian American Family*, for instance, the author reconnects the stories of her family to the poverty, deprivation, and abuse that forced them to leave Italy. For writers like Cris Mazza, Italian American ancestors have become a distant past. Her 2003 memoir, *Indigenous: Growing Up Californian*, implicitly interrogates what it means to be Italian Americans many generations after the departure from Italy: the word *indigenous* refers to Mazza's Californian origins—even if the text presents frequent echoes of her more remote Italian origins.

The intellectual autobiography also flourished among Italian Americans in the 1990s: the authors, generally separated by several generations from their country of origin, reflect on their intellectual development, in connection with or independently from their Italian American background. Marianna De Marco Torgovnick's 1994 *Crossing Ocean Parkway* is a collection of autobiographical essays in which the author recounts how, for her, embracing an intellectual life as a university professor required her to leave the conservative and claustrophobic Italian American community of Bensonhurst and, to a certain extent, distance herself from her culture of origin. In the 2006 *A Circular Journey*, also a collection of autobiographical essays, Helen Barolini writes about her development as a writer and an artist over years of intellectual activity but also about how she discovered her Italian American heritage and bridged Italian and American cultures. She presents her life in Italy, as the wife of an Italian poet and in close contact with Italy's finest intellectuals, together with the search for her origins in a small village in Calabria. Barbara Grizzuti Harrison's *An Accidental Autobiography*, published in 1996, is a collection of memories and reflections that, the author claims, are recorded in the same way memory functions: with no pattern or chronological order (although they are organized by theme). Raised in a dysfunctional Italian American family, with a violent father and a Jehovah's Witness mother who diminishes her in every possible way, Harrison manages to escape from this oppressive atmosphere and become a brilliant writer. The poet Diane di Prima tells a story of an unconventional life and of literary achievement in her 2001 *Recollections of My Life as a Woman: The New York Years*. Di Prima leaves her family and the institutionalized education of college to become part of the artistic scene in New York City. Along the way, she becomes an exceptional poet and collaborates with many of the intellectuals, artists, and poets of the New York cultural scene of the 1950s and 1960s.

While Italian American women often denounce the resistance of their families to their unconventional lives and their need to cut their connections with them if they want to become artists, male writers often have less conflicted relationships with their families. The lack of recognition of their intellectual work is generally related to the values of their working-class families, who identify work only with strenuous, physical activities. In Frank Lentricchia's *The Edge of Night: A Confession* (1994), a text that blends intellectual autobiography with literary and cultural criticism, the author, a prominent professor and critic, confesses his Italian American father's diffidence toward his intellectual activity. By defining the text as a confession, the author connects himself to his Catholic background. Lentricchia, however, seems to be on an existential quest, be it at a Trappist monastery or in Ireland. Gay Talese follows a different direction in *Unto the Sons* (1992), a text that combines autobiography and history. The text starts in the first person, recounting the family's migration to the United States before World War II, and then explores the history of the family in Italy, blending family stories with official and unofficial histories.

Contemporary gay and lesbian Italian American writers use memoir to expose the homophobic stigmatization they often face within their families and communities. In Mary Cappello's 1998 *Night Bloom*, the author publicly denounces her patriarchal and homophobic family, who violently punishes its members who refuse to accept traditional roles. The homosexual relationship in the background of Mary Saracino's 2001 memoir, *Voices of the Soft-Bellied Warrior*, constitutes a safe place for the author, unlike the family in which she was raised, where she suffered emotional and sexual abuse. In Frank DeCaro's *A Boy Named Phyllis: A Suburban Memoir* (1995) and in texts collected in anthologies such as the 1996 *Fuori: Essays by Italian/American Lesbians and Gays* (Mecca and Tamburri) and the 1999 *Hey Paesan! Writing by Lesbians and Gay Men of Italian Descent* (Capone, Leto, and Mecca), authors recount the different levels of rejection and marginalization they face both in American society and in their Italian American communities and families, which embrace traditional notions of femininity and masculinity.

Recently, Italian American authors—writers, historians, and filmmakers—have rewritten the story of racism and discrimination perpetrated against Italian Americans because of their dark complexion, which is associated both with the proximity of southern Italy to Africa and to their peasant origins. Kym Ragusa, who is of Italian American and African American descent, unravels a story of multiple discrimination in her memoiristic video *Fuori/Outside* (1997) and in her memoir *The Skin between Us: A Memoir of Race, Beauty, and Belonging* (2006). The author reveals the sense of displacement, ambiguity, denial, and rejection with which she grew up, in an environment where both sides of her family stigmatized the other. In *Are Italians White? How Race Is Made in America* (2003), the editors Jennifer Guglielmo and Salvatore Salerno collect contributions that problematize how Italian immigrants were at the same time victims of racial discrimination and perpetrators of the crime, mostly against African Americans and Latinos. In his memoiristic piece " 'Italians against Racism': The Murder of Yusuf Hawkins (R.I.P.) and My March on Bensonhurst," Joseph Sciorra remembers marching against racism in Bensonhurst in response to the killing of the African American Yusuf Hawkins by a group of predominantly Italian American men and realizing that his outrage at the racist killing was not shared by many in the Italian American community.

Other authors have explored in depth the political potential of the memoir by interweaving the narration of personal stories with the exposure of social abuses and harmful political practices. In DeSalvo's *Breathless: An Asthma Journal* (1997) and Suzanne Antonetta's *Body Toxic: An Environmental Memoir* (2001), the authors connect their diseases to their immigrant, working-class origins and to environmental abuse, while in Sandra Mortola Gilbert's *Wrongful Death* (1995), the author denounces the American health-care system, based exclusively on profit, and attacks the social politics of the American government.

In the past two centuries, Italian American writers have undertaken the necessary—at times nurturing and often painful—task of remembering their past and the past of their families, of parents and grandparents who had no access to writing and whose experience went unrecorded. The recovery of these writers' personal and collective memory has allowed them to gain a better understanding of their lives, of the reasons that prompted so many to leave their home country in search of a better future, and of their identities shaped between cultures.

Note

1. Giving an exact date for the beginning of the Italian American autobiographical tradition is difficult because the definition of *Italian American* is neither aproblematic nor transparent. The term usually indicates the masses of immigrants who came to the United States—mostly from the south of Italy, with no money or education, driven by poverty and deprivation, in different waves starting in 1880—and their descendants. The Italian literary critic Francesco Durante, however, has redefined the term to include those who left Italy before

the great migration, generally for personal or political reasons. In his two-volume *Italoamericana*, moreover, Durante includes texts written about the experience of the migration to the United States both in Italy and in America, both in English and in Italian. If we accept this extension of the term *Italian American*, then Da Ponte can be considered the first Italian American to have written an autobiography. The difference between *migrant* and *expatriate* here, however, seems relevant to me, and Da Ponte belongs to the second category. Thus Segale's text should be considered the first autobiography in the Italian American tradition. Since my intent here is not to establish an incontrovertible point of origin, I include both authors in this survey, because both their texts are relevant.

David Del Principe

Past and Present: Teaching the Family Memoir

Two works that I propose for instructors offering an introduction to Italian American memoir are Jerre Mangione's *Mount Allegro* and Frank DeCaro's *A Boy Named Phyllis*. By approaching these memoirs for their contrasting representations of the immigrant experience, instructors can raise topics of personal interest to students—family, gender, crime, and food—that also have cultural and literary relevance. These texts provide pedagogical models for reading and writing memoir. Further, this engagement with the genre can encourage a culturally informed discussion of representations of the Italian American family. The narrative shift from Mangione's evocative retelling of relatives' stories to DeCaro's bolder autobiographical voice and more inclusive formulation of identity also provides instructors with pedagogical opportunities to discuss various facets of the genre of the memoir.

   At Montclair State University, I teach Italian literature and culture to students who are predominantly first- and second-generation Italian Americans. Although these students may have a close connection to their ethnic background, they have little formal knowledge of the historical, political, and cultural contexts of immigration. This situation presents a distinct challenge for me as their instructor, since students sometimes react to ethnic stereotyping and cultural marginalization by adopting positions of indifference or cultural dominance or by defensively resisting exploring their families' immigrant experience. Teaching Mangione and DeCaro helps me meet these challenges because the memoirs explore diverse immigrant voices that students can, in turn, use as models for writing their own memoirs and as starting points for broader cultural explorations. By introducing Italian American memoir through works that represent a clash between old-world and modern-day immigrant experiences, I elicit a wide range of viewpoints that can lead to a more inclusive study of ethnic identity. Throughout the term, my students record personal reflections and observations from class discussions about family, ethnicity, and immigration in their journals. But it is when they make the transition from exploring literary topics to conducting intimate, oral interviews with family members that they develop their journals into memoirs that present in a reflective and organized manner a personal and cultural narrative of their relationship to their Italian American family and community. Students can use contrasting representations in *Mount Allegro* and *A Boy Named Phyllis*—Mangione's portrayal of traditional masculinity and organized crime against DeCaro's colorful portrayal of gay identity—as a catalyst to probe their families' views on topics such as gender roles, sexual orientation, and violence.

I introduce the study of memoir in an Italian cultural studies course because I find that this genre's elucidation of cultural hierarchies and ethnic oppression—what one student poignantly called "the silence of immigration"—can promote a broader understanding of the immigrant experience and the construction of ethnic identity. For example, an examination of the immigrant experience in a context that brings up the south-north migration of the 1950s and 1960s in Italy, the recent waves of African and eastern European immigrants to that country, and the Italian diaspora can provide the historical background necessary to validate students' immigrant stories.

Mount Allegro, set in Great Depression–era Rochester, New York, celebrates Mangione's Sicilian upbringing by evoking fond memories of family traditions, such as homemade cannoli, dinnertime toasts, *sirinatas* ("serenades"), and storytelling. The memoir also captures Mangione's dilemma: how to come to terms with the patriarchal attitudes of his father who establishes his identity as a "half-and-half" American Sicilian and with his family's involvement in organized crime while trying to "dispel some of the more spurious clichés pinned to the image of Italian Americans" (1, 302).

Two generations later, DeCaro makes no attempt to defend his family from stereotypes. Instead, he approaches stereotyping with a defiant sense of humor, focusing on his personal transition from New Jersey suburbanite to New York urbanite rather than on his relatives' stories about the transition from Italy to America. No longer the primary frame of reference for Italian American identity as in *Mount Allegro*, Italy and Italian receive only a passing mention from DeCaro, who, by fashioning his gay identity in New York with his parents' support, challenges traditional notions of Italian masculinity and the Italian American family.

In an early stage of the discussion, I ask my students to consider the generational and cultural contrasts in the two memoirs and to think of situations in which they have faced a contrast that heightened their difference in the family or a community. Students cite such examples as living or studying in Italy or speaking an Italian dialect. Personalizing a discussion of topics such as bicultural and bilingual heritage often makes students more disposed to discussing them theoretically and critically; as a result, students also write about the topics with a renewed sense of vigor in their journals. To complement such a discussion, I ask students to conduct oral interviews with family members using open-ended questions about what propelled their families' immigration to the United States, whether they consider English or Italian their dominant language, and how they have assimilated into American culture. The interviews are essential at this juncture. By providing students with a practical link from a literary to a cultural context and their personal situations, the interview project can break down resistance to exploring their families' immigration experience. Students gain firsthand knowledge about the history of immigration through vivid accounts of ethnic struggle against discrimination and of assimilation that lead to a heightened sense of cultural awareness and the expression of a stronger, more authentic autobiographical voice in their memoirs.

I also ask students to interview family members about how traditional gender roles are shaped by the immigrant experience and then to present their findings in class and write about them in further detail in their journals. Students are enthusiastic about this assignment and tap into gender- and crime-related topics in Mangione's and DeCaro's memoirs to express a wide variety of personal views about marriage, sexual conventions, and organized crime and gangsterism. Students seize on Mangione's depiction of men as domineering and aggressive and women as submissive—for example, Uncle Nino's attack on Mangione's father with a flatiron (30) and frequent use of *strafalaria* ("virgin-whore dichotomy") in his descriptions of women (152)—to contemplate personal notions of gender and sexuality. Using Mangione's conventional depiction of sexuality and DeCaro's open expression of homosexuality as a point of contrast, students enter freely into a discussion of their personal views about sexual orientation and conventions. Inspired by DeCaro's unapologetic portrayal of sexuality and dismissal of any male code of silence, or *omertà*, students become eager to debate sexual mores and ethnic morality, to relate them to their ethnic experience, and to incorporate these emerging thoughts and ideas into their journals.

Many students point out, for example, that while *Mount Allegro* depicts masculinity by making traditional associations to gangs or the Mafia, DeCaro rejects criminal activity as a construct of male identity, focusing instead on the absurdities of growing up as a gay Italian American in Little Falls, New Jersey, from the 1960s to the 1990s. They note that DeCaro, who uses his acting skills and newfound popularity to outwit the local gang, is depicted in an uncharacteristic expression of cerebral heroism for Italian Americans, eluding ethnic stereotyping as a mafioso or gangster. DeCaro's rejection of gangsterism becomes a rallying point for students, providing them with a sense of solidarity that can inspire a full-blown discussion of Italian American stereotypes in the contemporary media. They react enthusiastically to related projects that I assign, such as researching stereotypes of the Italian American family, masculinity, and criminal behavior in popular culture. They present and critique images in class from television sitcoms, movies, popular music, and the culinary world in which Italian Americans are regularly depicted as homogeneous, bigoted, violent, corrupt, and obsessed with food. Similarly, by focusing on DeCaro's critical awareness of crime and safety in suburbia—"*That* was where I feared for my life, not on Forty-sixth Street" (158)—instructors can help launch a provocative debate about suburban and urban crime and demographic shifts as they relate to students' lives.

The topic that perhaps conjures the most meaningful associations with the ethnic experience for students is food and eating rituals. Here, again, DeCaro parts ways with traditional conceptions of ethnic life, recasting the figure of the appetite-indulging grandmother as a reader of pornographic magazines and replacing family storytelling with a preference for television game shows. In DeCaro's world, the meal, the embodiment of the closely knit Italian family, has also given way to an American facsimile—"a huge plate of Celentano frozen manicotti" followed by Entenmann's pastries "with espresso and a shot of anisette" (145). Indeed, eating, which for Mangione's generation signified compensation for the loss of homeland and immigration hardship, leads to DeCaro's self-confessed addiction to food and the awareness that he must distance himself from his ethnic past by "put[ing] down the fork and pick[ing] up a pen" (*Boy*, acknowledgments). DeCaro's call to expand Italian American identity from the alimentary to the intellectual spurs a passionate debate among my students about topics such as the immigrant work ethic, the gender symbolism of food, and eating disorders and often results in their most original and prolific memoir writing. When students have a personal stake in their readings and are given assignments like the oral interview that foster a practical application of literary topics, they experience a connectedness that helps them move fluidly from their journals to a cohesive and organized expression of their autobiographical voice as memoir.

By adopting texts that serve as pedagogical models for reading and writing memoir, instructors can encourage a discussion of the literary and cultural representations of the Italian American family. Focusing on diverse immigration experiences in such memoirs, especially as they relate to students' lives, can arouse students' interest to record their own families' experiences as memoir and lead to a deepened exploration of their ethnic identity.

Bernadette Luciano

Oceans Away:
Rethinking Italian American
Autobiography in the Antipodes

By including a unit on Italian American women's autobiographical writing in my graduate course on autobiography at the University of Auckland, I faced the challenge of rendering these texts relevant to New Zealand students from a range of ethnic backgrounds. For Pakeha (European New Zealanders), Pacific Island groups, Asian immigrant groups, and South Africans, the North American and Italian cultures, not to mention the encounter between them, are foreign. My pedagogical approach, which cut across social and cultural specificity, proposed a critical reading of the texts as self-referential gendered autoethnographies to highlight the complexity and potential subversiveness of life writing. Autoethnographies, as defined by Mary Louise Pratt, are self-reflexive life narratives in which subordinate subjects describe themselves by engaging with and often talking back to the ways that dominant cultures have represented their cultural identities (7). In a similar, transgressive vein, feminist theories argue that women respond to the ways they have been constructed by patriarchal culture, from early essentialist theories distinguishing women's writing from male writing regarding content and style to later models exploring how women's writing is further complicated by issues of race, class, and ethnicity (Smith and Watson, "Situating").

The course readings included two memoirs by third-generation Italian American women—Diane di Prima's *Recollections of My Life as a Woman* and Louise DeSalvo's *Crazy in the Kitchen: Food, Feuds, and Forgiveness in an Italian American Family*. Both works, while constructing the writer-narrator's gendered and ethnic identity and writing from a privileged position of successful poet and academic, also look back and give voice to previous generations of silent, subordinate Italian Americans. In addition to the memoirs, we examined two autobiographical novels with a less obvious Italian American signature: Beverley Donofrio's *Riding in Cars with Boys* and Mary Saracino's *Finding Grace*. These novels, recounted from the point of view of rebellious young women, are more temporally and emotionally removed from the immigrant experience than the two memoirs and thus provide fewer cultural markers of Italian American ethnicity. In them, the focus shifts toward an authorizing of the self not so much through a negotiation with Italian culture as through a rebellion against patriarchal expectations and religious hypocrisy: Donofrio's "bad mother," Beverly, and Saracino's "bad daughter," Peanut, escape their violent and oppressive homes and lives to create a promising new future for themselves.

In their readings, my students were encouraged to search for similarity in difference, drawing on personal experiences to identify and understand how subordinate groups can engage with established discourses while also revising and critiquing them.

An Evolving Relation to Ethnicity

One of the two main points of entry into the texts was the exploration of the dynamic and evolving relation of the writer-narrator's ethnicity and her dominant culture. Ethnic identity, as scholars have suggested, is not fixed but dynamic and depends on many other factors, including geography, gender, sexuality, generation, and class (Goldman 292). I asked my students to approach the texts by considering the following questions: What evidence do the texts offer that generational distance from the immigration experience results in a different notion of Italian American identity? What are the (changing) markers of Italian American identity? How do these texts talk back to the dominant culture?

The two memoirs represent three generations of Italian Americans and reclaim a formerly marginalized and displaced ethnic history dating back to the beginning of the twentieth century and to the World War II period. Both texts reflect on key historical moments that shaped Italian American identity: the grandparents' immigration and World War II. Episodes such as di Prima's recollection of the racial discrimination experienced by her grandparents during the war and to DeSalvo's description of her grandmother's immigration papers illustrate how marginal subjects record and reflect on the way they have been branded as other in the dominant discourse. Cultural and geographical differences were used to facilitate rather than hinder an understanding of the textual tensions. Some students contrasted the primarily economic motivations behind the waves of late-nineteenth-century and early-twentieth-century Italian immigration to the reasons for their parents' more recent immigration to New Zealand. Students of Asian and South African origin identified their parents' powerful motivations as grounded in the desire for a better future for themselves and their descendants. They willingly sacrificed comfortable material existences for the opportunity for improved environmental or political conditions. By drawing parallels between immigrant motivations across cultures, my students were better able to perceive how these works did not just record first-generation experiences but highlighted and responded to the subjugation first-generation immigrants experienced in the dominant culture.

The experiences recounted by second-generation immigrants also spoke to my Asian students: they compared, for example, the representation of DeSalvo's mother's strong desire to be perceived as American with their own or their parents' attempts to assimilate. But what emerged strongly in our class discussions was the undeniable distinction between race and ethnicity. While assimilation and passing as members of the dominant culture are options available to white ethnic groups, they are not options for others, like Asians. Unlike DeSalvo's mother, one of my Asian students argued, most of them cannot simply change their diet or their neighborhoods to become invisible and exempt from racist victimization. Their identity is physically inscribed, and, even if they live in white suburban neighborhoods and speak English fluently, they remain potential targets of racism and other forms of exclusion. Race, like gender, is "from birth until death inextricably linked to one's personal identity and social status" (Goldman 292).

In their reading of these memoirs, my students identified more closely with the transcultural third-generation narrators with whom they share an educated and privileged view of the world. As DeSalvo revisits Italy, she discovers that she cannot fully identify with either American or Italian culture. My students understood this all-too-real and potentially unsettling notion of "in-between space" (Bhabha 38) or "contact zone" (Pratt 6). In this physical and textual space where cultures meet, the writer of auto-ethnography can explore his or her relation to the dominant culture, "not in terms of separateness . . . but in terms of copresence, interaction, interlocking understandings and practices, often within radically asymmetrical relations of power" (Pratt 7).

While ethnicity was at the center of our discussion of the two memoirs, several students thought that the autobiographical novels, *Riding in Cars with Boys* and *Finding Grace*, were devoid of a clear Italian American signature. One student argued that ethnicity, in both books, took the form of token references to Italian names and meals. To get my students to consider different expressions of ethnicity, I asked them to look for the social realities and values represented in these novels. They identified a working-class context that maintained traditional patriarchal values and a suffocating family environment. While these markers are not specifically ethnic, they represent values tied to Italian ethnicity and what the narrators need to escape to develop their identities. Both Beverly and Peanut (like the narrators of DeSalvo's and di Prima's memoirs) break away from their repressive homes to create promising futures for themselves. While Italian American culture offers only basic narrative devices for *Finding Grace* (limited to names and a few meal scenes in which typical Italian American dishes are prepared), both the solace and the hypocrisy offered by a Catholic upbringing permeate the novel. The former priest—who is selfish, self-centered, and violent, does not go to church, and criticizes Peanut's father for praying too much—epitomizes hypocrisy, while Peanut's faith in the church and the Virgin Mary are a last resort in moments of desperation. Ultimately, the Catholic virtue of grace, at first personified in the elderly woman and finally becoming a state of being, explains the title and provides the novel's resolution.

The Construction of a Gendered Self

Gender issues marked the second point of entry into the course readings. In reading these texts as articulations of women's life experiences, students were asked to focus on the highly relational features of women's life writing suggested by Mary Mason and others (Smith and Watson, "Situating" 17). How, in writing relationally, do women engage in and subvert the dominant discourse that has inscribed them? How, for example, do the narrators transgress the patriarchal scripts of their families and cultures? Di Prima's construction of a self at the junction of ethnicity and gender provided my students with a powerful response to this question. Di Prima speaks the culturally unspeakable: sexual relationships with both men and women, pregnancies and abortions, incidents of abuse and incest, attempts to alter her identification with her sexed body through clothes and appearance. Hence her text allows for a feminist reading that does not consign women to their bodies but locates the female body as it "emerges in, disrupts, redirects narrative practices" (Smith and Watson, "Situating" 36).

If my students recognized di Prima's representation of herself as a woman who saw the body as the site of transgression and of self-construction, they identified food and its preparation (as well as its association with the female and female spaces) as the transgressive, motivating, and unifying element of DeSalvo's *Crazy in the Kitchen*. Food is the narrator's means of exploring and understanding herself and her personal and collective history, from courtship to matchmaking to rituals of death. De-Salvo constructs herself and authorizes herself through the symbiotic relation of the two passions in her life, writing and food, and through the writing of food: "but without cooking, there can be no writing. . . . Cooking gets you out of your head. . . . I know that I couldn't write if I didn't cook" (226). While students recalled ways in which food appears in numerous literary and cinematic works about women's lives, they recognized DeSalvo's unique and subversive juxtaposition of writing and food and the double, interconnected construction of one's life in a domestic and a textual space. Ultimately, not only does food in women's writing provide "a language through which to express such an ambivalent view of the domestic space, it also becomes a vehicle through which to articulate ethnic identity" (Giunta, "Blending" 118).

My students loved Donofrio's *Riding in Cars with Boys*. They felt that the story and the language of this hip "bad-girl" narrative captured the rebellious spirit of the protagonist's generation. They identified Beverly's means of transgression—the car—as one that is prevalent in their own New Zealand automobile-centered, "boy-racer"–plagued culture. The car, with numerous and at times contradictory functions, is the central metaphor that framed their reading of the novel. While getting in a car with boys initially only suggests transgressing cultural norms for good girls, it later determines mobility, both geographical and social, and thus autonomy. A gendered reading reveals that, without a car, Beverly is the archetypal woman, trapped in oppressive domesticity. With a car, she breaks away from her family, the site of patriarchal oppression, as well as from her working-class world, and gains access to education, to a job, to a new life in New York City, and ultimately to female subjectivity. My students saw this text as a female bildungsroman in which the protagonist transgresses the patriarchal script by literally and metaphorically taking the driver's seat. At the end of the novel, she is still riding in a car with a boy, but this time he is the son she has successfully raised with her own values and against all odds.

Transgression as the path to self-discovery is also the central theme we used to read *Finding Grace*, which my students defined as a "good-girl narrative." Like Beverly, the novel's two sisters take their lives into their hands and run away from home. Their motivation, however, is not rebellion but the escape from patriarchal violence. The girls encounter a surrogate mother, Grace, who, though embodying the value suggested by her name, is another transgressive soul, perpetrator of a violent act committed to free herself and her child from the nightmare of domestic violence. My students noted that the novel critiques religious hypocrisy and the dark side of family life while positioning the Catholic values of grace and forgiveness as fundamental to the protagonist's acquisition of subjectivity. Though transgressive in its resistance to patriarchal scripts and its affirmation of female autonomy, this moralistic adolescent novel also restores and celebrates certain Italian American Catholic virtues.

Performing Gendered Autoethnography

The unit on Italian American autobiography provided my students with numerous examples of ways in which marginalized voices can engage in a dialogue that responds to the dominant culture that constructed them. At the end of the unit, my students applied their understanding of the texts to their own experiences by writing a gendered autoethnography (although I gave students who felt uncomfortable with this assignment the option to write a critical piece instead). In this assignment, they had to situate themselves in a marginalized, disempowered context and write from the acknowledged position of otherness. In their recounting of personal experiences, the students explored the way the dominant culture had marked their otherness and negotiated their constantly shifting relation to different cultures. One of the more sophisticated and mature students wrote a moving recollection of a personal and unanticipated loss.

She recorded the geographic mobility that defined the years of her youth and that had driven her from New Zealand to Russia and to the United States alongside the story of a friendship with a boy across continents and time. The discovery of his untimely death, revealed only years later in an encounter with a mutual friend, is accompanied by an unrelenting feeling of angst and displacement. Recounted in an engaging writing style and marked by memories of cold-war paranoia, her piece gives the reader access to both the narrated external events and the complexity of her confused and guarded feelings as she explores how the unexpected loss of a friend corresponds to the irretrievable loss of part of one's life. The tensions between mobility and displacement in this piece highlight the perennial sense of otherness that is part of the contemporary condition, a condition of inevitable intercultural encounters and a constant evolution of the self.

A young Korean New Zealand woman attempted to untangle her identity from a web of her transcultural experiences by examining emotions linked to her happy early childhood in Japan, her unhappy adolescent years in Korea, and her subsequent move to New Zealand. While she reluctantly accepts New Zealand as a provisional home (at least it is not Korea), she feels trapped by the identity inscribed on her body: "I was Asian and I would never be like them." She finds friendship or solace among other displaced Koreans but yearns for a return to Japan some day. In bravely talking back to her othered position, she shows in this text the difficulty of liberating ourselves from the dominant scripts that brand us and that keep us forever linked to a culture from which we may feel estranged.

Finally, an artistic Taiwanese New Zealander wrote and painted the story of a forbidden relationship between herself and a male teacher in Taiwan. The move away from home to New Zealand led to the loss of the lover to another woman but also to a voluntary separation from parental and cultural oppression, necessary for the acquisition of freedom and agency. While accepting the sense of loss of cultural identity, this student held on to elements of her parents' culture and, resisting assimilation, embraced transculturation as a possible avenue to the freedom and rights normally reserved for the dominant culture.

In their heartfelt and engaging works, my students demonstrated how the study of Italian American autobiography as gendered autoethnography helped them address conflicts in their personal and political histories, enabled them to make some sense of their stories, and helped them construct their identities through transgressive discourses. These Italian American autobiographical narratives, representing experiences that are oceans away, provided my students with the tools to talk back to the myths, taboos, expectations, and patriarchal scripts standing in the way of their agency.

Louise DeSalvo

When the Story Is Silence: Italian American Student Writers and the Challenges of Teaching— and Writing—Memoir

It is a bleak late January day in New York City. I am in a dingy classroom (battleship gray, black tile, broken blinds) at Hunter College, teaching an undergraduate memoir course. It's our second class, and twenty students sit in a circle, writing. Most work (some, full-time) to pay tuition; many are émigrés; many, second-generation Americans; many, older than traditional students.

To my right sits an Italian American woman. All the other students are free writing for ten minutes, but she (I will call her Carla) writes, stops, stares into space. Despite my instructions not to revise yet, Carla has crossed out a few sentences. If this is any indication, I believe she'll find it difficult to write memoir, and, if she is like other Italian American students I have taught, her challenge might be rooted in her culture, a challenge that I too have grappled with: how to write authentically about our lives if we come from a culture that insists we keep silent about our experiences.

In our next class, Carla doesn't hand in the assigned three pages. When I ask why, she responds that she has had family obligations. At the end of the first month, her work falls far short of the requirement. By the end of the second month, she has written a short first draft about her mother, whom she has described vaguely and idealistically. There is one moment, describing her sister, when the work comes alive. Then the silence of cliché takes over.

Carla is a composite of many of the Italian American student writers I have taught—some two dozen, over the years. Although there is surely no typical Italian American student, much writing about Italian American culture consistently raises the issue of the many people of Italian American descent who find it difficult to write about what they have freely chosen to write about: their families. I have discovered that teaching them poses special challenges (that other students might also share). Many are deeply rooted in Italian American culture and in the effects of the Italian diaspora.

The Challenge of the Cultural Imperative of Silence, *Omertà*

In my writing classes, I tell students to write about what concerns them deeply. Although I never mandate that students write about personal or family issues, most students choose to write about such matters. I believe the greatest challenge they face is the tradition of *omertà*—self-imposed silence (Gambino, *Blood*; Mangione and Morreale). Most Italian Americans have been taught not to discuss family matters publicly. "My father would kill me if he knew what I was writing," a student remarks. How can students break a silence so deeply rooted in Italian American (and Italian) culture if they believe that speaking about their lives is prohibited or dangerous? We as teachers should not underestimate this difficulty: in relation to the wealth of memoirs by authors from other ethnic and racial groups, there are few Italian American memoirs.

To help students understand the challenge of *omertà*, an instructor needs to discuss openly issues of silencing and self-censorship. Unless these are addressed—and most writing workshops don't address them, assuming that they are beyond the scope of the class—students must struggle alone, perhaps unsuccessfully, against a prohibition that, if named, they might be able to surmount.

I ask students to describe on paper or orally what prohibits them from writing authentically about their lives. I ask them to write about what will happen to them if they tell their story. Some believe they will be harmed; others, that they will be ostracized; still others, that their families will fall apart. After they articulate these imagined consequences, I ask them to imagine how they might tell their stories anyway. A few decide to use pseudonyms; a few decide to write fiction. I ask those who choose to write memoir to describe the story they would tell if they felt they could write freely.

Many of my Italian American students are afraid that they don't have anything important to say because many don't value their experience and don't see it as significant. Like many writing students, they are afraid to tell their stories, afraid of what their stories might reveal, afraid that they might fail. This fear can be disabling unless it is understood, worked with, and faced down.

Works like Ralph Keyes's *The Courage to Write: How Writers Transcend Fear* and Eric Maisel's *Fearless Creating* address this issue, describing how many famous writers do their work despite being afraid; one need not rid oneself of the fear to write. I also use Joyce Wycoff's *Mindmapping*, which teaches a strategy to tap into the nondominant hemisphere of the brain. Almost always, after students "mindmap," they discover what they want to write and that they have much to say.

In discussing cultural silencing, Italian American students discover that their inhibitions are often shared by others—Asian American students, students from Islamic countries, students from countries where their families were political dissidents. I also invite Italian American students to read about *omertà* in works about Italian American culture, such as Kym Ragusa's *The Skin between Us*, just as I ask students from other cultures to read about silence in their own culture in the diverse essays in Susan Richards Shreve's *Dream Me Home Safely*. Tillie Olsen's *Silences* treats this issue well; students learn that some great writers— such as George Eliot, Joseph Conrad, and Isak Dinesen—were silent until late in life. David Bayles and Ted Orland's *Art and Fear* examines silences by asking questions: "How does art get done? Why, often, does it not get done? And what is the nature of the difficulties that stop so many who start?" (1). Students are often helped by reading how "fears about yourself prevent you from doing your *best* work, while fears about your reception by others prevent you from doing your *own* work" (23). Julia Cameron's *The Artist's Way* presents a program designed to help writers overcome their inhibitions; I have used it both in my classes and to jumpstart my own work. By far the most successful strategy to overcome silence is to have students begin a piece with the phrase, "What I can't say." Students learn that memoir can address what they can't write and why they can't write. Silence itself, then, becomes the subject.

The Challenge of Not Having Models for Writing

Virginia Woolf once wrote that works of literature are not single births; they depend on previous works of art (65). Most of my Italian American students have never read a work by an Italian American. Whatever challenges African American, Latina and Latino, or Asian American students face, they have usually read several works by writers with shared backgrounds, and so they know that people like them write and publish their work. Often, they have read these works in literature courses, because of the success of efforts to expand the canon.

Most Italian American students are unaware of the important tradition of Italian American writing. Teachers can help all student writers find literary models to inspire them. Some models may be writers with backgrounds similar to theirs—one of my Latina students has found courage to do her work after reading Gloria Anzaldúa's *Borderlands / La frontera: The New Mestiza*. Other models may be from writers with different backgrounds—one of my Italian American students described how reading Maxine Hong Kingston's *Woman Warrior* inspired her. I often suggest starting with an anthology of Italian American writing. I suggest, too, that Italian American students read the book-length memoirs of Ragusa, Mary Cappello (*Night Bloom*), and Susanne Antonetta (*Body Toxic*).

Many Italian American families do not value writing; in fact, they often disdain it. ("What are you, queer?" an Italian American student writer is asked by his father. "It won't put food on the table," an Italian American student is told by her mother, when she says she wants to be a writer.) Selma Shapiro, a publicist, once told me that Italian Americans don't support Italian American writers in the same way, say, that many African Americans support African American writers or many Jewish Americans support Jewish American writers. And, because today's most well known Italian American icon is Tony Soprano, how can a young Italian American writer believe that her or his narrative about ordinary life is as worthwhile as one about a sensational and violent life?

Teachers of Italian American student writers can direct them to Maria Laurino's memoir *Were You Always an Italian?* or to Tina De Rosa's autobiographical novel *Paper Fish*. But Italian American educators must also press to have such works included in survey courses. Teaching these works in Italian American studies isn't sufficient; unless they are taught in survey courses, the work of Italian Americans will remain marginalized. Perhaps, too, programs in Italian American studies might include courses in writing and address the special challenges Italian American students face in the context of Italian American culture.

The Challenge of Family Demands

When I have asked working-class Italian American students why they find submitting their written work for class so difficult—and many do—they answer that their families place many demands on them or that they don't have a quiet place to work or that, when they are writing, their parents often interrupt them because they don't see writing as work.

I believe that Italian American—and all—students can benefit from writing in class. The classroom is that rare quiet place where they can work without interruption. If I can get them started, I know they will be more likely to continue outside class. I want them to experience what working in uninterrupted silence is like—something many of them can't do often. In-class writing usually takes the form of improvisational work: Stephen Nachmanovitch, in *Free Play: Improvisation in Life and Art*, for example, believes that such a stage is essential in the creative process. Students then take home what was begun in class, to rewrite, revise, polish, and complete the work.

If, like Carla, students find it hard to write, I give them prompts: sometimes from the memoir excerpts we are reading (from my memoir *Crazy in the Kitchen*, for example, to write about an object in a person's life that tells us something about him or her), sometimes from exercises in books like Jane Taylor McDonnell's *Living to Tell the Tale* or Ken Macrorie's *Searching Writing*.

The Challenge of Not Understanding the Writing Process

Throughout our work, I ask students to report about their challenges— "I can't find time to write"; "What I've written is garbage"; "I don't know what to write about." They speak, too, of their accomplishments— "I found that I remembered more about that incident than I thought I would"; "I know I'm going to write about third grade"; "It felt good to just write"; "I bought myself a special notebook." I ask students to help one another by suggesting possible strategies to handle challenges; I also ask students whether they shared the triumphs described by others. I often discuss the challenges published writers, including me, have faced, describing possible strategies: "Make a firm schedule, and stick to it, even if you can only write for half an hour a week"; "Don't judge what you've written, just write"; "It's common not to know what you want to work on; just keep writing, and a subject is bound to emerge." And I prepare students for what to expect at each stage of the creative process (confusion, but also elation at the beginning). I teach students how "real" writers work because many believe the ability to write is inborn and doubt they have what it takes to become a writer.

Underlying my pedagogy is the knowledge (based on three decades of teaching experience and on research in pedagogy, writing, and the creative process) that if students understand the creative process, if they learn what writers do when they write, if they learn to reflect on their own process, if they are rewarded for commitment to the process (rather than only for the final project), if they are permitted privacy to experiment at the beginning of the term, and if their early efforts are not graded, then each student will produce a memoir that will be the best work he or she has ever written.

A process-oriented pedagogy, eschewing judgment, I discovered early, works especially well with Italian American—indeed, all—students who need privacy to find their authentic voice, who may be working against a cultural prohibition against revelation, and who might take some time, perhaps even the whole semester, to get close to what they have to say. Taking a work through various stages replicates the way real writers work.

Though my work with my Italian American students has not been an unqualified success, the strategies outlined here have helped many succeed and tell their important stories. Unless we understand how prevalent the tendency is in Italian American students to silence themselves, the reality of Italian American life will continue to be underrepresented in American letters, and the only portraits we will continue to have are those that distort and misrepresent Italian American lives.

Luisa Del Giudice

Spoken Memories: Oral History, Oral Culture, and Italian American Studies

Oral History

It is the living members of an oral culture who become repositories of its knowledge, and it is this memory that forms the archive, both of oral culture (folklore) and of oral history. These disciplines, therefore, share an interest in collecting oral testimony and examining spoken memories, and they necessarily pivot on the personal interview.

Oral history has been variously described: "the interview of eyewitness participants in the events of the past for the purposes of historical reconstruction" (Grele, "Directions" 63); "hidden history" (Rowbotham); "history from below" (Evans 1); or "spoken memories" (Treleven). First-person oral narratives frequently reveal alternative perspectives, particularly if collected from groups previously excluded from the historical record for political, geographic, class, gender, or ethnic reasons. Just as the slave narrative collection *Born in Slavery*, which recorded surviving ex-slaves from 1936 to 1938, may be considered a "veritable folk history of slavery" (Southern 117), so too might a wide-ranging oral history campaign among Italian immigrants still yield an invaluable veritable folk history of immigration by allowing individual immigrants to "tell their own story, in their own way."

Such narratives give voice to an unlettered *gente senza storia* ("people without history"), such as the Italian peasants who immigrated to the United States. An Italian immigration narrative, assembled from viva voce testimonies of lived immigrant experience (and literally told from below, since many of the earliest immigrants traveled steerage class on transatlantic freighters), would surely enrich and enliven the statistical record of the migration phenomenon. Given the distinctiveness of spoken memories, layers of meaning can be explored in individual modes of expression, in the processes of self-interpretation and meaning making, and in the very reason for remembering or forgetting (see Portelli).

Not only does oral history supplement the historical record, but it may also create a historical record where none previously existed. And, not infrequently, oral history research leads to advocacy when a scholar attempts to come to terms with the question, Why has this story been excluded from the historical record? In Italian American scholarship, Lawrence Di Stasi's *Una Storia Segreta* ("A Secret Story [or History]") represents a notable example of giving voice, through oral testimonies, to just such a hidden story: for example, the internment of Italians, like the Japanese, as enemy aliens in the United States during World War II. This field-collecting campaign eventually led to proposed legislation to rectify the wrongs committed against Italian Americans and for the inclusion of this chapter of American history into the textbooks of California public schools (Public Law 106–451; see *Storia*), so that ephemeral or impermanent oral stories might be converted into a permanent written history.

Oral Culture and Folklore

Italian Mass Migration to the Americas

World War II proved a watershed for many Italian traditional cultures, as rapid industrialization and modernization, literacy campaigns, and social upheaval (e.g., emigration and internal migration) profoundly changed local communities in Italy. Those emigrants from towns and villages who left in the immediate postwar period never experienced such changes directly and, indeed, brought many archaic forms of folk culture and dialect to the Americas—aspects of culture that in their towns of origin were to undergo such radical change in the postwar era. Thus Italian emigrants abroad (the Italian diasporic periphery) continued many cultural practices long transformed in Italy (the center), making Italian American communities a focus of particular interest to folklorists.

But what, precisely, do folklorists study? Folklore studies cultural knowledge (lore) that is transmitted from one generation to the next by word-of-mouth or by example. There are few areas of traditional culture that did not rely on oral transmission: folksongs and folktales, of course, but also belief, celebration, culinary practices, and so forth. That this knowledge was communally shared and honored across generations accounts for its appeal, its meaning, and its cultural "authority" (see Del Giudice, "Italian American Folklore").

The Italian Folk Music Revival

Although certain genres of oral culture, dependent on Italian dialects, may not have fared well in America because of language loss, others, such as culinary practice, belief, and ritual, have. But even when apparently lost, important echoes remained at some generational distance—such as spoken memory about traditions and aspects of persistent peasant worldviews embedded in narratives from members of older generations. New forms of Italian American culture, of course, emerged: some without links to this cultural heritage; others with vague resonances of traditional culture; and still others that creatively transformed or translated such echoes into more contemporary idioms (see, e.g., Sciorra on rap and hip hop ["Language"]). Finally, at the tail end of this spectrum are the conscious acts of recovery, revival, and reclamation of cultural forms such as traditional music or folk ritual practice (see Magliocco on witchcraft). The Italian folk music revival of the 1960s presents a case in point.

The Italian folk music revival movement in Italy emerged from the sociohistorical context described above—rapid industrialization and the progressive disintegration of traditional society. Many scholars engaged in field-recording campaigns in an attempt to document traditional singers and musicians and to make these vernacular voices available to a wider audience through commercial recordings. Some, such as Joan Baez in the United States or Sandra Mantovani in Italy, performed them as revivalist folksingers. Sound recordings and concert performances became powerful tools in a movement that dealt not only with reviving cultural heritage "at risk of being lost . . ." but also with political advocacy. Scholars and performers brought the life struggles of ordinary "folk"—peasants, fisherman, shepherds, artisans, laborers—to the attention of the general public, so that their plight might be ameliorated and that they would not be forced to emigrate.

Did this Italian revival movement have much of an impact on those who had emigrated? Apparently not (Del Giudice, "Italian Traditional Song" 83). But more recent and emergent Italian folk music revivals in the United States, centered in New York in the late 1970s and in Los Angeles during the 1990s, may have had greater effects. The personal narratives of musicians, dancers, and ethnomusicologists still involved in this movement, such as John La Barbera, Alessandra Belloni, and Roberto Catalano and Enzo Fina, explore these questions in *Oral History, Oral Culture, and Italian Americans* (Del Giudice).

Recovering Traditional Knowledge and Direct Experience

It is through personal and collective acts of cultural recovery—field collection, recollection, or actual reclamation of cultural practices, commonly initiated through explorations of family life—that many Italian Americans encounter oral history and oral culture for the first time. But it is often direct experience of tradition (through dance, food, or ritual practice, for instance) that proves personally transformative to descendants of immigrants.

A large part of the task assumed by scholars of Italian American folklore is to recover such traditional knowledge and to present it to the general public through festivals, exhibits, and recordings, so that it might be experienced directly—all the while answering the questions of how and why cultural conservation or innovations occur. Folklore scholars may bring little-known forms of traditional culture to our attention (e.g., the *pizzica tarantata*, a form of "spider dance" ritual [Del Giudice, "Folk Music Revival" 218–20]), but it remains to be seen what long-term effects Italian Americans' encounters and engagements with traditional culture will have on the general public, on artistic and literary expression, and on Italian American scholarship.

Intersections between Oral History and Oral Culture Research

Oral history and oral culture research often intersect and prove mutually informing—as contiguous, porous, and overlapping fields. Robert Perks and Alistair Thomson (reminding us of the impact on American culture of Alex Haley's *Roots*) argue that "oral history recording taps into a vast, rich reservoir of oral traditions sustained through family, community and national memories" ("Critical Developments" 2), documenting the oral forms but also illuminating the oral process itself: how, why, and when cultural knowledge is passed along orally and how persons use spoken language to make sense of their life and times (see Vansina on the importance of oral historiography for nonliterate societies).

An exemplary study of the interplay between folklore and oral history may be found in Elizabeth Mathias and Richard Raspa's *Italian Folktales in America: The Verbal Art of an Immigrant Woman*. This collection presents the tales and storytelling practices of an immigrant woman, both in her native Dolomite village and as they were transformed through immigration to America, where, for example, traditional "c'era una volta" ("once upon a time") fairytales gave way to personal experience narratives of her life as an immigrant. Such research carefully analyzes the narrator's art and the personal meanings of her tales while setting the narratives and the cultural practice of storytelling in broader economic, political, and historical contexts. Mathias and Raspa thus not only provide an individual's narrative repertoire but also evaluate it against local and regional narrative traditions. They provide hard socioeconomic evidence to separate shared community experiences from unique aspects of the narrator's life. The best of current oral research engages in such "triangulation" of discourse (Lummis 274).

Many intersections at the boundaries of ethnography, oral history, and personal experience narrative have also been critical to my work on Italian and Italian American or Canadian cultures: on wine ("Wine"), song ("Italian Traditional Song," *Italian Traditional Song*, "Folk Music Revival"), architecture ("'Archvilla'"), and belief ("Cursed Flesh" and "Ethnography"). While researching concepts of food abundance, I discovered historical *paesi di Cuccagna* ("gastronomic utopias") but also a deeper truth about research methodology regarding personal history: it was in response to specific immigrant experiences—the persistent search for abundance—that I realized a need to look for traces of the awakening of a coherent and collective cultural past (Del Giudice, "Mountains"). Although it was in libraries and manuscript archives that I found the mythic land of plenty known as *Cuccagna*—which provided a historically sanctioned topos to which I might attach a collective cultural experience—it was through personal lived experience that I knew it to be true.

This dialogue between the present experience of traditional culture and written or visual documents, often spanning centuries, convinces me that a combined study of oral and written sources has the potential to create a significantly deeper understanding of our cultural tradition and that this methodology is critical to writing the history of a people who are, in large measure, without a written historical record. This work thus confirms the importance of gathering oral testimonies of personal experience—not only for folklore but for conventional historical research as well. Indeed, oral research methodologies, in conjunction with archival and bibliographic research, form a mutually sustaining and convincing partnership.

Fieldwork Methodologies, Applications, and Archives

With the growing interest in collecting oral testimonies, many practical guides to fieldwork now exist that treat such subjects as interviewing and transcription techniques, ethical and legal issues, and questions of archiving and preservation. Some focus on folklore (Bartis; Georges and Jones; Jackson); some on oral history (Bermani and De Palma; Dunaway and Baum; Grele, *Envelopes*; Ritchie; Truesdell); other on both (Hunt; Ives); and yet others on family history (Greene and Fulford). (Some helpful organizations supporting oral research are listed at the end of this essay.) But what can one do with these field-collected materials? The applications are many and diverse, since they are transformed into media— recordings, film, theater, exhibitions—for use in a wide variety of public settings, including museums, festivals, and Web sites. Darrell Fusaro, for instance, explores an unresolved murder in his own family history in the play *The Basement*; Beth Harrington, a documentary filmmaker on Italian American festivities, examines the process of ethnographic filmmaking and its moral dilemmas in *The Blinking Madonna*; while B. Amore transforms immigrant narratives and objects into artistic compositions in *An Italian American Odyssey: Life Line / Filo della vita* (exhibited at Ellis Island and elsewhere). An inherent value of an increasing multivocality in Italian American discourse—achieved partly through a diversity of oral testimonies recounting the varied experiences of the lives of actual Italian Americans—is its ability to counter and erode the ethnic stereotypes still prevalent in the popular media.

Perhaps some of the best known products of fieldwork are the sound recordings that capture the very voices producing oral genres like lullabies, vendors' cries, or folktales on Italian labels active during the Italian folk revival, such as Albatros, Fonit Cetra, and Dischi del Sole. Sound recordings of regional traditional music on such Italian labels may be found in the Del Giudice–Tuttle Collection in the University of California, Los Angeles, Ethnomusicology Archive. Alan Lomax (together with Diego Carpitella) made field recordings in Italy from the early 1950s, and many have been recently released as part of the Italian Treasury series by Rounder Records (*Italian Treasury*). In *Italian Traditional Song*, I provide an overview of traditional song, along with an annotated and translated anthology of sound recordings.

Finally, while memory functions metaphorically as an archive, actual archives frequently become public repositories of community memory and shared culture. They are critical to oral research. Ideally, primary documents are maintained in visual and sound archives that preserve the primacy of the original field documents, even though transcriptions of them may facilitate the ease with which they can be consulted. The number of physical and digital archives of sound recordings relating to the Italian American experience are growing as oral history projects on a variety of topics multiply. Such archives may document many aspects of the immigrant experience, specific community history, individual life histories, festivals and other traditions, and so forth. Only a fraction of their contents is ever digitized or published, so they remain a rich and frequently untapped source of primary materials for scholars.

Collections of oral materials on general immigration may be consulted in centers such as the Immigration History Research Center, at the University of Minnesota, or as part of specific projects such as the Ellis Island Oral History Project or on a publicly accessible Web site. *Italian Los Angeles: The Italian Resource Guide to Greater Los Angeles,* for instance, evolved from mapping the Italian presence in Los Angeles for the city's Cultural Affairs Department into a community-based oral history project (including university students) and finally into the Web site. Materials that form the basis of much of this site are now in the UCLA Ethnomusicology Archive's Italian Oral History Institute Collection. The Columbus Quincentennial project of the Library of Congress's American Folklife Center, *Italian-Americans in the West Project*, resulted in a traditional publication (Taylor and Williams) and a traveling exhibition that opened in 1992, both entitled *Old Ties, New Attachments: Italian-American Folklife in the West.* Sound archives scattered throughout Italy also provide vital contexts for fully understanding the Italian immigrant experience, on topics ranging from the world wars, fascism, and labor history to folk culture (see Barrera, Martini, and Mulè's guide to sound archives in Italy, *Fonti orali*). It is through this dialogue of spoken memories across continents and through time that the varied meanings of the Italian American experience can be more fully understood. This experience, too, is rooted in a long tradition of orally shared life and history. We must only learn to listen.

Note

A more extensive treatment of this topic may be found in my contribution to my edition *Oral History, Oral Culture, and Italian Americans* ("Speaking"). This edition presents selected papers from the thirty-eighth annual meeting of the American Italian Historical Association, in Los Angeles, 3–6 November 2005. This meeting represented the first for the AIHA (the organization most prominently representing the interests of Italian American scholars) to focus on such themes. I wish to thank Dorothy Noyes, Alessandro Portelli, Joseph Sciorra, and Edward Tuttle for their critical readings of earlier versions of this paper.

Appendix: Institutional Resources for Oral Research

Alan Lomax Archive (Association for Cultural Equity)
American Folklife Center, Library of Congress
American Folklore Society
Association of Personal Historians
Associazione Italiana Storia Orale
Center for Oral History Research, University of California, Los Angeles
Ellis Island Oral History Project
Immigration History Research Center, University of Minnesota
International Oral History Association (IOHA)
Italian Oral History Institute (IOHI)
Mediterranean Section, American Folklore Society
Museo Nazionale delle Arti e Tradizioni Popolari ("National Italian Folklife
     Museum"), Rome, Italy
Oral History Association (US)
Save Our Sounds: America's Recorded Sound Heritage Project
Society for European Anthropology (American Anthropological Association)
Una Storia Segreta
University of California, Los Angeles, Ethnomusicology Archive
University of Southern California Shoah Foundation Institute

Marisa Trubiano

From the Classroom to the Community and Back Again: Oral Histories and the Italian American Experience Course

Daniela: Who are some of the relatives in your family that you look to as a source of your Italian/American identity?
Anna: I guess my mother, she used to tell stories, you know, she's the one who let me in on everything. (Lombardi)

Daniela: What kind of objects and mementos has your family passed on over the years?
Anna: Oh, I believe I'm not sure, and I wish I was smart enough that I would have asked my mother more questions, and of my father too. That's why I think it's so important now to tell your children stories, which we never did, they did tell stories, we just never picked them up. But I'd like my children to learn from our experiences. (Lombardi)

The stories we tell are an intrinsic part of who we are, and they shape our private and public personas. When we speak freely about our lives, we may begin to shed the scripts that society imposes on us. Anna Lombardi's comments above have been culled from an oral interview submitted by the student Daniela Petruzzella as an assignment for my Italian American experience course at Montclair State University. While this course—The Italian American Experience: On the Margin or in the Mainstream?—

represents the only course in Italian American studies offered by the Italian section of the Department of Spanish and Italian, recent developments at Montclair are creating opportunities for the expansion of our offerings in Italian American studies across departments: the UNICO National and Montclair fund-raising campaign for a chair in Italian and Italian American studies, the founding of the Joseph and Elda Coccia Institute for the Italian Experience in America, and the recent hiring of a professor of American history with a concentration in Italian American history. Our Italian American experience course covers Italian American history, radicalism, labor and civil rights issues, education, politics, and representations of the Italian American experience in literature, film, and popular culture. Study field trips include visits to the Botto House American Labor Museum in Haledon and the Ellis Island Immigration Museum.

The oral history component of the course that I discuss here uncovers stories that make up the collective experience of the Italian American community of Montclair, New Jersey, while also encouraging students to investigate and share their ethnic experiences. The primary goal of this unit is to trace the history of Italian Americans in Montclair, the formulation of a local Italian American identity through time, and the advancement of multiculturalism in the local community. Students become local historians and contribute to the ongoing oral history project Montclair Memories: The Italians of Montclair Oral History Project, first conceived under the auspices of the Community Heritage Documentation component of the Community Outreach Partnership Center initiated by Montclair State and the Department of Housing and Urban Development in 2002. Copies of the products resulting from the oral history project will be donated to the Montclair Free Public Library's local history room and the Montclair Historical Society. The versatility and important implications of this kind of oral history unit make it applicable, with modifications, to other courses: Italian Cultural Studies and Cooperative Education in Italian and Twentieth-Century Civilization 1 Honors, for example. In the civilization course, my students and I address the formulation of ethnic identity globally as well as in an American context. We also study the intersection of war, identity, and politics of representation. The oral history component of each course directs students' attention to the "variations in human collective identity and their representations," to enhance "comprehension of identity and representation" (Stoeltje and Worthington 424).

"Don't ever forget where you came from" is a refrain that punctuates the over seventy-five oral interviews that my students and I have conducted, and where the students come from is the point of departure for this unit. We spend about five weeks on Italian American history—with a special focus on New Jersey—and on some representative texts of Italian American literature, like *The Milk of Almonds: Italian American Women Writers on Food and Culture*, edited by Louise DeSalvo and Edvige Giunta; *From the Margin: Writings in Italian Americana*, edited by Anthony Julian Tamburri, Paolo A. Giordano, and Fred Gardaphé; *Italian American Writers on New Jersey: An Anthology of Poetry and Prose*, edited by Jennifer Gillan, Maria Mazziotti Gillan, and Edvige Giunta; and *Crazy in the Kitchen,* by Louise DeSalvo. Then students learn to become storytellers. They report on cultural, religious, social, healing, and culinary traditions of their families, recounting personal and familial experiences, stories, jokes, and proverbs to classmates. They research their family histories and retell the stories that were orally transmitted from one generation to the next. I ask students to pay particular attention to how an oral account of one's life melds the personal with the collective experience, the past with the present, and fact with fantasy. They learn that, like the memoir, oral histories hold "the truth of memory, suspended between fact and imagination, a narrative that has often been filtered through a multiplicity of accounts" (Giunta, "Remembering" 2).

The oral history unit constantly moves from the voices of individuals to that of community, so students speak of themselves and then learn about others. The unit lasts four to five weeks, but students report on their progress throughout the remainder of the semester. Once students have acquired a general framework of the historical Italian American experience and reconnected with their individual and family histories, they examine materials that deal specifically with the history of Italians in Montclair. Required reading assignments include official documents that chronicle the Italian presence in Montclair, the development of the Italian national parish—Our Lady of Mount Carmel—and the traditions of the feasts of Our Lady of Mount Carmel and Saint Sebastian. In addition, they read the 1947 Civil Rights Audit (Montclair Forum), which highlights real estate proscriptions that negatively affected Italian Americans, African Americans, and Jewish Americans, as well as articles from the *Montclair Times* that report on school issues and recent developments in the community, such as the construction of the Midtown Direct New Jersey Transit train that has accelerated the fragmentation of the old

Italian and African American neighborhood, already discernible in the 1950s and 1960s. Students merge interview schedules into one master schedule that reflects the goals of the unit and the course in its entirety. They are then individually assigned interviewees and are provided with taping equipment from the Office of Instructional Technology or Language Learning Technology, if they do not own the appropriate equipment themselves. Before embarking on the project, students sign a consent form, approved by the Montclair State University Institutional Review Board, which states their rights and responsibilities as well as faculty expectations for student participation.

One major challenge of preparing this unit is the time-intensive initial work that must be done to bridge the gap that often exists between a campus community and the local community. Montclair Memories: The Italians of Montclair Oral History Project is the fruit of a collaboration with Donato Di Geronimo and Ruth Kunstadter, members of the Community Heritage Documentation Project, who introduced me to board members of groups like the Mount Carmel Seniors' Group, the Rosary Altar Society, the Saint Sebastian Society, and the Club Aquilonese. To ensure the successful outcome of the project, we spent considerable time organizing community presentations to introduce the project and garner local support. We spoke at the groups' monthly meetings and invited members to volunteer to be interviewed. We consulted with the staff at the Montclair Library and Historical Society and decided that oral interviews and materials gathered could be displayed at those two sites. Eventually, one early spring evening, the members of the Club Aquilonese on Pine Street and my Italian American experience class met over coffee and cake at the club, where initial contacts and appointments for formal interviews were made. Following the best practices in oral history collection—as outlined by the Oral History Association; the International Oral History Association; *Folklife and Fieldwork: A Layman's Introduction to Field Techniques*, by Peter Bartis; and the Indiana University Center for the Study of History and Memory—students provided the interviewees with a copy of the interview schedule and a release form. After the taped interaction, students worked on the transcription, remaining faithful to the structure and diction of the taped material. While the emphasis of this unit is primarily on orality, during this part of the process we also focus on the writing component. As William Bernard McCarthy states, the transcription of the oral interview heightens a student's sense of responsibility toward the content and empowers the student as an authentic writer (440). We aim to privilege the experience of a group whose stories have remained untold and unrecorded, to counter the loss of cultural memory in the community, as well as visible and invisible dividing lines in a multiethnic community like Montclair. As Edvige Giunta explains, "Appropriating memory is a crucial step for those who have been marginalized and denied access to public forums because of their gender, race, ethnicity, nationality, language, religion, sexuality, or class" (*Writing* 120). Kunstadter, one of our collaborators and interviewees, shares her hope that

> the neighborhood can become another type of thriving, interesting, close community, and perhaps this exhibit, and the publicity around it, will change the opinion some people have in Montclair of Pine Street as being just a blight on Montclair, and they will see the possibilities it has.

Once students have contacted their interviewees and have started conducting the interviews and transcribing them, the course content shifts again to more texts of Italian American literature and culture, analyzed under the lens of storytelling techniques, the presence and importance of orality in literature and everyday life, and the politics of representation. Toward the end of the course, the students finish their transcriptions and prepare a three-to-four-page commentary, which they present to the class. The result is a rich medley of voices relating accounts of personal, local, and national events. Sometimes diverging accounts of particular moments in the Italian American and American histories emerge—for example, accounts of World War II, the turbulent 1960s, the female experience, and generational differences. Indeed, like all oral texts and performances, the gathered oral histories speak to the impossibility of what Mark C. Amodio calls a "single, authorized version of a song against which the fidelity of all other versions can be measured" (100). After a discussion of the oral narrative of the Italian Americans of Montclair, students hand in the signed release form, the transcription of the interview in hard copy and on disk, the tape of the interview (audio, video, or digital), scanned photos and documents on disk, and their commentary.

Student reactions to the assignments for the oral history unit vary. Although some students find the time commitment and work load burdensome, most find the project rewarding. Numerous positive student comments cite memorable lessons. Assunta Scotto, a student involved in the project, remarked, "If I had to do the project over, I would do it happily. It opened my eyes to a world of Italian Americans of which I was not fully aware." Another student, Clair Long, commented on the value and time-sensitivity of the oral histories:

> The most enjoyable part of this project was meeting and listening to the stories of these people. . . . I have been asking about and listening to my mother's own stories as one of 8 children of immigrant parents for years. I never tire of them and I always seem to get a little piece of new information that I never heard before. Our ag[ing] population is such a stronghold of information, most times when we are younger, we're too caught up in our own lives to pay attention or care, then by the time we do, it's too late and they are gone.

Other observations indicate that student interviewers often see themselves in their interviewees' stories. That self-discovery frequently accompanies this kind of assignment yields rewards for the facilitator and student researcher alike.

The success of such a project can also be measured by how it motivates students to continue to do field research. Some students have taken additional related courses, like Cooperative Education, which offers students a self-designed internship or employment experience through the Center for Community Education, to become research assistants and exhibit curators, whose work is compensated through private and university grants. These students help organize "scanning parties" at the Montclair Free Public Library throughout the academic year, to which community members are invited to be interviewed and to bring documents and photos that are scanned while they wait. Students also research specific topics on file in the local history room. In addition, student assistants have been pivotal in the organization of the exhibits that opened at the Montclair Historical Society on 6 November 2004 and at the Montclair Free Public Library on 5 October 2005: they identified and prepared captions for photographs, documents, and artifacts, as well as digitized audio files.

In "Citizenship, Language, and Modernity," Iain Chambers argues, "Open to histories, memories, and possibilities from elsewhere, identities cannot be lived in a state of understanding that is already fully established. They become points of departure, openings on the continual elaboration of becoming" (29). Another of our collaborators and interviewees, Di Geronimo, writes about

> the enthusiastic response that our project has received from the Italian-American Community. Our work has stirred up many memories in this community, and, has served as a catalyst for many of these people to re-examine their family histories.

Indeed, Rosemarie Rabasca, an interviewee, comments that, because of this project, she has started researching her family's history and has finally begun to reclaim her cultural and linguistic heritage: "I am currently enrolled at the Language Institute to study Italian and I plan to take a trip to Italy in the future." The events surrounding the oral history project—scanning parties, student-conducted interviews, walking tours, exhibit openings—have re-created a sense of community for the Italian Americans of Montclair and revalorized their experiences. With each oral history, with each evocative performance and account, the identities of the Italian American community, of its storytellers, its student transcribers, its participants and observers alike are reelaborated, reinterpreted, and reconnected. This academic experience highlights the idea that, as we answer the question of how we identify ourselves, we open ourselves up to listening and understanding.

Theater and Performance

Emelise Aleandri

Italian American Immigrant Theater

The small number of Italian immigrants who traveled to America in the early part of the nineteenth century did so at the request of the Americans in need of Italian labor and skills. Musicians, singers, and other entertainers followed and were in turn joined by religious and political refugees and exiles, some of whom wrote for the theater. The first viable phase of Italian American theater emerged when Italian mass migration to the United States began in the 1870s. Playwrights reflected the tastes and concerns of the immigrant society. Audiences, composed of the displaced men and women of Italy, were hungry for entertainment, recognition, a support system, and social intercourse, all needs that the theater satisfied. The gradual assimilation of Italians would produce, by the late twentieth century, playwrights writing in English and giving voice to the emergence of a modern Italian American consciousness.

Italian American theater begins in New York City. In 1808, Lorenzo Da Ponte, to facilitate his teaching of Italian, adapted little comedies and short plays in Italian to be performed in his home by his twenty-four American students at Columbia University (*Memoirs*). These didactic pieces were adaptations of works he had done earlier in Europe. The true title of first Italian American playwright, however, goes to the political refugee Giuseppe Rocchietti for his *Ifigenia* (1842), the first extant published Italian American play, written in the style of classical tragedy. This play, too, was read aloud by his students as an exercise in the study of Italian. But Rocchietti's agenda was to uphold democracy and republicanism and overcome bigotry. Other playwrights who emerged, only after the mass migration, write an entirely different story, one that reflected their daily lives as immigrants or that celebrated their history and culture by resurrecting their mythology and folklore from the past (Aleandri [2006]). The example Rocchietti set for future playwrights, as a didactic writer of social conscience, was not replicated until the turn of the century, by Alessandro Sisca, known as Riccardo Cordiferro. Cordiferro's social dramas and satirical comedies differed from plays written by his contemporaries, who concentrated on vaudeville sketches, commedia dell'arte farces, the standard European melodramas, and the sensational plays often based on the scandalous headlines of the day (Cordiferro, "L'onore" and *Pezzente*; Aleandri [2006]).

During the nineteenth century, many dramatic forms and entertainments were displayed on the Italian American stage: comedy, farce, melodrama, tragedy, the history play, the *macchietta* ("character sketch"), the *drama giallo* ("mystery play"). In addition, the Italian American experience after 1880 furnished the subject matter for original plays written by Italian immigrant playwrights. New York's Italian-language newspapers, particularly *Il progresso italo-americano*, *Il telegrafo*, and *L'araldo italiano*, offer the most information on the day-to-day activity of the theater in the late nineteenth century, since they feature numerous theater advertisements, reviews, and notices of business and social activities. Despite their shortcomings—incompleteness, typographical errors, torn pages, misspellings of names, and illegible entries—the microfilm records remain the most valuable source for a major portion of this study and provide a large amount of the statistical data. The pages of the Italian dailies were more specific than any other sources about the details of a given performance (e.g., dates, places, actors, authors, play titles, theaters, ticket prices, and distribution points); they also provided clues regarding the social community and business roles pursued by the individuals discussed here.

For this kind of historical recovery, reading the Italian newspapers published in the United States is the best—and sometimes the only—way to discover not only what was being performed when and where but also the dominant attitudes toward the offerings, that is, why this drama was so important to the Italian immigrant community. The few additional articles by contemporaries or later commentators rarely include such detailed information and sometimes contradict one another on various points. Further confusion, sometimes caused by the fuzzy memory of a writer or performer as he or she wrote articles or memoirs in later life, can often be clarified through consultation of the newspaper record.

I searched the daily records on microfilm to unearth the data needed to create my studies of Italian immigrant theater—to be equipped to speculate about immigrant attitudes and to arrive at some conclusions. Often my archival research is the primary source because I have done the interviews and discovered some pieces of various puzzles from cellars and attics, photographs, anecdotes, letters, private collections, and newspaper microfilms. The fortuitous combination of newspaper records and personal collections, plus some additional articles, permits a reconstruction of the major events and minor incidents that shaped the history of Italian immigrant theater. But there is still much work to do. The women who acted in the theater, for example, also became writers, producers, and directors. While their names were mentioned in many press notices, there are no extant plays, just as there are no extant works of many early Italian American writers. Antonietta Pisanelli of San Francisco might have devised some skits that might be buried in an unknown archive in California (Seller).

The dominant nineteenth-century genres, primarily realism, naturalism (as well as its correlative, socialism), commedia dell'arte, and tragedy all contributed to the structures chosen by the writers for the Italian stage at this time. Key playwrights of the period include Rocchietti, Eduardo Migliaccio (pseud. Farfariello), Cordiferro, and Giovanni De Rosalia. Each employed a different dramatic genre: Rocchietti and Cordiferro wrote tragedy and social dramas; Farfariello and De Rosalia wrote vaudeville sketches, commedia dell'arte, dialect comedies, and *macchiette*. Their theatrical pieces reflect the dynamics of their immigrant community: the struggle and ideals of a society in transition in Rocchietti and Cordiferro and the individual's grappling with the new world in Farfariello and De Rosalia. These last two playwrights used many techniques from the Italian commedia dell'arte improvisational theater of the Renaissance, including slapstick, stock characters, music, and primal plots.

Migliaccio, whose stage name, Farfariello, means "Little Butterfly," made the Italian American immigrant the hero of his dramatic creations and became one of the most popular entertainers of the Italian American *caffè concerto* ("music hall") from the early 1900s until his death in 1946. Born in 1882 in Salerno, in 1897 he immigrated to the United States and worked at the bank of Don Pasquale Avallone on Mulberry Street, writing letters to Italy for the bank's clients, most of whom were illiterate Italian American laborers. This initiation into immigrant humanity supplied him with the subject matter of his future prodigious literary output. He performed the *macchietta,* a Neapolitan musical comedy sketch combining sung verses and spoken prose passages. Farfariello's original creation was the *macchietta coloniale,* or skit about the Italian immigrant community, in which he impersonated and satirized community figures recognizable to his audiences: Enrico Caruso, the bandleader, the *presidente della società* ("president of the community organization"), the Irish American, the *cafone* ("greenhorn" or "hick"), the wet nurse, the opera diva, the schoolgirl, the soldier boy, the bride, the street cleaner, the iceman, the fireman, the singer, the dancer, the soubrette, the policeman, the gangster, the bootlegger, the undertaker, the street vendor, and more. As Pasquale Passaguai, he showed immigrants how to avoid being duped by thieves, while his parody of *il presidente della società* cured many community leaders of their habit of wearing pretentious military uniforms at public functions.

These "photographs" of Italian American life earned their creator the title of "King of the colonial character sketch" (Aleandri [1999]). Farfariello wrote and spoke in the curious, newly evolving regional dialect of the Italian American community, *italo-americanese,* a linguistic soup of Italian and various dialect distortions of English and American slang. Farfariello wrote both the lyrics and monologues for all his skits. By 1914, he had a repertoire of 150 skits, which eventually increased to five or six hundred. Many were recorded by the Victor Company in 1916 and published by the Italian Book Company and the Italian newspaper *La follia.* During the heyday of Italian radio, he performed on many radio programs. Many of his recordings and *macchiette* are still available today, and a large collection can be found in the University of Minnesota Immigration History Research Center.

Cordiferro approached the problem of the Italian immigrant in a more serious mode. Cordiferro, the pen name for the poet, lyricist, journalist, editor, satirist, lecturer, and political activist Alessandro Sisca, was born in 1875 in San Pietro in Guarano, a province of Cosenza. He immigrated to the United States in 1892. In 1893, together with his father,

Francesco, and brother, Marziale, he founded the weekly literary newspaper *La follia*, which was widely read by the literati of the *colonie* in the major cities of the East. Cordiferro's plays concern the social conditions of the Italian immigrant. His first play, the three-act comedy in Martellian verse written in 1900, *Chi ha la testa di vetro non vada a battaglia di Sassi* ("If You Can't Take the Heat, Stay out of the Kitchen"), satirized the amateur theater groups who undertook plays beyond their abilities. The professional Maiori-Rapone-Ricciardi theater troupe (Ricciardi) mounted Cordiferro's earliest plays: the one-act *Il genio incompreso* ("The Misunderstood Genius"), another comic and satirical verse treatment of immigrant theater companies, advertised in *Il progresso italo-americano*, and the dramatic social monologue *Il pezzente* ("The Beggar"). His most significant dramatic work was the four-act social drama *L'onore perduto* ("Lost Honor"), adapted from his poem of the same title, which depicts the exploitation of Italian immigrants in Manhattan's Little Italy. Premiering on 20 February 1901, it played in many eastern cities until 1933. An analysis of *L'onore perduto* reveals its derivation from "Cecilia," a traditional Italian epic dirge sung for centuries in many dialect and musical variations. It laments the fate of Cecilia, an antiheroine who sacrifices her honor by giving sexual favors to the military official who promises to release her husband or lover either imprisoned or awaiting execution. The official treacherously executes the prisoner anyway. Cordiferro's domestic melodrama takes the familiar premise of Victorien Sardou's *Tosca*, places it in New York City's Little Italy in 1900, and manipulates the plot and speeches to illustrate his own topical social and political theses. The play examines the dishonesty of some Italian American bankers and its tragic effects on the immigrants; it also touches lightly on the emancipation of women. While Cordiferro's attitude toward the "woman problem" upholds the conventional double standard, it also validates the appropriateness of and necessity for the working wife and mother. His attitude toward prostitution is also in accord with the liberal, socialist, and naturalistic view of the time.

Another comic response to the immigrant experience were Sicilian dialect comedies featuring the halfwit Nofrio, created by De Rosalia (*Duello*; *Nofrio*). Born in Sicily in 1864, he became a professional actor with major companies in Italy before coming to New York sometime before 1903, when Cordiferro's *La follia* published his novel in Sicilian dialect, *Litteriu trantulia ovvero Lu nobili sfasulatu* ("Litteriu Trantulia; or, The Fallen Noble"). After 1903, De Rosalia started writing, directing, and performing independently. Also a journalist and teacher, he ran a school to teach English to Italian immigrants. In 1904 he performed his adaptation of *La balia* ("The Wetnurse") at Ferrando's Music Hall and became the impresario of his own theater company, La Compagnia Comico-Drammatica Giovanni De Rosalia, producing serious plays and comedies. The Sicilian *macchietta* "Piddu Macca" was written by De Rosalia and Filippo Dato for Farfariello (Fabbricatore). After 1907, De Rosalia abandoned the Italian prose theater and turned his energies to comedy. Most immigrants, illiterate and uneducated, were drawn more to farce and comedy than to De Rosalia's tragedy, so he formed a Sicilian dialect comedy theater to cater to the Sicilian immigrants in New York City. Nofrio made him very popular and became synonymous with De Rosalia, as Farfariello had become with Migliaccio and Cordiferro with Sisca. Nofrio, a Sicilian immigrant hick who always got himself into difficult situations, wore a big nose, a bushy head of black, curly hair, raggedy clothes, baggy checkered pants held up by suspenders, and a loose white shirt. De Rosalia himself interpreted Nofrio on the stage. Many skits were so popular that they were published, some by Cordiferro's *La follia*. Some of De Rosalia's plays and songs were recorded on the Columbia, Victor, and Okeh labels, as well as on his Nofrio label, in the 1920s. Between 1916 and 1928 almost two hundred three-minute recordings of his larger farces sold nationally (Accardi).

From the 1880s to the 1950s, Italian American playwrights continued to write in their own dialects. Most lived in New York City, and, although many of their scripts were never published, they nonetheless reached Italian immigrants in other American cities, as did Cordiferro, Farfariello, and, Eduardo Pecoraro. In the 1930s, 1940s, and 1950s, many dramatic works continued to make their way across the United States. They included the itinerant actor and writer Rocco De Russo's free adaptations of Italian dramas (at the University of Minnesota Immigration History Research Center), Clemente Giglio's bourgeois dramas (Flamma; Adelina Giglio; Alessandro Giglio), his son Sandrino Giglio's comedies and topical dramas (e.g., "The Death of King Umberto I"), Gennaro Cardenia's domestic melodramas, and Angelo Gloria's radio soap operas and comedies (Falbo; Gardenia; *Teatro*). The average audience, one can safely say, was quite unconcerned about whether a play was educational or socially relevant, but many of the writers were not. Some writers and directors imposed another role on the theater: it became a site of propaganda. The class struggle in New York City and throughout the world had become more desperate and the voice of reform more insistent, conditions that were reflected in the plays, particularly those of Cordiferro and of his contemporary, Salvatore Abbamonte (see "Attori," "Nei Primordi," and "Nella Colonia").

There was no direct line of evolution of immigrant Italian-language theater into Italian American theater in English from the community. The earlier immigrants were illiterate; their children were not. The assimilating second and third generations were leaving behind the old-fashioned topics, situations, and characters symbolic of their less sophisticated forebears. The Italian-language theater in America eventually died because the Italian-speaking audience disappeared, through attrition caused by death or assimilation. The need for a communal theater that the mass migration had created vanished when the acculturated second and third generations progressed to American entertainments. Italian American theater— everything from its architecture to its conventions to its styles of writing, acting, directing, and production—is virtually nonexistent today.

As the contemporary playwright Albert Innaurato explains, "Commercial survival depends on finding an audience, a particular audience that will come and see a particular work. . . . My [Philly] old people, 'i miei vecchi,' died off or moved far away" (qtd. in Shengold).

Joseph Sciorra

A Lived History under Scrutiny: Italian American Performance Art

Performance art is an arena of cultural production where Italian American artists provide alternative readings and often trenchant critiques of Italian American history and cultural practices, addressing topics such as immigration, family life and the home, Catholicism and spirituality, and neighborhood and social life. Gender roles, sexuality, and the body are areas of paramount concern for Italian American artists, as they are for other performance artists. As insiders-outsiders, these artists are both intimate with and estranged from their Italian American subject. This creative tension charges their work with the vibrancy of a lived history under scrutiny. Sites of Italian American vernacular expressive culture such as the family dinner table, the religious street *festa*, and the street corner inform the artists' themes and presentation styles. Much of this artistic production is motivated by an engaged cultural politics that challenges and reconfigures dominant discourses of Italian American identity, especially those perpetuated in the group.

Italian American performance artists are not heirs to the commercial Italian-language immigrant theater (1880s–1940s), which was defunct by the time they began working. Instead, their roots are in experimental and avant-garde art movements such as happenings and conceptual art that flourished in New York City during the 1950s and 1960s. Performance art emerged during the 1970s as a distinct art form, borrowing from poetry, theater, dance, stand-up comedy, and visual arts, and included video and site-specific installations. Autobiography became a vital source of material for performance artists; the one-person show and sustained monologue were key ingredients of this new art form.

Some artists explore the world of immigration and the resulting disaffection that immigrants and their descendants experience. New York resident Linda Mancini, granddaughter of Abruzzesi and Campanian immigrants to Montreal, Canada, developed the character of Angelina Contadina, an immigrant woman who arrives blindfolded on stage (to America).[1] Speaking to the audience in standard Italian, she expresses her disappointment with her new home and its inhabitants. She feeds her nineteen children—represented by tomatoes carried in a wicker basket—accompanied by the cacophony of English language lessons and vintage radio broadcasts of swing music and commercials, only to send her "boys" off to war by dropping the tomatoes to the floor with a kiss. Mancini's character eventually migrated into the work of other performance artists, such as Carmelita Tropicana, who contributed her Italian voice and perspective to New York's downtown multicultural art scene.

Third-generation LuLu LoLo, also known as Lois Evans née Pascale (Basilicata), bases many of her one-woman shows on historical and contemporary personages, both invented and real, in an act of rediscovery and reclamation. *Three Sisters in Soul: Saint, Solider, Seamstress* is a series of three monologues presented as part of an installation LoLo created at the Garibaldi-Meucci Museum in 2004. The solo piece is a rumination on three female personages from the historical past: Mother Cabrini; Anita Garibaldi, the Brazilian wife of Italy's "Great Liberator"; and, Esther Meucci, the wife of Antonio Meucci, whom the United States Congress recognized in 2002 as the inventor of the telephone. The piece reimagines these women's life stories as heroic exemplars for contemporary times. The following year, LoLo introduced another historically based, three-character feminist piece, *Soliloquy for a Seamstress: The Triangle Shirtwaist Factory Fire*, which focuses on the tribulations of working immigrant women.

The Italian American family has long fueled the American imagination as both a sociological subject and a myth. Italian American performance artists find the family and its primacy as a socializing agent to be a compelling source of inspiration. LoLo's *Macaroni and Mal Occhio* is a humorous set of interconnected character sketches of eleven family members—she is the daughter of the East Harlem community activist Pete Pascale—that evoke the lost world of immigrant familial practices and its labor intensive foodways, healing traditions and beliefs, and social networks.

Penny Arcade, also known as Susana Ventura, originally from Bridgeport, Connecticut, delves into the restrictive and stifling aspects of her Italian American family in her tour de force *La Miseria*. Named for the extreme poverty that was the impetus for millions of Italians' leaving their homes in search of work, the 1991 production centered on an Easter dinner table and involved over a dozen performers. Arcade's family members were not "Americans" but "peasant working-class southern Italians." As a teenager who snacked on focaccia stuffed with pickled eggplants, she realizes that she is not the "all-American girl" but the "other American girl." When Arcade's child self expresses her desire to be a dancer and an actress, she is chastised for being a *puttana* ("whore"). During the performance, members of the extended family sit around the table comparing the struggles of Italian immigrants with those of African Americans, Puerto Ricans, and Korean immigrants in racist and demeaning language. Characterizing her pugnacious Basilicata immigrant mother, who makes an appearance in a projected video, as the "Marlon Brando of mothers," Arcade acknowledges her mother's lasting influence on her life.

Several artists use autobiography to address issues concerning masculinity, patriarchy, and violence, especially at those locations where the domestic and the public converge. Marco Greco's one-man show *Behind the Counter with Mussolini* focuses on the relationship between a young boy and his Sicilian immigrant father with an affinity for the Italian dictator Benito Mussolini—his image is prominently displayed behind the counter of the family-owned deli—and calls into question values learned at the hands of a demanding and strict father. The authenticity of Greco's experiences is conveyed through the making of fresh mozzarella onstage during the performance. Chazz Palminteri's 1988 one-man show *A Bronx Tale*—which the actor Robert De Niro adapted to the screen in 1993 and Palminteri revived on Broadway in 2007—chronicles a boy's coming of age and his divided loyalties between a local gangster and his working-class father. Playing thirty-five characters, third-generation Palminteri (Sicily) dramatizes the historical influences and tensions surrounding masculine behavior and ideals. *Bless Them All* is a series of stories and characters written and performed by Johnny Lanz, also known as John Lanzillotto (Puglia), that portrays the gangsters, the junkies, and a traumatized and cruel World War II veteran father who served as masculine role models for a young boy growing up in a Bronx neighborhood, where "loyalty, honor, respect, and silence" was the code men lived by on the streets. Annie Lanzillotto (Puglia) mines the same family's legacy in *How to Wake Up a Marine in a Foxhole* and *Divine Wind*. The former performance work involves a stunning set piece in which Annie Lanzillotto, speaking in the voices of her working-class father and male relatives who proudly recount delivering ice to tenement walk-ups, chips at a spectacularly lit, 180-pound block of ice that she spins on a pedestal. For this Italian American family, "The house was a war zone, the kitchen a battleground, our bedrooms were foxholes," and a child's waking a father-veteran requires a soldier's strategy:

> If you nudge him awake he might think you're the enemy. You take the thumb, you press under the middle of the eyebrow, you let some light seep in to the eye.... You want him to know what he sees doesn't register with what's in his head.... You snatch the dream away from him. It all occurs in the cleft of a second. BOOM! The eye opens. He's awake!

To a large extent these artists' works counter the prevailing and nostalgic view of the Italian American family and its traditional gender roles as inherently life-affirming.

The Roman Catholic Church and Italian American manifestations of Catholicism exerted a major influence on the lives of Italian Americans. LoLo's transformation of herself into a "walking art piece" through the use of costume and sculptural headpieces is rooted in both Carmen Miranda's fanciful headgear and the pageantry of street processions in honor of the Virgin Mary and saints. Third-generation Linda Montano's (paternal grandparents from Molise) corporeal-centric performances of endurance are directly related to Catholic rituals performed as a child, as well as to Buddhist and Hindu meditative practices. Bronx-born conceptual artist Vito Acconci, son of an Abruzzesi father, created provocative and transgressive works that problematize the male body and the self, private and public spheres, domesticity, and violence. Arcade's *La Miseria* takes both a playful and critical look at the Catholic Church. Various saints—Saint Anthony of Padua, Saint Teresa of Ávila, Saint Sebastian, among others— descend from their church niches to banter as they wait for Jesus's Easter return, interacting like members of an extended family. Three priests celebrate mass in an operatic and campy fashion. Kneeling in confession to a priest (who is revealed to the audience as being a closeted homosexual), Arcade declares that she "hate[s] the Catholic Church" because of its lies, hypocrisy, misogyny, and persecution of homosexuals. When Arcade describes her rape and its aftermath in a disturbing moment in the performance, actors dressed as nuns silently fling mud at her, splattering her body and face, soiling her red dress. For these and other artists discussed in this essay, Catholic tenets and practices have fundamentally influenced concepts and presentations concerning spirituality, aesthetics, ritual, and the body.

The attention given to the body as both a site for and a subject of experimental performance art, also known as body art, uses the subjectivity of the artist in a climate of informed and acute gender politics. Acconci used his body as a medium in radical and often confrontational works that challenged viewers' understanding of the roles of the artist and audience. In *Conversion*, Acconci modifies the male body image by burning his body hair, concealing his penis between his legs, and pulling at his breast in a "futile attempt to produce female breasts." In his now famous work *Seedbed*, at the Sonnabend Gallery in New York City, the artist hid under a constructed wooden ramp, where he masturbated as visitors walked above. His sexual fantasies, triggered by the visitors' footsteps, were aired through an amplified speaker. Acconci enacts a topography of gendered and national identities in the ten-minute video *Shoot*. As he aggressively pushes his face, hand, stomach, and penis toward the camera, Acconci proclaims, "Yeah, I'm an American. I can't help it . . . I really do like Coca Cola." He makes childlike imitations of gunfire and explosions, then shifts gears, announcing, "No, I have an Italian name, my father's Italian. I'm not really American at all. I have a tradition. I have a culture." Pellegrino D'Acierno notes:

> [T]he themes associated with Italianness . . . seem to come into play in Acconci's art, albeit forced to an avant-garde extreme: the body—maculate and immaculate—territoriality; performance as self-display; the confounding of the public and private; violence, be it profane or sacred; and exorbitance. ("From Stella" 535)

The underlying intention of Montano's body-focused performances has been to erase the distinctions between art and life through ritual feats of endurance and sacrifice. In *Handcuff*, Montano and Tom Marioni were handcuffed together for three days, while in the now renowned collaboration *Art/Life: One Year Performance*, she and Tehching Hsieh were bound together with an eight-foot rope for a year while they avoided physical contact. For Montano, these experiential acts of intense corporeality and religious discipline induce moments of reflexivity and transcendence.

Women's sexuality and conventional roles are central to Arcade's work. Arcade developed *Bitch! Dyke! Faghag! Whore!* in 1990, during the culture wars that resulted, in part, from Congress's investigation of the National Endowment for the Arts. Arcade creates various characters who astutely comment on gay and lesbian culture, homophobia, AIDS, abortion, "academic feminism," repression, and sex as a "life force." At one point, she proclaims, "Love is the most political act you can make. It's the only one that changes the world." Toward the performance's end, Arcade strips naked, except for a sheer scarf imprinted with the American flag, to conclude her monologue. In *Bad Reputation*, Arcade examines girls and women who are stigmatized because of their sexual activity and, in particular, her rape and the lack of solidarity between women. As a woman's disembodied voice lambastes a rape survivor, Arcade swallows and vomits a dozen raw eggs onstage in the performance's disquieting finale.

Annie Lanzillotto also tackles gender, sexuality, and women's roles, but from the position of a working-class Italian American lesbian from the Bronx. In *Catholic School Kindergarten Sweethearts Turned Queer*, she and the Reverend John Edward Denaro recount their childhood crush and their eventual coming out as Denaro dresses in his clerical vestments and Lanzillotto slowly sheds her clothing. In *Confessions of a Bronx Tomboy: My Throwing Arm (This Useless Expertise)*, Lanzillotto repeatedly throws a ball against an X painted on a brick wall while musing on her tomboy childhood. In a 1995 series of performances—*A Passage of Oxygen, Pocketing Garlic (As If Skin Can Hold You)*, and *Uprooting Cement*—Lanzillotto, a childhood cancer survivor, explores "the voicelessness of illness," the healing properties of opera, and the "peasant wisdom of garlic." Many of these artists employ a neoburlesque style that revives older forms of popular entertainment to reframe women's bodies in a postfeminist era. In *Bitch! Dyke! Faghag! Whore!* and *Bad Reputation*, Arcade uses erotic dancers, declaring that the striptease is the most powerful feminine art form designed by women to control men. Two performing acts—the World Famous Pontani Sisters and Dirty Martini, also known as Linda Marraccini—are at the forefront of this neoburlesque movement. Knowledgeable about striptease's history, these performers present the eroticized female body in the conventions of this historically "low art" form with an ironic sensibility. With their tattooed bodies and heavy makeup, the Pontani trio—third-generation Angie and Tara (Umbria) and Helen Burkett—combine tap, Las Vegas showgirl routines, 1960s go-go dancing, and other forms in a postmodern mélange. Dance routines like "Mambo Italiano," featuring fruit-laden headdresses à la Carmen Miranda; "Italian Princess," a chair dance performed in tight short-shorts and cut T-shirts; and "Rat Pack," showcasing towering headgear sporting the visages of Frank Sinatra, Dean Martin, and Sammy Davis, Jr., reflect and reinforce popular notions of Italian American identity juxtaposed with other "exotic" types, such as "Chica Alborotada," "Jungle Exotica," and "Apache." Fourth-generation Dirty Martini, whom journalists describe as "zaftig" and "voluptuous," subverts the ideal feminine body type in her classic striptease routines: the fan dance, the balloon striptease dance, the dance of the seven veils, and others. In "St. Valentine's Day," Martini plays a woman who commits suicide after being stood up on a date, stripping down to panties and pasties as she falls dead on the floor. Presented in restaurants and cabarets, as well as in art galleries and festivals, neoburlesque illustrates how entertainment and performance art have converged to complicate the relation of artistic and commercial productions.

The urban neighborhood has figured prominently in the social construction of an Italian American identity, and performance artists have considered the interconnected concepts of belonging, exclusion, territoriality, and real estate. Annie Lanzillotto's two-year site-specific trilogy—*A'Schapett! (Wiping the Plate with the Heel of the Bread)*; *Mammamia! (You'll Never Get a Straight Answer Again!)*; and *How to Cook a Heart*—involved small business owners and their customers at the LaGuardia-era indoor Arthur Avenue Retail Market in the Bronx. This ambitious and multifaceted project dramatized local knowledge, collective memory, and lost community. Writing about the market in her essay "An Artist Journeys Home," Lanzillotto observed, "I watched the way the merchants and shoppers leaned over, creating a vital intimacy; the countertops morphed into confessionals, into stages" (68). In turn, the artist sought "to instigate, to load, to ignite performance, to provide a microphone for merchants and shoppers, to bring the scenarios to a level of dramatic intensity" (63), to enhance and exaggerate the market's everyday theatricality. Evoking the ancient agora and medieval marketplace, Lanzillotto invited trapeze artists, jugglers, musicians, opera singers, and prop and set designers from New York's downtown art world to the Bronx while creating the setting and encouraging customers and vendors to sing, play music, and tell personal narratives. A woman told stories of her laboring father who delivered ice to tenement apartments as she stood near a block of melting ice. A butcher and his wife (played by Lanzillotto) improvised a skit based on a true story about a former stall owner who, without a male heir, refused to leave his business to any of his three daughters, while they cooked lamb hearts that they later served to the audience-customers.

LoLo examines both the collapse of social life in the urban context and the creation of a new community around sexual orientation in *38 Witnessed Her Death, I Witnessed Her Love: The Lonely Secret of Mary Ann Zielonko*. The solo performance deals with the infamous murder of Catherine "Kitty" Genovese outside her Queens home in 1964, as thirty-eight neighbors observed yet failed to notify the police. Her lover at the time, Mary Ann Zielonko, came out about their lesbian relationship on the fortieth anniversary of Genovese's death. Based on research and a taped interview with Zielonko, LoLo's piece does not merely ruminate on a brutal death and the painful persistence of loss in the midst of metropolitan anonymity but more notably enacts memory and testimony in the dynamic work of community building.

Deanna Pacelli, originally from Illinois, scrutinizes the gentrification of a Brooklyn neighborhood in her 2003 one-woman show *There Goes the Neighborhood*, written by Mari Brown. With an uncanny ability for imitation, Pacelli performs, even inhabits, the words of Carroll Gardens residents taken from taped interviews. A series of intertwined and quickly paced talk by longtime and recent residents often tell the same story from different points of view. Pacelli probes current friction surrounding class, taste, and property, as well as older problems of organized crime, drug use, and racism. The changing Italian American neighborhoods and, ultimately, identity are presented in a humorous but keen fashion.

Works of performance art highlight artistic subjectivity to expose the socially constructed self. These new modes of aesthetic creation privilege race, gender, sexuality, and class as arenas for artists to scrutinize identity and representation. Italian American performance artists bring to bear "a matrix of perceptions, appreciations, and actions," what Pierre Bourdieu called habitus (82–83), that informs and fuels their work through style and subject, in combination with an array of additional influences. These unique artistic perspectives are catalysts for reflection, discussion, and cultural change.

Note

1. See the appendix, below, for references and critical responses to the performance art described in this essay.

Appendix: Review of Italian American Performance Artists

Joseph Sciorra and Stefania Taviano

The dates and locations given for each performance are those for each piece's first performance. Performances are presented in chronological order for each artist.

Vito Acconci

Acconci's official Web site, *Acconci Studio*, includes installations and contact information. Film and video documentation of the artist's performances is available at *Electronic Arts Intermix*.

Works

Trappings. Städisches Museum Batesburg, Mönchengladbach. 1971.

The artist crouches naked in a closet located in an industrial warehouse speaking to his penis and dressing it in doll's clothes.

Seedbed. Sonnabend Gallery, New York. 1972.

The artist hides beneath an enclosed ramp masturbating while describing his sexual fantasies, triggered by gallery visitors' footsteps above, through amplified speakers.

Critical Responses

D'Acierno, Pellegrino. "From Stella to Stella: Italian American Visual Culture and Its Contributions to the Arts in America." *The Italian American Heritage: A Companion to Literature and Arts*. New York: Garland, 1999. 499–552. Print. A portion of this article situates Acconci's work in an Italian American cultural praxis.

Poggi, Christine. "Vito Acconci's Bad Dream of Domesticity." *Not at Home: The Suppression of Domesticity in Modern Art and Architecture*. Ed. Christopher Reed. London: Thames, 1996. 237–52. Print. The author explores the artist's "rejection of the private self and the domestic sphere."

Penny Arcade (Susana Ventura)

Arcade's official Web site, *Penny Arcade*, includes a biography, reviews, photos, a listing of performances, MP3 files of performances, current projects in development, links to other Web sites, and the artist's blog. Video documentation of the artist's performances is available directly through the artist (e-mail parcade@aol.com).

Works

Bitch! Dyke! Faghag! Whore! Performance Space 122, New York. 1990.

A show about sex and censorship, blending "political humanism" and erotic dancers.

La Miseria. Performance Space 122, New York. 1991.

An autobiographical show dealing with the role of women, the hypocrisy of the Catholic Church, sex, homosexuality, and Arcade's rape as a teenager.

Bad Reputation. Performance Space 122, New York. 1999.

The show examines the experiences of young girls who are branded "bad" and are subsequently rejected by their families, peers, and society.

New York Values. Performance Space 122, New York. 2002.

A multimedia performance that looks at the death of bohemian New York and the cultural amnesia that occurs when rebellion itself is commodified and marketed.

Rebellion Cabaret. Gershwin Hotel, New York. 2004.

The artist takes on far right and far left politics, censorship, gentrification, and the commodification of alternative and counterculture practices.

Critical Responses

Arena, Patrick. "Penny for Your Thoughts." Rev. of *New York Values. A&E* 16–23 Jan. 2002: 7. Print.

Bruce, Keith. "The Proverbial Bad Penny." Rev. of *Bad Reputation. Herald* 8 Aug. 2001, arts sec: 14. Print.

Comwell, Jane. "Don't Cringe, Laugh." Rev. of *Bitch! Dyke! Faghag! Whore! Bulletin* 15 Feb. 1994: 79–81. Print.

Rubin, Ed. "Penny Arcade." Rev. of *Bitch! Dyke! Faghag! Whore! New Art Examiner* May 1997: 51. Print.

Sant, Toni. "Racy Reputation Delivers Dose of Reality." Rev. of *Bad Reputation. Washington Square* 12–14 Mar. 1999: 14. Print.

Talbot, Danielle, and John Mangan. "Everyone Is a Target for These One-Liners." Rev. of *Bitch! Dyke! Faghag! Whore! Age* 1 Apr. 1994: 14. Print.

Marco Greco

Video documentation of the artist's performance is available directly through the artist (e-mail theaternstuff@earthlink.net).

Work

Behind the Counter with Mussolini. Belmont Italian American Playhouse, New York. 1995.

One-man show about the relationship between a young boy and his Sicilian immigrant father behind the counter of a family-owned deli in the Bronx.

Critical Response

Gonzalez, David. "Growing Up with Il Duce the Deli Man." *New York Times* 4
　　Nov. 1998, metro sec: 7. Print. A feature article about the performance's
　　genesis. Quotes the artist and his father.

Frank Ingrasciotta

Ingrasciotta's official Web site, *Frank Ingrasciotta*, includes biography, educational background, directorial experience, contact information, and information on, reviews of, and video clips of excerpts of *Bloodtype Ragù*. Video documentation of the artist's performance is also available at this site.

Work

Bloodtype Ragù. Belmont Italian American Playhouse, New York. 2000.

A one-man show, featuring over thirty characters, focusing on the life of a second-generation Italian American who grows up between two cultures and comes to an understanding of his upbringing.

Critical Responses

Fontanella, Luigi. "Coguzze e brutte femmine." Rev. of *Bloodtype Ragù*.
　　America Oggi 21 Apr. 2002: 7. Print.
Gesslein Daniel. "Playwright Relates the Italian American Experience." Rev. of
　　Bloodtype Ragù. *Bronx News* 6–12 Apr. 2000: 7. Print.
Intrabartola, Lisa. "A Mentor and a Paesan." Rev. of *Bloodtype Ragù*. *Home
　　News Tribune* 3 May 2002: 12. Print.
Meyers, Joe. "Italian Family Plays Out on Polka Dot Stage." Rev. of *Bloodtype
　　Ragù*. *Connecticut Post* 20 June 2002: E1. Print.

Johnny Lanz (John Lanzillotto)

Video documentation of the artist's performance is available directly through the artist (e-mail johnny1009@yahoo.com).

Work

Bless Them All. Knitting Factory, New York. 1996.

A series of stories and characters drawn from masculine role models, including gangsters, junkies, and a World War II veteran father from a Bronx neighborhood.

Annie Lanzillotto

Lanzillotto's official Web site, *Annie Lanzillotto*, includes a biography, bibliography, the artist's blog, and streaming videos of performances. Video documentation of the artist's performances is available directly through the artist (e-mail lanzillotto@gmail.com).

Works

Cappuccinos and Cabrides. Performance Space 122, New York. 1994.

Solo performance in which the artist addresses the tensions of her working-class background and burgeoning art work and the difficulty of escaping one's ethnicity, class, familial violence, and work ethic.

Action Writing. Biblio's Books, New York. 1995.

Live improvised writings on scrolls of paper and immediate recitation.

A Passage of Oxygen. DIA Center for the Arts, New York. 1995.

A Raggedy Ann doll, wearing a permanent smile, is ill-treated and battered onstage, serving as a symbol for women's responses to domestic violence and childhood cancer.

Pocketing Garlic (As If Skin Can Hold You). Knitting Factory, New York. 1995.

Wrote, directed, and performed by a cast of seven, based on family oral histories of the healing uses of garlic.

Uprooting Cement. Dixon Place, New York. 1995.

This show is a multimedia "performance memoir," consisting of thirteen monologues based on the artist's childhood cancer, her mother's description of the tenacity of Italian immigrants, and her father's war stories, delivered while the artist mixes cement from a pink baby crib attached by a yoke to her shoulders.

La Scarpetta. Guggenheim Museum, New York. 1996.

A multigenerational cast of twenty—including merchants and customers from the Arthur Avenue Retail Market, actors, singers, musicians, dancers, and the artist's mother and ninety-six year old grandma—re-create a pushcart peddler market in the Guggenheim Museum's theater. Performers toss bread, salami, and cigars into the audience, while a video of the artist's grandmother's hands making cavatelli pasta are projected onto a thirty-foot screen for the performance's duration.

A'Schapett! (Wiping the Plate with the Heel of the Bread); *Mammamia! (You'll Never Get a Straight Answer Again!)*; and *How to Cook a Heart.* Arthur Avenue Retail Market, New York. 1996–97.

Site-specific community-based performances based on the oral histories of Bronx pushcart peddlers, neighborhood residents, and the diaspora of shoppers.

How to Wake Up a Marine in a Foxhole. Kitchen, New York. 1998.

Solo show based on the oral history of Lanzillotto's father, a World War II veteran who returned to the ice business in the Bronx after combat in Okinawa.

A Stickball Memoir. Smithsonian's Folk Life Festival, Washington. 2001.

Solo performance and installation of text on sculpture about growing up as a tomboy in the Bronx.

Stories from the Lives of Italian-American Women. Ellis Island Museum of Immigration, Ellis Island, New York and New Jersey. 2001.

A series of site-specific tableaus, creating interaction with museum visitors, in B. Amore's *Life Line.*

Sul 'Occh du Schapp. Graduate Center, City University of New York. 2002.

Written, directed, and performed by Lanzillotto. A bilingual play in English and southern Italian dialect, based on the oral histories of her family in southern Italy.

Divine Wind. Marquee Theater, New York. 2004.

A "memoir performance" that explores issues of indelibility and inheritance in a painful parental divorce.

Critical Responses

Cosper, Darcy. "Community Action." *Metropolis* Nov. 1996: 63. Print. Feature article on *A'Schapett!*

Gonzalez, David. "Where Hearts Are Worn on Their Sleeve." *New York Times* 15 Feb. 1997, metro sec.: 25. Print. Feature article about the production of *How to Cook a Heart.*

Lanzillotto, Annie. *Annie and Marco: How to Cook a Heart: Verbatim.* N.p.: Lanzillotto, 1997. Print. Partial transcription of improvised dialogue between Lanzillotto and the butcher cum actor Mario Ribaudo from a performance of *How to Cook a Heart.*

———. "The Fall and Decline of Ancient the Bronx." *Art Journal* 56.4 (1997): 59–61. Print. Feature article on *A'Schapett!, Mammamia!,* and *How to Cook a Heart.*

———. "An Artist Journeys Home." *Works of Heart: Building Village through the Arts.* Ed. Lynne Elizabeth and Suzanne Young. Oakland: New Village, 2006. 60–75. Print. The author describes the genesis and production of *A'Schapett!, Mammamia!,* and *How to Cook a Heart.* The article contains excellent photographs of the performances.

Silverman, Francine. "Music in the Market." Rev. of *A'Schapett!, Mammamia!,* and *How to Cook a Heart. Bronx Press Review* 29 Aug. 1996: 11. Print.

LuLu LoLo (Lois Evans née Pascale)

Video documentation of the artist's performances is available directly through the artist (e-mail lululolo@rcn.com).

Works

LuLu Lolo Takes Her Hat Off to the Fair Sex—Unfair Victims. Tenement Theater, Lower East Side Tenement Museum, New York. 2001.

The artist portrays three historical women: a madam discussing the 1836 murder of the prostitute Helen Jewett in New York City; an immigrant seamstress who died in the 1911 Triangle Shirtwaist Factory fire; and a woman who fought in the Civil War disguised as a man.

Macaroni and Mal Occhio (Evil Eye): Food, Faith, and Family—Growing up Italian-American. Brooklyn Public Library, Leonard Branch, New York. 2002.

A one-woman show presenting interconnected character sketches of the artist's family members in a humorous exploration of growing up Italian American in East Harlem.

Lucille Consorti. Metropolitan Playhouse, New York. 2004.

Based on a taped interview, the artist interprets the words of Lucille Consorti, the owner of a family pipe-covering business in New York's East Village.

38 Witnessed Her Death, I Witnessed Her Love: The Lonely Secret of Mary Ann Zielonko. Provincetown Fringe Festival. Davis Center, Columbus. 2004.

Based on research and a taped interview, the artist interprets the words of Mary Ann Zielonko, whose lover Kitty Genovese was murdered outside her Queens home in 1964 as thirty-eight neighbors looked on without notifying the police.

Three Sisters in Soul: Saint, Soldier, Seamstress. Garibaldi-Meucci Museum, New York. 2004.

A series of three monologues in keeping with traditional theater practices that portrays the lives of Saint Mother Cabrini; Anita Garibaldi, the Brazilian wife of Italy's "Great Liberator"; and Esther Meucci, wife of Antonio Meucci, who is credited with being the original inventor of the telephone.

Critical Responses

Kaiser, Bill. "2004 Columbus National Gay and Lesbian Theatre Festival." Rev. of *38 Witnessed Her Death. On The Purple Circuit.* 1 Nov. 2004. Web. 25 June 2009.

McKanic, Arlene. "Lulu LoLo at Tenement Museum." Rev. of *LuLu Lolo Takes Her Hat Off. Greenwich Village Gazette* 9 July 2001. Web. 25 June 2009.

———. "Macaroni and Mal Occhio." Rev. of *Macaroni and Mal Occhio. Greenwich Village Gazette* 15 Nov. 2002. Web. 25 June 2009.

Linda Mancini

Works

Bone China. Tangente Danse Actuelle, Montreal. 1985.

A nonverbal piece about loneliness in which the artist portrays a character waiting for her date who never arrives and slowly losing her composure.

Angelina Contadina. Home for Contemporary Art, New York. 1989.

This is a one-woman show in Italian that brings a woman's critical perspective to the Italian American experience of migration.

Not Entirely Appropriate. Performance Space 122, New York. 1991.

The title is a play on words referring to the initials of the National Endowment for the Arts and is a reaction against censorship of the artists.

Good As It Gets. Dance Theater Workshop, New York. 1993.

A tragic comedy about abortion focusing on a teenage character who gets pregnant in the 1970s and is sent to Tokyo by her parents to get an abortion.

Tip or Die. HERE Arts Center, New York. 1995.

A full-length piece, set in a restaurant with a series of characters, about the human condition and how much you can learn about a person when food and money are involved.

Love You, Gotta Go. Blue Heron Theater, New York. 2001.

A series of shorts written and performed with David Deblinger and directed by John Rubin Gould.

Critical Responses

Bruckner, D. J. R. "The Unseen Characters Emerging by Invention." Rev. of *Tip or Die. New York Times* 16 Sept. 1994: C26. Print.
Sims, David. "Stripping Away the Veneer." *Seacoast Times* 23 Jan. 1994: 14. Print. A feature article about Mancini's performances, with quotations from the artist.

Dirty Martini (Linda Marraccini)

Martini's official Web site, *International Burlesque Sensation: Dirty Martini*, includes biography, photo gallery, listing of upcoming performances, press kit, links to burlesque-related Web sites, and contact information.

Works

No known documentation of performances exists, but some are discussed in the publications list below.

Critical Responses

Baldwin, Michelle. *Burlesque, the New Bump-n-Grind*. Denver: Speck, 2004. Print. A popular review of neoburlesque addressing topics like feminism, body type, "drag and queer" burlesque, and the male gaze; includes references to Dirty Martini, as well as the World Famous Pontani Sisters.

Glasscock, Jessica. *Burlesque, from Gaslight to Spotlight*. New York: Abrams, 2003. Print. A history of striptease and burlesque, with a final chapter on neoburlesque, a paragraph about Dirty Martini, and a photo sequence of her balloon dance.

Kourlas, Gia. "Where Performance Art and Pasties Meet." *New York Times* 25 May 2003, arts and leisure sec.: 8. Print. An overview of neoburlesque in New York City, including Dirty Martini.

Shalia, Dwan. "(Not) For His Eyes Only." *New York Times Magazine* 5 Oct. 2003: 35. Print. An overview of neoburlesque in New York City, including Dirty Martini.

Linda Montano

The Web site *Linda M. Montano* documents the *7 Years of Living Art + Another 7 Years of Living Art = 14 Years of Living Art* project and includes a "Virtual Residency" with the artist, contact information, and the artist's bio, complete with bibliography, videography, and a list of performances. Video documentation of the artist's performances is available through the Video Data Bank.

Works

Handcuff. Museum of Conceptual Art, San Francisco. 1973.

Montano and the artist Tom Marioni are handcuffed for three days.

Three Days Blindfold. Women's Building, Los Angeles. 1974.

Montano lives three days blindfolded in an art gallery.

Art/Life: One Year Performance. New York City. 1983–84.

Montano and the artist Tehching Hsieh are bound together with an eight-foot rope for a year while they avoid physical contact.

7 Years of Living Art +Another 7 Years of Living Art = 14 Years of Living Art. 1984–98.

Each year for seven years Montano wore clothing of a single color associated with Hindu's seven *chakra*, the body's energy points (e.g., red for energy, green for compassion, white for joy), engaged in a series of daily rituals, and provided "art/life" counseling at the New Museum in New York City. After seven years, she repeated the project for a total of fourteen years.

Critical Responses

Montano, Linda. *Art in Everyday Life*. New York: Station Hill, 1981. Print.
Includes descriptions (divided into "Art" and "Life") and photographs
of performances dating from 1964 to 1980, transcribed audio tracks and
photographs from videos, transcribed interviews, and a "Vita."

Montano, Linda. *Letters from Linda M. Montano*. Ed. Jennie Klein. New York:
Routledge, 2005. Print. The author writes about her performances and
philosophy regarding art and life. Also includes interviews about the
performances *Art/Life: One Year Performance* and *7 Years of Living
Art +Another 7 Years of Living Art =14 Years of Living Art,* among
others. The chapter "How-To Manual" includes sections discussing
teaching performance.

Deanna Pacelli

Video documentation of the artist's performance is unavailable.

Work

There Goes the Neighborhood. Bar Below, New York. 2003.

Written and directed by Mari Brown, created by Deanna Pacelli and Mari Brown.
One-woman show depicting various characters discussing gentrification in the
Brooklyn neighborhood Carroll Gardens.

Critical Response

Bahrampour, Tara. "A Play on Words: Brooklyn Accents and Trends Are
Central to One-Woman Show." *New York Times* 14 Nov. 2003, metro
sec.: 1+. Print. A feature article on performance's genesis and its
response among neighborhood people depicted.

Calogero "Chazz" Palminteri

Work

A Bronx Tale. West Coast Ensemble Theater, Los Angeles. 1989.

A one-man show, featuring thirty-five characters, chronicling a boy's coming of
age and divided loyalties between a local gangster and his working-class father.

Critical Responses

Gardaphé, Fred L. *From Wiseguys to Wise Men: The Gangster and Italian
American Masculinities*. New York: Routledge, 2006. Briefly discusses
the 1993 cinematic adaptation of Palminteri's show and representations
of Italian American masculinity.

Tedesco, Jo Ann. "Sacraments: Italian American Theatrical Culture and the
Dramatization of Everyday Life." *The Italian American Heritage: A
Companion to Literature and Arts*. New York: Garland, 1999. 353–86.
A portion of this article discusses Palminteri's *Bronx Tale* in the context
of Italian American culture.

The World Famous Pontani Sisters

The official Web site, *Greetings from Angie Pontani and the World Famous Pontani Sisters!*, includes listings of past and upcoming performances, newspaper reviews, photo gallery, merchandise, and contact information.

Critical Responses

Romano, Tricia. "Bombshells Away! The New Burlesque Hits Gotham." *Village Voice* 5–11 Mar. 2003. Web. 25 June 2009. An overview of neoburlesque, including the World Famous Pontani Sisters.

Shapiro, Rebecca, dir. *Showy and 5 Foot 2: The World Famous Pontani Sisters.* 2004. Film. This video documentary includes performances and interviews with the artists, as well as their parents.

Note

The research by Stefania Taviano for this appendix was supported by the British Academy.

Stefania Taviano

Uncovering and Performing Italian American Stories

> It was my mother's broken heart that brought me to this market in the first place. In 1993, she suffered an aortic aneurysm while she was making pasta. . . . Then came the day she was to take her first "day-trip", six months later. . . . I witnessed this weird pilgrimage, back to the salamis, back to the Bronx where her father is buried, where her mother first stepped into shoes into this country, where something began, that is not yet finished. And today at Mario's heart-stand, it is the heart I come back to. The visceral, muscular, heart itself.
> (Lanzillotto, *How*)

Annie Lanzillotto's account of the origins of the site-specific, community-based performances *A'Schapett*, at the Arthur Avenue Retail Market, illustrates how the artist's physical and artistic voyage to the market, which parallels her mother's personal experience as an Italian American, testifies to the vital role that cultural traditions play in the lives of Italian Americans. In *A'Schapett*, what happens at the heart stand where the butcher Mario sells and cooks the heart conveys the strong cultural and human significance that food has for Italian Americans. The transcript of a live dialogue between Annie and Mario, *How to Cook a Heart*, sheds light on the symbolic value that recipes can take in performance.

200

Here I discuss the pedagogical opportunities offered by the work of Italian American performance artists such as Lanzillotto and Penny Arcade. I describe what these opportunities are and how I have developed them in a course on performing Italian American culture. While students are initially attracted to performance art because they are interested in acting, they soon learn to reflect on the relation of art and cultural images, first by analyzing how Italian American performance artists reinforce or challenge these images onstage and then by creating performances using research in the Italian American community.

The course is divided in two main parts: the first part, devoted to the study of Italian American performers, who are invited to come to class, prepares students for the second and more demanding part, in which they interview members of the local community and write performance texts from their interviews. In the first part, I use Lanzillotto's and Arcade's work as examples of performance art documenting the Italian American experience. I begin with sessions devoted to an overview of these performers' work, in which we analyze primary and secondary sources—such as transcripts of performances, video recordings, performers' critical writings about their performances as well as press coverage and reviews. I then invite performers to come to class and present their work to the students. We ask artists who cannot feasibly come to the class to take part in a videoconference, which similarly allows students and performers to communicate. If neither of these options is available, some class time can be given over to live readings of performers' work as well as showing videos in class.

Students study Lanzillotto's work by analyzing transcripts and viewing a video recording of *A'Schapett*; they also read other writings by Lanzillotto ("Artist" and "Fall") and reviews of her work. I then divide students into small groups and ask them to analyze the creative process underlying each piece, to reflect on how Lanzillotto uses personal experience—in this case her mother's heart attack—as a springboard for the performance at the Arthur Avenue Retail Market. Finally, I ask them to consider how the performance revolves around food as a powerful cultural image of the Italian American experience. I pose specific writing questions:

What is the role of cultural images in Lanzillotto's performance?
Does Lanzillotto reinforce or question stereotypes of Italian American culture? How?
How does your perception of Italian Americans affect your response to this particular performance?

Each group presents its responses to the class. The resulting debate prepares students for their meeting with the artist and allows them to reflect on particular issues they might want the artist to address.

During the artist workshop, which follows this introductory part of the course, each performance artist discusses his or her work and explains how a particular piece is put together. While many students have shopped at a market—or even the Arthur Avenue Retail Market—Lanzillotto chooses to go back to the market not just to shop but to confront the working-class Italian American, somewhat chauvinist context she left and to use theater as a tool to promote interaction with the merchants and stimulate them to tell their stories.

Lanzillotto's choice to immerse herself in the market's life by renting an empty fruit stall (where she brought a piano, which became "The Opera Stand") introduces students to forms of communication and cultural interaction that are only possible in performance. *A'Schapett* demonstrates the power of performance within a performance piece as it creates a spectacle delving into the history of the market where "the fourth wall is not even a remote possibility" (Lanzillotto, "Fall" 61). As an interactive performance, based on "direct observation and interviews in the market" (*A'Schapett*), Lanzillotto's work, instead of offering stereotypical representations of Italian Americans, points to ways to undercut stereotypes and enhance people's lives through performance. *A'Schapett* transforms a common market into an opera house and, among other things, gives Mario, the butcher, an opportunity to combine the art of selling hearts with that of singing in public for the first time in his life. Students learn that performance can subvert common images of cultural identity and social roles by bringing out the artistic side of the market.

Performers' workshops can open students' eyes to how a performer transforms and transposes events from everyday life into a performance. In this sense, Lanzillotto's strategy to use surreal images and absurd settings, such as a trapeze artist performing over the butcher's counter while the butcher is cooking, helps students understand how performance complicates the representation of real life. As Lanzillotto argues, she gives herself and all the artists working with her a challenge: "Go Home" and "work with the mentalities you fled in your development" ("Fall" 61).

As with *A'Schapett*, I ask students to analyze Arcade's *La Miseria* by first reflecting on how the artist's personal experience is transformed into a disturbing satire that addresses social issues such as gender inequality, the hypocrisy of the Catholic Church, heterosexuality, homosexuality, and rape. *La Miseria* opens with two women onstage: a woman speaking Italian and an actress playing the young Penny. Penny, the narrator, tells the story of her life and also translates the other woman's words for the audience, commenting on her attitude. After viewing video recordings of the performance and reading critical accounts of Arcade's work, students address specific issues. They analyze the metatext that results from the juxtaposition of the Italian-speaking woman and the actress playing Penny with the presence of Arcade herself onstage throughout the performance.

Moreover, by being exposed to Arcade's work, students are confronted with challenging performances aimed at shocking theater audiences and forcing them to address disturbing issues. Students also watch videos of other Arcade shows that bring problematic social events in all their brutality and violence to the stage; *Bitch! Dyke! Faghag! Whore!*, for example, deals with the rape of a mildly retarded woman by a group of boys at Saint John's University. These troubling shows are pedagogically useful because they encourage students to reflect on events that are ignored in society and to share their personal opinions about such events—something they may never have done.

One technique particularly successful in helping students examine the controversial and deeply important issues raised by Arcade (and other performance artists) is requiring them to engage in live readings of parts of the performance text. Doing a live reading of the trial transcript, as Arcade does in *Bitch! Dyke! Faghag! Whore!*, and then asking students to reflect on Arcade's closing act of swallowing and throwing up a dozen raw eggs can generate intense discussions of audience's identification with the woman's violation. Again, I pose questions about the performance during live readings:

> Have you seen other performances dealing with disturbing social events, such as rape?
> What was your reaction?
> What was the reaction of other members of the audience?
> Do you believe that theater should entertain rather than shock its audiences?

Such questions encourage students to reflect on, among other things, the political role that theater plays in our society.

After this first part of the course, students interview members of local Italian American communities and write performance pieces. Each student gets in touch with an Italian American through personal contacts, if they have any, or through organizations such as the Sons of Italy and the Garibaldi Society. Once they have established the contact, students asks the interviewees for permission to use their stories as the basis for a performance piece (a formal permission form is filled out at the first meeting). If consent is given, the student and the interviewee decide where to hold the interview. It is important to choose a quiet place, so that the student and interviewee can be undisturbed and the interview can be recorded without interruptions. The student can ask the Italian American interviewee to tell his or her personal or family immigration story or can decide to focus on a topic of interest to the interviewee. After transcribing the interview, the student may contact the person interviewed to ask any further questions.

This particular assignment is very exciting to students because, having viewed examples of performance art based on "the ordinary," they are primed to listen carefully to the people they interview—when given the chance, people almost always want to tell stories, especially about themselves. It is important that the workshops with the performers precede the students' creative assignment, so that, by the time students are working on their projects, they feel comfortable interviewing people. If students still have any doubts, we spend some time discussing the kind of questions they may ask during the interviews to encourage people to tell their stories, and we reflect on the importance of maintaining the spoken language when transcribing the interviews to reproduce it in performance.

Contacting members of the community, interviewing them, and convincing them to recount some of their experiences promote a sense of responsibility in the students. Students feel the significance of "owning" their learning process and of being personally committed to their education (Brandes and Ginnis 26). Moreover, the task of turning immigrants' stories into performances makes students understand their responsibility toward the people interviewed and motivates them to do well. This sense of responsibility explains the positive reaction of students to this assignment in a course on documentary performance I team-taught in the Department of Theater and Drama at Wesleyan University, in Middletown, Connecticut. The course was connected with a project aimed at documenting oral histories of immigrants from the Sicilian village of Melilli, who compose about fifty percent of Middletown's large Italian community. Students were first introduced to models of documentary performance through the work of performance artists such as Ann Deavere Smith by reading the performers' writing as well as critical reviews of the performances. Later, students contacted and interviewed members of the local community to learn about their individual and common stories. In class, each student presented a brief solo performance created from the transcription of his or her interview. The other students were then asked to comment on the solo performance and give feedback and suggestions. These separate works eventually became an integral part of the collaboratively written performance, entitled *Over There*, a phrase that describes the elusive quality of the immigrants' place of origin, Melilli (see Taviano).

My Wesleyan students were enthusiastic about studying Sicilian culture and learning about immigrants' experiences and Middletown local history. They also appreciated that this last phase of the course became an opportunity to gain insights into the practicalities of literary and theatrical production. One student, a very skilled actor, impersonated Frank Lentini, nicknamed the three-legged man because he was born with a third leg attached to his spine and had sixteen toes. Lentini, the first Sicilian to move to Middletown, became one of the legendary attractions of the P. T. Barnum Circus. The student was not able to interview Lentini, but he created his performance from the recollections of members of the immigrant community (Lentini was renowned in the community for turning his handicap into a show and managing to lead a normal and successful life).

Another student wrote and performed the memories of a woman who, as a little girl attending the local school, was asked by her teacher, a nun, to dress as a saint on All Saints' Day. Yet another student became fascinated by the tradition, typical of Sicilian villages, of calling people by their nickname. The following opening lines of a character in *Over There* testify to the importance of such a tradition:

The Cannatas, the Mazzottas, the Tomassis, the Milardis, the De Mauros, the Petrosellis . . . half the people in Middletown came from over there in Melilli, but you know people better from their nicknames. Like Pagghia 'nculo. His name was Rano, but if you said Mr. Rano, they didn't know what you were talking about. But if you said Pagghia 'nculo, "Ehhh, u canuscemu, avi dill'Italia cu canuscemu a chistu." Sure we know him. You're talking about Pagghia 'nculo. *Pagghia* means straw, so maybe he got the name because he used to sleep on straw and the straw went up his rear end. I don't know.

The combination of these two main phases of the course on Italian American performance—a direct and personal interaction with performance artists and their work and students' active involvement in the process of interviewing, artistic writing, and production—contributes to its pedagogical value and uniqueness. Such complexity and the requirement to go well beyond the printed page make this material an enriching and illuminating addition to the study of the Italian American experience. Moreover, the pedagogical principles informing the course promote active and engaging methods of teaching and learning.

Note

My research for this essay was supported by the British Academy.

Part III

Revisiting Italian American Film and Popular Culture

Anthony Julian Tamburri

A Contested Place: Italian Americans in Cinema and Television

Italian Americans occupy a strong, if often contested, place in American media. Stereotypical representations of Italian Americans as overly sexual, violent, and sentimental began in the early twentieth century. Such depictions generated debates in the Italian American community at the end of the twentieth century about the casting of non–Italian Americans in Italian American roles, the media's role in creating and maintaining stereotypical representations of Italian Americans, and the lack of films about Italian Americans by Italian American directors.

Films such as F. A. Dobson's *The Skyscrapers of New York* (1905), Wallace McCutchen's *The Black Hand* (1906), and D. W. Griffith's *The Avenging Conscience* (1914) are early vessels for such stereotyping. *Skyscrapers* first offered Dago Pete, a small-time crook who steals his boss's watch while shifting blame onto a coworker; the second film underscored the stereotype of the Black Hand; and the Italian in this third film is an ill-reputed blackmailer. Even in his earlier film *At the Altar*, Griffith underscores, in an apparently positive storyline, sexuality and violence as part of the Italian character. During the silent era of cinema in the United States, Italians and Italian Americans were repeatedly portrayed by non-Italians. Thomas Ince and Reginald Baker's *The Italian* is sensitive to the immigrant's plight. The film follows the trials and tribulations of Beppe Donnetti—portrayed by the non-Italian George Beban—in his unsuccessful search for good fortune and well-being in the United States. Trapped in the immigrant ghetto from which he longed to escape, he helplessly watches his infant son succumb to disease. Compared with Griffith's film, *The Italian* does prove sympathetic to the predicament of Italian immigrants without engaging in a stereotypical semiotic.

It was not until the arrival of Rudolph Valentino that an Italian actor played a prominent role on the screen, even though Valentino rarely portrayed an Italian in a central role. As a handsome Italian actor of international fame, he was one of the first sex symbols of the silver screen. The characters he portrayed were sexually charged, exotic, and rebellious. Valentino's popularity in such roles may have powerfully reinforced the stereotypes of Italian Americans within the dominant culture, as they "encapsulated the archetypal Italian in the mainstream psyche" (Russo, "Unacknowledged Masterpiece" 227).

The non-Italian representation of Italians in America continued throughout the 1930s and 1940s, with Mervyn Leroy's *Little Caesar*, whose lead character, Rico Bandello, was played by Edward G. Robinson; or Richard Wallace's *The Fallen Sparrow*, in which William Edmunds played Papa Lepetino. During these same years, however, the presence of directors of Italian descent rose dramatically, though few films depicted the Italian in America in a central role. These were the boom years for directors such as Frank Capra and Vincente Minnelli, two of the more prolific and successful filmmakers of the first half of the twentieth century.

Italian American actors and characters became central to the film industry only in the mid-1940s, when actors such as Richard Conte starred in a nongangster role as Lieutenant Angelo Canelli in Lewis Milestone's *The Purple Heart*; similarly, Jimmy Durante played Nick Lombardi in Richard Whorf's *It Happened in Brooklyn*. During this same period, Ida Lupino began making films. She wrote and directed five films between 1949 and 1953, before moving into a directorial career in television. Her behind-the-camera work includes, for the big screen, *Not Wanted*, *Outrage*, and *The Bigamist*, and, for television, episodes for *The Donna Reed Show*, *GE Theatre*, *The Untouchables*, and *The Twilight Zone* over three decades.

After the 1960s, which brought a new positive mindset to the United States about ethnicity, young directors such as Michael Cimino, Francis Ford Coppola, Brian De Palma, Penny Marshall (née Carole Penelope

Marsciarelli), and Martin Scorsese made their mark with such films as *The Godfather, Mean Streets, The Conversation, Carrie, The Deer Hunter, Raging Bull, Scarface, Year of the Dragon, Big,* and *A League of Their Own.* They lay the groundwork for those to follow, such as Greg Mottola, Nancy Savoca, Nick Stagliano, Sylvester Stallone, and Stanley Tucci.

The themes of the films of these Hollywood directors vary. The Mafia recurs in the films of Coppola (*The Godfather* films) and Scorsese (*Mean Streets* and *Goodfellas*) and is transformed into generalized, organized—and sometimes small-town—crime by filmmakers such as De Palma (*Scarface*), Stallone (*Paradise Alley*), and Stagliano (*The Florentine*). Marshall and Mottola instead offer insights into family matters and gender issues. Working-class issues and the young woman's plight become fundamental for the early period of Marshall's film direction, whereas Mottola's *Daytrippers* examines marital relations with Italian Americans as the family backdrop. Savoca and Tucci confront their Italian American heritage head-on. Savoca interrogates old-world values in an Italian American neighborhood (gender, work, us versus them) in *True Love* and *Household Saints.* Tucci, in turn, in his codirected *Big Night,* explores the trials and tribulations of the new immigrant as two brothers try to integrate themselves into a postwar United States.

Among the newest artists are Rachel Amodeo (*What about Me*), Tom DeCerchio (*Celtic Pride*), Helen De Michiel (*Tarantella*), Tony Piccirillo (*The 24th Day*), and Marylou Tibaldo-Bongiorno (*Little Kings*). Amodeo's *What about Me* explores the tragic results of the homelessness of a reincarnated Lisa Napolitano. Having already suffered death in her first life, Lisa now endures the hard life of the streets and all that can befall her, short of a second death. Amodeo succeeds in combining the tragic with the comedic, keeping the viewer on a constant rollercoaster. After a tour-de-force debut with his short, *Nunzio's Second Cousin,* DeCerchio debuted on the big screen with *Celtic Pride,* a film that looks at exaggerated fandom among the working class. Piccirillo's *The 24th Day,* a psychological thriller, addresses the notion of individual responsibility for one's actions. De Michiel and Tibaldo-Bongiorno focus on being Italian American: *Tarantella* deals with a young woman's return home for her mother's funeral and her emotional encounter with her Italian heritage; *Little Kings* examines the rapport among three brothers as well as their relationships with the women in their lives. All four directors represent, to a certain degree, a new *visione del mondo* ("worldview") for today's generation of Italian Americans. While we still find the mafioso in such films as

Michael Corrente's *Federal Hill*, we also find the desire to take up issues such as gender, sexuality, working-class identity, and ethnicity in a much more direct and profound manner than in the past.

In addition to De Cerchio's *Nunzio's Second Cousin*, worthy of mention are the fictional shorts of Diane Frederick, Joseph Greco, and Dina Ciraulo. De Cerchio and Frederick deal directly with their Italian heritage. *Nunzio's Second Cousin* invites its viewers to reexamine notions of sexuality and race in the Italian American community, whereas Frederick's *Che bella famiglia* presents its viewers with a portrait of Italian America as seen through the lens of gender and family. Greco and Ciraulo offer films that, at best, make subtle references to their heritage. Greco's *Lena's Spaghetti* addresses early female adolescence, in which things Italian are literally relegated to the margins of the screen in the form of realia such as postcards. Ciraulo's *Touch* is void of Italian American imagery and addresses themes like class and family relations.

Many of the directors mentioned above have also been involved in documentary filmmaking. In *Italianamerican*, Scorsese sits down with his parents and, in the guise of an afternoon visit for what seems like a Sunday dinner, has them recount their experiences growing up as children of immigrants in New York's Little Italy. Of the younger generation, Tibaldo-Bongiorno, Mariarosy Calleri, and Kym Ragusa also turned to the documentary. Tibaldo-Bongiorno's *Mother-Tongue: Italian American Sons and Mothers* shows how a special group of seven Italian American men—including Scorsese, John Turturro, and Rudy Giuliani—relate to their mothers. Calleri's experimental documentary *Uncovering* explores issues of gender, race, and ethnicity as articulated by a series of voice-overs and added songs. Ragusa's eight-minute documentary *Passing* explores the issue of racial identity as we follow the story of her fair-skinned, African American grandmother's trip down south in 1959, while *Fuori/Outside* uses the author's relationship to her Italian American grandmother as a springboard to contextualize racism among Italian Americans.

Other noteworthy filmmakers have extensive experience in documentary work. Tony DeNonno has dedicated his decades-long career primarily to this genre. From *Part of Your Loving* to his more recent *Heaven Touches Brooklyn in July*, DeNonno's films have captured many facets of Italian Americana, especially in the Northeast. Michael Angelo DiLauro has produced a series of documentaries for regional and national television. In 1986, *The Family Caring* garnered him his first regional Emmy. In

2003, his *Prisoners among Us: Italian-American Identity and World War II* gained much notice for its rehearsing of the Italian experience in the United States through the lens of Proclamation Number 2527 (December 1941), which categorized nonnaturalized Italians as potential "enemy aliens," a chapter of the Italian experience in the United States that has only recently become known, thanks to the work of both DiLauro and, previously, the historian Lawrence Di Stasi.

Susan Caperna Lloyd has contributed to the filmography of Italian American documentaries with two powerful shorts: her award-winning *Processione: A Sicilian Easter* and *The Baggage*. *Processione* records the yearly festival in Trapani, Sicily, of the Procession of the Mysteries and examines the *ragion d'essere* ("raison d'être") of such a festival, as it has been celebrated throughout the centuries. *The Baggage* is a visual collage of old photographs and movie footage that recounts the story of an immigrant family and its three generations through a gendered lens. The viewer witnesses both the glories and the tribulations endured by this family. Sicily as a theme continues in the work of Calleri and Gia Marie Amella. In *Hidden Island / L'isola sommersa*, Calleri reads her family's narrative of emigration through the Sicilian myth of Persephone. Amella's *My Sacred Island* explores multifaceted Sicily, its eastern Mediterranean past that collides with its more western present, and how this historical contamination has informed a society and its people through the centuries. Amella's *Simply Slow Food* features a spot on central Italy's cuisine. Like Amella in her candid exposé of the world of waitresses, *Serving with Dignity*, Renata Gangemi explores the plight of ethnic women in two of her documentaries. *Talking Back* is an experiential analysis of the service industry and how it treats its women, Latinas especially. In like fashion, she brings to the screen the emotional effect pregnancy can have on women's lives in *Among Women*. In this mixture of documentary film and creative reenactment, Gangemi also juxtaposes the medical profession's modern techniques of prenatal care and delivery with midwifery. Luisa Pretolani examines the plight of the working class in *Italian American Presence(s)*, in which she documents the difficulties Italian immigrants face as they settle into an American way of life. By looking at the experiences of two Indian women, *Things I Take* explores the predicament of the immigrant who both holds on to and surrenders the ties to her homeland.

The history of Italian Americans' roles in television differs somewhat from that of those on the silver screen. From the outset of the television age, Italian Americans have been a presence both in front of and behind the camera, and distinctions between Italian American and non–Italian American actors have been more blurred. *Life with Luigi* and *Bonino*, for example, both portrayed single Italian American fathers raising children alone. In *Life with Luigi*, the widower Pasquale is played by the non-Italian American Alan Reed, whereas widower Bonino is played by the Italian American actor Ezio Pinza. Television did not appear to reject Italian or Italian American actors as cinema did at the beginning of its century-long existence.

As with cinema, television represented Italians and Italian Americans stereotypically. An early stereotype was the Latin lover, as portrayed in *The Continental*, the nickname of the suave, debonair, Italian-born Renzo Cesana, promoted as an Italian count and member of Rome's high society. Instead, The Continental was an obnoxious gigolo who engaged in a one-way flirtatious conversation with the housewives who presumably watched the show. Such a seemingly innocent, yet image-damaging comical performance inspired spin-offs by the likes of Ernie Kovacs, Billy Crystal, and Christopher Walken. *The Untouchables* added to the mythology of Italians and Italian Americans as members of the Mafia. The series highlighted the criminal element of Chicago during the Roaring Twenties, featuring Al Capone and Frank Nitti as staple hoodlums.

While stereotypical representations in television, as in film, decreased to some extent after the civil rights movement of the 1960s, Italians and Italian Americans continued to appear fairly regularly in negative and reductive roles: men were still depicted as gangsters, villains, buffoons, or inarticulate blue-collar workers; women as subservient wives, sexy but unintelligent mistresses, or factory workers. Cesare Danova was a con man in *Garrison's Gorillas*; Kaye Ballard played an interfering mother-in-law in *The Mothers-in-Law*; Richard Castellano played an Italian American sheet-metal worker in *Joe and Sons*; and, of course, some tried to keep the Mafia image alive, as in *The Gangster Chronicles*, which presented the Italian American mobster from his own point of view (actors included Michael Mouri [Charles "Lucky" Luciano], Louis Giambalvo [Al Capone], and Richard Castellano [Giuseppe "Joe the Boss" Masseria]). At the same time, the stereotype of the Italian American criminal was morphing into the Italian American crime fighter, policeman, or detective: beginning with Columbo (played by Peter Falk), then Toma (played by Tony Musante), then Petrocelli (played by Barry Newman), then Baretta (played by Robert Blake), and culminating with Captain Frank Furillo (Daniel Travanti) in *Hill Street Blues*, known to his mistress, the public defender Joyce Davenport (Veronica Hamel), as "pizza man," a moniker suggestive of the blue-collar worker.

Italian Americans were also depicted in worlds far removed from crime, though not necessarily from stereotypes. In the 1970s and 1980s, Italian Americans relived the 1950s and 1960s with Fonzie (Henry Winkler), the lovable "guido" figure of *Happy Days*, and Laverne De Fazio (Penny Marshall) in *Laverne and Shirley*. In both cases, we witness familiar stereotypes: Fonzie as the streetwise high school dropout, a greaser from the old neighborhood who is also the working-class answer to the Latin lover; Laverne as the street-smart, occasionally wise-cracking woman who suggests a certain sexuality that, for the show's setting, might be considered a bit risqué. These two characters also share working-class employment: Fonzie is an auto mechanic and Laverne works on an assembly line in a beer factory.

At this time, we also find a generation of single parents, such as the above-mentioned Joe Vitale (Richard Castellano) and the more novel Italian American Ann Romano (Bonnie Franklin) of *One Day at a Time*. Not wanting to be anyone's daughter or wife, Ann Romano ends up divorcing her husband and moving back to her hometown with her two daughters. There, desirous of proving her independence as a woman, Ann lands a job as an account executive, a profession that surely raised the professional bar among Italian Americans on screen, placing them outside the standard civil service jobs when they eventually transitioned from the working class.

But the one television genre in which Italian Americans most broke out of stereotypes was the variety show. Starring in such programs were singers, actors, and musicians such as Tony Bennett, Perry Como, Jimmy Durante, Dean Martin, Julius La Rosa, Liza Minnelli, Henry Mancini, Guy Lombardo, Frank Sinatra, and Sonny Bono. Como, Durante, Martin, and Sinatra, for example, each had successful runs of variety shows that featured theirs talents and those of other, non-Italian singers. La Rosa and Minnelli were frequent visitors, if not regulars, on others' variety shows. Lombardo ushered America into many a New Year's Eve, and Mancini serenaded viewers through his numerous scores for television. Finally, Sonny Bono, along with his wife, Cher, transformed the classic variety show into a more hip rock-and-roll program. These entertainers and others who appeared on the small screen contributed to a more positive image of the Italian American: men were no longer gangsters or dimwits; women were no longer wives, factory workers, or gum-snapping girlfriends. Both Italian American men and women were seen as stars, as American success stories.

While it might be argued that the negative depiction of Italians and Italian Americans has been mitigated to some degree by the new ethnic sensitivity that seems to have its origins in the civil rights movement of the 1960s, one might counter such argument by pointing to some of the Mafia movies by Coppola and Scorsese and more recent portrayals such as *The Sopranos*. The jury is surely out on this matter, as it is still out on the validity of arguments against the Mafia films and shows, since one might resort to the old adage that bad publicity is better than no publicity at all, further lending fuel willy-nilly to the ongoing debate.

Peter Bondanella

Palookas, Romeos, and Wise Guys: Italian Americans in Hollywood

Italian American representations in Hollywood cinema can be broken down into four large categories, each associated with genres that include many films not specifically about Italian Americans: depictions of the immigrant experience and life in the Little Italys, predominantly but not exclusively associated with large East Coast urban areas; depictions of "palookas," Italian American prizefighters; treatments of Italian American Romeos or Latin lovers; and the inevitable representations of Italian American wiseguys. There is also a subcategory of wiseguy films that propose comic parodies of works depicting serious Italian American criminals. Hollywood Italians thus appear in thematic clusters of films that are both Hollywood genre films and specific illustrations of Italian American versions of such traditional genres. An important task of any course devoted to Italian Americans in cinema and television is to distinguish the general generic conventions of these works and the extent to which they accept, reject, modify, or transcend generic conventions of the larger group of works to which they belong.

Such films as *The Italian, Christ in Concrete, The Rose Tattoo, Marty, Love with the Proper Stranger, Italianamerican, Moonstruck,* and *A Bronx Tale* are first and foremost family romances, following the conventions of that popular film genre. Films involving palookas appear in the genre films featuring prizefighters, such as *Golden Boy, Somebody Up There Likes Me, Raging Bull,* and the *Rocky* franchise. Latin lovers (not all of whom are Italian American) naturally are a special category of the romantic male Hollywood star: the Italian American version of this is well illustrated by the Valentino silent films, such as *The Sheik, Son of the Sheik,* and *Cobra;* by the films made by the Rat Pack, which included the Italian Americans Frank Sinatra and Dean Martin; and by *Saturday Night Fever,* the film that made John Travolta a superstar, defined for all time the Italian American "guido," and launched the disco craze that dominated pop culture in the 1970s. Like all star vehicles, Latin lover films raise interesting questions about masculinity. The Hollywood film genre that Italian American images have dominated is, of course, the gangster film and its comic variant. Genre films in Hollywood often have more to do with one another than with films in other genres. Thus the Hollywood Italian prizefighter in such works as *Golden Boy, Raging Bull,* or *Rocky I–V* develops its own cinematic tradition, drawing inspiration more from other fight films than from Hollywood Italians in gangster or Latin lover movies. The same may be said of the development of the Hollywood Italian gangster film, from *Little Caesar* and the first *Scarface* to *The Godfather* trilogy and *Goodfellas:* these key films develop more in relation to one another within the conventions of the gangster genre than in reaction to Hollywood films about Italian American society that depict real or imaginary Little Italys. Thus writing the history of representations of Hollywood Italians is complicated by the existence of these Hollywood genres outside the artistic development and growth of the Little Italy picture, the first genre depicting Italian Americans' immigrant experience. In some respects, the genres of the palooka, the Romeo or Latin lover, and the wiseguy constantly toy with the status of the ethnic stereotype, but a history of the Little Italy genre reveals that in depicting the life of more ordinary Italian Americans, other stereotypes sometimes prevail (the Italian American as racist and bigot, as in the films of Spike Lee; the Italian American as the emotional, unsophisticated, or uncouth "guido," as in any number of works from the silent era to the present).

Since the 1970s, many Italian American directors (Martin Scorsese, Francis Ford Coppola, Brian De Palma, and Quentin Tarantino, to mention only the most famous) and Italian American actors (such as Robert De Niro, Joe Pesci, John Turturro, Stanley Tucci, Al Pacino, Marisa Tomei, and James Gandolfini) have played key and even dominant roles in Hollywood cinema production. In addition, these directors and performers have made a valuable contribution to the growth and complexity of the image of Italian Americans in American cinema. Yet two enormously important Italian American directors of a different generation—Frank Capra and Vincente Minnelli—never emphasized their ethnic origins (in fact, no lasting trace of obvious Italian Americana can be found in their major works), but both men helped define the American dream of the classic Hollywood film, the image of America that more contemporary Italian American directors may sometimes call into question. That two different generations of filmmakers of Italian American descent treat their backgrounds in entirely different ways raises interesting questions about the relation of ethnic identity and artistic creation.

Negative stereotypes exist in the representation of Hollywood Italians, but the quality of so many of the great films depicting Hollywood Italians is so high that for many such films (*The Godfather* is the best example) it is impossible to reject these great works as merely perpetuating stereotypes, just as it is impossible to ignore the literary values of such Shakespeare plays as *Othello* and *The Merchant of Venice* on the grounds that they are politically incorrect expressions of racial or religious prejudice. This consideration also applies to the single most important television representation of Italian Americans—David Chase's HBO series, *The Sopranos*. But stereotyping remains a critical problem in this field, a problem that is common to all studies of ethnic representation in cinema, television, or popular culture in general.

Some examples from films I have used in classroom discussions—*Christ in Concrete, Marty, A Bronx Tale*, and several episodes of *The Sopranos*—can shed light on practical methods of teaching about ethnic stereotypes that are typically associated with Italian Americans: stereotypes resting on views of Italian working-class values and their tradition-bound Little Italys, on conflict between Italian first-generation immigrants and their offspring born in the United States, and on the Italian American link to organized crime. The three films in question all have as their protagonists working-class Italians: construction workers, a butcher, and a bus driver. Here the students might well examine the dominant representation of this stereotype now that it is no longer accurate. While the vast majority of Italian Americans in the Hollywood cinema remain members of the blue-collar classes, demographically, according to the 2000 census, Italian Americans have moved into the middle and upper classes. Many of the Little Italys located in specific ethnic neighborhoods of large urban centers may play a more important role in our fictional and cinematic imaginaries than in our actual society today, as demographic changes have changed their character. Although these films present extremely sympathetic and complex characters, they may be said to relate more accurately to the past than to the present.

Geremio in *Christ in Concrete* embraces the American dream of the first-generation immigrant, tries to make a better life for his family, but is destroyed by his ambition to rise above the level of a simple bricklayer. Geremio is emblematic of the clash of immigrant expectations and stark American realities. The title character of *Marty* lives with his first-generation Italian mother, who looks askance at Clara, the non-Italian college graduate he brings home on a date. This timid butcher clearly shows how Italian values about family and *la via vecchia* ("the old way") change when confronted by a different and more modern society. Marty's ideas about the family and the role of women obviously differ from those in the old-world mores that his mother blindly embraces. Whereas his mother remains content to confine women to the traditional role of household management and raising a family, Clara wants to join the postwar generation of women who envision other careers outside the family structure.

Lorenzo of *A Bronx Tale* is the most complex figure of the three working-class Italian Americans because he must contend with Sonny, a neighborhood Mafia boss, for his son's affections. The perfect vehicle for discussing stereotypes of Italian Americans, *A Bronx Tale* juxtaposes the gangster with the respectable second-generation immigrant who believes in honesty and hard work rather than wiseguy shortcuts to success, and it is the mafioso who quotes Machiavelli and instructs the honest father's son, Calogero, that he must avoid choosing the career path Sonny has taken.

Christ in Concrete, Marty, and *A Bronx Tale* all relate to earlier times— the Great Depression era and the period immediately following World War II. During this era, Italian Americans indeed predominantly belonged to the working class, before they had succeeded in reaching higher socioeconomic status through increased emphasis on higher education. The value of selecting several episodes from *The Sopranos* for a discussion of ethnic stereotyping is that these inhabitants of New Jersey are decidedly upper middle class (in economic status if not in behavior) and are several generations removed from the original immigrants who arrived at Ellis Island from the old country. Even though Tony Soprano once exclaims to his daughter Meadow (a name that reeks of ethnic assimilation), "Out there, it's the nineties, but in this house it's 1954!" nothing could be further from the truth, and the producer David Chase knows this well. He presents the entire debate over ethnic stereotypes in a comic and even cynical light.

A few key episodes can stimulate classroom discussion—"Forty-Six Long," "Commendatori," and "Christopher." In the first episode, Paulie "Walnuts" delivers a diatribe against the "rape" of Italian culture in America, but of course he is an Italian American gangster (the most obvious stereotype imaginable) and actually knows very little about Italian culture. Moreover, his complaint about American exploitation of Italian cuisine is followed by his theft of an espresso maker, supposedly an attempt to balance the accounts. In the second episode, Paulie and Tony visit business partners in Naples, enabling Chase to juxtapose contemporary Italian culture with that of Italian Americans. In Chase's view, Italian Americans and Italians—even gangsters—are completely different breeds. Once again, Paulie shows his ignorance of his cultural heritage and longs for his particular Italian American "gravy" on his pasta, even when confronted with the most refined culinary delicacies available in Naples. Here Chase undermines the idea that Italian Americans and Italians are related in any meaningful cultural way. Finally, in the third episode, Chase critiques the sense of victimhood felt by various ethnic groups (including Italian Americans) and also takes aim at contemporary attempts to paint Christopher Columbus as a genocidal murderer of indigenous peoples after his discovery of America. Once again, Chase's take on this kind of argument treats Italian Americans critically: ultimately the New Jersey descendants of this so-called mass murderer miss their Columbus Day Parade and abandon their intention of making a political statement about Italian American culture in America to instead gamble away the holiday at an Indian casino.

Much of the opposition among Italian American groups to *The Sopranos* derives not from the producer's manipulation of ethnic stereotypes but from Chase's presentation of a perspective on Italian American culture that is not completely positive. Further, most audiences reacted to *The Sopranos* as more than just another continuation of the gangster stereotype (although this aspect is certainly present); they enthusiastically followed the lives of a group of Italian Americans who were so completely assimilated into American society that they became universal representations of us all, even if some of their activities took place outside the law.

I believe it is important not to use a course on Hollywood Italians merely to lament the existence of ethnic stereotypes. True, Hollywood cinema sometimes represents Italian Americans in unflattering ways, and the fact that Americans of Italian descent virtually dominate the pantheon of gangsters in the cinema tends to confirm the worst suspicions of those in the Italian American community who see prejudice at the bottom of such artistic choices. But any close examination of even the most stereotyped image can lead to interesting cultural and historical questions, and the problem of ethnic stereotyping requires that some films be screened that may, indeed, embody such a perspective.

Giulia Centineo

Language and Dubbing
in the Filmic Representation
of Italian Americans

What role does language play in the portrayal of Italian American characters in Hollywood films? What linguistic conventions should we analyze when studying the cinematic representation of Italian Americans? How does language usage in both American films and their dubbed Italian versions promote and reinforce Italian American stereotypes? These are some of the questions I ask students to consider in The Italian American Experience, an upper-division film course I teach at the University of California, Santa Cruz. The course enrolls an average of twenty-seven students, evenly divided between men and women and coming from a wide range of academic and ethnic backgrounds, of whom thirty-three to forty percent are of Italian descent.

In this essay, I refer frequently to *The Godfather* trilogy because it provides the widest range of linguistic devices in the representation of Italian Americans in film. While in my course I also investigate such issues as register and style and code elaboration, I limit my discussion here to my pedagogic approach to three noteworthy linguistic conventions: the use of English spoken with an Italian accent, the use of code switching, and the loss of accent. Finally I discuss how Italian American language is transposed in the dubbed Italian versions of American films.

English with an Accent

In *The Godfather*, Amerigo Bonasera's heavily accented English frames the narrative as an ethnic epic, as a struggle toward the loss of that accent and thus toward assimilation. To help students begin to think about the use and impact of accented English in filmic contexts, I ask them to remember their first experience with foreign accents in the media. They invariably mention cartoons, providing examples such as *Aladdin* (Arabic), *Pinocchio* (Italian), and *Beauty and the Beast* (French). We then discuss how accented English often gives the viewer the impression of traveling through time and place, rendering exotic ("orientalizing") the speaker. I invite my class to think about possible relationships between the accent and the personalities or life styles of characters and finally to reflect on the possible interpretations of such a usage. Students then provide examples of "undesirable" foreign accents from cartoons, like Boris's and Natasha's Russian accent in *The Bullwinkle Show* and *Aladdin*'s Arabic accents, which I ask them to interpret in the larger contexts of the cold war and the first Gulf War, respectively. Such activities enable students to make explicit the implicit, unanalyzed, and therefore unconscious assumptions about language and its contextual interpretations; they also teach students to reflect on language use and linguistic choices in the media, particularly in Italian American cinema. Students gradually become aware, aided by reading Rosina Lippi-Green's *English with an Accent*, of how cinema subtly asserts the linguistic hegemony of English while reducing other languages to mere accents, markers of imperfection and otherness.

Code Switching

The Godfather trilogy contains several scenes in which all or some of the characters, typically Italians or first-generation Italian Americans, speak exclusively in Italian or one of its dialects. In the opening scene of *The Godfather: Part II*, for example, Vito Corleone's mother says to Don Ciccio, "ma u figghiu miu è siccu" ("but my son is frail"), to which Don Ciccio replies, "E si quannu crisci, crisci forti?" ("And if when he grows up, he gets strong?"). When I ask students to reflect on the use of Sicilian here and in those scenes depicting the life of Vito Corleone as a young man in the United States, they note that only conversations set either in Sicily or in an ethnic American neighborhood are conducted entirely in Sicilian. They believe this usage is limited because of the Americans reluctance to

read subtitles. Ultimately, then, the use of Sicilian contributes a picturesque flavor to the narrative, just as the convention of accented English
does.

Italian American characters, by contrast, tend to "code switch" between Italian or a dialect and English. "Johnny, Johnny, canta'na canzone.
Sing a song," Mrs. Corleone pleads at Connie's wedding (*Godfather*). And
in what is the first (in the chronology of the story) utterance of the now
famous phrase, young Vito reassures Clemenza, "Un ti scantari, sono si-
curu: I'll make him an offer he don't refuse" (*Godfather: Part II*). More
commonly, Italian Americans begin with English and switch to Italian:
"What are you, a dance judge or something? Va va fatti i cazzi toi" ("Go
mind your business"), Clemenza says to Paulie at Connie's wedding (*Godfather*); and "I am not taking a picture without Michael. Le fotografie, più
tardi," Don Vito says when the family is assembling for a group photo
(*Godfather*).

Because some students may initially misinterpret the practice of code
switching as a sign of linguistic deficiency, I discuss everyday examples of
this phenomenon before we proceed with the analysis of specific filmic examples. When students consider their own experiences of parents' switching to their native language as a strategy to avoid their children's eavesdrop-
ping, they understand that code switching can be a meaningful linguistic
strategy. Essays from Peter Auer's work on code switching provide essential
theoretical background. After students are comfortable with the concept
and its usages, I ask them to analyze video clips for which I provide a textual transcription and to focus on the contextual occurrence of code
switching, such as the status, generation, and age of the participants or the
type of speech event. Through such close contextual analysis, students
come to understand that first-generation immigrants use code switching
extensively, while those of second and third generations, primarily English
monolinguals, use their heritage language in a more limited set of culturally specific situations, to display emotions and in ceremonial language
(e.g., thanking, toasting, swearing, greeting).

When asked to think about the contexts in which code switching appears in *The Godfather* films, students are quick to point out that code
switching into Sicilian or Italian recalls old-world values and traditions
and affirms group membership. In a scene from *The Godfather II*, for example, Michael says, "Tom, sit down. Che c'è?" ("What's wrong?"), and
Tom replies, "Ma nenti, perché?" ("Nothing, why?"). Having thus established a familial connection with this use of Italian, Michael switches back

to English to talk about business: "Our friend and business partner Hyman Roth is in the news." In the ensuing class discussion, students further elaborate that, at the symbolic level, Michael's usage of Italian ("Che c'è?") reminds Tom of their common "family" background and reciprocal loyalties. They also notice that Tom's answer ("Ma nenti, perché?") reaffirms their relationship, while at the same time literally challenging the implication of any deviation from an expected code of conduct. Michael's subsequent switch back to English ("Our friend and business partner") symbolically marks a change in his relationship with Tom, from a familial one to a business—and potentially antagonistic—one, at least until they come to an understanding and reconcile. Michael asks, "Allora, tu stai?" ("So, are you staying?"), and Tom answers, "Sì, io staiu" ("Yes, I am staying"). Once again, the switch back to the ancestral language reaffirms and seals their familial bond.

Students also realize, through a review of a large sample of code-switching instances that I make available in handouts, that in *The Godfather* trilogy, the expressive and metalinguistic range of code switching becomes progressively more narrow. Specifically, by the third film, the use of Sicilian almost exclusively signals crime, betrayal, deception, and the underworld. For instance, we look at the scene in which Vincent, pretending to betray Michael Corleone, meets Don Lucchesi and asks him, "How can I help?" Don Lucchesi responds by inviting him to speak privately with the command "Vieni!" ("Come!"), adding "Tu parli italiano un poco?" ("You speak a little Italian, right?"). In a very different kind of scene, Vincent calls Mary his "bella cugina, tesoru miu" ("beautiful cousin, my treasure"). The use of Italian here underscores the fact that the two are not just engaged in the sweet talk of love but are defying Michael's paternal command not to see each other. These and other examples illustrate that, in the last chapter of the saga, a switch into Sicilian indicates primarily a change in context and register, that is, the passage from this world to a world of crime, betrayal, and sin. Sicilian, which in *The Godfather* and *The Godfather II* was used by all characters, good or bad, has here become conventionalized as the language of deviance.

The Loss of Accent

Analyzing the loss of accent allows students to examine a linguistic convention that is intertwined with key themes of Hollywood representations of immigrants. In *The Godfather* trilogy, second- and third-generation

Italian Americans speak nearly uniformly with an "uneducated" East Coast urban accent, mostly the dialect spoken in the working-class neighborhoods and boroughs of the New York City area. My California students can easily point out some of the distinctive traits of this accent, such as the absence of the final or preconsonantal *r*, as in "car" or "beard"; the raising of the low-front vowel in words such as "bad" to a mid-front vowel, similar to the vowel sound in "bed"; the pronunciation of dental-alveolar fricatives as dental-alveolar stops (e.g., "them" as "dem"), and the use of double negatives and contractions such as the now ubiquitous "fuggedaboudit." These examples alone enable students to see that this exclusive linguistic choice traps Italian American fictional characters within the boundaries of their ethnic enclave and social class.

When discussing linguistic prejudice and stereotypes, I struggle with identifying stereotypes without engendering and reinforcing them. I find it imperative that students understand that a particular language or any variety of language is neither good nor bad per se and that all language varieties are perfectly logical systems. Rather, the social and cultural status of a linguistic variety derives from its persistent and consistent association with positive or negative traits of its speakers and their lifestyles. To explore these connections, I ask students to describe in a short essay the language used by Italian Americans in scenes they select from *The Godfather* and to associate particular linguistic traits with a speaker's physical and moral characteristics. Students who focus on the character Sonny discover that his nonstandard and coarse language use—revealed in lines like "Goddam FBI don't respect nothing" and "That Turk shows a hair on his ass, he's dead"—correlates with his violent temper and criminal lifestyle, while the more standard language spoken by Michael correlates with his higher education and businessman's identity.

At this point, students begin to reflect on how the use of a particular language variety contributes to the perception of Italian Americans. I ask them to consider whether speakers are usually aware of the stigma attached to their manner of expression. We watch scenes from *Saturday Night Fever*, a film that skillfully represents the loss of accent and the adoption of a different speech style as a way to reject one's stigmatized social identity. In particular, I ask students to quickly jot down their observations of Tony Manero's and Stephanie Mangano's speech in scenes in which the two characters interact (e.g., when she practices ballet and when they go out for coffee). Tony says, "You was looking at me, I was looking at you, remember?" and Stephanie quips, "What is this? I look at a guy for a millionth of a second and he already gets delusions of grandeur." Students do not fail to notice the sharp contrast between their speech patterns and point explicitly to their individual differences. One student will notice that Stephanie's lexical choices—"grandeur," "remarkable"—along with her affected pronunciation of *r*s, correlates with her name dropping, ballet lessons, and tea drinking; another student will point out that Tony's nonstandard use of grammar ("You was looking at me"), his use of contractions such as "howyoudoin," and his pronunciation of words such as "coffee" correlate with his bad table manners, low-paying job, and limited education. Students can easily find reasons for Stephanie's struggle to lose her accent, as illustrated by her self-correction ("Well it *ain't* Manhattan, it *isn't* Manhattan") in her unconditional love for "everything Manhattan," a place where, as she sees it, "People are beautiful, offices are beautiful . . . the lunch hours are beautiful too." Students also note her overt disdain for her Bay Ridge community and people like Tony: "Look, where I work the people are remarkable and not like these Bay Ridge people at all," and "You are a cliché, you're nowhere, on the way to no place." Students point out that Stephanie wants nothing to do with a world inhabited by uneducated brutes and recall Stephanie's linguistic coaching by her Manhattan boyfriend: "Stephanie, I told you not to say 'super.' Nobody says 'super' anymore." As Stephanie is claiming membership in a more prestigious neighborhood and higher social milieu, she is also distancing herself linguistically from her community.

Close linguistic and cultural analysis of films like these enables students to understand that the rendering of Italian American language in film is not merely a matter of mimetic accuracy; rather, it crucially contributes to the construction of a certain stereotypical Italian American character. Students realize how the speech of Italian American characters is recast as a monolithic and unnuanced form of expression that stigmatizes those who use it and contributes to their representation as a definitive other, not only in the United States but also abroad.

Italian American English Dubbed in Italian

In the additional Italian-language section of this course, we turn to the Italian version of *The Godfather* trilogy, along with scenes from other dubbed English-language originals. I also require that students read Sergio Raffaelli's and Nicoletta Maraschio's work to understand the role of dubbing in the wider context of dialect use in Italian national cinema. Students learn that the practice of dubbing, inspired by linguistic purism, emerged in the 1930s during the years of the fascist dictatorship and remained essentially unchanged, expunging all forms of low register and dialectal inflections, until 1973. In fact, it was not until the release of *Il Padrino*, the dubbed version of *The Godfather*, in 1973 that the sociolinguistic variation present in the original films started to be systematically reflected in their dubbed foreign versions. In *Il Padrino*, which has become the model for dubbing Italian Americans, Italian American characters speak almost exclusively a variety of a southern Italian dialect, mostly Sicilian, that is coded as uneducated. At one point, for example, Sollozzo addresses the kidnapped Tom Hagen, saying, "Perciò tu ci devi parlare con Sonny e devi quietare anche i caporreggime, ddru Tessio ddru panzuni di Clemenza, l'affare è bonu, credi a me" ("So, you gotta talk to Sonny, you gotta talk to the caporegimes, that Tessio and that fat Clemenza. . . . It's good business, Tom"). In this scene and many others throughout the film, characters speak with a rather artificial and at times stereotypical Sicilian intonation and pronunciation (e.g., *caporreggime, panzuni, bonu*) and with a dialectal use of syntax and morphosyntax (e.g., *ci, ddru*), lexicon, and word order.

Although *Il Padrino* represents the official beginning of the convention of dubbing Italian American speech with southern dialects, there were notable precursors to this tradition. In class, we analyze scenes—for which I provide the dubbed Italian text and its International Phonetic Alphabet transcription—from a few earlier films such as *Midnight Cowboy* (*Un uomo da marciapiede*)—and *My Fair Lady*. As a result of this analysis, students learn that, rather than exceptions, these earlier uses of southern accents and dialects represent stages in the long development of a linguistic stereotype of which *Il Padrino* is its point of arrival and legitimization. In fact, students notice that the choice of a particular dialect and the intensity of an accent correlate to perceived negative traits of the character and not necessarily to a southern origin at all. In the dubbed Italian version of *My Fair Lady*, for example, Eliza speaks with a heavy southern (Pugliese) accent. Since Eliza is obviously a Londoner, the choice of a southern accent to dub her voice indexes her humble origin and lack of formal education.

As a teacher and researcher, I feel that it is imperative to situate our discussion of the dubbing of Italian American speech into southern Italian in a broad political and social context, as, for instance, that provided by Jane Schneider in *Italy's "Southern Question": Orientalism in One Country*. An exposure to dubbed Italian American cinema provides students with a disturbing and vivid picture of past and contemporary Italian stereotypes about southern Italy and about those who emigrated mostly from the south to the United States. Overall, the examples drawn from both older and newer films and television series, including fairly recent imports (such as *The Sopranos* or *The Nanny*), provide students with rich data illustrating the widespread use of southern Italian dialects and accents to signal criminality, emigration, poverty, ignorance, backwardness, vulgarity, marginalization, and, in the best cases, quaintness.

By the end of the term, my students see that cinema, with its myths about prestige and stigmatized language varieties, is a powerful tool to promote language ideology. This type of linguistic and cultural analysis enables students to identify the subtle workings of racism and to understand how speech in cinema, operating at a deep and almost unconscious level, serves as a potent means of creating, disseminating, and magnifying stereotypes and prejudice—a relevant exercise that can also be applied to other national and ethnic contexts.

Courtney Judith Ruffner

Cultural Stereotyping in
Happy Days and *The Sopranos*

"What are you really? Have you ever thought about that? If I say pizza, what do you think of? If I say *gangster* or *ethnicity*, what comes to mind?" These are the questions I ask twenty-five students on the first day of my composition class at Manatee Community College in south Florida. I ask my students to consider these questions as they take turns telling the class a bit about themselves. The course focuses on representations of ethnicity. The students range from traditional seventeen-year-olds to nontraditional students, some my grandmother's age. Several of these students were born and raised in Florida and consider themselves white or black, while others have moved here from somewhere else in the States but also call themselves white or black. When I ask one African American student what her ethnicity is, she replies, "I'm black." At first, her answer seems so obvious that the class, including this student, laughs. I then ask her if she is sure, whether she has completed a family tree, and she responds, "No, we haven't done that. Hmmm . . . that makes me wonder." This exchange excites the class as they continue with their introductions, only now they are responding without certainty about their ethnic backgrounds. The class has a vast makeup of racial and ethnic identities: Caucasian, African American, Asian, Russian, and Hispanic. What these students do not know at this point is that they are about to become steeped in ethnic research while learning how to write. It is in this writing class that students begin to understand how cultural stereotyping shapes the construction of ethnic identity. And, as a result, they become aware of their biases and transform their vocabulary and their ways of reading and writing from simple and uninformed positions to more critical and nuanced perceptions of ethnicity.

Here I concentrate on one assignment that I require, the compare-and-contrast paper, designed to complicate the idea of the Italian American (the image that the class has been defining thus far in the course). I introduce Arthur Fonzarelli from *Happy Days*, otherwise known as Fonzie or the Fonz, by showing three episodes of the show. Fonzie serves as a fine example of an Italian American stereotyped character because he is cast as a dangerous greaser, a rebel more dangerous than the non-Italian characters on the show. In the series's first episode, "All the Way," Fonzie only appears in scenes that depict him as a sexual, brooding womanizer. He does not speak to anyone until the last scene, after Richie lies about "going all the way" with a girl, and Fonzie makes a date with her. When Richie finally tells the truth about not having had sex with the girl, Fonzie tells him he is angry, but he will let this one slide if Richie does not lie anymore. He says: "I'll do all the lying." In the composite "Fonzie Loves Pinky," we see Fonzie growing into a man, still depicted as sexual and womanizing but with a steady job and more common sense than the other characters his age. And in the episode "A Woman Not under the Influence," Fonzie's character is transformed from the highly sexualized Italian American thug to the teacher-father-husband figure he becomes over time.

I assign Maria Laurino's article "Italians on TV: From the Fonz to *The Sopranos*, Not Much Evolution" to ground a discussion about Italian American stereotypes. Many students respond to Laurino's central question, "Are Italian Americans ever allowed to evolve?" They begin to recognize that calling an Italian American a "greaser thug," as one student referred to Fonzie, is stereotyping. In addition to Laurino's article, I add the idea of the hyphenated society by assigning Louise DeSalvo's article, "Color: White / Complexion: Dark." DeSalvo discusses the experiences of naturalization for her Italian grandmother and also analyzes the question of the skin color of Italians in relation to African and white races. Laurino and DeSalvo help provoke a discussion of Fonzie among my students that addresses issues such as the stereotyped masculine gangster (thug) and the treatment of this character in relation to the other non-Italian characters. Our discussion centers on the process of Fonzie's "colonization," that is, the changes he undergoes as a regular at the white middle-class American Cunningham family table during the course of the show. The students begin to recognize the transformations that Fonzie undergoes to become a part of the ideal white family. They comment on the changes he makes to his vocabulary, wardrobe, and occupation to become part of the establishment of the time.

To conceptualize Fonzie's initial otherness, I divide the whiteboard into two columns: Fonzie and the Cunninghams. I ask the students to begin calling out attributes of the different characters. After about twenty minutes, Fonzie's column reads: leather jacket, tough, sexy, wild, motorcycle, Italian, orphan, *dawg*, exotic, attitude, loner. The Cunningham column reads: happy, family, typical, white, middle-class, balanced, conservative. Using these lists, we then chart Fonzie's change in the three episodes we have viewed. Some students observe that the first episode shows the Cunninghams and their family values as the primary voice of reason in the show. They help get Fonzie off the streets and into a respectable but subjugated environment, the apartment over their garage. Their interference is necessary to save Fonzie from his own hapless errors and to guide him to the path of the colonizer's ideal, the moral majority.

Fonzie gradually loses his "otherized" identity: he parts with his office, the vulgar men's room at the local teen hangout Arnold's; he leaves his angst-ridden, tortured rebellion behind when he becomes a teacher; his sexy womanizing attitude melts away when he falls in love and begins to build a relationship in which he adopts the traditional 1950s role of provider. It is this transformation from rebel to rehabilitated member of the dominant class that charts the progress of the Italian American on the show. Ironically, the ratings for *Happy Days* began to decline as the Fonz made his transformation. Once Fonzie is integrated (namely as teacher at Jefferson High, proprietor of Arnold's, and adoptive father) into multiple layers reserved only for colonizers, my students suggest that either he is deemed to be a threat to the already established orders of the viewers or that, once reformed, he is just boring. In either case, the rehabilitation of the Fonz is the likely cause of the declining ratings.

We turn next to a more contemporary representation of the Italian American and view three episodes of HBO's *The Sopranos*. I ask my students to pay particular attention to the character of Paulie Gualtieri, played by Tony Sirico. I require them to write a short paper, given the prompt "Who, really, is Peter Paul 'Paulie Walnuts' Gualtieri?" As the first episode is about to begin, I encourage the students to consider what being named Walnuts represents for Paulie and what being nicknamed the Fonz or Fonzie represented for a man named Arthur (a not-so-cool first name) Fonzarelli.

It is clear from the episode's title, "I Dream of Jeannie Cusamano," when Paulie admits that he has seen a therapist because he lacks "coping skills," that his character is complex. We are able to see his anger before we have a chance to experience it in almost every scene. David Chase casts him as violent to reflect his stereotyped appearance: rough skin, slicked-back black hair trimmed with white on the sides, and, although described by Chase on the official HBO Web site as "the most meticulously coiffed and manicured capo in the Soprano crew," an old-fashioned gangster's sense of dress. We are privy to the fact that "he's highly superstitious and has a violent—at times literally murderous—temper, as well as a distrust of others that borders on the paranoid" ("Paulie Walnuts"). As walnuts are tough nuts to crack, so is Paulie: he has always struggled with his identity as a member of the Soprano crime family and with personal problems—not only his anger but also his sexuality. Several students make a connection between Paulie and Fonzie and their need to belong to a family unit.

As the students transition into the second episode of *The Sopranos*, I hand out the Cindy Donatelli and Sharon Alward article " 'I Dread You'? Married to the Mob in *The Godfather*, *Goodfellas*, and *The Sopranos*." The students read and annotate it based on themes we have discussed, specifically stereotypes and identity. At this point, the class viewings of *Happy Days* and *The Sopranos* begin to coalesce into a unified narrative for the students as they draw connections among the characters. The one theme that students notice is the obvious dichotomy between the stereotyped masculine thug Fonzie and the feminized gangster Paulie. In fact, after the first episode of *The Sopranos*, one student remarked that Paulie seems "a bit . . . gay." Others agreed immediately and suggested that "he's different from the other Italian Americans we have been discussing." Students point out that where both Fonzie and Paulie are seemingly superstitious in nature, Paulie sees a therapist because his superstition borders on paranoia. They associate this paranoia with Paulie's softer side. Fonzie, however, maintains his masculine demeanor and refuses to go to therapy because it is a sign of weakness. This refusal helps solidify Fonzie's conventional masculinity in the students' view. Students go on to point out that while both characters are close to their families and have an above-average intimacy with the mother figures in their lives, Paulie's attachment to his mother seems unnaturally close (for example, he refers to his mother using terms of endearment while he touches her face). Actions like these are what confuse the students as they try to read Paulie. They mistake Paulie's tender mannerisms and affection for his mother for what they consider to be traditionally represented gay behavior. Although they are unable to fully explain the difference between the characters of Fonzie and Paulie, the students have recognized a change in Italian American characterization. Not only are they confused by instances of gentle behavior in Paulie, such as his ideas of women in *la Cosa Nostra* or his kindness to his mother (both directly linked to his older, more traditional Italian upbringing), but they are equally perplexed by his contradictory good-versus-evil actions.

In the episode entitled "Eloise," Paulie breaks into the home of his mother's friend to steal her "mattress money," her savings. When she finds him in her bedroom, he suffocates her with a pillow, takes the money, and leaves. We know that being a gangster is the life Paulie has chosen; therefore, he must do whatever he needs to in order to "kick up" money to Tony each week, even if it means "whacking" an old woman. Yet several students cringe at the murderous Paulie. One student says: "I feel bad for him. He has to do these terrible things because if he doesn't, he'll be killed by Tony." But other students suggest that the "masculine gangster" role does not appear to suit Paulie. Further, they note that while Fonzie does not possess this type of blatant "gangster masculinity" because he is more domesticated from the start, he nonetheless does display a certain stereotyped masculinity that, like Paulie's, is ultimately called into question. Early in the show, Fonzie carved his name in the table at Arnold's with his fingernail, and he inspired fear in everyone by simply walking into a room, not to mention that he allegedly could have great power over women simply by snapping his fingers. But as Fonzie became more conventional, students note that he also became less masculine, perhaps because he became part of the establishment. There is no place for aggression or violence in the establishment; therefore, Fonzie must keep his anger in check while standing as a role model not only to the kids in his Jefferson High classroom but also to the viewing audience.

The final episode of *The Sopranos* that I show in class, "Pine Barrens," heightens the students' awareness of their biases concerning sexuality. The opening scene features an angry Paulie having to make a collection from a

Russian for fellow gangster Silvio. Visibly enraged, Paulie channels his emotions into violence when he shows up at the Russian's apartment. To regain control of his conflicting identity (a somewhat feminine Paulie versus a masculine gangster), he taunts the Russian by calling him names, turning "rubles" into a derogatory term of otherness, and making fun of Russian toilet practices. When the Russian responds, "go fuck your mother," Paulie reverts to violence to control the situation and to solidify his masculine persona. In our discussion of the episode, the students point out: "Paulie is caught between taking up the roles of his crew and the more feminine actions he demonstrates when he is not with them. Of course, these [feminine] actions are unacceptable in his world." So, after having seen three episodes, I ask students again, "Who is Peter Paul Gualtieri?" They give conflicting responses: "he is a stereotype of a real Mafia criminal"; "he is a violent man with issues"; "he is just a guy trying to make a living who likes his nails to look good"; and "he is the last of the old guard in the Soprano crew, and that makes him do the things he does."

Students eventually begin to ask larger questions such as: "Why would Chase depict a gangster like this, in such a feminine way?" and "Don't any of the guys in Paulie's crew see that he seems feminine?" I am thrilled that the study of Paulie has led the class into an unexpected realization of their sexual stereotyping. Their vocabulary changes from *gay* to *feminine* as we continue our discussion of Paulie. The students' language becomes more critical and analytic over the semester, largely because they have read critical essays along with viewing television episodes. Students also begin to question their images of what they consider to be gay in their lives. They have come to understand that simply because a man chooses to get a manicure, to respect his mother, or see a therapist, he should not be stereotyped as *gay*, a term indicating sexual preference. Most important, my students learn to engage in a discourse that asks them to consider others in a way that they have not previously been asked to do. They learn to challenge and complicate their responses to television, film, and literature and to question the working of stereotyping not only in cultural representations but also in their personal lives.

Part IV

Historical and
Interdisciplinary
Approaches

Jennifer Guglielmo

Situating Italian Immigrant Women's Radical Writing in American History

I include Italian American history and literature in all my classes on United States history. In one class—Women Writing Resistance—I devote two weeks to the testimonial writing of working-class Italian immigrant women anarchists from the early twentieth century. I discovered this material in my archival research: writing produced in the first decades of the twentieth century, which the Italian-language anarchist presses published and circulated in the United States and beyond. Taking the form of short essays in newspapers or longer treatises in pamphlets, such writing was generated by women with very little formal education and few economic resources, and thus it exposes students to the political cultures of women on the margins.

This material works particularly well in Women Writing Resistance, a course designed to give students a sense of United States history in the nineteenth and twentieth centuries from the perspective of women's cultural work. We study how women have creatively unmasked power relations in their confrontations with colonialism, racism, patriarchy, war, and capitalism to envision and enact alternative ways of being. Our focus is on women's writing, including speeches, journalism, letters, and memoir, in connection with other forms of creative expression such as music, spoken word, visual art, dance, and political action.

The writing of Italian immigrant women comes in the second section of the course, which explores working-class, immigrant and migrant women's cultural work in the radical social movements of the turn of the century. We begin the second section with material documenting Chinese, Puerto Rican, Cuban, and Mexican immigrant and migrant women's writing in the transnational feminist, anticolonial, and labor movements at the turn of the twentieth century, to understand women's diasporic political cultures in San Francisco, Puerto Rico, New York City, Tampa, and along the Mexico–United States border (Yung; Sánchez-Gonzalez; Mirabal; Hewitt; Lomas). The writing by Italian women anarchists is another layer of this history. By the time students delve into this literature, they have learned how systems of power are shifting and impact women's lives in multiple ways. We study how women are positioned in racialized processes of nation building in vastly different ways: Chinese immigrant women were formally denied United States citizenship and barred from entering the country, while Puerto Rican and Mexican women were marginally included as colonial subjects. By attending to the structural processes that shape patterns of migration, settlement, labor, and politics, students learn that Latina and Latino and Asian American subjectivity has been shaped by contradiction: while these groups reside in and contribute their labor to the United States, they are marked as perpetually foreign, alien, and unassimilable. This history helps students understand how citizenship in the United States has been conflated with whiteness and that assimilation for Europeans meant both Americanizing and whitening.

We study Italian immigrant women's radical writing after having established this history of race making. This choice reflects my pedagogical commitment to deconstructing the mythic "up-by-the-bootstraps" European immigrant that has become iconic in classic history texts and the mass media and used as the yardstick by which to measure other ethnic groups in the United States: the poverty-stricken but determined and hardworking immigrant who triumphs against all odds to assimilate in the land of milk and honey. This highly individualist narrative not only tends to erase women (or positions them as appendages to men), it also elides the very power relations that give rise to and shape patterns of immigration, settlement, and adjustment. Students learn that history cannot be comprehended without an attention to power and how a great deal of women's cultural work was intended to make those ideologies and structures more visible. There are many blind spots in the creative work, of course, and I encourage students to explore these silences as well, since they are especially revealing about who can afford to ignore particular manifestations of power and why.

I begin the lesson with some classic photographs of Italian immigrant women—those by Jacob Riis and Lewis Hine—so students can analyze some of the more popular representations that continue to inform our collective memory of this past. In this way, they meet the garment worker and factory girl of the tenements and sweatshops. They see her represented as the hardy peasant, dexterously balancing huge bundles of clothing on her head, seated before a sewing machine or loom, or holding an infant in her arms amid the chaos and filth of the modern industrial metropolis. Her face is often obscured either by her focused concentration on the work at hand or by her heavy load. On occasion, I give students copies of a quintessential photograph and ask them to write one page outside class on their impressions, so they can interpret the document on their own first. I have also had students write in-class stream-of-consciousness pieces with the photograph projected on a screen, to give them a chance to reflect on the image before our class conversation begins. These photos help us answer a series of questions that we take up together in discussion: How is she portrayed? Why might this be? What is highlighted and what is occluded? What is the message that this image conveys? How might an early-twentieth-century middle-class audience interpret this image? What signals her race, class, and gender? We explore how these images restrict Italian immigrant women to a particular persona, one that women's testimonial writing will challenge. I make a point to infuse the class discussion with information concerning the relationship between Progressive Era middle-class native-born reformers in the United States who generated and consumed such images and the European immigrant women who are portrayed, to situate the photographs in their historical context. This can also be done by assigning material on or by Hine and Riis or by including scholarship on Progressive Era reform (Friedman-Kasaba; Ewen; Newman; Frankel and Dye).

Building on our past discussions, I ask students to consider how these photographic images advance, reconcile, or refute the United States' nation-building project of that period and encourage them to identify the particular location of Italian women in the United States at this time. Italian immigrant women were, for example, heavily recruited by clothing manufacturing firms to come to New York City for low-wage labor in the burgeoning industrial capitalist economy. They were classified as white by the federal government and were therefore permitted to enter, reside, and become citizens (which meant that their families could represent themselves in a court of law, vote, and own property). They were also not subjected to systematic racialized segregation at the levels experienced by African Americans, American Indians, Mexican Americans, or Latin American and Asian immigrants. Yet southern Italians were perceived popularly and by government officials as racially suspect and biologically inferior to northern and western European Americans. Identifying how Italian women entered the United States' economic and racial order is essential to understanding their cultures of resistance. This understanding can also be facilitated with assigned readings from Thomas A. Guglielmo's book, *White on Arrival: Italians, Race, Color, and Power in Chicago, 1890–1945*; the anthology *Are Italians White? How Race Is Made in America* (J. Guglielmo and Salerno); and recent scholarship by Matthew Frye Jacobson (*Barbarian Virtues*; *Roots*; *Whiteness*) and David R. Roediger (*Working*). We also compare and contrast the experiences of Italian immigrant women with those of the Chinese, Mexican, Cuban, and Puerto Rican women we studied, to explore differing processes of racialization and their various legal, political, and economic positions.

We then turn to the essays, manifestos, testimonies, and letters produced by Italian immigrant women between 1897 and 1907, many of whom resided in New York City and northeastern New Jersey. The writing is all in Italian. I have translated several essays for students, two of which have been reprinted in the anthology *Italian American Writers on New Jersey: An Anthology of Poetry and Prose* (Gillan, Gillan, and Gunta). The essays are typically short, often only a few paragraphs in length, and they usually begin with a dramatic call to action: "Alle donne, emancipiamoci!" ("To women, let's emancipate ourselves!") and "Alle mie sorelle proletarie" ("To my proletarian sisters"). Hundreds of women's essays survive because they were published in two anarchist newspapers from Paterson, New Jersey, and New York City, two important centers of Italian immigrant radicalism. While radicals constituted a minority among Italian immigrants, they were highly visible and vocal in all the major Italian enclaves through at least the 1920s. Most of the women authors were self-identified anarchists and socialists who were active in local grass-roots, revolutionary, working-class movements. They were also mothers, grandmothers, factory workers, performance artists (they wrote and performed short plays and skits), and labor organizers. Many left school as children to work in neighborhood factories, like other Italian immigrant women, since their wages were necessary for their family's survival. So the lectures, neighborhood discussions, study circles, newspapers, and pamphlets of the radical subculture provided a way for women to continue and deepen their education. This involvement, combined with their experiences as marginalized and itinerant workers, taught them a great deal about the world around them. As Alba Genisio wrote, her insight into "women's emancipation" was derived not from formal study but from her lived experiences: "I am not an intellectual but the daughter of a discredited and oppressed people."

One position that Italian immigrant women radicals consistently articulated in this writing is that revolutionary activism required their dreams and insights. Like other working-class anarchist and socialist women, they developed a *femminismo* (this was the word they used) that refuted liberal feminism's demands for political and legal inclusion and instead developed a materialist analysis of power. They circulated treatises from their anarchist-feminist comrades around the world, such as an essay by Luigia Reville in which she declared: "We are not feminists in the manner of the bourgeoisie, who claim the equality or supremacy of our sex and would be satisfied with the realization of these dreams." To them, feminism meant that working and poor women's struggles, concerns, and strategies informed revolutionary practice. Virginia Buongiorno was one of many who added her voice to the discussion:

> It is not enough to struggle for the vote (as do the bourgeois women in this hardly free America). We want to tear down all the false prejudices that infest the world. It is not with changing certain laws that we can call ourselves free. . . . You see, my sister workers, these laws are made by the bourgeoisie for their interests.

As anarcho-syndicalists, they sought revolutionary change to end all systems of oppression and hierarchical authority, whether in the form of industrial capitalism, the government, the church, or the men in their families and communities.

They also spoke out against the aggressive actions of the Italian government in Africa and opposed the United States' imperialism in Asia and Latin America. Italian anarchists also opposed nationalism because they believed that it was the root of the problem. In one of her early essays on what it was like to be an immigrant in the United States, Ersilia Cavedagni, author and noted activist in both the United States and Italy, noted:

> How evil is this, a society in which its members have developed a stupid aversion to others who do not speak the same language or are born under another sky and wear different clothes. . . . Ah, this damned and miserable concept of country separates so stupidly, uselessly, and ferociously those who nature intended to be brothers.

These women also wrote essays exposing the routine mob lynching of African Americans by white Americans, the deplorable conditions under which Chinese immigrants were forced to work and live, and what they called "yankee barbarism" more generally. In this way, they educated one another about how class oppression was not only rooted in nationalism and imperialism but connected to histories of slavery and colonialism and to the continued practices of segregation, racial terror, disfranchisement, and economic exploitation.

The women's most common theme was the impact of dangerous, grueling, low-wage labor on their psyches and bodies. Women workers most often addressed their writing to other women workers, as seen here in Maria Barbieri's 1905 essay:

> We have become human machines who stay locked in the immense industrial prisons, where we lose our strength, our health and youth, where our rights are shattered before the greed of the bourgeoisie. And we don't rebel against these abuses to our right to live? We don't shake with rage before the pompous and contemptuous lady, who because of us wears a silk skirt from our humble labor?

They often dedicated their essays to their "sorelle di fatica" ("sisters of drudgery"): "We who produce all the social riches . . . the silk, the lace, and the embroidery of great luxury must skimp in our own lives just to wear cotton. . . . Why is it that this life, which should be a paradise, is for us a torment?"

Students are generally surprised by the women's transnational and radical feminism and their attention to subjects often associated with later social movements: imperialism, militarism, racism, labor practices, abuse by church officials, liberatory education, free love, nonoppressive parenting, equitable gender relations, and class struggle. To help students understand this history, I complement the primary documents with scholarship on Italian American radicalism (Gabaccia, *Italy's Many Diasporas*; Cannistraro and Meyer; Gabaccia and Iacovetta; Gabaccia and Ottanelli; A. Cameron; J. Guglielmo, "Italian Women's Proletarian Feminism" and "Sweatshop Feminism"). To help this culture come alive, I bring photocopies of the radical newspapers and pamphlets to class, as well as photographs of the communities and strikes in which these authors played a role. Such material is available in secondary sources like Steve Golin's *The Fragile Bridge*, but much is in archives such as the American Labor Musuem / Botto House National Landmark, in Haledon, New Jersey, and the Immigration History Research Center at the University of Minnesota.

Taken together, these documents teach students about anarchism and socialism from the perspective of those who devoted themselves to these movements. In the effort to analyze why these activists and their ideas became criminalized and stigmatized, I contrast the self-representations with popular and official depictions of anarchists from such texts as Salvatore LaGumina's *WOP! A Documentary of Anti-Italian Discrimination in the United States.* This comparison helps students understand how Italians were racialized through an imagery and discourse of othering that hinged on notions of their inherent criminality. Students learn from the scholarship of Salvatore Salerno, for example, that the newspapers that published the most essays by Italian immigrant women anarchists were targeted for censorship by the federal government during the red scare of World War I, in large part because of their bold stance against white supremacy and racist violence. Students learn how the widespread suppression of civil liberties during the red scare was motivated, in part, by the federal government's fear of the alliances that working-class people were forming across racial lines (Kornweibel).

Since much scholarly writing during the 1980s and 1990s advanced an image of Italian immigrant women as uninterested in politics and without a history or culture of resistance, these primary documents force students to ask why this stereotype has persisted. Students often remark that this first generation of immigrant women activists seems more radical, more subversive, and less willing to sacrifice their revolutionary visions to assimilate into American society than later generations. These documents challenge progressivist notions of American history—that over time each generation is more cosmopolitan, more open-minded, more involved in the political life of their community than the last. They teach students to deconstruct popular notions of immigrant women as backward compared with their more Americanized daughters. Moreover, they offer inspiration as students continue to confront the impact of war, imperialism, class and race inequality, and other forms of systemic oppression in their lives.

Kimberly A. Costino

Recrossing Ocean Parkway: Teaching Italian American Literacy Narratives and Racial Formation in First-Year Composition Courses

In the field of composition studies, literacy narratives are generally considered to be any narrative account of how a person has "become" literate in a particular cultural context. Such narratives, like Marianna De Marco Torgovnick's "On Being White, Female, and Born in Bensonhurst," have been staples in composition classrooms since the 1980s, when David Bartholomae and Anthony Petrosky urged writing teachers to introduce their students to texts that would reflect their experiences crossing languages and cultures. Many instructors believe that by asking students to read and write literacy narratives they will make visible, and therefore work toward a valuing of, multiple kinds of literacies, multiple kinds of identities, and the dialectical relation among them. In so doing, they believe they are working to deconstruct the limiting literacy/illiteracy binary that has historically linked literacy with whiteness and illiteracy with the racialized other. I disagree. To begin to shake loose the ideological articulations between literacy and whiteness and illiteracy and racialized otherness, we cannot only read and discuss literacy narratives from a variety of cultures and perspectives with our students; we also need to examine how these cultures and identities have been historically and ideologically constructed through public discourse. We need to engage students in what the feminist philosopher and historian Joan W. Scott has referred to as the process of historicization, the practice of "mak[ing] visible the assignment of subject-positions" and "trying to understand the operations of the complex and changing discursive processes by which identities are ascribed, resisted, or embraced" (65). This essay illustrates the ways that Italian American literacy narratives, when examined in their historical contexts, can be particularly effective in engaging students and teachers in the process Scott describes. Not only does teaching Italian American literacy narratives work to historicize the genre of the literacy narrative and the racialized literate/illiterate binary that it unwittingly constructs, but it also highlights the imbrication between literacy and immigration, examines how identity categories—including whiteness—are socially and rhetorically constructed, and exposes the role literacy plays in this process of racial formation.

The traditional approach to teaching literacy narratives usually involves providing students with samples from a wide variety of cultures, asking them to consider the role language and moving between languages plays in shaping the protagonists' identities, and then asking them to consider those issues in terms of their own lives. We see this, for example, in the literacy scholar Mary Soliday's description of her composition course. After reading a variety of perspectives on identity and literacy,

> the students in this class composed a list of twelve questions, which we then used as the assignment for writing; students chose questions such as "Do you feel you are losing your own culture's language when you are learning a different language? How do you feel talking two or more languages?" and "Why does sounding educated seem to people of color to be associated with being white? Why does black and white have to be an issue?" (516)

My approach to teaching literacy narratives is similar. Students read texts from a variety of cultures, including Richard Rodriguez's *Hunger of Memory*, the story of how the son of Mexican immigrants, a "boy who first entered the classroom barely able to speak English," came to conclude his education "in the stately quiet of the reading room in the British Museum" (43); bell hooks's "Keeping Close to Home," which frames literacy as enabling movement between the "materially underprivileged" world of her African American home and the "materially privileged" white world of academia (75); and Torgovnick's "On Being White, Female, and Born in Bensonhurst," which discusses the implications of the fact that her education "removed" her "from the fundamental economic and social conditions of Bensonhurst" (10), an Italian American community, to a middle-class life that has allowed her the "freedom—to experiment, to grow, to change" (11). I want my students to be able to see the consistencies in the narrative structures of these texts despite their differing cultural contexts and to consider the ideological, generic, and rhetorical roots of such consistencies.

I raise questions similar to the ones Soliday discusses in her course. Particularly salient to my students is the link between school discourse (i.e., "sounding educated") and "sounding white" and/or "being rich." We therefore spend time examining the role of this equation between school literacy, race, and class in the question of whether learning a new language and becoming educated means leaving one's home culture behind and whether or why race in general has to "be an issue." In addition to these questions, however, we also spend a great deal of time identifying and analyzing how racialized categories have come to be; the discursive and ideological processes that create, maintain, or alter them; and the role that school literacy plays in the process.

Because time constraints make it difficult to have students historicize all the literacy narratives that we read in this way, we only conduct an extensive intertextual analysis as a class for Torgovnick's essay. I focus on this text for several reasons. First, Italian American literacy narratives are particularly effective for exposing and examining the instability of racial categories and literacy's role in the process of racial formation because of the various relations Italian Americans and Italian immigrants have had historically to both whiteness and education. Indeed, one student wrote in response to a quotation about the Yusuf Hawkins murder that "the Italians in Bensonhurst are white, but they don't really 'talk white.'" While a similar argument could be made for other white ethnic communities in America, I focus on Italian American literacy narratives because Italian American history and literature is still relatively unknown to the culture generally and to this particular Southern California student population specifically. In addition, I believe that if, as a teacher, I ask students to consider their privileges and how they are implicated in the processes of racial formation that structure our world, then I must be willing to do the same. I have found that teaching these texts enables me to accomplish these goals.

The notion that Italian Americans see themselves as white is nowhere more evident than in the media representations of the racially motivated murder of Yusuf Hawkins (see, e.g., Blumenthal, "Black Youth" and

"Police"; Bohlen; Johnson; Kaufman; "Murder"; Ravo, "Marchers" and "Two Hundred Fifty Whites"), the impetus for Torgovnik's narrative of Bensonhurst, as well as two other Bensonhurst essays my students read: Joseph Sciorra's " 'Italians against Racism': The Murder of Yusuf Hawkins (R.I.P.) and My March on Bensonhurst" and Maria Laurino's "Bensonhurst." I assign these essays, as well as the news accounts of the Hawkins murder, because I want my students to see multiple constructions of Bensonhurst and to consider their implications in shaping our ideas about racial meanings and their relation to literacy and education. The essays work well together because these three authors all wish to make sense of Bensonhurst, but not, as Torgovnik puts it, "in the manner of a news account or a statistical sociological analysis" (9), and to consider their identities in relation to the Bensonhurst community.

We read the news accounts first, so that students can see the representations of Bensonhurst to which Torgovnick, Sciorra, and Laurino respond. During a class conversation about these media reports, one student likened "the Bensonhurst mentality" to the "gang mentality" we hear about in the Southern California news: "It's almost like the people in Bensonhurst are like a gang, trying to protect their territory from outsiders; the only difference is they're white." After discussing the similarities and trying to problematize the assumption that gangs are not white, I draw students' attention to the characterization of the Bensonhurst Italian Americans as white. When I ask them if they think of Italian Americans as white, of *me* as white, they have slightly varying responses. Some look uncomfortable because I have drawn attention to race in our actual classroom, but most look at me as if I am crazy and say, "yeah," in the tone of "isn't that patently obvious?" At this point I ask how they know. What makes Italians white? After all, my complexion is as dark as many Latinos. We discuss the intricacies of race and complexion at greater length later; here, I play on the dominant cultural conflation between complexion and racial identity.

To the question of why Italian Americans are white, silence generally ensues, so we turn to primary and secondary sources that address the history of race and immigration in the United States, such as *New York Times* articles from 1907–11 that address the immigration restriction debates and the literacy test that was repeatedly proposed to restrict the new, racialized, "undesirable" immigrants from southeastern Europe (see, e.g., "Future Americans"; "Illiteracy"; "Immigrant"; "Northcliffe"; "Test"; "Unread Immigrants"); excerpts from the congressional debates concerning the literacy test provided in E. P. Hutchinson's *Legislative History of American Immigration Policy*; charts cataloging the characteristics of all the "racial types" included in the 1911 report of the United States Immigration Commission; and information from pamphlets about Darwinism, social Darwinism, and eugenics (see Quigley).

My students are surprised to learn that what we now think of as white ethnics (e.g., Italian Americans, Irish Americans, Polish Americans) were, according to the 1911 report, considered different, "undesirable races." We read through essays from Jennifer Guglielmo and Salvatore Salerno's *Are Italians White? How Race Is Made in America*. Specifically, we first look at Thomas A. Guglielmo's " 'No Color Barrier': Italians, Race, and Power in the United States," which argues that the "many perceived racial inadequacies [of Italians] aside, they were still largely accepted as white by the widest variety of people and institutions" (30). Then, to highlight the way language use works to construct and establish racial identity, we look at Caroline Waldron Merithew's "Making the Italian Other: Blacks, Whites, and the Inbetween in the 1895 Spring Valley, Illinois, Race Riot," which illustrates how in the particular incidence of the Illinois race riot of 1895 Italian immigrants relied on whiteness for power, but they had to aggressively assert such whiteness to create their difference from African Americans. And we finish this portion of the sequence with Louise DeSalvo's "Color: White / Complexion: Dark," which both complicates our discussions about race, ethnicity, and color by adding and distinguishing the notion of complexion and makes students aware of the ideological link between being "not quite white" and being uneducated or illiterate (27). During these discussions, we note the ideological conflation between a lack of school literacy and lack of intelligence; many students can get passionate about its inaccuracy, citing examples of members of their own families who are "not stupid, just because they don't have an education." We also note the cultural power of this conflation between school literacy and "being smart" and turn our attention back to Bensonhurst and Sciorra's and Laurino's essays on this community.

Students thus compare the relation of Italian Americans and race, color, and complexion in Sciorra's and Laurino's representations, in the media reports on Hawkins, and in the arguments presented by Guglielmo, Merithew, and DeSalvo. They note the similarities in the way whiteness is used by the Italian Americans in the 1895 Illinois race riot and by the Bensonhurst residents that Sciorra describes. According to my students, both groups are racist. Rather than suffer racial discrimination, these groups of Italian Americans assert their whiteness as a way of constructing themselves as superior to African Americans. I point out that understanding why this happens is the impetus for these essays on Bensonhurst. Sciorra states, for example, that he wanted to "understand why Italians in New York had come to base their identity in direct opposition to people of color" and to find out "if it was necessary to physically and spiritually abandon one's community in search of a more complete and holistic self" (201, 202). Similarly, Laurino claims that she kept returning to and trying to write about Bensonhurst to understand the Italian American identity from which "geography and education" had made her "different" (154).

Like Torgovnick's literacy narrative, then, these essays aim at exploring how and why Bensonhurst has come to identify itself so forcefully as white and to understand how these writers are, or can be, connected to this community and the sense of being Italian American that it represents when their educations—and politics—have carried them far away and made them other. As my students note almost immediately, Torgovnick, Sciorra, and Laurino do not assert their whiteness as aggressively and are embarrassed and ashamed of the racism expressed by many of the Bensonhurst residents. As one student wrote in a reading-response journal entry, these writers don't need to insist on their whiteness because "they're educated and have money. That does it for them."

Comments like these lead us back to the questions we started with: "Is it necessary to abandon one's home community as one becomes literate?" "Does this question have to be about race?" They also bring us back to the link the students started to make earlier among school literacy, race, and economic class, but as a result of having historicized Torgovnick's narrative and examined the processes of identity construction, racial othering, and the role language and literacy plays in these processes, the students see the articulation between literacy, whiteness, and middle-class status not as natural and inevitable but as a function of the interplay between racial politics, language, privilege, and power. They have a greater understanding of how the separate, racialized worlds that structure so many literacy narratives have been created, maintained, and sometimes altered. They come to realize that, as Edvige Giunta puts it, "race . . . is a slippery concept, part of a story made up by those in charge of language" ("Figuring" 228). Such a realization, I hope, encourages them to be more critical and more in charge of their language use and, in turn, their identities, which, in the end, is a primary purpose of any composition course.

Roseanne Giannini Quinn

Teaching Italian American Literature through Popular Culture and Intersectionality in an Ethnic Studies Class

Students who self-select ethnic studies courses are usually intellectually and personally oriented to embrace marginalized literatures. However, while these students may welcome the study of Italian American authors and issues, they often declare that they have never knowingly read an Italian American book (although some have asked if Dan Brown's *The Da Vinci Code* qualifies). Precisely because of such limited exposure to an Italian American literary tradition, I have begun to introduce the study of Italian American writing in my ethnic literature survey course from the more easily accessible and student-directed entry point of Italian American representations in popular culture. When teaching two very different works of the Italian American canon, the classic *Christ in Concrete*, by Pietro di Donato, and *AVA*, by Carole Maso, I have seen students make connections between art and life that are sparked by their investment in moving from their cultural turf to the complexity of Italian American literature.

In general, students know much more than I do about what representations are currently being seen, heard, downloaded, and consumed in popular culture. In the context of studying ethnic literature, having students bring in examples from popular culture that they perceive are useful for analyzing race, ethnicity, sexuality, and gender can create a shared discourse of intersectionality that we can then compare with the more complex and often contradictory issues raised by literary texts. In the age of post-*Sopranos* influences, students frequently frame their articulation of Italian American culture in direct correlation to what they have seen or know of the HBO television series. When I asked students in my course on American ethnic literature to write words that describe "Italian American," almost all responded with "Tony Soprano." Repeatedly, they seemed only able to access stereotypical terms about Italian Americans such as "loud," "passionate," "big families," "criminals," "greasy," "wop," "mobsters"; one student wrote that the word most associated with Italians was "fuck (the word they use so much)." After collating their anonymous responses and typing them up for the class to review, I saw clearly that students felt comfortable using descriptive words that ranged from simple stereotype to ethnic slur—perhaps, not surprisingly, because they often interpreted these designations as positive.

Since almost every student identified criminality as quintessentially Italian American and not necessarily *la cosa mala* ("a bad thing"), I asked them to write a response to a follow-up question: Were there places where the Italian American Mob paradigms appeared in popular cultural forms other than on television? They directed me to consider rap and hip-hop music and video, especially the Tupac Shakur song "Me and My Girlfriend," where the sound of old-school (i.e., Italian American) machine-gun fire can be heard over the chorus. To many, Shakur's self-identified thug persona (displayed in a tattoo across his body) as well as his music actually pays homage to Italian American culture. When pressed by me to explain how they know this reference, many male students seemed well aware that Brian De Palma's film *Scarface*, in which Al Pacino stars as the Cuban mobster Antonio Montana, is a remake of an earlier film with the Al Capone–like gangster Tony Camonte. They felt that such knowledge of a film's history gave them an understanding of Italian Americans in context—even if they could not identify the year (1932) or director (Howard Hawks) of the film. A 2003 DVD release of the De Palma film includes a short documentary produced by Def Jam entitled *The Origin of Gangsta*, in which contemporary rap and hip-hop artists describe their devotion to both films. In the same exercise, students said that they wanted to watch and analyze more current representations, so we made a list of possible selections, and they chose to view 50 Cent's music video for his song "Wanksta," in which the image of the urban don (as 50 Cent looks directly into the camera and proudly announces "Me, I'm the Gang-sta") to many students seems cross-culturally empowering: he has money, cars, women, influence.

These images directed us toward a challenging set of questions that I had students discuss in small groups before moving to *Christ in Concrete*: What constitutes masculinity for Italian American men? for men of color? for Anglo men? Why do images of violence persist as a desired metaphor for masculinity in popular culture, and what negative effect can this association have on American men? How is all consumer culture coded by race and gender? Is it possible to undo our association between crime and masculinity? Starting with representations of Italian Americans in popular culture, students were able to identify prevailing images of manhood and violence that crossed Italian ethnicity into African American and Latino spheres.

After this discussion, we moved to *Christ in Concrete*. Di Donato's poetic immigration novel follows Paul in his effort to work, provide for his family, and retain his sense of manhood under the harsh, discriminatory conditions of the construction industry in New York. Students had never heard of this book, but many of them had come from families in which fathers and other male relatives earned their living doing manual labor in construction and field work. Because we had already spent class time analyzing popular cultural imperatives of Italian American manhood, students brought a more sophisticated theoretical, indeed contemporary, approach to analyzing an actual old-school text. They seemed prepared to investigate what is Italian American about a book without a gangster. And perhaps, too, many students reappraised the vulnerability of the men in the book who literally sacrificed their lives, some buried in concrete, as reconfigured manhood. An Italian American protaganist who struggles in poverty and mourns over his dying mother thus becomes a counternarrative to the masculinity that students had most likely expected or previously valued.

Toward the end of the course, when we were about to read Maso's postmodern novel *AVA*, I decided to begin with a discussion of Madonna as arguably the most pervasive popular-culture example of Italian American womanhood. Before I could show my fraying VHS film clips from the rockumentary *Truth or Dare*, a female Italian American student, who had coincidentally the night before attended Madonna's Confessions tour concert, interrupted and told the class all about how Madonna hung herself from a disco cross while singing about the need for worldwide AIDS funding and research. Another student actually asked her, "What's with Italians and this Christ stuff?" What followed was a student discussion about the beginning of our course and how di Donato's book, depicting life struggle and spiritual sacrifice, was still all too alive and well; they found Madonna's critique of greedy politicians' disregard for AIDS to be uncannily similar to di Donato's criticism of how the working class was treated—through the Christ metaphor. To my surprise, many students supported the original student when she expressed her admiration for Madonna as a woman who did what she wanted even though she was Italian American.

I asked students to identify a contemporary, younger entertainer who could be compared with Madonna. Many students, Italian American or not, chose Gwen Stefani, whom they saw as a powerful and sexually independent businesswoman, much like Madonna. The students suggested that we watch the music video "It's My Life," with Stefani and her group, No Doubt. In the video, a remake of the 1980s song originally performed by the band Talk Talk, Stefani plays a gangster-era moll who systematically murders various men (played by her bandmates). After we viewed the video, I asked students to get together in groups and discuss the representations of Italian American womanhood in the video. One group stated confidently, "Gwen is taking the gangsters' power away, taking it for herself, and for all Italian American women." As soon as the seemingly tired gangster motif reappeared, these students applied a feminist analysis to it; in a context where organized crime still has so much cultural currency, Stefani's taking the reins is seen as liberating. Since the metaphor of the Mob still resonates, being a female don certainly supplants being the exploited moll. Another group made the interesting observation, "She looks like Madonna and is sampling her image to gain power," a concept that they would go on to apply to our understanding of Maso's book.

Maso's tour-de-force text *AVA* is a difficult book to teach because of its form. The poetic novel tells the story of the last day of Ava Klein's life. Maso incorporates popular references of the time of the book's writing through newspaper headlines, references to contemporary artists, statistics about AIDS, classical music titles, and other examples. She also included quotations from women authors and feminist theorists, from Emily Dickinson to Virginia Woolf to Hélène Cixous. When I had previously attempted to teach the book in other courses, I had only discussed the feminist theory as a postmodern backdrop to the book and had virtually ignored the power of popular culture for Ava in her last day. My students suggested that Maso was sampling just as musicians do. The group who understood how Gwen Stefani was using Madonna's image to establish her narrative authority brought us a similar approach to Maso. They said that she was sampling from Woolf, Cixous, and Dickinson to establish her feminist authority and that, as Maso says over and over again, Ava's story is, after all, a "song cycle." When we read an excerpt from Maso's *The Bay of Angels*—"And the angels say like your mother did once when you brought home triple stars, despite the force of the closed book, despite the persistence of x—you can fly"—students said that they understood Italian American literature to be about both the struggle to assert fuller identities and what it has meant to be an Italian American woman or man historically, because representations in the popular imagination are still so limiting ("From *The Bay*" 337).

The value of approaching Italian American literature from a student-directed pedagogy does not just benefit Italian-descended students. It also has deep resonances for African American, Latino and Latina, Asian or Pacific Islander, and mixed-race students who come to ethnic studies courses eager to find intersecting cultural relations both with neighboring communities and with differing and overlapping forms of artistic expression and political action. It may also be equally significant for Anglo students who do not identify themselves as raced or ethnic subjects, because they too listen to this music, watch these films, absorb and begin to counter these stereotypes. Together, I believe that my students and I can work to create a classroom environment where it is possible not only to contemplate the representations confronting us of what it means to be Italian American but also to realize that we can develop the power and the knowledge to analyze, resist, and understand the implications of such representations.

Clarissa Clò

"How Is Sicily Like Jamaica?": Gendered Multiethnic Identities and Cross-Cultural Encounters

"How Is Sicily Like Jamaica?" a poem by the New York–based Italian American author Rosette Capotorto, invites us to consider the links between the two islands—washed by different seas in two different continents—and the experiences of their people. This question forces the reader to explore connections that may not be immediately detectable, and it is the kind of question that I want to address and unpack with students in my class. I am an assistant professor of Italian—with interdisciplinary training in cultural studies, women's studies, and Third World literature—working in the Department of European Studies at San Diego State University. By "European" we mean a cultural and political entity, comprehensive of colonial legacies and postcolonial accountabilities, that has shaped and been shaped by histories and identities far beyond the territorial boundaries of the geographic construct called Europe. This essay reflects on how I plan to use some works by Italian American women writers in a European studies course I am designing on Europe and its others, including "Italy's many diasporas" (Gabaccia 176).

The texts in question are Susanne Antonetta's *Body Toxic: An Environmental Memoir*, Pamela E. Barnett's "Other People's Food"—included in Louise DeSalvo and Edvige Giunta's *The Milk of Almonds*—and some poems by Capotorto. My goal is to show how these texts insert themselves in a larger transnational framework, primarily Atlantic and Mediterranean, that debunks the notion of homogeneous and separate nations, communities, and movements, including feminism, and insists on the interconnectedness, interdependence, and inequalities among and between the local and the global, the personal and the political, the First World and other worlds, us and them (Alexander and Mohanty xix; Mohanty 13; Grewal and Kaplan; Roach 4). By emphasizing the interrelationship in the lives of different women, I do not mean to suggest that the experience of women in the Third World and of women of color in the West is the same as that of white women, nor do I intend to appropriate Third World and postcolonial feminist critique for liberal Western feminist causes or agendas. Rather, my comments propose to take their criticism seriously and apply it to the study of Italian American women's literature, which by virtue of its ambiguous ethnic status poses interesting and productive challenges to these theories. In this respect, two fundamental questions that I will encourage students to address during my course are, What is the significance of the multiethnic cross-cultural encounters figured in these women's texts? How do these marginal stories contribute to understanding and shaping the core of United States, European, and world history?

Because my students are mostly undergraduates, I know that these questions can be overwhelming and might only become meaningful if I lay out a critical context that clarifies how literature and culture work and why they matter in societies. Initial class discussion will need to explore how culture, including literature, is a terrain of both struggle and pacification in which we all intervene, as individuals, families, communities, and nations (Anderson 5–7; Eley and Suny; L. Lowe 1–36; R. Williams, *Marxism* 11–20, 45–54). In particular, I hope to enable students to explore how these overlapping, often contradictory, multiple narratives that "interpellate" us all are encoded in Antonetta's, Barnett's, and Capotorto's works (Althusser 174). From here, it is my hope that my students may be able to recognize in their lived experiences many of the same sites of cultural struggle and contradiction that these writers reveal.

One of the most striking features of the literature of these particular Italian American authors is their emphasis on the costs that the ideology of the American dream has had on their families and on them as women. I want students to realize how, far from being celebrated, the narrative of immigration and assimilation is demystified and deconstructed by these authors. They should understand why these writers are often critical of the institution of the family as the site where individual histories get rewritten by the older members: through exclusions and inventions, younger generations are required to alter their lives to match the dominant American narrative of struggle and success, a narrative that requires the adherence to middle-class, white, patriarchal, and heteronormative values predicated on "hard work" and "self-denial" (Antonetta 225). Ideally students will become aware that while these dominant narratives may legitimize and authorize certain family stories and memories and validate the ideology of national belonging, they do so at great costs to ethnic communities and especially to women (Guglielmo, "White Lies" 8; Giunta, *Writing* 15–33). I also want us to explore some of the specific literary strategies these authors use in attempting to make an intervention into a larger cultural context: why is a story told in a particular way? How does it rhetorically manipulate us into identifying or not identifying with certain characters and for what purpose?

Body Toxic exposes the artifice and pain involved in Antonetta's multiracial—Italian, English, and Barbadian—family's construction of a story that relies on "elaborate silences, mantras of unspeech" to fit the American narrative of assimilation (8). The narrator's body is represented as an allegory of the failure of the American dream that could not be realized in the cold-war polluted New Jersey environment in which she grew up. But her and her family's stories are by no means confined to the Garden State or even to the United States. From one perspective, Antonetta's disease-ravaged body is the result of American internal and external militaristic culture and parallels the damages inflicted on the local landscape and its community. Moreover, it simultaneously encodes the contradictory histories of colonialism and indentureship in the Caribbean part of her British heritage and of migration and poverty on her Italian side.

It is crucial that students see the connections the author draws between her personal life story—"the story of a body" (186)—and the larger national and transnational histories that also shape it. I plan to require as one of the first written assignments a critical essay about the argument made by the author in a text. In this course, students will need to be able to analyze how Antonetta positions her and her family's experiences at the intersection of multiple histories. Further, they must understand why she can claim that "when I say 'myself' I lie by simplification" (227). To help students read the text simultaneously from these multiple perspectives, I realize that I will need to spend a significant amount of time in class discussing the text with my students and conducting close readings of relevant passages.

For instance, the first chapter of Antonetta's memoir, "First Words" (which puns with "First Worlds"), encapsulates all the entangled issues surrounding the political implications of her personal life, issues that the author obsessively returns to throughout the rest of the book: the complex Italian and Barbadian family histories; her coming of age as a woman in a polluted landscape; the relevance of writing and its subsequent suppression; the role, intrusion, and abuse of scientific and other public authorities on misinformed and powerless communities. I will ask students to draw a list of themes and topics covered in this chapter, and collectively we will unpack the chapter and make a chart of all of them. I imagine that such themes and topics will be disparate, some even apparently unrelated non sequiturs, because of how Antonetta presents them to the reader. Yet, it is precisely their apparent scatteredness, as messy as Antonetta's life and the world we live in, that will propel us into the rest of the book and guide class reading and discussion. We will add to the chart at every class meeting. Perhaps the most powerful and revealing image of the chapter, and one I am confident students will notice because of its concreteness, is that of Kotex sanitary napkins. They are used to recall the day of young Antonetta's much awaited first period, which, far from granting independence and womanhood, marks the beginning of the control imposed on women's sexuality by a patriarchal society ("my life ordered by the demand of the Kotex" 22). The same image is paralleled in the following page by her later discovery that Kotex napkins were also paradoxically used in a local nuclear power reactor to contain radioactive spillage ("what keeps a nuclear plant running is lots of Kotex" [24]). Through such chilling and sarcastic statements, Antonetta not only brings together the personal and the political but also shows the power of language and storytelling to expose and alter an oppressive reality.

While it is Antonetta's physical body that cannot reconcile her family's abridged narratives, the author suggests that, in remembering and in writing, she possesses a strategic tool to subvert and potentially reverse erasures: "I was given silence" (44), yet "out of an utter silence anything can come" (50). Her memoir is the counternarrative to the silence and unreliable history passed down to her from her family, a history that erases the family's racial identity. Instead of following the typical rags-to-riches narrative she has inherited from her family, she begins her story over again in each chapter, repeating information already given in a previous one or inserting new information without introduction, making it difficult for the reader to follow the connections or the intended gaps between parts of the story. This strategy may initially baffle students, who in general tend to be content- and plot-oriented and often disregard the significance of form. So I plan to spend some time unpacking how this story is told. Antonetta's memoir takes unexpected turns and repetitions while dropping clues on how to interpret its purposeful fragmentation. The process of recording her life story exposes how stories, personal and collective, are actually created: rather than direct, linear accounts of what "really" happened, stories, histories, and memories are always constructed through selective processes of inclusion and exclusion.

To help students experience the selectivity of narrative and thus to understand Antonetta's points about the significance of what is included and what is excluded from a story, I will require students to write an auto-biographical essay on a particular event or set of events in their life. Such writing will require them to reflect on why Antonetta states that "memory is a form of lying. Autobiography is a literary form devoted to the ceremonial lie" (185). I hope students will realize that the way we tell a story impacts our sense of self as well as our sense of the larger culture. The way we talk about ourselves in large part determines whether we will capitulate to or resist our culture's hegemonic narratives. I also want students to be able to find the intersections of multiple local and global forces in their histories and to see how their ways of writing make them both the products and the producers of these forces.

Whereas the body as the physical manifestation of one's life history is central in Antonetta's narrative—"my family legacy happened in the body" (68)—Barnett's memoir "Other People's Food" contests the primacy of blood in determining one's affiliations, calling such a belief "culture's most dangerous fiction" (142). When read contiguously, these two texts can bring the discussion of multiethnic intersections and encounters to a new interpretative level. They juxtapose the inescapability of one's family history and the choices of identification we can make along the way. If Antonetta uses the body strategically to reclaim a repressed history, a tangible ancestral trace that cannot be undone, Barnett exposes the dangers in relying too heavily on narratives of kin and consanguinity in the construction of identity, at the expenses of other forms of identification based on commonalities of interests, behaviors, and practices. The different ways of understanding the self and of forming community that these texts expose are well worth unpacking and debating in class discussions, perhaps by providing examples of coalition building on campus or in the local community.

Barnett recounts her experience of bonding with a Palestinian family in a refugee camp near Jerusalem. While she is welcomed among them as kin because she is Italian American and therefore shares "Mediterranean blood" with them ("[t]he Italians and the Greeks are the Arabs of Europe" [135]), she hides from them that she is Jewish too and that her features and habits are more heavily influenced by this side of the family. The paradox in the story is that her Italian grandmother spent her life trying to emulate the WASP lifestyle and to erase her Italian identity through the fabrication of "a contained genealogy" that "would deny any capillary that linked her to these dark people living among olive trees" (140, 142). Instead, Barnett remarks that "If I learnt how to be 'Mediterranean,' I learnt it from Ashkenazi Jews" (137). Barnett resorts to "passing" so that she will not upset her hosts who so willingly share their food and hospitality with her. She feels "sure that this intimacy could not withstand a confession" (142), and she is well aware of the historical reasons why the Palestinian family might be less welcoming were they to know her full identity. Yet, at the same time, she insists on the importance of multiple identifications over "policed identities" and on the necessity to "collapse boundaries" to appreciate the "tapestry of connection" that links people to one another for reasons far beyond ethnic purity (142, 142, 135).

The most radical potential of the course lies in the opportunity to debate with students how these texts may encourage them to interrogate their personal localized experience and the web of interrelated connections and communities that contribute to form their identities through affiliations or antagonisms. The solidarity with other communities around the globe affirmed in these authors' works provides viable alternative models to the myth of uniform families contained in homogeneous nations.

Capotorto's poem "How Is Sicily Like Jamaica?" imagines alternatives that stress the affinities among oppressed groups that share, according to the poet, comparable "radical politics," "history of anarchism," and "walking walking/everywhere." In "Some White Guy Guru Type Talks On and On" Capotorto reinvents her "imagined" ancestral lineage:

the ancestors live if their name is called
bob Marley bob Marley
eternally beautiful bob Marley

does my Sicilian grandmother
walk the same heaven as he

Through this figuration, Capotorto comments on how contemporary multiethnic politics could be changed:

if we begin to believe that
all the ancestors
of all the people
live in the same afterlife
surely that is a place
where borders are
no longer
necessary
where communication is not
hindered by barriers of language
and other stonewalls

I cannot imagine a rich heaven
and a poor heaven
a black heaven
and a white heaven
a japanese heaven and
a chinese heaven
a new york and new jersey heaven
a california and a mexican heaven
what do you do if you are a halfie?
mulatto heaven

it simply makes no sense

The poem exposes the paradoxes inherent in most constructions of unified identities and communities. It could lead the way for a final, collaborative, ethnographic group project that would require students to explore cross-cultural encounters in a local community by collecting interviews and analyzing the rhetorical strategies used by their subjects. Archival research in the library or in nearby institutions would help students historically locate the transnational processes (i.e., colonial and migrant trajectories) that along with local forces are shaping the life of that community.

Through these texts and this pedagogical approach, I hope to counteract the impulse to read literature as the representation of individualist and insular personal concerns and to encourage students to understand literature as globally interconnected to other communities' histories. As Capotorto writes in her poem "In the Real World," "*the world must be made round.*" Written in the aftermath of 9/11, it challenges us to build "round" alliances based on common histories and political affinities.

Teresa Fiore

Class and Ethnicity:
An Interdisciplinary Approach
to Teaching *Christ in Concrete*

> *English, German, or Africano—who pays and pays for the music?—*
> *The working asses who are we . . . !*
>
> —Pietro di Donato, *Christ in Concrete*

I first taught the course Italian American Culture at California State University, Long Beach, as part of the Italian studies program, housed along with the Graziadio Center for Italian Studies in the Department of Romance, German, Russian Languages and Literatures. The university and the local Italian American community collaborate to help the program and the center support Italian American studies through course offerings and public events.

This upper-division class was attended by students of mixed ethnic backgrounds (from such places as Honduras, Armenia, and Iran): only one-fifth of it claimed Italian origins. They were all majors or minors in Italian and had taken comparative and ethnic literature classes, so they were already conversant in literature and film. Yet on the first day of class, none of them could name a single Italian American writer, whereas they were all familiar with several films by Italian American directors, such as *The Godfather* or *Goodfellas*.

In designing the syllabus, I started from the premise that a course on ethnicity is embedded in a class-based discourse. Therefore, while organizing the weekly topics on the Italian American experience, ranging from food and family to religion and sexuality, I included several materials that would elicit a discussion of class-related matters. The examination of the working-class history of the Italian American community allows the students to reposition this ethnic group in a set of social dynamics (labor protests, civil rights' defense) that is not fully apparent when they simply consider the current integrated status of this community in the United States. In addition, an approach that is sensitive to working-class culture triggers a reevaluation of Italian American history away from the stereotypical crime-related figurations and opens a space for interethnic readings of such history. In this sense, many of the questions raised in this class can be addressed in a working-class studies course by using Italian American texts like the ones I discuss here.

I adopted three main textbooks: *La Storia*, Jerre Mangione and Ben Morreale's overview of the Italian American experience; *The Italian American Reader*, edited by Bill Tonelli, an anthology of Italian American literature; and *The Milk of Almonds*, a collection of women's writings, edited by Louise DeSalvo and Edvige Giunta. The reading list also comprised several shorts and feature films as well as the novels *Ask the Dust*, by John Fante, and *Christ in Concrete*, by Pietro di Donato. In this essay, I map out an interdisciplinary approach to teaching the latter novel, a powerful narrative that documents the struggles and losses experienced by immigrants on American construction sites. My approach included comparative readings of filmic and visual texts inspired by the novel. In this specific course section, students watched Edward Dmytryk's 1949 film *Christ in Concrete*, a long-neglected rendition of di Donato's novel, and analyzed the novel in connection with paintings by two artists who infused their works with a social ethos, albeit through different styles. The Works Progress Administration artist Osvaldo Louis Guglielmi (1906–58) responded to the socioeconomic pressure of his time through a marked symbolism intended to render the profound suffering of the working class, while the trade unionist turned painter Ralph Fasanella (1914–97) expressed an explicit social denunciation in his primitive art.

Rediscovered by working-class studies scholars such as Michael Denning, di Donato's autobiographical novel became a book of central importance for Italian American studies in the early 1990s. Set during the Depression era, the novel recounts the experience of a group of Italian immigrant bricklayers in New York City, toiling to survive in a new hostile environment at odds with their traditional Catholic values. The plot revolves around the tragic death of Geremio, which causes a clash between his wife's traditional sense of fatalism and his son Paul's budding need for a politically conscious reaction to injustice that develops along interethnic lines. I gave the students specific suggestions to critically analyze two basic dynamics at work in the book: religion as a source of both cohesion and paralysis and class consciousness as a cause for both collective progress and community disintegration. I also invited students to pay special attention to the novel's innovative literary quality: its experimental language brings together working-class migrants' lingo and echoes from Italian dialects and weaves with ease several stylistic registers.

We centered our discussion of the book on religion and class as key focuses for the understanding of Italian American history at large. The sharp tensions elaborated in the novel were partially lost on the students whose affiliation to religious and class groups was tenuous: some reported that they could not identify with the dramatic tone of the religious crises described by the author since, in their secular world, disassociation from a religious tradition was not perceived as a rupture. Food and gender as other pivotal issues in di Donato's work proved to be more immediately accessible for students to explore forms of belonging. Yet once we inserted *Christ in Concrete* in the historical context of the 1930s, the clash between a religious creed informed by passive acceptance and the pressure to reject social exploitation on the basis of class consciousness became meaningful.

Although the avant-garde character of the novelist's language and narrative structure made the reading fairly challenging, students recognized an unexpected modernity in the text. Prompted to reflect on the inextricable relations between form and content, they realized that the aesthetic solutions of the novel (such as stream-of-consciousness writing and blocks of text in capital letters set off from the main text) signaled the author's purposeful representation of the process of writing as building and consequently of the function of literature as a tool to document and denounce social evils in a creative manner. At the end of the course section devoted to *Christ in Concrete*, students reported that the meta-literary level of the text was one of the most fascinating aspects of the novel. In general, they found the novel appealing for its theme and style and, in the final evaluations, most of them stated that it was their favorite book in the course.

We further discussed issues of ethnic and class belonging after the screening of Dmytryk's filmic adaptation of the novel. This black-and-white film shifts the focus away from the religious theme and the mother-son relation and embraces an artificial love plot that to a degree erases the book's complexity. In the film, Geremio's struggle as a disenfranchised worker is burdened by his attraction to a woman whose lifestyle erroneously creates in him the illusion of escaping the demands of the socioeconomic system. Because of the director's affiliation with the Communist Party, the film was censored, although its analysis of class dynamics is far from revolutionary and its overall message does not come across as propagandistic. While Geremio's tragic ending in the film is read in moral terms rather than through class-conscious filters, the representation of the workers' lives on the construction site mirrors the novel's experimental narrative: Dmytryk adopted a fast editing technique in his collages of close-up shots of raw materials, machinery, and dynamic bodies. Both the writer's and the director's choice of avant-garde languages offers readers and viewers the opportunity to consider, on the one hand, the risks of aestheticizing work, even of presenting technology and labor as freeing forces, and, on the other, the liberating opportunity to use art to condemn progress as inhuman. Such considerations turned out to be rather difficult to tackle. To discuss the political relevance of visual and literary tools in a more productive way in the future, I intend to invite students to search for artwork (visual, theatrical, and filmic) produced around issues of immigration in Los Angeles and evaluate their effect, as part of a group assignment. Once they draw connections with local artists and identify their modes of expression ranging from realism to postmodern irony, students will be better equipped to assess the relevance of the artists' ability to produce a strong reaction to such social problems as discrimination against and exploitation of immigrants. Students will therefore be more comfortable in evaluating the aesthetic modes of the film and the novel *Christ in Concrete*, two texts that provide a cultural response to the Depression era's social conflicts, while eliciting reflections on similar subjects in contemporary society.

In the second part of the cross-disciplinary exercise, students compared literature and paintings about workers' oppression. They started by analyzing a series of works by Guglielmi (see J. Baker): *Festa* (1940), *Job's Tears* (1947), and *The Tenements* (1939) are surrealist and expressionist translations of di Donato's experimental language onto the canvas and, like his novel, a denunciation of the misery of the working class. The paintings bear the same titles of the novel's chapters and convey as effectively the sense of loss and deprivation experienced by poor workers during the Depression, even at moments of celebration. Students also looked at a later response to *Christ in Concrete*, Fasanella's *The Iceman Crucified* autobiographical series (see D'Ambrosio), which includes large canvasses produced between 1948 and 1956. The direct analogy between toiling at work and dying on a cross signals a denunciation of religious fatalism and functions as a call to a class-based action that embraces the recuperation of ethnic values. Depicting crowded scenes in a dense primitivist style, the series is a tribute to Fasanella's family and neighbors, to the workers of the world, and to authors such as di Donato who verbalized the workers' plea through a strong symbolism. Students found it interesting to explore the paintings' composition, their chromatic qualities, and the relation between persons and living or working spaces depicted in them. They were particularly impressed by the influence that the novel *Christ in Concrete* has had on filmmakers and painters over a long period of time—a sign, they concluded, of the enduring force of di Donato's book in the artistic and social arena.

On the basis of students' responses to these works, I believe that moving from one medium to another in the same framework represented a productive pedagogical practice to break traditional separations among disciplines and to understand the social implications of the arts at large in their genesis and fruition. In their effective engagement with *Christ in Concrete*, these works open new ways to read the fervor and ethos of the 1930s and 1940s through an ethnic filter. Such works also allow for a reevaluation of di Donato as the model for a rhetoric of class struggle that, as Denning suggests in *The Cultural Front: The Laboring of American Culture in the Twentieth Century*, provided a vision of change to the oppressed in its reinterpretation of progress and capitalism in the United States regarding ethnic formations (249). These critical concepts made students aware of the constant overlapping of issues of class and ethnicity or race and of the possibilities that this double take opens up in terms of crosscultural encounters and alliances. As Janet Zandy has pointed out in her introduction to *Calling Home*, a seminal text on these topics, "as a body of work, working-class literature is about possibility, not despair" (11). The texts addressed in the class were therefore presented and eventually perceived not simply as the products of a self-contained ethnic group (Italian American) but as the expression of the complex intersection of ethnic conditioning, religious legacy, class belonging, and gender positioning. In this way, students systematically examined and understood the history of ethnic groups on the basis of socioeconomic relations.

Class assignments included three short papers in specific formats (magazine review, academic essay, and creative piece), written in response to readings and screenings: the genre variety was meant to highlight the differences in register, scope, and intentions of each text according to what had already surfaced through the discussion of literary, nonfictional, filmic, and artistic materials during the semester. At the end of the course, students prepared a final project based on an oral history that encouraged them to collect information about their families' or acquaintances' Italian American history and compare it with the texts included in the syllabus. Before the conclusion of the course, students took part in an out-of-class activity designed to give them direct exposure to the questions at hand: How do artists shape their immigrant experience? Who is the subject of their works' fruition? In what forms do their works leave a mark over time? To tackle such questions with immediacy, students were asked to participate in a guided tour of Simon Rodia's Watts Towers, located in South Los Angeles, a unique example of outsiders' arts in which the Italian migratory experience translates into a creative project charged with intense political meaning (see Goldstone and Goldstone). Indeed, this visit allowed them to set up parallels with the artwork on toiling manual workers discussed in class and to contextualize it in a real contemporary environment. In this depressed neighborhood, some of the main issues we addressed in the course acquired concrete tangibility: class belonging, art for the community, access to social opportunities, and, last but not least, "edification" as a synonym for the manual work of building as well as for the act of creatively constructing an identity and a sense of being.

In general, students appreciated this class for the opportunity they were given to explore their backgrounds as Italian Americans or the history of Italian Americans at large in a context that overcame the simplistic dichotomy between condemnation of Italians as criminals and blanket defense of them through antidefamation campaigns. Students found the class demanding because of its interdisciplinary approach and the anthologies challenging because they were not designed as textbooks with biographical introductions and textual analysis. Yet they were all pleased to explore an often neglected field of study, and some of them continue to attend the center's Italian American studies programs.

In the future, I will consider adopting *Voices of Italian America: A History of Early Italian American Literature with a Critical Anthology*, edited by Martino Marazzi, for its combination of primary and secondary sources and its inclusion of less commonly taught authors. In addition, I am thinking about devoting more time to an in-depth exploration of

John Fante's representation of working-class issues in *Ask the Dust*, a novel in which class-based identifications are recognized and rejected with subtle irony and cross-cultural empathy invests individuals rather than the collective ethos. Other texts that might be relevant for a working-class studies course incorporating Italian American authors are *The Letters of Sacco and Vanzetti*, written in the 1920s, and Montaldo's film *Sacco and Vanzetti*, both viable teaching tools for analyzing forms of social struggle and marginalization, this time in the context of a case that received and continues to receive much international attention.

Regardless of the texts used in class, what remains central to all approaches to arts and literature on the working-class experience in its intersection with ethnicity, gender, and religion is their mythopoeic and social functions. In a metaliterary passage of *Christ in Concrete*, di Donato expressed this fear:

> No poet would be there to intone meter of soul's sentence to stone, no artist upon scaffold to paint the vinegary sweat of Christians in correspondence with the red brick and gray mortar, no composer attuned to the screaming movement of Job and voiceless cry in overalls. (143)

Yet his novel as well as Dmytryk's film and Guglielmi's and Fasanella's paintings are tangible accounts of the important experience and contribution of immigrant workers, otherwise often unnamed in official historical records. In this sense, the course, when taught in a program of Italian studies, can also incorporate references to writings by current immigrants based in Italy (see Parati, *Mediterranean Crossroads*) on the premise that a country of emigration turned into one of immigration in the past few decades is a case in point to understand the international, transhistorical, and multiethnic frame of labor issues.

Elvira G. Di Fabio and Carol Bonomo Albright

The Immigrant Question in the Italian American Experience Course

The Harvard Extension School course Italian-American History, Literature and Issues of Identity is offered under humanities and meets two evening hours every week for fifteen weeks. (Before 2002, the ethnic studies offerings at Harvard College and at the Harvard Extension School focused mainly on the African American, Asian American, and Latino or Latina experiences.) The course covers modules on Italian history prior to the mass migration; Italian immigration to the United States; representations of Italian Americans in art, theater, film, the popular media, and literature; and the effects of religion on the community. The enrollment ranges from nine to twenty students, mostly adult learners; some are bachelor or master's of arts candidates in the humanities, but most are there for general continuing education. The class has never been ethnically homogeneous: over the years, Jewish, Armenian, Cajun, French Canadian, Polish, Vietnamese, Scottish, English, and Italian American students have enrolled in the course.

The Italian American Immigrant Experience:
Interdisciplinary Focus on Workers' Issues
Using History, Film, and Art

In line with the Italian American immigrant experience of the early twentieth century, the course content revolves around workers' issues. We begin our course with historical texts, films, and art works that are accessible and provide a quick immersion into key issues of immigrant experience that we then explore in greater depth throughout the term. We start with a lecture on Giuseppe Mazzini—his political philosophy and his ideas about health care and other social measures as well as the actions he took to implement them, such as founding a workers' night school while he was in exile in England (D. M. Smith). We continue with a discussion of the failure of the Risorgimento in the south of Italy. Finally, we show Mario Monicelli's Oscar-winning film, *I compagni* (*The Organizer*), which examines Italian workers' rights and organization in a recently industrialized city in the north in the 1890s. We assign Pascal D'Angelo's *Son of Italy* because it gives a firsthand testimony to the injustices suffered by the disenfranchised, especially in his description of the *mezzadria* sharecropping system that led to the "great hemorrhaging" of Italy. We discuss D'Angelo's indictment of the dehumanizing conditions that awaited the Italian workers in the "land of opportunity" and the role of the padrone in getting work for the migrant work gangs: students realize how, already in the early twentieth century, the political conscience sustaining the labor movement was being articulated by authors like D'Angelo.

After discussing the rural Italian colonies in America and the work that brought the immigrants to specific locales, we focus on the nineteenth-century mining strikes in the Midwest so that students can see that Italian immigrants did not settle only in the urban Northeast. We show Frank Capra's *Mr. Deeds Goes to Town*, which displays the admirable qualities of the common man. Longfellow Deeds serves as the forerunner of Capra's populist banker, much in the vein of A. P. Giannini, who founded what is today the Bank of America. We recommend that students read *Dark Tide: The Great Boston Molasses Flood of 1919*, Stephen Puleo's journalistic retelling of the tragedy that still haunts Boston's North End. Puleo's exposé on the great Boston molasses flood underscores the plight of the disenfranchised in the immigrant neighborhood. He puts the event into the larger historical context of the red scare, anarchism, and the Sacco and Vanzetti arrest. This tale provokes spirited reactions from the students who have heard references to this event from relatives.

We continue with a discussion of the central presence of the worker in the paintings of Joseph Stella and Ralph Fasanella and the photographs of Tina Modotti. Stella's early portraits of immigrant workers in the Pittsburgh coal processing plants, which are part of his *Pittsburgh Types* series (1908–09), feature Croatian, Irish, Herzegovinian, and Russian immigrants, among others. We also include Stella's *Workers at Rest*, formerly titled *Laid Off*; *In Bread Line at Wood's Run;* and *Back of a Man Working* (Haskell). Students are shocked and moved by representations of workers' tools as devices of workers' torture in Fasanella's paintings. In *Family Supper* (1974), for example, the father is depicted on the right on a cross with a crown of thorns constructed of ice tongs, and in the rear the mother is bound to a cross by spools of thread (Watson). Modotti's photography makes similar use of crucifixion imagery in *Workers* (1926–29): her workers carrying boards recall Christ's carrying his cross. Students are responsive to the range of her photographs: *Hands Holding Tools*, which depicts the dignity of workers; her well-known *Workers on Parade*, taken from above a group of Mexican workers defined by the concentric circles of their sombrero hats; and *Poverty and Elegance*, which shows a worker sitting on the edge of a sidewalk with a sign above him of a couple in evening clothing (S. Lowe).

To further develop the historical context of these pictorial representations of working people on the lowest rung of the ladder, we discuss the lynching of eleven Italian immigrants in New Orleans in 1891 (Gambino, *Vendetta*) and the trial of Nicola Sacco and Bartolomeo Vanzetti (Mangione and Morreale 130, 249–50, 294, 296–301). We also direct students to Felix Frankfurter's book about the trial and Francis Russell's analysis of the case. While many of the books we refer to are on reserve for students, students do buy and read Jerre Mangione and Ben Morreale's *La Storia: Five Centuries of the Italian American Experience.* This comprehensive and readable book establishes the basic historical context for the weekly class lectures and discussions. (An alternative to Mangione and Morreale is Choate, *Emigrant Nation.*) Carol Bonomo Albright and Elvira G. Di Fabio's research on Giuseppe Rocchietti explores the correspondences between and the melding of two cultures as well as how an immigrant becomes an American (students read extracts: 52–56, 67–70, 106–30, 141–46). Much like Puleo's text on the Boston molasses flood, Robert Orsi's *The Madonna of 115th Street*, which we introduce early in the term, rings true to those students who have attended the religious feasts that animate the North End during the summer months.

Focus on Literature: Random, Canonical, and Contemporary Reading

In the first third of the course, students read about fifty pages from one of two literary anthologies—Regina Barreca's *Don't Tell Mama!* or Bill Tonelli's *The Italian American Reader.* (An alternative to Barreca is Albright and Herman, *Wild Dreams.*) We place students in groups of three or four and ask them to discuss what they have read initially by listing the themes they discovered in their particular selections. The small-group discussions are guided by the instructors and eventually brought into a plenary discussion of commonly discussed themes. Quickly, students discover common themes such as work ethic, generational differences, passionate expressiveness, and family lexicons among the different texts they have read. This rich discussion builds in the class an incipient sense of familiarity with Italian American literature.

We then ask students to attempt to define Italian American literature, even broadly. We ask, "What qualifies as Italian American literature?" Most students argue that Italian American literature includes not simply texts written by Italian American authors but rather texts with particular inflections. Some students try to break these inflections down by time period, suggesting that in an early work such as Pietro di Donato's *Christ in Concrete* economics determines views toward education and work, most tellingly through Paul's choices. The debate between work and education is further underscored through the cultural differences between Paul and his Russian American, Jewish friend, Louis. In later works, this debate can lead to generational divergences, as seen in the relationship between Lucia and her daughter in Mario Puzo's *The Fortunate Pilgrim.* Other students look for more subtle cultural characteristics and values, such as the use of respect for elders as a deterrent to a child's self-actualization. Still others argue for a more general approach and attempt to define Italian American literature through overarching leitmotifs, including family and food (see, e.g., Gabaccia, "Italian-American Cookbooks"; Helstosky). Students are amazed that what they would have previously considered mundane occurrences—descriptions of neighborhoods, descriptions of work inside and outside the home, female chatter over food preparation, the peculiar lexicon of an immigrant grandmother—can constitute literature.

In addition to a literary anthology, students read a book from two categories of works: the canonical voices of Italian American literature (John Fante's *Wait until Spring, Bandini*; di Donato's *Christ in Concrete*; Marie Hall Ets's *Rosa: The Life of an Italian Immigrant*; Mari Tomasi's *Like Lesser Gods*; Puzo's *The Fortunate Pilgrim*) and representative texts from the last three decades (Helen Barolini's *Umbertina*; Rita Ciresi's *Sometimes I Dream in Italian*; Tina De Rosa's *Paper Fish*; Maria Laurino's *Were You Always an Italian?*; Kenny Marotta's *A Piece of Earth*). These readings serve as the basis for an oral report, small-group discussions, and a written synthesis of themes in Italian American literature. Throughout the course, we emphasize the centrality of work and workers, whether it is the consequences of Bandini's winter idleness, the death of Geremio in *Christ in Concrete*, or the work of six-year-old Rosa in the silk factory of northern Italy.

The readings develop the objective of the course: to give students a usable past by focusing on the early immigrants' work lives and their heroic endeavors to improve their lives and the lives of their children. Since the readings consider the flexibility the immigrants displayed in acculturating to new modes of work, a new language, and new living conditions, we hope the course fosters a renewed sense of identity, especially for those of our students who come from a generation of immigrants who sought to stifle their immigrant identities outside the home.

Content is continually recycled, and the course moves forward in a circular rather than a linear progression. Though the weekly classes may have a specific topic, there are always references to matters that were brought up in previous lectures. The experiences and values of the community identified in Monicelli's *I compagni* come into play later when the class discusses Capra's *Mr. Deeds*. The echoes of D'Angelo's experience are remarkable in Stella's *Pittsburgh Portraits*.

Reflection Papers

Students submit three short (450–600 word) reflection papers on what it means to be Italian American at three different points in the semester. The students incorporate references to materials they have read and the themes discussed in class. The grade for this series of assignments is cumulative.

We expect students to move away from an initial superficial, often stereo-typical, reflection on what it means to be Italian American (food, family, ethnicspeak) to a more informed and scholarly consideration that de-essentializes Italian American identity. As one young woman wrote in her final reflection, "Being Italian American is about denying stereotypes and fulfilling them, breaking away from one's culture and finding oneself in it again."

The cooperative learning that results from small-group discussions broadens perspectives, and the experience of others inevitably unveils truths about each student's life experiences. One student thought her Abruzzese grandmother's strange home remedies were shameful throwbacks to old-world superstitions; the course helped her celebrate her grandmother. She now realized that she had inherited her grandmother's special powers of observation and creativity. As another student put it, "It was only when I stopped searching for something I thought I knew . . . that I found some-thing better than what I had been looking for all along."

Peter Kvidera

Imagining the Italian: Nineteenth-Century American Literature, Italian Immigrant Writing, and the Power of Literary Representation

When discussing representations of Italian Americans in literature and film, I remind students that Americans had been thinking about Italian culture long before the great influx of immigrants from Italy in the late nineteenth century. Shortly after the American Revolution, tours to Italy gained popularity, and so many Americans went that Nathaniel Hawthorne wrote in his 1860 novel *The Marble Faun* (perhaps with tongue in cheek), "Everybody, now-a-days, has been to Rome" (70). Those who could not get their knowledge firsthand had increasing access to textual representations of Italy, including newspaper and magazine articles, paintings, photographs, travel guides, and fiction. With great enthusiasm, Americans attended Italian opera and hung Italian art on their walls. Italy, thus, settled firmly into the American imaginary; Americans saw Italy not simply as a place but as a complex aesthetic, cultural, and moral construct.

Considering why this construct may have influenced Italian American authors—and may influence our interpretations of their writing—is a starting point for my course Italy and the American Imagination: Comparing the "Italian" in American and Italian American Literature. I structure this course with two units. The first unit introduces various representations of Italy, Italians, and Italian Americans with a combination of canonical, nineteenth-century American literary texts and lesser-known Italian immigrant writing. The second unit explores later responses to these representations in Italian American novels written in the middle and late twentieth century. Although the second unit of this course covers a larger part of the term, I focus this essay on the earlier canonical and immigrant texts to demonstrate how literature can establish, fix, and challenge certain images discursively. Because students begin by focusing on these images, they are better able to understand the social and political power of later Italian American fiction, especially as writers address standard (and superficial) stereotypes of Italians that persist in American culture. Because the Italian American authors I teach—Pietro di Donato, John Fante, Raymond DeCapite, Helen Barolini, Jerre Mangione, and Tina De Rosa—all negotiate Italian American identity to move from stereotype to more complex readings of character, I use the first part of this course to uncover origins of common stereotypes and the subsequent need to interrogate them. My goal is for students to discover a longer history of the Italian in our literary imagination, as well as the structure of the Italian stereotype, which arises from oversimplifications that both romanticize and vilify the Italian character.

We begin the course by spending approximately five weeks examining nineteenth-century representations of Italy and Italians in the work of Margaret Fuller, William Dean Howells, Mark Twain, Nathaniel Hawthorne, and Henry James, all of whom visited or lived in Italy and wrote about their impressions in a variety of genres. Then to deepen our analysis of these representations—and to provide a bridge to the course's second unit—we conclude this part of the course with Italian immigrant writing published at approximately the same time. These texts, which I take from Martino Marazzi's anthology of early Italian American literature, *Voices of Italian America*, present an alternative picture of Italian identity and thereby provide an important critical apparatus for the course. When placed alongside the American canonical texts, Italian American writers such as Camillo Cianfarra demonstrate, for example, how the one-dimensional Italian of Henry James differs from the complicated and conflicted Italian of immigrant writers. Paying attention to such intertextual dialogue between canonical and immigrant writing, I find, proves instructive later in the course when we examine the Italian in the twentieth-century American imaginary.

To establish a foundation for that intertextual dialogue, I divide this first unit of the course into five sections that allow students to delineate carefully how literary representation creates, perpetuates, and interrogates stereotypes. I assign a variety of readings, and, to assist students in analyzing the literature, I provide study questions throughout. These questions inevitably shape our class discussions.

Impressions of Italy through Politics

I introduce this first part of the course by assigning selections from Joseph P. Cosco's *Imagining Italians: The Clash of Romance and Race in American Perceptions, 1880–1910*. Cosco presents an excellent history of American writing on Italy and explains the social and political events that dominated nineteenth-century Italy. With this history as a background, we turn to the writing of Margaret Fuller for the unit's first section, "Impressions of Italy through Politics." While most of her American contemporaries ignored Italy's political volatility, Fuller embraces this subject for letters that she published in the *New York Tribune* while residing in Italy. I assign several of these letters—those printed on 1 January 1848, 4 May 1848, 26 January 1849, 11 August 1849, and 13 February 1850—and ask students to write on two questions in response: What political, social, or cultural issues does Fuller emphasize? How does such emphasis affect her representations of both Italy and Italians? In class, I divide the students into groups, assign each group one letter, and have them share their responses to the questions. Most groups remark on Fuller's political sympathies: each letter, the students usually find, outlines the struggles and heroism of Italians fighting against foreign aggression. I ask them to examine how Fuller structures her letters, and students at first usually see her only rambling from point to point. Yet some gradually notice that even when Fuller opens by reflecting on the weather or a landscape, she is never long in getting to a social or political issue.

Regarding politics, one group of students offered a more nuanced reading. They observed that when Fuller reports on the battle for Italian unification, she positions her discussion within a tour of Rome. When she reflects on an assassination, for example, she ventures from church to church, and as she does so, her thoughts turn from national politics to the Papacy. The group decided that at this point her letter reads like a guidebook of sorts. I asked them to consider why she would make this narrative choice. One student thought that if travel writing was then popular (it was), it would make sense to use this form to interest readers in the significance of Roman politics. Another student noticed a similar style in a different letter: a passage that walks readers through the splendors of the piazza of Saint John Lateran and ends by declaring, "The sun was setting, the crescent moon rising, the flower of the Italian youth were marshaling in that solemn place" (426). Fuller uses the guidebook structure, he claimed, to blend the beauty of Rome with a representation of Italian independence. In other words, Fuller makes her politics palatable by merging contemporary realities with an aesthetic appreciation of ancient Rome.

Noting Fuller's reference to the Italian youth, students examining another letter said Fuller also blends people and place: the Romans are "injured," just like the city. I asked the class if they felt that Fuller sympathized completely with the Italian people. Most agreed that she did. One student, however, was not so sure of this empathy when she recalled an earlier observation by Fuller that casts doubt on Italian courage and dignity when her characters face foreign occupation: "Their hands fall slack, their eyes rove aimless, the beggars begin to swarm again, and . . . emerge daily more and more frequent from their hiding places," and the men of Rome slip back toward a natural "effeminacy" (431). This student felt that even Fuller's enthusiastic portrait of the Roman contains a veiled critique, especially when reality does not meet an idealized view of Italian heroism. The student response touched on an issue that returns in the subsequent units: representing Italians is a complicated business, especially when contemporary Italy is subsumed by a desire to recapture the Golden Age.

Italy and the Tour

The search for Italian antiquity is one point with which we begin the second part of this unit, "Italy and the Tour," which focuses on two travelogues: *Italian Journeys*, by William Dean Howells, and *The Innocents Abroad*, by Mark Twain. Our goal here is to consider how travel writing creates its own images of Italy and Italians, perhaps different from Fuller's politically focused reports. I ask students to keep track of how Howells and Twain describe the natives that they, as tourists, encounter: where the Italians appear and how they are characterized. Students often note that both authors seem less interested in people than in architecture, but in comparison to Twain's biting wit, Howells appears positive in his representation of them. One student pointed to Howells's chapter "Between Rome and Naples," in which Howells comments on the laboring class:

> They were straight and handsome girls, and moved with a stately
> grace under the baskets of earth balanced on their heads. Brave

black eyes they had such as love to look and to be looked at; they were not in the least hurried by their work, but desisted from it to gaze at the passengers whenever the train stopped. They all wore their beautiful peasant costume—the square white linen head-dress falling to the shoulders, the crimson bodice, and the red scant skirt; and how they contrived to keep themselves so clean at their work, and to look so spectacular in it all, remains one of the many Italian mysteries. (149–50)

The mysteries continue with a "beggar-boy at Isoletta" who was "perfectly beautiful and exceedingly picturesque" (150). These descriptions appear benign, but when pressed, students may discover further nuances in the characterization. Soon this class saw the oddity of using "picturesque" and "spectacular" to paint a real picture of economic deprivation. The local people become something like art objects, one student suggested. Another student noted that the tourist-writer, gazing out of the window of the train, literally looks down on the peasants and, from that distance, creates them as he wishes. I felt that observation was apt but wanted to encourage more depth of thought about the construction of the identity of the Italian other. I asked the student to consider the position of the American reader, a person likely well versed in the discourse of American capitalism. After some reflection the student said that, to such a reader, the peasant who stopped to look at every train might be seen as lazy. After further deliberation, the class concluded that Howells's description is notable because it demonstrates a culturally conditioned response to peasants as somewhat naturally indolent, as well as a desire to turn them into aesthetic objects.

Having read Twain's chapters on his Italian travels (chs. 17–31) alongside Howells, the students often make comparisons between narratives, especially representations of the people and places. Occasionally a student will correlate Howells's idealized peasants with Twain's idealized place. But as we often note, Twain's relation to tourist sites is complex. To explore this issue, I ask students to select one location and track Twain's comments: Are Twain's portrayals positive or negative or both? What has Twain learned or taken away from the experience at this place? What guide does he offer his readers for interpreting Italy and Italians? The student responses were as varied as the places Twain visited. Most commonly, students came to class with lists of negative characterizations of the chosen place: the once magnificent Venice is now "fallen a prey to poverty, neglect, and melancholy decay" (217); modern Rome is "gifted" only with sloth and superstition (267). Students are usually amused and often surprised at Twain's negativity, and when they respond this way, I refer them back to Cosco, who finds that Twain's humor undermines all efforts to know precisely how he feels about the country. I also suggest that Twain's portrayals are perhaps contradictory by design. I use his discussion of Lake Como as an example. He finds it breathtaking but point for point believes that it cannot match his beloved Lake Tahoe—at least at first comparison.

Contradictions arise when expectations and reality fail to match. The students often find this dilemma throughout Howells's narrative. To analyze how Howells registers his disappointment, I divide students into groups to interpret a passage from *Italian Journeys* that in some manner compares past and present. We examine this description of the castle of the dukes of Ferrara:

> I think that the moonlight . . . could have fallen on nothing else in all Italy so picturesque, and so full of the proper dread charm of feudal times, as this pile of gloomy and majestic strength. The daylight took nothing of this charm from it; for the castle stands isolated in the midst of the city, as its founder meant that it should, and modern civilization has not crossed the castle moat, to undignify its exterior with any visible touch of the present. (32–33)

Each group considers the tension between what Howells sees and what he would like to see. Students are quick to observe that he has little patience with modernity. Like his desire for the people, this writer hopes for the picturesque in the landscape, even if that quality means deterioration and stagnation. I also ask the students to observe the imagery in the passage. From this example, a student noticed "moonlight" and "daylight." While the latter suggests some clarity of vision, he believed that Howells associates the former with charm and some altered perspective. The charm that moonlight casts over the scene may indicate that, for Howells, the real Italy of value is the Italy of memory and imagination.

The Romance of Italy

I dwell on the power of imagination as we move into our third section, "The Romance of Italy," which explores an Italy that also resides in the imagination, but in fiction as well. Our central text is Hawthorne's *The Marble Faun*, and it is worth telling students about the novel's popularity at the turn of the twentieth century. In the introduction to a 1902 printing, Katharine Lee Bates notes that "no good American visits Rome without it" (ix); in fact, Howells pays homage to the novel several times in *Italian Journeys*. To structure our discussions of excerpts from this novel, I provide topics for students to track, such as Hawthorne's presentation of art and artifacts, the prominence of tourist locations, and the force of history and the past. Regarding art, many students find Hawthorne's Rome to be nothing but a museum—the plot moves characters from masterpiece to masterpiece. Indeed, one student mentioned that the novel operates like the travelogues we read previously (and another slyly mentioned that he found it to be a much better guide). But art remains at the center, and students never fail to remark that the lone Italian among the four main characters is himself a work of art. Not only does Donatello resemble the marble Faun of Praxiteles, but, to his American friends, he becomes that statue. As such, he connects art with history, another topic about which students have much to say. One student used the following observation by Kenyon to suggest that Donatello represents both classical art and classical Italy:

> There is something very touching and impressive in this statue of the Faun. In some long-past age, he must really have existed. . . . What a pity that he has forever vanished from the hard and dusty paths of life—unless . . . Donatello be actually he! (13)

Hawthorne's Americans, the class finally concluded, desire the Italian to be only art and myth.

A student asked if Hawthorne uses imagination to avoid contemporary social and political concerns. Several members of the class felt that he did, but others were not completely satisfied with that assessment. Like Howells's, Hawthorne's tourist-artists also find Rome polluted and corrupt. Some students focused on passages such as the following: "To Kenyon's morbid view, there appeared to be a contagious element, rising fog-like from the ancient depravity of Rome, and brooding over the dead and half-rotten city, as nowhere else on earth" (412). The bleakness here refers to the very real danger of malaria, or "Roman fever," a dread malady to those unused to the Roman climate. Some students began to wonder if the "threat" of Italy augments the romance of the place. As one noted, Hawthorne does not necessarily condemn Rome or the Roman; rather, he uses the unpleasant features of Italian life to position people and places in the aestheticized realm of legend. Hawthorne's novel invites deeper analysis of the rhetoric and language used to describe the foreign and the foreigner.

Italian Tradition and American Concerns

Prompted by Hawthorne's use of "contagious," I have students brainstorm possible implications of this term as we move to the unit's fourth part, "Italian Tradition and American Concerns," which focuses on Henry James's "Daisy Miller." For some students, contagion simply represents a physical threat; for others, it registers mystery and adventure and denotes an emotional response to the people and place. These replies signal how a literary text can take the real, cast a new light on it, and expand its meaning. In this part of the course, I hope to interrogate that power of fiction further and investigate directly a feature we have come across in other texts: the desire not only to idealize Italy but also to examine America through the Italian experience.

James represents this trend, specifically how writers use Rome as a cosmopolitan backdrop that foregrounds contemporary American socioeconomics. The first assignment I give my students is to write a short reflective piece that bridges the material they read earlier in the course and this fictional account of the American social elite residing in Rome. As a guide, I ask them to reflect on the ways James's characters interact with Roman people and places. Many students assert, at first, that the novella has little to do with Italy—they do not see any meaningful association between the tourists and their adopted home. Others remark that Romans appear but as marginal and shadowy figures, either as ornaments to the scene or as lascivious threats to innocent American girls. I also ask my students to think about the setting: though it is often eclipsed by social maneuvering, might the setting still play a significant role? I refer to a scene near the novella's conclusion, set in the ruins of the Colosseum, and have students examine the following three passages: "When on his return from the villa . . . Winterbourne approached the dusky circle of the Colosseum, it occurred to him, as a lover of the picturesque, that the interior, in the pale moonshine, would be well worth a glance" (45); "The historic atmosphere was there, certainly; but the historic atmosphere, scientifically considered, was no better than a villainous miasma" (46); and after Winterbourne "cuts" Daisy, whom he detects in the shadows with Giovanelli: " 'This is the way people catch [Roman fever]. I wonder,' he added, turning to Giovanelli, 'that you, a native Roman, should countenance such a terrible indiscretion'" (47). I have students mark words that begin to look familiar. While "picturesque" often stands out again, students usually begin to associate this designation with "historic," "miasma," and "indiscretion." One student decided that in James's hands, the charm of the setting takes on different meaning when placed in the context of American societal expectations: Rome is still defined by beauty and tradition, she argued, but the decay of the ruins can be transferred to one of this social set who refuses to follow the rules. Daisy cannot survive because she embraces the "miasma" of the real, complex Rome, to the chagrin of those following traditional social protocol. James, therefore, reveals an important correspondence: the modern American girl's demise reflects a refusal (by American tourists and authors and readers) to accept a view of Italy and the Italian that is equally modern, a view that includes the messier realities of contemporary life. Thus the American viewpoint on Italy ultimately presented in "Daisy Miller" is significantly narrower than my students might have thought on first reading it.

If we can get to this point in our discussion, students will notice how James's novella follows other writers' inclination to view Italy through an American perspective and, at the same time, America through the lens of the Italian journey. We need only glance back at Fuller, writing to an America heading toward civil war and urging her readers to meditate on Italian unification efforts, to see how representations of Italy and Italians were shaped (to a degree) by American concerns. Each of these writers therefore demonstrates to students that seeing Italy and the Italian means taking into account many issues beyond the country and its people.

Early Italian American Alternative Representations

We turn finally to the Italian immigrant writing from the Marazzi anthology. Keeping in mind the tendency to cast Italians narrowly, as art object or physical threat, or to view Italy only through American concerns, we look to these texts for alternative representations. I ask students to note if and how these stories complicate and deepen the characterizations of Italians in them. Inevitably, students find contrasts with the American texts. For example, in "The Kid from Genoa," an anonymous piece published in *L'eco d'Italia*, they often observe that the stereotypical image of the uneducated, dangerous, and depraved Italian is supplanted with a kindhearted and sincere beggar-child who strives to return the handout he received. In Bernardino Ciambelli's *The Mysteries of Mulberry*

Street, students make note of the joint (and equal) effort by American and Italian policemen to fight evil on New York streets. When reading the extract from Camillo Cianfarra's memoir, *The Diary of an Immigrant*, students comment on the complex characterization of the immigrant facing both adversity and triumph in a new environment. In Caterina Avella's *The Flapper*, students discover an Italian American woman portrayed not as an exotic figure to be objectified but as an active participant of mainstream, modern American society.

It is my hope that by reading and discussing the literature of canonical writers and their lesser-known Italian American contemporaries (or near contemporaries), students will be prepared for richer analysis of the twentieth-century Italian American novels we subsequently study. And it is my further hope that they will be prepared for continued interrogations of all constructions of identity.

Ilaria Serra

Travel Literature: Negotiating the Gaze between Italy and America

Italy and the grand tour: Venice, Rome, Florence. United States and Route 66: Chicago to Los Angeles. These words can evoke a particular atmosphere in the classroom on the first day of the course Travel Literature: Italy to America and Back. The course focuses on travel writings by Italian, American, and Italian American authors visiting the United States or Italy. It is not a creative writing workshop, even though travel journals can be a helpful requirement (especially if the course is taught in a term-abroad program). The course can encourage students to develop critical thinking and pursue analysis of the texts through questions concerning the semiotics of place, personalization of space, self-discovery, symbolic geography, and gendering. For every reading, I have designed an anthology of images, relating to the place to be studied, that is used in a classroom activity.

Introduction to the Course

Spreading out large maps of Italy and the United States on the first day of the course can be a helpful device to invite students to begin exploring notions of travel. Students can brainstorm as they look at the maps and point out familiar locations. I ask them to articulate the symbolic value of each location, not only as a physical place (mountains, lakes, narrow streets, skyscrapers, dust, dampness, chill) but also as a symbolical topos (ancient, young, passionate, cultured, romantic, rural, ignorant). I also introduce the key concepts of the course: the meaning of *toponomastica* (especially interesting in cases such as Venice in California or Civitavecchia in Lazio); the notion of mental topos; the merging of reality and imagination in travel literature; and the connections between style, identity, and agenda and one's perception of place. The motivations underlying travel writing should frame the discussion throughout the term, addressing everything from the urgency of penning what may seem volatile and short to travel as instability and discovery. Discovery often becomes a self-discovery: "we must say 'I,' whether in words or in any other semiotic system, in order to enter into dialogue with others" (Bartkowski 85).

The Italian on America, the Italian American on Italy, the American on Italy

The threefold distribution of the material—Italians traveling to the United States; narratives of Americans in Italy; and travel journals of Italian Americans discovering their roots in Italy—allows students to compare and contrast the myths about the two countries while also realizing the mutable quality and definitions of travel.

The first section of the course, "Italians Traveling to America," includes readings from Giacomo Beltrami's *A Pilgrimage in America* and Francesco Arese's *A Trip to the Prairies*, older accounts of the discovery of the West through Italian "imperial eyes" (Mary Louise Pratt's definition) in addition to Andrew Torrielli's *Italian Opinion on America*, which offers examples of nineteenth-century travel writing with some historical background. An interesting but still untranslated travel book is Giuseppe Giacosa's *Impressioni d'America*, for which I suggest reading Benjamin Lawton's article in *Abroad in America*. (Advanced Italian students can read an extract of this and other works in the original language.) In these works, students can search for themes such as the "discovery" of the new continent; the myth of the noble savage (the portrayal of American Indians as ancient Romans); the criticism of taste, chaos, inhumanity, and lawlessness but also the praise of freedom. Other twentieth-century Italian authors who can be read in conjunction with these authors include Emilio Cecchi (*America amara*), Giuseppe Prezzolini (*America in pantofole* and *Tutta l'America*), Mario Soldati (*America, primo amore*), Guido Piovene (*De America*), Luigi Barzini (*O America*), and Beppe Severgnini (*Ciao, America!*). Collectively, these texts offer an overview of America—spanning a century—as seen by Italian intellectuals. Students may find Piovene's descriptions of old Florida in his chapter "Il vecchio sud" or Soldati's caustic sketch of American professors especially compelling.

The Italian American travel narratives section, which encompass the second part of the course, opens with Helen Barolini's *More Italian Hours and Other Stories*. This work represents a particular kind of Italian American encounter with Italy, where the discovery of a place is also a discovery of self and the place is a reflection of the writer's self. For Barolini, as for other Italian American authors, the encounter with Italy promotes a personal exploration and acceptance of fractured cultural identities. In *Immigrant's Return*, Angelo Pellegrini uses the trip to Italy to measure how American he has become; in contrast, in "Amalfi Days," Jay Parini discovers the Italian embedded in his American persona. Barbara Grizzuti Harrison's *Italian Days*, Theresa Maggio's *The Stone Boudoir* and *Mattanza*, Mark Rotella's *Stolen Figs*, Susan Caperna Lloyd's *No Pictures in My Grave*, Mary Russo Demetrick and Maria Famà's *Italian Notebook*, and Anne Calcagno's edited essay collection *Italy: True Stories of Life on the Road* provide an interesting cluster of texts to examine issues of identity and culture, mythology and history, gender, religion, family, and nostalgia. Students have the opportunity to investigate how a particular Italian American vision of Italy—either as an ancient, patriarchal, and primitive country; a welcoming home encouraging self-discovery; or a place of disquieting alienation in its non-Americanness—often shapes the perception of Italy, particularly for Italian Americans.

The third section of the course centers on Americans traveling to Italy. Students consider the way in which the discovery of Italy often represents the encounter with a world of ancient beauty, backwardness, and community. Early in this section, Paul Baker's *The Fortunate Pilgrims* provides a historical excursus on American travelers in Italy and offers an interesting take on common themes, such as the American view on Italian religion or art or the general "meaning" of Italy. Henry James's *Italian Hours* demonstrates a finesse of observation and a passionate love for the country, especially for Venice, Florence, and Rome, cities that the author visited from 1869 to 1907. Ernest Hemingway's article "Italy 1927" allows students to revisit Italy in an important period of its history, during the fascist regime, through his perky account of the writer's automobile trip. Three essays—on Capri, Tarquinia, and the Vatican—from the recent *Conde Nast Traveler Book of Unforgettable Journeys* nicely complement the other readings (Glowczewska).

By this time, students have acquired all the necessary material to compare writers and writings, which will be the topic of their last written requirement. For example, reading James's *Italian Hours* with Barolini's *More Italian Hours* can generate a comparative discussion of the American gaze and the Italian American gaze: James is a male observer, an uninvolved judge standing at a flowered balcony and (despite his declarations of love for Italy) looking at Italy from the perspective of what he has studied about it, as if the country were still something in a book. Barolini, in contrast, is an Italian American woman writer and a vibrant participant in Italian life and culture who chooses living symbols of Italy to tell her stories.

Semiotics of Place, Symbolical Geography, Seeing and Gendering of Travel Writing

The semiotics of place offers a useful theoretical frame for the course as students explore questions such as, What is the meaning of a place? How does a specific place create metaphors and symbols? Luigi Monga's comprehensive articles on the history of travel writing ("Travel and Travel Writing"), and on balancing truth and creativity ("The Unavoidable 'Snare of Narrative'") give a basis for students to begin thinking about their final writing assignment. They examine travel writing as any of these categories: as a metaphor for human life, as a religious experience, as pedagogy, as a trade tool, as a phallic voyage or female activity, as confrontation of the self, or as leisure. The observations of the Italian immigrants Adolfo Rossi and Angelo Pellegrini can help students understand and compare the transformation of the physical into the abstract—the process of the symbolization of geography. Here, for example, is Rossi's description of Italy in 1893, after his return from America, through which he traveled both as an immigrant and as an Inspector of Immigration. He writes that, in comparison with America,

> Italy looks like a nice cemetery. With a few cars, rare tramways, lack of railways inland, our major cities seemed silent and almost sleeping. The streets appeared extraordinarily narrow. . . . The river Po, Adige and Tevere had become small brooks for me. I found all small, petty and belittled. (167)

Rossi's description of Italy is especially compelling if juxtaposed to Pellegrini's. Pellegrini transfigures the American landscape into the American spirit of freedom in this passage:

> It was the vastness and the freedom and the impersonality of what we saw that seduced and bewildered and troubled us. . . . Is it any wonder that . . . we felt that we ourselves had been released from narrow prison walls, into a freedom the immensity of which frightened us a little? (39–40)

These authors' reflections can be the springboard for exploring questions on the semiotics of place and binary oppositions such as Italy and its history versus America and its youth; Italy and its narrow spaces versus America and its breadth; Italy, overpopulated and man-made, versus America, wild and nature-dominated; Italy, stiff and heavy with tradition, versus America, young and free and ready to change.

The gendering aspect of travel writing is another central topic in the course, largely dedicated to women's writings, of which there are only a few examples from the past (Eric Leed [*Mind* and *Shores*], Marilyn Wesley, Nancy Walker, and Mirella Scriboni tackle this aspect). Wesley's argument that journeys are a means of change can be one way of reading authors such as Clotilde Giriodi, Amy Bernardy (*America* and *Paese*), and Irene Di Robilant, the first Italian women to turn their eyes and minds toward America, for them a contradictory symbol of both freedom and inhumanity. In contrast, American women living in Italy construct an Italian myth of country life, cuisine, and alternative lifestyle, as indicated by Frances Mayes's *Under the Tuscan Sun*, Mary Taylor Simeti's *On Persephone's Island*, and Susan Neunzig Cahill's *Desiring Italy*, a collection of women's writing on Italy. Finally, Susan Caperna Lloyd's *No Pictures in My Grave: A Spiritual Journey in Sicily* focuses on the author's transformative journey and her encounter with ancient forms of female spirituality represented by Demeter and the Black Madonna. Adria Bernardi describes walking in Florence in her unique clogs as an identity search in "The Errant Steps of Wooden Shoes," and Theresa Maggio ponders symbolic drinking at her Sicilian "source" in *The Stone Boudoir*.

Students' Discovery of Italy

Several critical texts tackle the implications of the "eyes of the beholder": Mary Louise Pratt's *Imperial Eyes*, for example, can help students become aware of hidden values embedded in travel literature, such as the presence of an underlying imperialistic gaze and the role of power involved in the act of seeing. Another recurring theme in Italian American travel writing is the difference between the traveler and the tourist. Eric Leed examines this difficult identity in *Shores of Discovery*, in which he charges the tourist with negative characteristics of superficiality, and *The Mind of the Traveller*, in which he defines travel as experience, noticing the same root of *travel* and *travail*. Voyage is ordeal, suffering, and a test.

The ultimate goal of this course is to lead students to reflect on what it means to be Italian, American, and Italian American by looking at how these identities crisscross in travel narratives. A course like this may also provide students with a cultural overview to enhance their understanding of Italy, as well as give them the instruments to consciously enjoy any kind of travel they may undertake.

Part V

Resources

RoseAnna Mueller and Dora Labate

A Review of Anthologies for Teaching Italian American Studies

This listing of Italian American anthologies includes an overview of collections of critical essays, anthologies of mixed genres (creative and critical works), an encyclopedia, and special issues of journals.

Barolini, Helen, ed. *The Dream Book: An Anthology of Writings by Italian American Women.*
    The first of its kind, this groundbreaking anthology features the writings of fifty-six Italian American women. The entries are grouped into chapters presenting memoirs, nonfiction, fiction, drama (the one-act play *Pizza*, by Michele Linfante), and poetry. The anthology contains a preface to the revised edition, and a long introduction broken into such sections as "The Historical and Social Context of Silence," "Seed of Doubt: The Internal Blocks," and "Literary Hegemonies and Oversights: The External Blocks." Barolini provides a brief introduction for each writer. In addition to authors clearly identifiable as Italian American, the anthology features writers such as Mary Gordon and Frances Winwar, whose Italian American backgrounds may go unrecognized by the general reader.
Barreca, Regina, ed. *Don't Tell Mama! The Penguin Book of Italian American Writing.*
    This anthology features ninety authors (from 1800 to the present) who examine the social and political lives of Italian Americans through poetry, memoir, essay, and fiction. Organized alphabetically, entries include entertainers such

as Ray Romano and Jay Leno; nationally recognized poets such as John Ciardi, Diane di Prima, and Lawrence Ferlinghetti; and novelists such as Don DeLillo, Tina De Rosa, Evan Hunter, and Wally Lamb. Barreca also includes a number of lesser-known writers. Some of the selections are reprints, while others are original contributions.

Barreca, Regina, ed. *A Sitdown with the Sopranos: Watching Italian American Culture on TV's Most Talked-About Series.*
This anthology contains eight essays that explore the hit television show from a variety of angles: religion, ethnic culture, masculinity, the role of the family, and psychotherapy, among others. Contributors include Sandra M. Gilbert, E. Anthony Rotundo, Jay Parini, Fred L. Gardaphé, Michael Flamini, Carla Gardina Pestana, and George Anastasia.

Barreca, Regina, ed. Spec. issue of *LIT: Literature Interpretation Theory.*
Essays examine Italian American classics such as Pietro di Donato's *Christ in Concrete* and popular television shows such as *The Sopranos.* Contributors include Mary Jo Bona, Carol Bonomo Albright, Elvira Di Fabio, Susan Leonardi, Rebecca A. Pope, and Kenneth Scambray.

Birnbaum, Lucia Chiavola, ed. *She Is Everywhere! An Anthology of Writing in Womanist/Feminist Spirituality.*
This anthology includes writings by women of diverse cultural and spiritual traditions. In the introduction, the editor explains that the subject of this book is the African dark mother. Adopting a womanist or feminist spirituality as a theoretical approach, contributors explore the symbolic presence of the African dark mother in such figures as the Spanish Goddess, the Sardinian Dea Madre, the Mujer Azul, the Guatemalian Virgin Maria, and the Black Madonna. Italian American contributors include Chickie Farella, Marguerite Rigoglioso, Mary Saracino, and Louisa Calio.

Bona, Mary Jo, ed. *The Voices We Carry: Recent Italian/American Women's Fiction.*
The fiction of fourteen writers is divided into such sections as "The Recreation of Historical Lives," "The Intersection between America and l'Italia," "*La Famiglia* in America," and "The End of a Generation." The works are rooted in Italian culture, the integration of and conflict between Italian and American customs, and familiar traditions in the United States. The writers explore the role of ethnic memory in identity formation, especially for second- and third-generation writers. Contributors include Rachel Guido De Vries, Susan J. Leonardi, Dorothy Bryant, Adria Bernardi, Daniela Gioseffi, and Phyllis Capello.

Camaiti Hostert, Anna, and Anthony Julian Tamburri, eds. *Scene italoamericane.*
An Italian translation of the volume below.

Camaiti Hostert, Anna, and Anthony Julian Tamburri, eds. *Screening Ethnicity: Cinematographic Representations of Italian Americans in the United States.*
The essays collected in this volume explore the representations of Italian Americans in film beginning with the silent era and extending to the HBO series *The Sopranos.* The essays cover Italian American directors such as Frank Capra, Michael Cimino, Francis Ford Coppola, Martin Scorsese, and

Nancy Savoca and non–Italian American directors who depict Italian Americans in their films, such as Norman Jewison and Spike Lee.

Capone, Giovanna, Denise Nico Leto, and Tommi Avicolli Mecca, eds. *Hey Paesan! Writing by Lesbians and Gay Men of Italian Descent.*

Divided into three parts, "Reclaiming: A Lifeline to Our Cultural Identity," "Coming Out: Guinea Queers," and "Mezz' e Mezz': Weaving Two Identities," this collection of essays explores homophobia and the silencing of lesbian and gay members in the Italian and Sicilian communities in North America. *Hey Paesan!* is the first book in which the writers have appeared in such a context. It includes essays, poems, fiction, memoir, and interviews by Mary Saracino, Dodici Azpadu, Rachel Guido deVries, Chris Lombardi, Theresa Carilli, Vittoria Repetto, Maria Fama, and Tim Cavale, among others.

Ciatu, Nzula Angelina, Domenica Dileo, and Gabriela Micallef, eds. *Curaggia: Writings by Women of Italian Descent.*

Hoping to break the code of *omertà*—the conspiratorial silence that imposes secrecy, self-censorship, and a refusal to betray family secrets—the editors assemble poems, stories, journal entries, essays, visual art, and photos by American and Canadian women writers, including Rosette Capotorto, Nancy Caronia, Joanna Herman, Maria Mazziotti Gillan, Giovanna (Janet) Capone, K. Freeperson, Michelle Alfano, Daniela Gioseffi, Nzula Angelina Ciatu, Joanna Clapps Herman, Vittoria Repetto, Edvige Giunta, Diane Raptosh, and Gabriella Micallef. While the anthology's main concern is to demonstrate and celebrate the diversity of the Italian American experience, several pieces foreground the tensions and frictions in immigrant families and their intergenerational struggles. Themes include mother-daughter relationships, domestic violence, incest, and sexual coming out. The works are presented in seven sections, each of which is introduced by its editor.

Ciongoli, A. Kenneth, and Jay Parini, eds. *Beyond the Godfather: Italian American Writers on the Real Italian American Experience.*

Congioli, a neurologist and president of the National Italian American Foundation, and Parini, a writer, poet, and professor, put together this anthology in response to the question posed by Gay Talese in his notorious *New York Times* article "Where Are the Italian-American Novelists?" The essays by twenty-three Italian American writers include personal reflections and critical analyses of Italian American authors: Dana Gioia examines Italian American poetry; Linda Hutcheon writes about "crypto Italians" like herself and Sandra M. Gilbert, who lost their Italian last names through marriage; Fred L. Gardaphé reflects on the works of Pietro di Donato, John Fante, and Mario Puzo; and Edvige Giunta considers Tina de Rosa's *Paper Fish* as a landmark text in American literature. Other contributors include Matilda Cuomo, Gay Talese, Sandra M. Gilbert, Maria Laurino, and Frank Lentricchia.

Crispino, Anna Maria, with Edvige Giunta and Caterina Romeo, eds. *Italiane d'America.* Spec. issue of *Leggendaria.*

The special issue groups together interviews, critical articles, and creative pieces that deal with identity and *italianità* as conflictual themes. Anna Maria Crispino's interview of Francesco Durante and Andreina De Clementi's "Quando partirono le donne" explore migration from two different angles: Durante stresses the centrality of language as a mark of the immigrant displacement and as an instrument to re-create this experience at a literary level. De Clementi's work explores the immigrants' experience as an essentially male phenomenon. In "Memoir e scrittura: Il viaggio delle parole," Giunta and Romeo discuss the memoir as the preferred genre of Italian American women writers. "Bugie bianche, verità nere" by Jennifer Guglielmo deconstructs ethnic identity by renegotiating the concepts of "whiteness" and "blackness." Other contributors include Marisa Trubiano, Anna Camaiti Hostert, Anthony Julian Tamburri, Robyn Pastorio-Newman, Aglaia Viviani, and Kym Ragusa.

D'Acierno, Pellegrino, ed. *The Italian American Heritage: A Companion to Literature and Arts.*

This invaluable cultural history documents the development and growth of Italian American opera, drama, film, and literature and analyzes Italian American identity through essays about the works of musicians, filmmakers, writers, and other artists. Featuring twenty-seven original essays, the work is divided into four parts: "Identity," "Roots and Traditions," "Writing," and "The Italian American Presence in the Arts." The first appendix, "The Italian American Experience, 1492–1998," presents a time line of significant personages and events in Italian American history. The second appendix, "Cultural Lexicon: Italian American Terms," defines Italian terms, which are cross-referenced to highlighted words in the essays. The book also includes a filmography.

DeSalvo, Louise, and Edvige Giunta, eds. *The Milk of Almonds: Italian American Women Writers on Food and Culture.*

This collection of Italian American women's writing showcases fifty-four well-known authors—such as Rita Ciresi, Lucia Perillo, Diane di Prima, Maria Mazziotti Gillan, and Carole Maso—as well as emerging writers—including Pamela E. Barnett, Loryn Lipari, and Cheryl Burke—who draw on personal and cultural memory in which food becomes a touchstone for their poetry, fiction, and memoirs. Attempting to dismantle racist, classist, and sexist discourse, the contributors contextualize food in situations such as birth, motherhood, family relationships, death, and sexuality. The anthology is divided into eight sections: "Beginnings," "Ceremonies," "Awakenings," "Encounters," "Transformations," "Communities," "Passings," and "Legacies."

Durante, Francesco, ed. *Italoamericana: Storia e letteratura degli italiani negli Stati Uniti.* Vol. 1: *1776–1880* and vol. 2: *1880–1943.*

This anthology, written in Italian, is a substantial work that includes fifty-five Italian authors writing from America and presented in three sections. The first section, "Nella patria degli eroi," includes the reflections and impressions of Italians living in the United States in the late eighteenth century to the late nineteenth century, from priests to adventurers. Francesco del Verme discusses the United States in the 1780s; Paolo Andreani writes about Washington; and Carlo Vidua describes Boston, his favorite city. Six entries (letters and poetry) are by Lorenzo Da Ponte, Mozart's librettist. The second and largest section, "Le retrovie del Risorgimento," contains twenty-seven selections. Some are travel accounts such as Francesco Arese Lucini's voyage to the plains of the Sioux, the South Pass, the Great Salt Lake, and San Francisco (published in French in 1894) and Filippo Manetta's report on the living conditions on southern plantations, based on his six-year experience in the mid-nineteenth century. The third section, "La frontiera della fede," features fifteen authors who write about religious themes and the founding of missions, including two women, Suor Blandina and Umilia Capietti. Each section has a substantial introduction and a one-to-three-page biography on each author.

Fazio, Venera, and Delia De Santis, eds. *Sweet Lemons: Writings with a Sicilian Accent.*

This anthology includes over fifty North American writers of Sicilian heritage: approximately one-third of the writers are Canadian, two-thirds are from the United States, and a small selection of Sicily's best known authors—Salvadore Quasimodo, Bartolo Cattafi, Guiseppe Pitre, and Fortunato Pasqualino—are also included in translation. The volume includes folktales, plays, short stories, poems, memoirs, essays, and one film script—Susan Caperna Lloyd's *The Baggage*—by well-established and emerging authors. Among the authors included are Gianna Patriarca, Salvadore Ala, Tony Ardizzone, Kirk Bonner, Gabriella Micallef, Louise Rozier, Kenneth Scambray, Johanna Barca Mastrototaro, Joseph Farina, and Maria Fama.

Gillan, Jennifer, Maria Mazziotti Gillan, and Edvige Giunta, eds. *Italian American Writers on New Jersey: An Anthology of Poetry and Prose.*

This anthology reflects the diversity of the artistic achievements of Italian Americans who write about their ethnic experience in New Jersey, which has been home to many Italian immigrants. It contains fiction, poetry, memoirs, oral histories, and journalistic pieces by well-known authors such as Pietro di Donato, Gay Talese, Louise DeSalvo, Frank De Caro, Bill Ervolino, Tom Perrotta, Susanne Antonetta, and Maria Laurino, as well as emerging writers. The texts, which explore the relation of ethnicity, culture, and place, are organized in four sections: "Looking Back" (which also includes a separate section on Paterson); "Blending In"; "Crossing Bridges" (which includes the subsection "Interstate Commerce: New York and New Jersey Bound"); and "Changing Direction."

Gillan, Maria Mazziotti, and Jennifer Gillan, eds. *Unsettling America: An Anthology of Contemporary Multicultural Poetry.*

This anthology features poetic responses by American ethnic poets to the stereotyping, discrimination, and bigotry suffered by minorities who live in an intolerant society. The anthology is divided into five sections: "Uprooting," "Performing," "Naming," "Negotiating," and "Re-envisioning." Both emergent and established poets write about issues such as loss of home, stereotypes, self-perception, assimilation, and the erosion of customs. Italian American poets in this collection include: Lawrence Ferlinghetti, Daniela Gioseffi, Mary Jo Bona, Justin Vitiello, and Sandra M. Gilbert.

Giordano, Paolo A., and Anthony Julian Tamburri, eds. *Beyond the Margin: Readings in Italian Americana.*

Nine years after their first collaboration on *From the Margin*, two of the editors update the state of Italian American studies, which flourished in the 1990s, continued to grow through conferences, developed associations—such as the American Italian Historical Association—endowed chairs, writing groups, and inspired a sizable output of talented second- and third-generation Italian American writers. The essays in "Part One: General Considerations" examine the question of what Italian American literature is. "Part Two: Reading Literature" includes critical essays about such writers as Emmanuel Carnevali, John Fante, Helen Barolini, Don DeLillo, and Sandra M. Gilbert. "Part Three: Reading Film" includes an essay on representations of African Americans in the works of Coppola, De Palma, and Scorsese and an essay on Scorsese and Ferrara. In "Part Four: Further Readings," the editors include essays on the state of Italian American writing in the United States and the place of Italian American letters in ethnic studies.

Giordano, Paolo A., and Anthony Julian Tamburri, eds. Spec. issue of *Canadian Journal of Italian Studies.*

The essays, written by scholars who have been instrumental in the creation and dissemination of Italian American studies, include "Here Are the Italian/American Writers!" by Fred L. Gardaphé; "Nino Ricci's Narrative and the Search for the Collective Unconscious of the Italian-American," by Stelio Cro; "Talese's *Unto the Sons:* An Inward Journey to Italian/American 'Roots,'" by Mario Aste; "Narratives of Loss: Voices of Ethnicity in Agnes Rossi and Nancy Savoca," by Edvige Giunta; "Gianna Patriarca's 'Tragic' Thought: *Italian Women and Other Tragedies,*" by Anthony Julian Tamburri; and interviews with the writers Maria Mazziotti Gillan, Mary Jo Bona, Luigi Fontanella, Peter Carravetta, Paolo Valesio, and Robert Viscusi.

Giunta, Edvige, ed. *Italian American Women Authors.* Spec. issue of *VIA: Voices in Italian Americana.*

Giunta groups together Italian American authors under the categories of criticism, fiction, poetry, memoir, and reviews. In addition to creative work such as memoirs by Louise DeSalvo and Mary Cappello, fiction by Rita Ciresi and Renee Manfredi, and poetry by Sandra M. Gilbert, Phyllis Capello, Maria Mazzotti Gillan, Daniela Gioseffi, Kathleen Ossip, and Tina De Rosa, this special issue also includes critical essays and reviews on literature, film, and art by Italian American women.

Giunta, Edvige, and Caterina Romeo, eds. *Origini: Le scrittrici italo americane.* Spec. issue of *TutteStorie.*

This special issue of the Italian feminist journal gathers interviews, critical articles, and creative pieces by Italian American women writers, poets, and scholars in Italian translation. As in *Leggendaria*, the Italian translation of creative works by such Italian American writers as Kim Addonizio, Mary Cappello, Tina De Rosa, Louise DeSalvo, Carole Maso, Mary Saracino, Gioia Timpanelli, Mary Hall Ets, Rosette Capotorto, Maria Mazziotti Gillan, Maria Laurino, Kym Ragusa, and Janet Zandy are made available in Italian translation for the first time. The editors highlight the absence of full translation of books by these and other Italian American women. This special issue aims to break this silence. Giunta's "Ai confine dell'identità," Linda Hutcheon's "Criptoetnicità," Jennifer Guglielmo's "Pietre, parole e circoli politici," and Romeo's "A casa senza casa: La relazione con lo spazio" open up academic discussions on identity politics. By organizing the creative works around two categories—the present and the past—the editors offer a diachronic perspective into the history of Italian American women's literary production.

Guglielmo, Jennifer, and Salvatore Salerno, eds. *Are Italians White? How Race Is Made in America.*

Sixteen personal and critical essays examine the position of Italian Americans in the history of race making by exploring how race is defined, categorized, and confronted and how Italian Americans have asserted, challenged, or subverted whiteness. The anthology is divided into four sections: "Learning the US Color Line" includes essays by Louise DeSalvo, Thomas Guglielmo, Donna Gabaccia, and Vincenza Scarpaci; "Radicalism and Race" contains essays by Caroline Merithew, Michael Topp, Salvatore Salerno, Franklin Rosemont, and Manifest; "Whiteness, Violence and the Urban Crisis" has essays by Gerald Meyer, Stefano Luconi, and Joseph Sciorra; "Toward a Black Italian Imaginary" includes essays by Kym Ragusa, Edvige Giunta, John Gennari, Ronnie Mae Painter, and Rosette Capotorto. The book concludes with an afterword by David R. Roediger.

Guglielmo, Jennifer, and Salvatore Salerno, eds. *Gli Italiani sono bianchi? Come l'America ha costruito la razza.*

Italian translation of text above.

Gutkind, Lee, and Joanna Clapps Herman, eds. *Our Roots Are Deep with Passion: Creative Nonfiction Collects New Essays by Italian American Writers.*

The actor Joe Mantegna wrote the foreword and provided the title for this collection of twenty-one nonfiction narratives by prizewinning and new writers who draw on their Italian roots. The subjects addressed range from writing about the love of herbs and garlic (Sandra M. Gilbert and Stephanie Susnjara) to the relationship with grandparents (Louise DeSalvo, Edvige Giunta, Peter Selgin, Jeanna Lucci Canapari) and reminiscences and reflections about growing up Italian American and the Italian American family (Christine Palamidessi Moore, Maria Laurino, Carol Bonomo Albright, Annie Rachele Lanzillotto). Herman's "Words and Rags" is an etymological lesson and a panegyric to the common dishrag. The essays are infused with Italian words and dialects, explanations of the origin of nicknames, and recipes. The wide range of emotions—jealousy, sacrifice, revenge, and injustices suffered in Catholic school—will touch every reader who has had to measure up against the dominant culture and been an other.

Italian American Literature. Spec. issues of *MELUS.*

These two issues together demonstrate how far Italian American literature has come in its attempts at challenging stereotypes of Italian Americans and evolving into a field confident in its own status. Volume 14 (1987) brings together articles and reviews whose main interest can be appreciated at a historical level as a survey of the literature at that time. Two representative articles include. "The Re-visioning of New York's Little Italies: From Howells to Puzo," by Lawrence J. Oliver, and "Italian-American in Film: From Immigrants to Icons," by Carlos E. Cortés. Volume 28 (2003), edited by Mary Jo Bona, includes articles that cover a full array of theoretical approaches, from feminist postcolonial theory—"The Willingness to Speak: Diane di Prima and an Italian American Feminist Body Politics," by Roseanne Quinn—to ethnic studies—Josephine Gattuso Hendin's "Social Constructions and Aesthetic Achievements: Italian American Writing as Ethnic Art."

LaGumina, Salvatore J., Frank J. Cavaioli, Salvatore Primeggia, and Joseph A. Varacalli, eds. *The Italian American Experience: An Encyclopedia.*

With contributions from over one hundred sixty scholars, this encyclopedia presents an account of the history of Italians in the United States from the colonial period to the present, listing their contributions to American history, pop music, labor unions, and other organizations. From "agriculture" to "Joseph Zappulla," this encyclopedia-format volume provides information about people, places, and objects that are part of the Italian American experience in the United States. There are entries about prominent Italian Americans—Mario Cuomo, Robert De Niro, and John Fante—and lesser-known Italian Americans such as Candido Jacuzzi, and not so obvious or "encrypted," Italian Americans such as Anne Bancroft and Bobby Darin. The encyclopedia features one hundred original photos, bibliographies at the end of the entries, an introduction, notes on contributors, suggestions for further information, and an index.

Mannino, Mary Ann, and Justin Vitiello, eds. *Breaking Open: Reflections on Italian American Women's Writing.*

Seventeen essays by scholars and writers treat themes such as ambivalence, power, and the influence of ethnicity on Italian American women writers. Some of the authors draw on childhood memories as a foundation for their creativity. The works show how, despite conflict and separation from their families, the authors remain anchored to their Italian American heritage. The anthology includes an introduction written by Mannino and Vitiello and essays by Mary Cappello, Rachael Guido De Vries, Rita Ciresi, Maria Famà, Josephine Hendin, as well as many other well-known Italian American academics who share their perspectives on growing up Italian in the United States.

Marazzi, Martino. *Misteri di Little Italy: Storie e testi della letteratura italoamericana.*

This book provides a view of Italian American studies as seen from the motherland, written by a Milan-based scholar. It is divided into four sections: "Narratori," which examines lesser-known figures of the origins of the literature as well as recognized authors of the 1930s such as Pietro di Donato and John Fante; "Poeti," which discusses the poetical production of the colonies as well as the anarchist poet Arturo Giovannitti; "Prose di testimonianza," which looks at various narratives of witness, from reportages to autobiographical writings; and "Il punto di vista italiano," in which Marazzi studies the initial exclusion and delay in Italian scholars' interest in Italian American writing in Italy.

Marazzi, Martino. *Voices of Italian America: A History of Early Italian American Literature with a Critical Anthology.*

An English translation of Marazzi's Italian anthology, above.

Mecca, Tommi Avicolli, and Anthony Julian Tamburri. *Fuori: Essays by Italian/ American Lesbians and Gays.*

This book includes six essays, by Tommy Avicolli Mecca, Giovanna Capone, Theresa Carilli, Philip Gambone, Rachel Guido De Vries, and Mary Cappello, that explore gay and lesbian identity in the contexts of Italian American family and culture. It includes a preface by the editor. Mary Jo Bona's introduction examines the links among multiple forces shaping the identity of Italian American gay and lesbian writers—ethnicity, gender, sexuality, and class—and how coming out as gay specifically "influences, showcases, modifies, and reinvents" Italian American ethnicity (4).

Messina, Elizabeth G., ed. *In Our Own Voices: Multidisciplinary Perspectives on Italian and Italian American Women.*

This anthology includes essays originally presented at a symposium on Italian and Italian American women organized by the Collective of Italian American Women at New York University in 2001. It also includes other essays not presented at the symposium. Essays are not comparative, but each focuses on either Italian or Italian perspectives. Contributors include Flavia Alaya, Annette Wheeler Cafarelli, Dawn Esposito, Josephine Gattuso Hendin, Joanne Mattera, Laura Ruberto, and Rudolph Vecoli.

Scapp, Ron, and Anthony Julian Tamburri, eds. Spec. issue of *Differentia: Review of Italian Thought.*

The special issue promotes critical and interpretive thinking about current topics in Italian American culture such as identity politics, race, and gender, and it conveys the compelling force of a new field of study. The book is divided into three sections: "Studies and Essays," which includes essays by scholars such as John Paul Russo, Robert Viscusi, Ben Lawton, Fred Gardaphé, and Francesca Canade Sautman; review essays by Mary Jo Bona, Alessandro Carrera, Peter Carravetta, and Paolo Giordano; and book reviews of Italian American critical and creative works, from Tamburri's *To Hyphenate or Not to Hyphenate* to Giose Rimanelli's *Benedetta in Guysterland*. Creative work by Maria Mazziotti Gillan, Claudia Menza, Christine Perri, Felix Stefanmile, and others is interspersed throughout the issue.

Tamburri, Anthony Julian, Paolo Giordano, and Fred L. Gardaphé, eds. *From the Margin: Writing in Italian Americana.*

This groundbreaking anthology, updated since its first appearance in 1991, is divided into the sections "Creative Works," "Poetry," and "Critical Essays";

the third section is subdivided into discussions of the characteristics of Italian American literature, analyses of specific writers, and essays about films. Most stories, poems, plays, and essays collected in this volume appear for the first time. The introduction examines the cultural concept of *italianità* and its diverse artistic manifestations. The extensive and updated critical bibliography and selected filmography make it a valuable research and teaching tool.

Tonelli, Bill, ed. *The Italian American Reader: A Collection of Outstanding Stories, Memoirs, Journalism, Essays, and Poetry.*

This collection of sixty-eight stories, poems, and excerpts from memoirs and novels is organized in thematic sections: "Home"; "Mom"; "Sex, Love and Good Looks"; "Food"; "Pop"; "Work"; "Death"; "God"; "Each Other"; and "Everybody Else." It aims to include outstanding works by American writers who are of Italian ancestry, even if their subject matter has nothing to do with being Italian. The volume includes the works of Dana Gioia, Don De-Lillo, Ed McBain, Frank Lentricchia, Richard Russo, and Josephine Gattuso Hendin. An essay by Tonelli discusses the contributions of Italian American singers, musicians, actors, and film directors to American culture.

Notes on Contributors

Carol Bonomo Albright taught Italian American studies at Harvard Extension School. She is editor of *Italian Americana*; coeditor of *Wild Dreams: The Best of* Italian Americana, *Italian Immigrants Go West*, and an annotated edition of Joseph Rocchietti's works; series editor of Italian American Autobiographies and has published essays in numerous books and journals. Her most recent book is *American Women, Italian Style:* Italian Americana's *Best Writings on Women*.

Emelise Aleandri is the author of the first volume of the history series The Italian-American Immigrant Theatre of New York City, as well as other books and numerous articles. The original creator, producer, and host of the nationally syndicated cable television program *Italics: The Italian American Magazine*, she has also produced three documentaries: *Teatro: The Legacy of Italian-American Theatre*; *Festa: Italian Festival Traditions*; and *Circo Rois: Che Bella Vita!* Aleandri is artistic director of Frizzi & Lazzi, the Olde Time Italian American Musical Theatre Company and has performed in major feature films, television, and theatrical productions.

Mary Jo Bona is professor of Italian American studies and directs its program at Stony Brook University. Bona wrote *Claiming a Tradition: Italian American Women Writers*, edited *The Voices We Carry: Recent Italian American Women's Fiction*, and coedited, with Irma Maini, *Multiethnic Literature and Canon Debates*. Her monograph, *By the Breath of Their Mouths: Narratives of Resistance in Italian America*, is forthcoming.

Peter Bondanella is Distinguished Professor Emeritus of comparative literature, film studies, and Italian at Indiana University; past president of the American Association of Italian Studies; and a member of the European Academy of Sciences and Arts. He is the author of *Hollywood Italians: Dagos, Palookas, Romeos, Wise Guys, and Sopranos* and numerous books and translations dealing with Italian literature and cinema, including the forthcoming "A History of Italian Cinema."

Giulia Centineo is lecturer in Italian at the University of California, Santa Cruz, where she teaches language courses and Italian culture through cinema. Her publications include work on the semantics of Italian auxiliary selection, the distribution of the morpheme *si* in Italian transitive/inchoative pairs, and the alternation between *passato prossimo* and *passato remoto* in oral narratives. She is working on language and prejudice both in film and in the press.

Clarissa Clò is assistant professor and director of the Italian program at San Diego State University. She teaches courses in Italian language, literature, culture, and cinema. She is also developing digital media archives on San Diego's Little Italy and Italian artists in the diaspora. Her research interests include feminist, migration, and postcolonial studies; film; music; and popular culture. Her work has been published in *Annali d'Italianistica, Diacritics, Diaspora, Forum Italicum, Italica, Italian Culture*, and *Il lettore di provincia*.

Kimberly A. Costino teaches English at California State University, San Bernardino, where she is associate professor, composition coordinator, and director of Gateway, a program for first-year students. Her interest in cultural studies and Italian American literature infuses her approach to teaching composition in the first-year writing program and in the master of arts composition programs.

Peter Covino is assistant professor of English and creative writing at the University of Rhode Island. He is the author of the poetry collection *Cut off the Ears of Winter*, winner of the 2007 PEN/Osterweil Award for emerging poets, and of the chapbook *Straight Boyfriend*, which won the Frank O'Hara Poetry Prize. His poems and translations have appeared or are forthcoming in numerous books and journals.

Rose De Angelis is professor of English at Marist College, where she teaches ethnic and American literature courses, and is a past editor of the book series Anthropology and Literature. Her work on Italian American studies has appeared in *Forum Italicum* and *Italian Americana*, and she has edited a volume of essays entitled *Between Anthropology and Literature: Interdisciplinary Discourse*.

Luisa Del Giudice is an independent scholar, founder and director of the Italian Oral History Institute, and past professor of Italian folklore. She has published widely on Italian and Italian American and Canadian folklore and oral history and produced conferences and public programs on Italian and Mediterranean cultures. She was named Fellow of the American Folklore Society and knighted (cavaliere) by the president of Italy in 2008.

David Del Principe is associate professor of Italian at Montclair State University. He is the author of *Rebellion, Death, and Aesthetics in Italy: The Demons of Scapigliatura* and various essays on nineteenth-century Italian and gothic literature. He is at work on an ecofeminist study of gothic allegories of consumption in nineteenth-century Italian and European literature.

Louise DeSalvo is the Jenny Hunter Endowed Scholar for Creative Writing and Literature at Hunter College. Among her publications are *Virginia Woolf*; *Writing as a Way of Healing*; *The Milk of Almonds* (coedited with

Edvige Giunta); the memoirs *Vertigo* (winner of the Gay Talese Prize and the Premio Acerbi Award), *Breathless, Adultery, Crazy in the Kitchen,* and *On Moving.* She is writing "Reading My Father's War," a memoir about her father's experiences in World War II.

Elvira G. Di Fabio is senior preceptor and associate director of undergraduate studies for Romance languages and literatures at Harvard University. She directs Italian language instruction at the college and teaches courses in Italian language and culture and Italian American studies, including a course on the Italian American image from Broadway to Hollywood. She coauthored, with Carol Bonomo Albright, *Republican Ideals in the Selected Works of Italian-American Joseph Rocchietti, 1835–1845,* which introduces and reproduces two of Rocchietti's published works: the earliest known Italian American novel and an essay on national literature.

Teresa Fiore is associate professor of Italian at California State University, Long Beach. Her teaching and research areas include Italian American studies, nineteenth- and twentieth-century Italian culture, and Italian language pedagogy. Her essays on issues of migration, space, ethnicity, and identity have appeared in the journals *Diaspora, Annali d'Italianistica,* and *VIA* and in the volume *Comparative Sites of Ethnicity.* She is the editor of the 2006 issue of *Quaderni del '900,* devoted to John Fante.

Donna R. Gabaccia is Rudolph J. Vecoli Chair at the University of Minnesota, where she is also the director of the Immigration History Research Center. A specialist on international migrations, she has a particular interest in immigrant life in the United States and in Italian migration around the world. Her book "Foreign Relations: An International History of U.S. Immigration" is forthcoming.

Fred Gardaphé is Distinguished Professor of English and Italian American studies at Queens College and the John D. Calandra Italian American Institute. His books include *Italian Signs, American Streets: The Evolution of Italian American Narrative*; *Dagoes Read: Tradition and the Italian American Writer*; *Moustache Pete Is Dead!*; *Leaving Little Italy*; and *From Wiseguys to Wise Men: The Gangster and Italian American Masculinities.* He is cofounder and coeditor of *VIA: Voices in Italian Americana* and editor of the Italian American Culture Series of State University of New York Press.

Edvige Giunta is professor of English at New Jersey City University and coeditor of *Transformations: The Journal of Inclusive Scholarship and Pedagogy.* She is the author of *Writing with an Accent: Contemporary Italian American Women Authors* and coeditor of *The Milk of Almonds: Italian American Women Writers on Food and Culture* and *Italian American Writers on New Jersey.* Her memoir and poetry have appeared in journals and anthologies. She is at work, with Joseph Sciorra, on "Cut Threads, Embroidered Lives: Domestic Needlework in the Italian Diaspora," an anthology of critical and creative writing.

Jennifer Guglielmo is assistant professor of history at Smith College. Her publications include *Are Italians White? How Race Is Made in America* (coedited with Salvatore Salerno), which has been translated into Italian, and *Living the Revolution: Italian Women's Everyday Resistance and Radicalism in New York City, 1880–1945*, which was awarded the Organization of American Historians' Lerner-Scott Prize in U.S. Women's History.

Josephine Gattuso Hendin is professor of English and Tiro A Segno Professor of Italian American Studies at New York University. Her novel, *The Right Thing to Do*, won an American Book Award from the Before Columbus Foundation. She is the author of *The World of Flannery O'Connor*; *Vulnerable People: A View of American Fiction since 1945*; and *HeartBreakers: Women and Violence in Contemporary Culture and Literature* and editor of Blackwell's *Companion to Postwar American Literature and Culture*. She is president of the American Italian Historical Association.

Peter Kvidera is associate professor of English at John Carroll University, where he teaches courses in nineteenth- and twentieth-century American literature, immigrant and ethnic literatures of the United States, and Japanese literature. His articles have been published in *New England Quarterly, American Literature*, and *American Quarterly*, and he is working on the book "Americanizations: U.S. Immigrant Writing at the Turn of the Twentieth Century."

Dora Labate is completing her doctorate in Italian at Rutgers University. She is working on a dissertation on contemporary Italian American women's voices with an emphasis on memoir writing. Her research and interests include twentieth-century and contemporary Italian literature.

Bernadette Luciano is associate professor of Italian and head of the School of European Languages and Literatures at the University of Auckland. She has written articles and book chapters on Italian cinema, film adaptation, Italian women's historical novels, women's autobiographical writing, and literary translation. She has coedited an interdisciplinary book on New Zealand–European cross-cultural encounters and has written the book *The Cinema of Silvio Soldini: Dream, Image, Voyage*. She is working on a book on contemporary Italian women filmmakers.

Kathleen Zamboni McCormick is professor of literature and pedagogy at Purchase College. Her books include *The Culture of Reading and the Teaching of English*, which won the MLA's Mina Shaughnessy Award, and *Approaches to Teaching Joyce's* Ulysses (coedited with Erwin Steinberg). She is currently working on a book-length memoir, "Why Is God in Daddy's Slippers?" on growing up as a half-Italian and half-Irish American.

RoseAnna Mueller is associate professor of humanities and foreign languages at Columbia College, Chicago, and the Santa Reparata International School of Art in Florence. Her publications include articles and book reviews in *VIA: Voices in Italian Americana, Italica*, and *Annali d'Italianistica*. Her book chapter "Machiavelli in the Modern World" appears in *Seeking Real Truths: Multidisciplinary Perspectives on Machiavelli*. Her poetry translations have appeared in *Italian Poetry Today*.

Mark Pietralunga is the Victor B. Oelschlager Professor of Modern Languages and Linguistics at Florida State University. His areas of interest are twentieth-century Italian literature and culture, translation studies, and Italian American studies. Among his books and editions are *Beppe Fenoglio and English Literature: A Study of the Writer as Translator*; *Beppe Fenoglio e l'esaltante fatica del tradurre*; *Prometeo slegato: Pavese traduttore di P. B. Shelley*; *Quaderno di traduzioni: Beppe Fenoglio*; and *Cesare Pavese and Antonio Chiuminatto: Their Correspondence*.

Roseanne Giannini Quinn teaches English, ethnic studies, and women's and gender studies at Santa Clara University, where she is also a California Legacy Project Scholar. She has researched and published in Italian American studies with a focus on women's multigenre narratives and on the work, in particular, of Diane di Prima and Carol Maso. She is writing a book on contemporary avant-garde and popular writing by Italian American women and the development of Italian American feminist theory.

Caterina Romeo is assistant professor at the University of Rome, Sapienza, where she teaches gender studies and migration studies. She is the author of *Narrative tra due sponde: Memoir di italiane d'America* and the coeditor of special issues of *Dialectical Anthropology* and *tutteStorie*. She has translated into Italian Louise DeSalvo's *Vertigo* and Kym Ragusa's *The Skin between Us*. She is working on a book project on migrant and postmigrant women writers in contemporary Italy.

Courtney Judith Ruffner is assistant professor of English at State College of Florida. She was contributing editor to the Edgar Allan Poe book in Harold Bloom's BioCritiques series and has an article on Poe forthcoming for EBSCO Publishing's Critical Insights series. She is a founding editor of the literary journal *Florida English* and is writing her dissertation on the postcolonial Italian American and the commodification of Italian Americans in film and television.

John Paul Russo is professor of English and classics at the University of Miami. His books include *Alexander Pope: Tradition and Identity* and *I. A. Richards: His Life and Work*; his *Future without a Past: The Humanities in a Technological Society* received the 2006 Bonner Prize for a study of the liberal arts, with special attention to bridging the gap between the "two cultures" of the sciences and the humanities. He has been awarded three

Fulbrights to Italy, where he has taught at the universities of Palermo, Rome, Genoa, and Salerno.

Joseph Sciorra is associate director at Queens College's John D. Calandra Italian American Institute, where he conducts original research and conceptualizes and implements the institute's academic and cultural programs. As a folklorist, he has published extensively on religious practices, cultural landscapes, material culture, and youth culture and has curated several exhibitions in these areas. He is coeditor of the poet Vincenzo Ancona's bilingual *Malidittu la lingua / Damned Language* and author of *R.I.P.: Memorial Wall Art*, a collection of photographs by Martha Cooper documenting memorial graffiti.

Ilaria Serra is assistant professor of Italian at Florida Atlantic University, where she teaches Italian cinema, Italian American cinema, Italian Literature, and Italian language. Her research spans from Italian cinema and literature to the history of Italian immigration to the United States. She is the author of *Immagini di un immaginario: L'emigrazione italiana negli Stati Uniti fra i due secoli: 1890–1925*; *The Value of Worthless Lives: Writing Italian American Immigrant Autobiographies*; and *The Imagined Immigrant: Images of Italian Emigration to the United States between 1890 and 1924.*

Anthony Julian Tamburri is dean of the John D. Calandra Italian American Institute and professor of Italian and Italian American studies. He is codirector of Bordighera Press, past president of the American Italian Historical Association, and president of the American Association of Teachers of Italian. His books include *Italian/American Short Films and Music Videos*; *Narrare altrove: Diverse segnalature letterarie*; and *Una semiotica dell' etnicità*. He is also the executive producer of *Italics, the Italian American TV Magazine*, produced by the Calandra Institute and CUNY-TV.

Stefania Taviano is assistant professor of English at the University of Messina. She is author of *Staging Dario Fo and Franca Rame: Anglo-American Approaches to Political Theatre* and editor of *Migrazione e identità culturale*. She is also a translator and has contributed to the translation of Dario Fo's *Johan Padan and the Discovery of the Americas*. Her monograph "Translating English as a Lingua Franca" is forthcoming.

Marisa Trubiano is associate professor of Italian at Montclair State University, where she teaches courses on Italian language, literature, cinema, and cultural studies; translation; and Italian American literature and cultural studies. Her book on the Italian screenwriter, journalist, and novelist Ennio Flaiano, "Ennio Flaiano and His Italy: Postcards from a Changing World," is forthcoming. She is co-coordinator of the ongoing Italians of Montclair Oral History Project.

Robert Viscusi is the author of the novel *Astoria*; the long poem *An Oration upon the Most Recent Death of Christopher Columbus*; the poetry collection *A New Geography of Time*; and the critical history *Buried Caesars and Other Secrets of Italian American Writing*. He is Broeklundian Professor and executive officer of the Wolfe Institute for the Humanities at Brooklyn College. In 2008 he was awarded the Giuseppe Acerbi Award for criticism of Italian American writing.

Works Cited

Print, Electronic, and Miscellaneous

Aaron, Daniel. "How to Read Don DeLillo." Lentricchia, *Introducing* 67–82.

Abbamonte, Salvatore. "Attori e Filodrammatici della vecchia Colonia Italiana di NY." *La follia* 24 Mar. 1940: 9. Print.

———. "Nei Primordi del Teatro Coloniale." *La follia* 11 Feb. 1940: 5. Print.

———. "Nella Colonia di Quarantacinque Anni or Sono." *La follia* 14 Jan. 1940: 5. Print.

Accardi, Joseph. "Giovanni De Rosalia: Playwright, Poet, and Nofrio." *Italian Americana* 19.2 (2001): 176–200. Print.

Addonizio, Kim. *Tell Me: Poems.* Rochester: BOA, 2000. Print.

———. *What Is This Thing Called Love.* New York: Norton, 2005. Print.

Affron, Mirella Jona. "The Italian-American in American Films, 1918–1971." *Italian Americana* 3.2 (1977): 233–55. Print.

Alaya, Flavia. *Under the Rose: A Confession.* New York: Feminist, 1999. Print.

Alba, Richard D. *Italian Americans: Into the Twilight of Ethnicity.* Englewood Cliffs: Prentice, 1985. Print.

Albright, Carol Bonomo. "Definitions of Womanhood: Class, Acculturation, and Feminism." Barolini, *Dream Book* 125–39.

Albright, Carol Bonomo, and Elvira G. Di Fabio, eds. *Republican Ideals in the Selected Works of Italian-American Joseph Rocchietti, 1835–1845.* Lewiston: Mellen, 2004. Print.

Albright, Carol Bonomo, and Joanna Clapps Herman, eds. *Wild Dreams: The Best of Italian Americana.* New York: Fordham UP, 2008. Print.

Aleandri, Emelise. *The Italian American Immigrant Theatre of New York City.* Dover: Arcadia, 1999. Print.

———. *The Italian-American Immigrant Theatre of New York City, 1746–1899.* Lewiston: Mellen, 2006. Print.

Alexander, M. Jacqui, and Chandra Talpade Mohanty. "Introduction: Genealogies, Legacies, Movements." *Feminist Genealogies: Colonial Legacies, Democratic Futures.* Ed. Alexander and Mohanty. New York: Routledge, 1997. xiii–xlii. Print.

Alfonsi, Ferdinando. *Dictionary of Italian-American Poets.* New York: Lang, 1989. Print.

———. *Poesia italo-americana: Saggi e testi / Italian American Poetry: Essays and Texts.* Catanzaro: Carello, 1991. Print.

———. *Poeti italo-americani: Antologia bilinigue / Italo-American Poets: A Bilingual Anthology.* Expanded ed. Catanzaro: Carello, 1994. Print.

Allen, Beverly, and Mary Russo, eds. *Revisioning Italy: National Identity and Global Culture.* Minneapolis: U of Minnesota P, 1997. Print.

Althusser, Louis. *Lenin and Philosophy and Other Essays.* Trans. Ben Brewster. New York: Monthly Rev., 1971. Print.

Amodio, Mark C. "Contemporary Critical Approaches and Studies in Oral Tradition." Foley 95–105.

Amore, B. *An Italian American Odyssey: Life Line / Filo della vita: Through Ellis Island and Beyond.* New York: Center for Migration Studies, 2006. Print.

Anderson, Benedict. *Imagined Communities: Reflections on the Origin and Spread of Nationalism.* New York: Verso, 1991. Print.

Antonetta, Susanne. *Body Toxic: An Environmental Memoir.* Washington: Counterpoint, 2001. Print.

Anzaldúa, Gloria. *Borderlands / La frontera: The New Mestiza.* San Francisco: Aunt Lute, 1999. Print.

Arcade, Penny. *Bitch! Dyke! Faghag! Whore!* Performance Space 122, New York. 1990. Performance.

———. *La Miseria.* Performance Space 122, New York. 1991. Performance.

Ardizzone, Tony. *In the Garden of Papa Santuzzu.* New York: Picador, 1999. Print.

Arese, Francesco. *A Trip to the Prairies and in the Interior of North America.* 1838. Trans. Andrew Evans. New York: Harbor, 1934. Print.

Ariès, Philippe. *Western Attitudes towards Death from the Middle Ages to the Present.* Trans. Patricia M. Ranum. Baltimore: Johns Hopkins UP, 1974. Print.

Arigo, Christopher. *In the Archives.* Richmond: Omnidawn, 2007. Print.

———. *Lit Interim.* Montpelier: Pavement Saw, 2003. Print.

Astarita, Tommaso. *Between Salt Water and Holy Water: A History of Southern Italy.* New York: Norton, 2005. Print.

Auer, Peter, ed. *Code-Switching in Conversation: Language, Interaction, and Identity.* London: Routledge, 1998. Print.

Avella, Caterina Maria. *The Flapper.* 1923. Marazzi, *Voices* 78–91.

"Awards for 'The Sopranos.'" *International Movie Database.* IMDb, 2009. Web. 4 Mar. 2009.

Azara, Nancy. *Fire.* 2000. Collage. Collection of Azara.

Baker, Aaron, and Juliann Vitullo. "Mysticism and the Household Saints of Everyday Life." *VIA: Voices in Italian Americana* 7.2 (1996): 55–68. Print.

Baker, John. *O. Louis Guglielmi: A Retrospective Exhibition.* New Brunswick: Rutgers UP, 1980. Print.

Baker, Paul. *The Fortunate Pilgrims: Americans in Italy, 1800–1860.* Cambridge: Harvard UP, 1964. Print.

Baldassaro, Lawrence. "Dashing Dagos and Walloping Wops: Media Portrayal of Italian American Major Leaguers before World War II." *NINE: A Journal of Baseball History and Culture* 14.1 (2005): 98–106. Print.

Banfield, Edward C. *The Moral Basis of a Backward Society.* 1958. New York: Free, 1967. Print.

Barbieri, Maria. "Ribelliamoci!" *La questione sociale* 18 Nov. 1905: n. pag. Print.

Barnett, Pamela E. "Other People's Food." DeSalvo and Giunta 135–42.

Barolini, Helen. "Becoming a Literary Person out of Context." *Massachusetts Review* 27.2 (1986): 262–74. Print.

————. *Chiaroscuro: Essays of Identity.* 1997. Madison: U of Wisconsin P, 1999. Print.

————. *Chiaroscuro: Saggi sull'identità.* Milan: Guerini, 2004. Print.

————. *A Circular Journey.* New York: Fordham UP, 2006. Print.

————. "A Circular Journey." *Texas Quarterly* 21.2 (1978): 109–26. Print.

————, ed. *The Dream Book: An Anthology of Writings by Italian American Women.* 1985. Syracuse: Syracuse UP, 2000. Print.

————. *More Italian Hours and Other Stories.* Boca Raton: Bordighera, 2001. Print.

————. *Passaggio in Italia.* Rome: Avagliano, 2003. Print.

————. *Umbertina.* 1979. Afterword by Edvige Giunta. New York: Feminist, 1999. Print.

Barone, Dennis, ed. *Furnished Rooms: Emanuel Carnevali.* New York: Bordighera, 2006. Print.

Barreca, Regina. *Don't Tell Mama! The Penguin Book of Italian American Writing.* New York: Penguin, 2002. Print.

————, ed. Spec. issue of *LIT: Literature Interpretation Theory* 13.3 (2002): 167–248; 14.1 (2003): 1–67. Print.

————, ed. *A Sitdown with the Sopranos: Watching Italian American Culture on TV's Most Talked-About Series.* New York: Palgrave, 2002. Print.

Barrera, Giulia, Alfredo Martini, Antonella Mulè, eds. *Fonti orali: Censimento degli istituti di conservazione.* Rome: Archivi di Stato, 1993. Print. Quaderni della rassegna degli archivi di Stato.

Barresi, Dorothy. *All of the Above.* Boston: Beacon, 1991. Print.

————. *The Post-rapture Diner.* Pittsburgh: U of Pittsburgh P, 1996. Print.

————. *Rouge Pulp.* Pittsburgh: U of Pittsburgh P, 2002. Print.

Bartholomae, David, and Anthony Petrosky, eds. *Facts, Artifacts, and Counterfacts: Theory and Method for a Reading and Writing Course.* Upper Montclair: Boynton, 1986. Print.

Bartis, Peter. *Folklife and Fieldwork: A Layman's Introduction to Field Techniques.* 1979. *Library of Congress.* Lib. of Cong., 2002. Web. 15 Apr. 2008.

Bartkowski, Frances. *Travelers, Immigrants, Inmates: Essays in Estrangement.* Minneapolis: U of Minnesota P, 1995. Print.

Barzini, Luigi. *O America, When You and I Were Young.* New York: Penguin, 1977. Print.

Bates, Katharine Lee. Introduction. *The Marble Faun; or, The Romance of Monte Beni.* By Nathaniel Hawthorne. New York: Crowell, 1902. v–xxi. Print.

Bayles, David, and Ted Orland. *Art and Fear: Observations on the Perils (and Rewards) of Artmaking.* Santa Barbara: Capra, 1993. Print.

Belloni, Alessandra. "Alessandra Belloni: In Her Own Words." Interview and trans. Luisa Del Giudice. Del Giudice, *Oral History* 193–251.

Belluscio, Stephen, ed. *Constructing a Bibliography: American Italian Historical Association, 1968–2003.* Boca Raton: Bordighera, 2004. Print.

————. "Sixty Years of Breaking Silences: A Brief History of Italian American Literary Criticism." *Italian Americans: A Retrospective on the Twentieth Century.*

Ed. Paola Sensi-Isolani and Anthony Julian Tamburri. Staten Island: Amer. Italian Hist. Assn., 2001. 241–67. Print.

———. *To Be Suddenly White: Literary Realism and Racial Passing.* Columbia: U of Missouri P, 2006. Print.

Beltrami, Giacomo Costantino. *A Pilgrimage in America, Leading to the Discovery of the Sources of the Mississippi and Bloody River; with a Description of the Whole Course of the Former, and of the Ohio.* 1828. Chicago: Quadrangle, 1962. Print.

Benasutti, Marion. *No Steady Job for Papa.* New York: Vanguard, 1966. Print.

Bender, Daniel E., and Richard A. Greenwald, eds. *Sweatshop, USA: The American Sweatshop in Historical and Global Perspective.* New York: Routledge, 2003. Print.

Bermani, Cesare, and Antonella De Palma, eds. *Fonti orali: Istruzioni per l'uso.* Venice: Soc. Mutuo Soccorso Ernesto de Martino, 2008. Print.

Bernardi, Adria. "The Errant Steps of Wooden Shoes." *Travelers' Tales Italy: True Stories.* Ed. Anne Calcagno. San Francisco: Travelers' Tales, 2001. 280–95. Print.

———. *In the Gathering Woods.* Pittsburgh: U of Pittsburgh P, 2000. Print.

Bernardy, Amy. *America Vissuta.* Torino: Bocca, 1911. Print.

———. *Paese che vai: Il mondo come l'ho visto io.* Firenze: Le Monnier, 1923. Print.

Betocchi, Silvio, ed. *Giuseppe Prezzolini: The American Years, 1929–1962.* New York: Vanni, 1994. Print.

Bevilacqua, Piero, Andreina De Clementi, and Emilio Franzina, eds. *Storia dell'emigrazione italiana.* 2 vols. Rome: Donzelli, 2001–02. Print.

Bhabha, Homi K. *The Location of Culture.* London: Routledge, 1994. Print.

Birnbaum, Lucia Chiavola, ed. *She Is Everywhere! An Anthology of Writing in Womanist/Feminist Spirituality.* New York: iUniverse, 2005. Print.

Biskind, Peter. *Easy Riders, Raging Bulls: How the Sex-Drugs-and-Rock-'n-Roll Generation Saved Hollywood.* New York: Simon, 1998. Print.

Blumenthal, Ralph. "Black Youth Is Killed by Whites; Brooklyn Attack Is Called Racial." *New York Times* 25 Aug. 1989, late ed.: A1. Print.

———. "Police Search for Eighteen-Year-Old in Killing of Brooklyn Youth." *New York Times* 26 Aug. 1989, late ed., sec. 1: 1. Print.

Boelhower, William. *Immigrant Autobiography in the United States (Four Versions of the Italian American Self).* Verona: Essedue, 1982. Print.

———. *Through a Glass Darkly: Ethnic Semiosis in American Literature.* New York: Oxford UP, 1986. Print.

Boelhower, William, and Rocco Pallone. *Adjusting Sites: New Essays in Italian American Studies.* Stony Brook: Forum Italicum, 1999. Print. Filibrary 16.

Bohlen, Celestine. "In Bensonhurst, Grief Mixed with Shame and Blunt Bias." *New York Times* 28 Aug. 1989, late ed.: A1. Print.

Bona, Mary Jo. *Claiming a Tradition: Italian American Women Writers.* Carbondale: Southern Illinois UP, 1999. Print.

———, ed. *Italian American Literature.* Spec. issue of *MELUS* 28.3 (2003): 3–237. Print.

―――. "*Mater Dolorosa* No More? Mothers and Writers in the Italian/American Literary Tradition." *VIA: Voices in Italian Americana* 7.2 (1996): 1–19. Print.

―――, ed. *The Voices We Carry: Recent Italian/American Women's Fiction.* New York: Guernica, 1994. Print.

Bonaffini, Luigi, ed. *Dialect Poetry of Southern Italy: Texts and Criticism: A Trilingual Anthology.* New York: Legas, 1997. Print.

―――, trans. *Phrases and Passages of a Salutary Song, Mario Luzi.* Toronto: Guernica, 1999. Print.

―――, trans. *Variable Star, Vittorio Sereni.* Toronto: Guernica, 1999. Print.

Bonaffini, Luigi, and Achille Serrao, eds. *Dialect Poetry of Northern and Central Italy: Texts and Criticism: A Trilingual Anthology.* New York: Legas, 2001. Print.

Bonaffini, Luigi, Achille Serrao, and Justin Vitiello, trans. *Via Terra: An Anthology of Contemporary Italian Dialect Poetry.* Brooklyn: Legas, 1999. Print.

Bondanella, Peter. *Hollywood Italians: Dagos, Palookas, Romeos, Wise Guys, and Sopranos.* New York: Continuum, 2004. Print.

Born in Slavery: Slave Narratives from the Federal Writers' Project, 1936–38. Manuscript Div. and Prints and Photographs Div., Lib. of Cong., 23 Mar. 2001. Web. 27 Mar. 2009.

Bourdieu, Pierre. *Outline of a Theory of Practice.* New York: Cambridge UP, 1991. Print.

Boyle, Kay, ed. *The Autobiography of Emanuel Carnevali.* New York: Horizon, 1980. Print.

Brandes, Donna, and Paul Ginnis. *A Guide to Student-Centred Learning.* Oxford: Blackwell, 1986. Print.

Brizzolara, Andrew. "The Image of Italian Americans on U.S. Television." *Italian Americana* 6.2 (1980): 160–68. Print.

Brock, Geoffrey, trans. *Disaffections: Complete Poems 1930–1950 by Cesare Pavese.* Port Townsend: Copper Canyon, 2002. Print.

―――. "Italian Poetry Portfolio—Some Recent Italian Poems." *Poetry* 191.3 (2007): 209. Print.

Brodkin, Karen. *How Jews Became White Folks and What That Says about Race in America.* New Brunswick: Rutgers UP, 1998. Print.

Brown, Dan. *The Da Vinci Code.* New York: Doubleday, 2003. Print.

Bryant, Dorothy Calvetti. *Miss Giardino.* 1978. Afterword by Janet Zandy. New York: Feminist, 1997. Print.

Buongiorno, Virginia. "Alle compagne lavoratrici!" *La questione sociale* 15 Oct. 1895: n. pag. Print.

Burke, Cheryl. "Bone, Veins, and Fat." DeSalvo and Giunta 105–12.

Burns, Jennifer, and Loredana Polezzi, eds. *Borderlines: Migrazioni e identità nel Novecento.* Isernia: Iannone, 2003. Print.

Bush, Mary Bucci. *Drowning.* Berkeley: Parentheses Writing Series, 1995. Print.

Cahill, Susan Neunzig, ed. *Desiring Italy.* New York: Fawcett, 1997. Print.

Calandra, John D. *A History of Italian American Discrimination at CUNY.* Albany: New York State Senate, 1978. Print.

Calcagno, Anne, ed. *Italy: True Stories of Life on the Road*. San Francisco: Travelers' Tales, 1998. Print.

Camaiti Hostert, Anna. "Filming on the Hyphen: Gender and Ethnicity in Italian/American Cinema." *VIA: Voices in Italian Americana* 17.1 (2006): 59–68. Print.

Camaiti Hostert, Anna, and Anthony Julian Tamburri, eds. *Scene italoamericane. Rappresentazioni cinematografiche degli italiani d'America*. Rome: Sossella, 2001. Print.

———, eds. *Screening Ethnicity: Cinematographic Representations of Italian Americans in the United States*. Boca Raton: Bordighera, 2002. Print.

Cameron, Ardis. *Radicals of the Worst Sort: Laboring Women in Lawrence, Massachusetts, 1860–1912*. Urbana: U of Illinois P, 1993. Print.

Cameron, Julia. *The Artist's Way: A Spiritual Path to Higher Creativity*. New York: Putnam, 1992. Print.

Cammett, John, ed. *The Italian American Novel*. Staten Island: Amer. Italian Hist. Assn., 1969. Print.

Canadé Sautman, Francesca. "Grey Shades, Black Tones: Italian Americans, Race and Racism in American Film." Camaiti Hostert and Tamburri, *Screening* 1–31.

———. "Women of the Shadows: Italian American Women, Ethnicity and Racism in American Cinema." *Differentia* 6-7 (1994): 219–46. Print.

Cannistraro, Philip, and Gerald Meyer, eds. *The Lost World of Italian American Radicalism: Politics, Culture, History*. Westport: Praeger, 2003. Print.

Capello, Phyllis. "Factory Girls, Bangkok." *Paterson Literary Review* 27 (1998): 405. Print.

———. "A Song for the Girls at the Triangle Shirtwaist Factory." "Embroidered Lines and Cut Threads." Ed. Edvige Giunta and Joseph Sciorra. Forthcoming.

Capone, Giovanna, Denise Nico Leto, and Tommi Avicolli Mecca, eds. *Hey Paesan! Writings by Lesbians and Gay Men of Italian Descent*. San Francisco: Three Guineas, 1999. Print.

Caponegro, Mary. *Materia prima*. Rome: Leconte, 2004. Print.

———. *The Star Café and Other Stories*. New York: Macmillan, 1990. Print.

———. *Tales from the Next Village: Fictions of Mary Caponegro*. Providence: Lost Roads, 1985. Print.

Caporale, Rocco, ed. *The Italian-Americans through the Generations*. New York: Amer. Italian Hist. Assn., 1986. Print.

Capotorto, Rosette. *Bronx Italian*. Hoboken: Pronto, 2002. Print.

———. "How Is Sicily Like Jamaica?" "Take My Redheaded Word for It." 2004. MS.

———. "In the Real World." MS.

———. "Some White Guy Guru Type Talks On and On." MS.

Cappello, Mary. *Night Bloom: A Memoir*. Boston: Beacon, 1998. Print.

Carnevale, Nancy. *A New Language, a New World: Italians in the U.S.* Urbana: U of Illinois P, 2009. Print.

Carnevali, Emmanuel. *A Hurried Man*. Paris: Contact, 1925. Print.

Caroli, Betty Boyd, Robert F. Harney, and Lydio F. Tomasi, eds. *The Italian Immigrant Woman in North America*. Toronto: Multicultural Hist. Soc. of Toronto, 1978. Print.

Caronia, Nancy. "Go to Hell." DeSalvo and Giunta 95–100.

Carravetta, Peter. "Con/Texts before the Journeys: Migration, Narration, Historical Identities." *L'esilo come certezza*. Ed. A. Ciccarelli and P. A. Giordano. West Lafayette: Bordighera, 1998. 246–83. Print.

Carravetta, Peter, and Paolo Valesio, eds. *Poesaggio: Poeti italiani d'America*. Quinto di Treviso: Pagus, 1993. Print.

Carrera, Alessandro, and Alessandro Vettori. *Binding the Lands: Proceedings of the Third Annual Symposium of the Italian Poetry Society of America*. New Brunswick: Italian Heritage Studies, 2004. Print.

Casella, Paola. *Hollywood Italian: Gli italiani nell'America di celluloide*. Milan: Baldini, 1998. Print.

Casillo, Robert. "Catholicism and Violence in the Films of Martin Scorsese." Tropea, Miller, and Beattie-Repetti 283–304.

———. *Gangster Priest: The Italian American Films of Martin Scorsese*. Toronto: U of Toronto P, 2006. Print.

———. "Reflections on Italian American Cinema." *VIA: Voices in Italian Americana* 17.1 (2006): 1–27. Print.

Casillo, Robert, and John Paul Russo. *The Italian in Modernity*. Vol. 1. Toronto: U of Toronto P, forthcoming.

Catalano, Roberto, and Enzo Fina. "Simple Does Not Mean Easy: Oral Tradition Values, Music, and the *Musicàntica* Experience." Del Giudice, *Oral History* 119–35.

Cavallero, Jonathan J. "Gangsters, Fessos, Tricksters, and Sopranos: The Historical Roots of Italian American Stereotype Anxiety." *Journal of Popular Film and Television* 32.2 (2004): 50–63. Print.

Cavallo, Diana. *A Bridge of Leaves*. 1961. Toronto: Guernica, 1997. Print.

Cavedagni, Ersilia. "Straniera." *La questione sociale* 31 Dec. 1898: n. pag. Print.

Cecchi, Emilio. *America amara*. Firenze: Sansoni, 1943. Print.

Ceramella, Nick, and Giuseppe Massara, eds. *Merica. Forme della cultura italo-americana*. Isernia: Iannone, 2004. Print.

Ceravolo, Joseph. *The Green Lake Is Awake: Selected Poems*. Saint Paul: Coffee House, 1994. Print.

Chambers, Iain. "Citizenship, Language, and Modernity." *PMLA* 117.1 (2002): 24–31. Print.

Choate, Mark I. *Emigrant Nation: The Making of Italy Abroad*. Cambridge: Harvard UP, 2008. Print.

Ciambelli, Bernardino. *I misteri di Mulberry*. New York: Frugone, 1893. Print.

———. *The Mysteries of Mulberry Street*. 1893. Marazzi, *Voices* 52–61.

Cianfarra, Camillo. *The Diary of an Immigrant*. 1904. Marazzi, *Voices* 113–21.

Ciardi, John. *As If: Poems New and Selected*. New Brunswick: Rutgers UP, 1955. Print.

———, trans. The Divine Comedy, *Dante Alighieri*. New York: Norton, 1977. Print.

Ciardi, John, and Edward M. Ciefelli. *The Collected Poems of John Ciardi*. Fayetteville: U of Arkansas P, 1997. Print.

Ciatu, Nzula Angelina, Domenica Dileo, and Gabriela Micallef, eds. *Curaggia: Writings by Women of Italian Descent*. Ontario: Canadian Scholars, 1998. Print.

Ciefelli, Edward M. *John Ciardi: A Biography*. Fayetteville: U of Arkansas P, 1997. Print.

Cinel, Dino. *The National Integration of Italian Return Migration, 1870–1929*. New York: Cambridge UP, 1991. Print.

Cinotto, Simone. *Una famiglia che mangia insieme: Cibo ed etnicità nella comunità italoamericana di New York, 1920–1940*. Turin: Otto, 2000. Print.

Ciongoli, A. Kenneth, and Jay Parini, eds. *Beyond the Godfather: Italian American Writers on the Real Italian American Experience*. Hanover: UP of New England, 1997. Print.

———. Preface. Ciongoli and Parini, *Beyond* xiii–xiv.

Cipolla, Gaetano. *Siciliana: Studies on the Sicilian Ethos*. New York: Legas, 2005. Print.

Cipriani, Lisi. *The Cry of Defeat*. Boston: Gorham, 1906. Print.

Ciresi, Rita. *Sometimes I Dream in Italian*. New York: Delacorte, 2000. Print.

Citino, David. *The Book of Appasionata: Collected Poems*. Columbus: Ohio State UP, 1998. Print.

Clemente, Carole A. "The Italian-American Woman: Searching for a Sense of Identity through Literature." *VIA: Voices in Italian Americana* 9.1 (1998): 163–73. Print.

Collins, Richard. *John Fante: A Literary Portrait*. Toronto: Guernica, 2000. Print.

Conzen, Kathleen Neils, David A. Gerber, Ewa Morawska, George E. Pozzetta, and Rudolph J. Vecoli. "The Invention of Ethnicity." *Journal of American Ethnic History* 12.1 (1992): 3–41. Print.

Cooper, Stephen. *Full of Life: A Biography of John Fante*. New York: Farrar, 2000. Print.

Cordiferro, Riccardo [Alessandro Sisca]. "L'onore perduto." N.d. TS.

———. *Il pezzente*. New York: Cocce, n.d. Print.

Corsi, Edward. *In the Shadow of Liberty: The Chronicle of Ellis Island*. New York: Macmillan, 1935. Print.

Corso, Gregory. *Mindfield: New and Selected Poems*. New York: Thunder Mouth, 1989. Print.

Corso, Paola. "Girl Talk." *Feminist Studies* 31.3 (2005): 616–17. Print.

Cortes, Carlos. "Italian-Americans in Film: From Immigrants to Icons." *MELUS* 14.3-4 (1987): 107–26. Print.

Cosco, Joseph P. *Imagining Italians: The Clash of Romance and Race in American Perceptions, 1880–1910*. Albany: State U of New York P, 2003. Print.

Costanzo, Gerald. *Nobody Lives on Arthur Godfrey Boulevard*. Brockport: BOA, 1992. Print.

Covello, Leonard. *The Social Background of the Italo-American School Child: A Study of the Southern Italian Family Mores and Their Effect on the School Situation in Italy and America*. 1944. Totowa: Rowman, 1972. Print.

Crispino, Anna Maria. Editorial. Crispino, Giunta, and Romeo 3.

Crispino, Anna Maria, with Edvidge Giunta and Caterina Romeo, eds. *Italiane d'America*. Spec. issue of *Leggendaria* 46-47 (2004): 1–56. Print.

Cutrufelli, Maria Rosa. *Canto al deserto: Storia di Tina. Soldato di mafia*. Milano: Longanesi, 1994. Print.

Dabbene, John. "CSJ Calls on Hollywood to Stop Perpetrating Native Stereotyping of Italian-Americans." *Justice* July-Aug. 1998: n. pag. Web. 14 July 2009.

D'Acierno, Pellegrino. "Cinema Paradiso: The Italian American Presence in American Cinema." D'Acierno, *Italian American Heritage* 563–690.

———. "From Stella to Stella: Italian American Visual Culture and Its Contribution to the Arts in America." D'Acierno, *Italian American Heritage* 499–552.

———, ed. *The Italian American Heritage: A Companion to Literature and Arts*. New York: Garland, 1999. Print.

D'Agostino, Guido. *Olives on the Apple Tree*. New York: Doubleday, 1940. Print.

D'Agostino, Peter. "Craniums, Criminals, and the 'Cursed Race': Italian Anthropology in U.S. Racial Thought." *Comparative Studies of Society and History* 44.2 (2002): 319–43. Print.

D'Ambrosio, Paul S. *Ralph Fasanella's America*. Cooperstown: Fenimore Art Museum, 2001. Print.

D'Angelo, Pascal. *Son of Italy*. 1924. Buffalo: Guernica, 2003. Print.

Daniels, Roger. *Not Like Us: Immigrants and Minorities in America, 1890–1924*. Chicago: Dee, 1997. Print.

Da Ponte, Lorenzo. *Memoirs of Lorenzo Da Ponte Mozart's Librettist*. Trans. L. A. Sheppard. Boston: Houghton, 1929. Print.

———. *Le memorie di Lorenzo Da Ponte, da Ceneda, scritte da esso*. New York: Gray, 1923. Print.

De Capite, Michael. *Maria*. New York: Day, 1943. Print.

DeCaro, Frank. *A Boy Named Phyllis: A Suburban Memoir*. New York: Viking, 1996. Print.

Delamater, Jerome H., and Mary Ann Trasciatti, eds. *Representing Sacco and Vanzetti*. New York: Palgrave, 2005. Print.

Del Giudice, Luisa. "The 'Archvilla': An Italian Canadian Architectural Archetype." Del Giudice, *Studies* 53–105.

———. "Cursed Flesh: Faith Healers, Black Magic, and Death in a Central Italian Town." *Italian American Review* 8.2 (2001): 45–56. Print.

———. "Ethnography and Spiritual Direction: Varieties of Listening." *Rethinking the Sacred*. Proceedings of the 9th SIEF Conference, 2008, Derry. Ed. Ulrika Wolf-Knuts. Abo: Abo Akademi UP, 2009. 9–23. Print.

———. "The Folk Music Revival and the Culture of *Tarantismo* in the Salento." Del Giudice and Van Deusen 217–72.

———. "Italian American Folklore, Folklife." LaGumina, Cavaioli, Primeggia, and Varacalli 237–45.

———, ed. *Italian Traditional Song*. 1989. Los Angeles: Italian Heritage Culture Foundation and the Istituto Italiano di Cultura, 1995. Print.

———. "Italian Traditional Song in Toronto: From Autobiography to Advocacy." *Journal of Canadian Studies* 29.1 (1994): 74–89. Print.

———. "Mountains of Cheese and Rivers of Wine: *Paesi di Cuccagna* and Other Gastronomic Utopias." Del Giudice and Porter 11–63.

———. "Speaking Memory: Oral History, Oral Culture and Italians in America." Del Giudice, *Oral History* 3–18.

———, ed. *Oral History, Oral Culture, and Italian Americans.* Selected papers from the 38th annual meeting of the American Italian Historical Association, 3–6 Nov. 2005, Los Angeles. New York: Palgrave, 2009. Print.

———, ed. *Studies in Italian American Folklore.* Logan: Utah State UP, 1993. Print.

———. " 'Wine Makes Good Blood': Wine Culture among Toronto Italians." *Ethnologies* 23.1 (2001): 1–27. Print.

Del Giudice, Luisa, and Gerald Porter, eds. *Imagined States: National Identity, Utopia, and Longing in Oral Cultures.* Logan: Utah State UP, 2001. Print.

Del Giudice, Luisa, and Nancy Van Deusen, eds. *Performing Ecstasies: Music, Dance, and Ritual in the Mediterranean.* Ottawa: Inst. for Medieval Music, 2005. Print. Claremont Cultural Studies.

DeLillo, Don. *Cosmopolis.* New York: Scribner's, 2003. Print.

———. *Mao II.* New York: Viking, 1991. Print.

———. *Underworld.* New York: Random, 1997. Print.

———. *White Noise.* New York: Viking, 1985. Print.

Demetrick Russo, Mary, and Maria Famà. *Italian Notebook.* Syracuse: Hale Mary, 1995. Print.

Denning, Michael. *The Cultural Front: The Laboring of American Culture in the Twentieth Century.* New York: Verso, 1996. Print.

De Rosa, Tina. *Paper Fish.* 1980. Afterword by Edvige Giunta. New York: Feminist, 1996. Print.

———. *Pesci di carta.* Trans. Laura Giacolone. Pref. Caterina Romeo. Afterword by Edvige Giunta. Roma: Nutrimenti, 2007. Print.

De Rosalia, Giovanni. *Il Duello di Nofrio.* New York: Italian, 1918. Print.

———. *Litteriu trantulia ovvero Lu nobili sfasulatu.* New York: Follia, n.d. Print.

———. *Nofrio al Telefono.* New York: Italian, 1918. Print.

DeSalvo, Louise. *Breathless: An Asthma Journal.* Boston: Beacon, 1997. Print.

———. "Color: White/Complexion: Dark." Guglielmo and Salerno, *Are* 17–28.

———. *Crazy in the Kitchen: Food, Feuds, and Forgiveness in an Italian American Family.* New York: Bloomsbury, 2004. Print.

———. " 'Mbriago." Gutkind and Herman 1–14.

———. *Vertigo.* 1997. Introd. Edvige Giunta. New York: Feminist, 2002. Print.

———. *Vertigo.* Italian trans. Rome: Nutrimenti, 2006. Print.

DeSalvo, Louise, and Edvige Giunta, eds. *The Milk of Almonds: Italian American Women Writers on Food and Culture.* New York: Feminist, 2002. Print.

De Stefano, George. *An Offer We Can't Refuse: The Mafia in the Mind of America.* New York: Farrar, 2006. Print.

De Vito, Anthony J. "The Struggle for Existence in the Work of Giovanni Verga." *Italica* 18.4 (1941): 179–85. Print.

De Vries, Rachel Guido. *Gambler's Daughter.* Toronto: Guernica, 2002. Print.

———. *How to Sing to a Dago.* Toronto: Guernica, 1996. Print.

di Donato, Pietro. *Christ in Concrete*. 1939. New York: Signet, 1993. Print.

Di Geronimo, Donato. Message to Marisa Trubiano. 29 Nov. 2004. E-mail.

Di Pasquale, Emanuel. *Escapes the Night*. Stony Brook: Gradiva, 2001. Print.

———, trans. *Silvio Ramat's Sharing a Trip: Selected Poems*. Lafayette: Bordighera, 2001. Print.

Di Piero, W. S. *Brother Fire*. New York: Knopf, 2004. Print.

———. *Chinese Apples: New and Selected Poems*. New York: Knopf, 2007. Print.

di Prima, Diane. *Memoirs of a Beatnik*. 1969. New York: Penguin, 1998. Print.

———. *Pieces of Song: Selected Poems*. San Francisco: City Lights, 1990. Print.

———. *Recollections of My Life as a Woman: The New York Years*. New York: Viking, 2001. Print.

Di Robilant, Irene. *Vita americana*. Torino: Bocca, 1929. Print.

Di Stasi, Lawrence. "How World War II Iced Italian American Culture." *Multi-America: Essays on Cultural Wars and Cultural Peace*. Ed. Ishmael Reed. New York: Viking, 1997. 169–78. Print.

———. *Una Storia Segreta: The Secret History of Italian American Evacuation and Internment during World War II*. Berkeley: Heyday, 2001. Print.

Donatelli, Cindy, and Sharon Alward. "'I Dread You'? Married to the Mob in *The Godfather, Goodfellas*, and *The Sopranos*." Lavery, *This Thing* 60–71.

Donofrio, Beverly. *Looking for Mary; or, The Blessed Mother and Me*. New York: Viking, 2000. Print.

———. *Riding in Cars with Boys: Confessions of a Bad Girl Who Makes Good*. New York: Penguin, 1990. Print.

Dunaway, D. K., and W. K. Baum, eds. *Oral History: An Interdisciplinary Anthology*. Walnut Creek: Altamira, 1996. Print.

Durante, Francesco, ed. *Figli di due mondi. Fante, Di Donato & C.: Narratori italoamericani degli anni '30 e '40*. Rome: Avagliano, 2002. Print.

———, ed. *Italoamericana: Storia e letteratura degli Italiani negli Stati Uniti*. 2 vols. Milano: Mondadori, 2001–05. Print.

Eco, Umberto. *Art and Beauty in the Middle Ages*. New Haven: Yale UP, 1986. Print.

"1891: New Orleans Prejudice and Discrimination Results in Lynching of Eleven Italians, the Largest Mass Lynching in United States History." *Milestones of the Italian American Experience*. Natl. Italian Amer. Foundation, 2003. Web. 4 Mar. 2009.

Eley, Geoff, and Ronald Grigor Suny. "Introduction: From the Moment of Social History to the Work of Cultural Representation." *Becoming National: A Reader*. Ed. Eley and Suny. New York: Oxford UP, 1996. 3–37. Print.

Equi, Elaine. *Ripple Effect: New and Selected Poems*. Saint Paul: Coffee House, 2007. Print.

Ermelino, Louisa. *The Sisters Mallone*. New York: Simon, 2002. Print.

Esposito, Dawn. "Gloria, Maerose, Irene, and Me: Mafia Women and Abject Spectatorship." *MELUS* 28.3 (2003): 91–109. Print.

———. "The Italian Mother: The Wild Woman Within." Camaiti Hostert and Tamburri, *Screening* 32–47.

Esposito, Michael D. "The Travail of Pietro di Donato." *MELUS* 7.2 (1980): 47–60. Print.

Ets, Marie Hall, ed. *Rosa: The Life of an Italian Immigrant.* 1970. Madison: U of Wisconsin P, 1999. Print.

———. *Rosa: Vita di una emigrante italiana.* Cuggiono: Ecoistituto della Valle del Ticino, 2003. Print.

Evans, George Ewart. *Ask the Fellows Who Cut the Hay.* London: Faber, 1956. Print.

Ewen, Elizabeth. *Immigrant Women in the Land of Dollars: Life and Culture on the Lower East Side, 1890–1925.* New York: Monthly Review, 1985. Print.

Fabbricatore, Giovanni. "L'artista De Rosalia." *L'araldo italiano* 18 Oct. 1905: 3. Print.

Falbo, Italo C. "Figure e scene del teatro popolare italiano a New York." *Il progresso italo-americano* 3 May 1942: 5S. Print.

Falcone, Giovanni, with Marcelle Padovani. *Cose di cosa nostra.* Milano: Rizzoli, 1991. Print.

Fante, John. *Ask the Dust.* 1939. New York: Harper, 2006. Print.

———. *Romanzi e racconti.* Milan: Mondadori, 2003. Print.

———. *Wait until Spring, Bandini.* 1938. Santa Rosa: Black Sparrow, 1983. Print.

Farrell, James T. "The End of a Literary Decade." *Literature at the Barricades: The American Writer in the 1930s.* Ed. Ralph Bogardus and Fred Hobson. Tuscaloosa: U of Alabama P, 1982. 204–10. Print.

Fazio, Venera, and Delia De Santis, eds. *Sweet Lemons: Writings with a Sicilian Accent.* Mineola: Legas, 2004. Print.

Ferlinghetti, Lawrence. *A Coney Island of the Mind.* New York: New Directions, 1958. Print.

———. *These Are My Rivers: New and Selected Poems, 1955–1993.* New York: New Directions, 1993. Print.

Ferraro, Thomas. *Feeling Italian: The Art of Ethnicity in America.* New York: New York UP, 2005. Print.

Flamma, Ario, ed. *Italiani di America.* New York: Cocce, 1936. Print.

Foley, John Miles, ed. *Teaching Oral Traditions.* New York: MLA, 1998. Print.

Fontanella, Luigi. *Land of Time: Selected Poems, 1972–2003.* New York: Chelsea, 2006. Print.

———. *La parola transfuga: Scrittori italiani in America.* Fiesole: Cadmo, 2003. Print.

Forgacs, David, and Robert Lumley, eds. *Italian Cultural Studies: An Introduction.* New York: Oxford UP, 1996. Print.

Forgione, Louis. *The River Between.* New York: Dutton, 1928. Print.

Foscolo, Ugo. *Le ultime lettere di Jacopo Ortis.* 1930. Chapel Hill: U of North Carolina P, 1970. Print.

Foster, George M. *Culture and Conquest: America's Spanish Heritage.* New York: Wenner-Gren Foundation, 1960. Print.

Frankel, Noralee, and Nancy S. Dye, eds. *Gender, Class, Race, and Reform in the Progressive Era.* Lexington: UP of Kentucky, 1991. Print.

Frankfurter, Felix. *The Case of Sacco and Vanzetti: A Critical Analysis for Lawyers and Laymen.* 1927. New York: Universal Lib., 1962. Print.

Franzina, Emilio. *Dall'Arcadia in America: Attività letteraria ed emigrazione transoceanica in Italia (1850–1940)*. Torino: Fondazione Giovanni Agnelli, 1996. Print.

———. "Emigrazione transoceanica e ricerca storica in Italia: Gli ultimi anni (1978–1988)." *Altreitalie* 1 (1989): 6–56. Print.

Friedman-Kasaba, Kathie. *Memories of Migration: Gender, Ethnicity, and Work in the Lives of Jewish and Italian Women in New York, 1870–1924*. New York: State U of New York P, 1996. Print.

Frisardi, Andrew, trans. *Selected Poems of Giuseppe Ungaretti: A Bilingual Edition*. New York: Farrar, 2002. Print.

Fuller, Margaret. *The Essential Margaret Fuller*. Ed. Jeffrey Steele. New Brunswick: Rutgers UP, 1992. Print.

Fusaro, Darrell. *The Basement*. Dir. Peter Budevski. *The Basement*. Web. 30 Apr. 2008.

"Future Americans Will Be Swarthy." *New York Times* 29 Nov. 1908. Late ed., sec. 2: 7. Print.

Gabaccia, Donna R. *From Sicily to Elizabeth Street: Housing and Social Change among Italian Immigrants, 1880–1930*. Albany: State U of New York P, 1984. Print.

———. "Italian-American Cookbooks: From Oral to Print Culture." *Italian Americana* 16.1 (1998): 15–23. Print.

———. *Italy's Many Diasporas*. Seattle: U of Washington P, 2000. Print.

———. "Race, Nation, Hyphen: Italian-Americans and American Multiculturalism in Comparative Perspective." Guglielmo and Salerno, *Are* 44–59.

Gabaccia, Donna R., and Franca Iacovetta, eds. *Women, Gender, and Transnational Lives: Italian Workers of the World*. Toronto: U of Toronto P, 2002. Print.

Gabaccia, Donna R., and Fraser M. Ottanelli, eds. *Italy's Workers of the World: Labor, Migration, and the Making of Multi-ethnic Nations*. Urbana: U of Illinois P, 2001. Print.

Galassi, Jonathan, trans. *Eugenio Montale, Collected Poems, 1920–1954*. New York: Farrar, 1998. Print.

Gambino, Richard. *Blood of My Blood: The Dilemma of the Italian Americans*. New York: Doubleday, 1974. Print.

———. *Vendetta: The True Story of the Largest Lynching in U.S. History*. 1977. Buffalo: Guernica, 2000. Print.

Gardaphé, Fred L. *From Wiseguys to Wise Men: The Gangster and Italian American Masculinities*. New York: Routledge, 2006. Print.

———. *The Italian American Writer: An Essay and Annotated Checklist*. Spencertown: Forkroads, 1995. Print.

———. *Italian Signs, American Streets: The Evolution of Italian American Narrative*. Durham: Duke UP, 1996. Print.

———. *Leaving Little Italy: Essaying Italian American Culture*. Albany: State U of New York P, 2004. Print.

———. *Moustache Pete Is Dead! Eviva Baffo Pietro! The Fra Noi Columns, 1965–1988*. Boca Raton: Bordighera: 1997. Print. *VIA* Folios 13.

Il genio incompreso. Il progresso italo-americano 18 Sept. 1894: 2. Print.

Genisio, Alba. "Alle donne proletarie." *La questione sociale* 7 Mar. 1908: n. pag. Print.

Georges, Robert A., and Michael Owen Jones. *People Studying People: The Human Element in Fieldwork.* Berkeley: U of California P, 1980. Print.

Gerstle, Gary. *American Crucible: Race and Nation in the Twentieth Century.* Princeton: Princeton UP, 2000. Print.

Giacosa, Giuseppe. *Impressioni d'America.* 1899. Padova: Muzzio, 1994. Print.

Giaimo, Mary. "Mary Giaimo: Three Poems." *Italian American Writers.* Ed. Daniela Gioseffi. Italian Amer. Writs., 2001. Web. 2 May 2008.

Gianini Belotti, Elena. *Pane amaro: Un immigrato italiano in America.* Milan: Rizzoli, 2006. Print.

Gibson, Mary. *Born to Crime: Cesare Lombroso and the Origins of Biological Criminology.* Westport: Praeger, 2002. Print.

Giglio, Adelina. Interviews by Emelise Aleandri. 1995.

Giglio, Alessandro. Interview by Emelise Aleandri. 29 May 1971.

Gilbert, Sandra M. *Kissing the Bread: New and Selected Poems, 1969–1999.* New York: Norton, 1999. Print.

———. "*Piacere Conoscerla*: On Being an Italian-American." Tamburri, Giordano, and Gardaphé 116–20.

———. *Wrongful Death: A Memoir.* New York: Norton, 1995. Print.

Gillan, Jennifer, Maria Mazziotti Gillan, and Edvige Giunta, eds. *Italian American Writers on New Jersey: An Anthology of Poetry and Prose.* New Brunswick: Rutgers UP, 2003. Print.

Gillan, Maria Mazziotti. *All That Lies between Us.* Toronto: Guernica, 2007. Print.

———. *Italian Women in Black Dresses.* Toronto: Guernica, 2004. Print.

———. *Where I Come From: Selected and New Poems.* Toronto: Guernica, 1995. Print.

Gillan, Maria Mazziotti, and Jennifer Gillan, eds. *Unsettling America: An Anthology of Contemporary Multicultural Poetry.* New York: Penguin, 1994. Print.

Gioia, Dana. *Interrogations at Noon.* Saint Paul: Graywolf, 2001. Print.

———. "Low Visibility: Thoughts on Italian American Writers." *Italian Americana* 12.1 (1993): 7–37. Print.

———. "What Is Italian American Poetry?" Ciongoli and Parini 167–74.

Gioia, Dana, and Michael Palma. *New Italian Poets.* Brownsville: Story Line, 1991. Print.

Giordano, Paolo A., ed. *Joseph Tusiani: Poet, Translator, Humanist: An International Homage.* West Lafayette: Bordighera, 1994. Print.

Giordano, Paolo A., and Anthony Julian Tamburri, eds. *Beyond the Margin: Readings in Italian Americana.* Cranbury: Fairleigh Dickinson UP, 1998. Print.

———, eds. Spec. issue of *Canadian Journal of Italian Studies* 19.53 (1996). Print.

Giorno, John. *Subduing Demons in America: Selected Poems, 1962–2007.* Berkeley: Soft Skull, 2008. Print.

Gioseffi, Daniela. *Blood Autumn / Autunno di sangue: Poems New and Selected.* Trans. Elisa Biagini and Luigi Bonaffini. Boca Raton: Bordighera, 2006. Print.

———. *Eggs in the Lake: Poems.* Rochester: BOA, 1979. Print.

Giovannitti, Arturo. *Arrows in the Gale.* Riverside: Hillacre, 1914. Print.

———. *The Collected Poems.* New York: Arno, 1975. Print.

Giriodi, Clotilde. *Una signorina italiana in America.* Torino: Roux, 1893. Print.

Giunta, Edvige. "Blending 'Literary' Discourses: Helen Barolini's Italian/American Narratives." Giordano and Tamburri 114–30.

———. *Dire l'indicibile. Il memoir delle autrici italo americane.* Arezzo: U degli Studi Siena, 2002. Print. Quaderni di studi sulle donne.

———. "Figuring Race." Guglielmo and Salerno, *Are* 224–33.

———, ed. *Italian American Women Authors.* Spec. issue of *VIA: Voices in Italian Americana* 7.2 (1996): 1–315. Print.

———. "Persephone's Daughters." *Creative Nonfiction.* Spec. issue of *Women's Studies: An Interdisciplinary Journal* 33.6 (2004): 767–86. Print.

———. "The Quest for True Love: Ethnicity in Nancy Savoca's Domestic Film Comedy." Camaiti Hostert and Tamburri, *Screening* 259–76.

———. "Remembering Ourselves, Writing Our Histories: Memoir, Oral History, and Global Communities." *Proceedings of the XIII International Oral History Conference, 23–26 June 2004.* Rome: Comune di Roma and Intl. Oral History Assn., 2004. CD-ROM.

———. "'They Cut off Our Tongues When We Came Here': Cultural Mutilation and Healing in Italian American Literature and Film." MLA Annual Convention. Marriott, Philadelphia. 30 Dec. 2004. Address.

———. *Writing with an Accent: Contemporary Italian American Women Authors.* New York: Palgrave, 2002. Print.

Giunta, Edvige, and Caterina Romeo, eds. *Origini: Le scrittrici italo americane.* Spec. issue of *TutteStorie* 8 (2001): 1–80. Print.

Glowczewska, Klara, ed. *The Conde Nast Traveler Book of Unforgettable Journeys: Great Writers on Great Places.* New York: Penguin, 2007. Print.

Gnisci, Armando. "Conclusioni." *Alì e altre storie. Letteratura e immigrazione.* Ed. Raffaele Genovese et al. Rome: Rai Eri, 1998. 99–102. Print.

Golden, Daniel. "The Fate of *La Famiglia*: Italian Images in American Film." Miller, *Kaleidoscopic Lens* 73–97.

Goldman, Anne E. "Autobiography, Ethnography, and History: A Model for Reading." Smith and Watson, *Women* 288–98.

Goldstone, Bud, and Arloa Paquin Goldstone. *The Los Angeles Watts Towers.* Los Angeles: Getty Museum, 1997. Print.

Golin, Steve. *The Fragile Bridge: Paterson Silk Strike, 1913.* Philadelphia: Temple UP, 1988. Print.

Gramsci, Antonio. *The Southern Question.* Trans. and introd. Pasquale Verdicchio. West Lafayette: Bordighera, 1995. Print.

Green, Rose Basile. *The Italian-American Novel: A Document of the Interaction of Two Cultures.* Rutherford: Fairleigh Dickinson UP, 1974. Print.

Greene, Bob, and D. G. Fulford. *To Our Children: Preserving Family History for Generations to Come.* New York: Doubleday, 1993. Print.

Grele, Ronald J. "Directions for Oral History in the United States." Dunaway and Baum 63–78.

———. *Envelopes of Sound: The Art of Oral History.* 1975. Chicago: Precedent, 1985. Print.

Grewal, Inderpal, and Caren Kaplan. *Scattered Hegemonies: Postmodernity and Transnational Feminist Practice.* Minneapolis: U of Minnesota P, 1994. Print.

Guglielmo, Jennifer. "Italian Women's Proletarian Feminism in the New York City Garment Trades, 1890s–1940s." Gabaccia and Iacovetta 247–98.

———. "Sweatshop Feminism: Italian Women's Political Culture in New York City's Needle Trades, 1890–1919." Bender and Greenwald 185–202.

———. "White Lies, Dark Truth." Introduction. Guglielmo and Salerno, *Are* 1–14.

Guglielmo, Jennifer, and Salvatore Salerno, eds. *Are Italians White? How Race Is Made in America.* New York: Routledge, 2003. Print.

———, eds. *Gli italiani sono bianchi? Come l'America ha costruito la razza.* Milan: Saggiatore, 2006. Print.

Guglielmo, Thomas A. "'No Color Barrier': Italians, Race, and Power in the United States." Guglielmo and Salerno, *Are* 29–43.

———. *White on Arrival: Italians, Race, Color, and Power in Chicago, 1890–1945.* New York: Oxford UP, 2003. Print.

Guida, George. *Low Italian.* Lafayette: Bordighera, 2006. Print.

———. *The Peasant and the Pen: Men, Enterprise, and the Recovery of Culture in Italian American Narrative.* New York: Lang, 2003. Print.

Gutkind, Lee, and Joanna Clapps Herman, eds. *Our Roots Are Deep with Passion: Creative Nonfiction Collects New Essays by Italian American Writers.* New York: Other, 2006. Print.

Haley, Alex. *Roots: The Saga of an American Family.* New York: Doubleday, 1976. Print.

Haller, Hermann. *The Hidden Italy: A Bilingual Edition of Italian Dialect Poetry.* Detroit: Wayne State UP, 1986. Print.

———. *Una lingua perduta e ritrovata: L'italiano degli italo-americani.* Firenze: Nova Italia, 1993. Print.

———. *The Other Italy: The Literary Canon in Dialect.* Toronto: U of Toronto P, 1999. Print.

Harrison, Barbara Grizzuti. *An Accidental Autobiography.* Boston: Houghton, 1996. Print.

———. *Italian Days.* New York: Weidenfeld, 1989. Print.

———. *Off Center: Essays.* New York: Dial, 1980. Print.

Haskell, Barbara. *Joseph Stella.* New York: Whitney Museum of Amer. Art, 1994. Print.

Hawthorne, Nathaniel. *The Marble Faun; or, The Romance of Monte Beni.* Introd. Richard H. Brodhead. New York: Penguin, 1990. Print.

Helstosky, Carol. "The Tradition of Invention: Reading History through *La Cucina Napoletana.*" *Italian Americana* 16.1 (1998): 7–15. Print.

Hemingway, Ernest. "Italy 1927." *New Republic* 131.21 (1954): 46–49. Print.

Hendin, Josephine Gattuso. "The New World of Italian American Studies." *American Literary History* 13.1 (2001): 141–57. Print.

———. *The Right Thing to Do.* 1988. Afterword by Mary Jo Bona. New York: Feminist, 1999. Print.

Hewitt, Nancy A. *Southern Discomfort: Women's Activism in Tampa, Florida, 1880s–1920s.* Urbana: U of Illinois P, 2001. Print.

Himsel, Deborah. *Leadership Sopranos Style: How to Become a More Effective Boss.* Chicago: Dearborn, 2004. Print.

Hine, Lewis Wickes. *Women at Work: One Hundred Fifty-Three Photographs.* New York: Dover, 1981. Print.

Hobsbawm, Eric J., and Terence O. Ranger. *The Invention of Tradition.* 1983. Cambridge: Cambridge UP, 1992. Print.

hooks, bell. "Keeping Close to Home." *The Presence of Others: Voices and Images That Call for Response.* Ed. Andrea A. Lunsford and John J. Ruszkiewicz. New York: Bedford–St. Martin's, 1996. Print.

Howells, William Dean. *Italian Journeys.* Boston: Houghton, 1899. Print.

Hunt, Marjorie. *The Smithsonian Folklife and Oral History Interviewing Guide.* Washington: Smithsonian Inst., Center for Folklife and Cultural Heritage, 2003. Web. 30 Apr. 2008.

Hutchinson, E. P. *Legislative History of American Immigration Policy, 1798–1965.* Philadelphia: U of Pennsylvania P, 1981. Print.

Ignatiev, Noel. *How the Irish Became White.* New York: Routledge, 1996. Print.

"Illiteracy and Its Significance." Letter. *New York Times* 12 Jan. 1912, late ed., sec. 8: 3. Print.

"Immigrant Type Low, but 1,100,735 Get In." *New York Times* 7 Jan. 1907, late ed., sec. 5: 5. Print.

Ingle, Bob, and Sandy McClure. *The Soprano State: New Jersey's Culture of Corruption.* New York: St. Martin's, 2008. Print.

Italian-American Literature. Spec. issue of *MELUS* 14.3-4 (1987): 1–170. Print.

Italian Americans in the West Project Collection. Rev. Sarah Bradley Leighton and Rona R. Razon. Amer. Folklife Center, Lib. of Cong., Sept. 2005. Web. 30 Apr. 2008.

"Italian (Includes Sicilians)." *TV Acres.* TV Acres, n.d. Web. 19 Feb. 2009.

Italian Los Angeles: The Italian Resource Guide to Greater Los Angeles. Italian Oral Hist. Inst., 2005. Web. 30 Apr. 2008.

Italian Treasury: Folk Music and Song of Italy. Rounder Records, 1999. CDs. Alan Lomax Collection.

Ives, Edward D. *The Tape-Recorded Interview: A Manual for Field Workers in Folklore and Oral History.* 1980. Knoxville: U of Tennessee P, 1984. Print.

Jackson, Bruce. *Fieldwork.* Urbana: U of Illinois P, 1987. Print.

Jacobson, Matthew Frye. *Barbarian Virtues: The United States Encounters Foreign Peoples at Home and Abroad, 1876–1917.* New York: Hill, 2000. Print.

———. *Roots Too: White Ethnic Revival in Post–Civil Rights America.* Cambridge: Harvard UP, 2006. Print.

———. *Whiteness of a Different Color: European Immigrants and the Alchemy of Race.* Cambridge: Harvard UP, 1999. Print.

James, Henry. "Daisy Miller." 1892. *Tales of Henry James.* Ed. Christof Wegelin. New York: Norton, 1984. 3–50. Print.

———. *Italian Hours. Collected Travel Writing: The Continent.* New York: Lib. of Amer., 1993. 279–620. Print.

Johnson, Kirk. "A New Generation of Racism Is Seen." *New York Times* 27 Aug. 1989, late ed., sec. 1: 32. Print.

Juliani, Richard N., ed. *The Family and Community Life of Italian Americans.* New York: Amer. Italian Hist. Assn., 1983. Print.

———. "The Image of the Italian in American Film and Television." Miller, *Ethnic Images* 99–104.

Kaufman, Michael T. "Despair Comes Twice to a Brooklyn Family." *New York Times* 26 Aug 1989, late ed., sec. 1: 26. Print.

Kessner, Thomas. *The Golden Door: Italian and Jewish Immigrant Mobility.* New York: Oxford UP, 1977. Print.

Keyes, Ralph. *The Courage to Write: How Writers Transcend Fear.* New York: Holt, 2003. Print.

"The Kid from Genoa." 1869. Trans. Ann Goldstein. Marazzi, *Voices* 47–52.

Kingston, Maxine Hong. *The Woman Warrior: Memoirs of a Girlhood among Ghosts.* New York: Vintage, 1989. Print.

Kornweibel, Theodore. *"Seeing Red": Federal Campaigns against Black Militancy, 1919–1925.* Bloomington: Indiana UP, 1998. Print.

Kraut, Alan. *The Huddled Masses: The Immigrant in American Society, 1880–1921.* Wheeling: Davidson, 2001. Print.

Kunstadter, Ruth. Message to Marisa Trubiano. 28 Nov. 2004. E-mail.

La Barbera, John T. "That's Not Italian Music! My Musical Journey from New York to Italy and Back Again." Del Giudice, *Oral History* 101–17.

LaFemina, Gerry. *The Parakeets of Brooklyn / I parrocchetti di Brooklyn.* Trans. Elisa Biagini. Boca Raton: Bordighera, 2005. Print.

LaGumina, Salvatore J. *WOP! A Documentary of Anti-Italian Discrimination in the United States.* San Francisco: Straight Arrow, 1973. Print.

LaGumina, Salvatore J., Frank J. Cavaioli, Salvatore Primeggia, and Joseph A. Varacalli, eds. *The Italian American Experience: An Encyclopedia.* New York: Garland, 2000. Print.

Lamantia, Philip. *Bed of Sphinxes: New and Selected Poems, 1943–1993.* San Francisco: City Lights, 1997. Print.

Lanzillotto, Annie Rachele. "An Artist Journeys Home." *Works of Heart: Building Village through the Arts.* Ed. Lynne Elizabeth and Suzanne Young. Oakland: New Village, 2006. 60–75. Print.

———. *A'Schapett.* Arthur Avenue Retail Market, New York. 1996–97. Performance.

———. "The Fall and Decline of Ancient the Bronx." *Art Journal* 56.4 (1997): 59–61. Print.

———. *How to Cook a Heart.* Arthur Avenue Retail Market, New York. 1997. Print. Transcript.

Lapolla, Garibaldi M. *The Grand Gennaro.* New York: Vanguard, 1935. Print.

La Sorte, Michael A. *La Merica: Images of Italian Greenhorn Experience.* Philadelphia: Temple UP, 1985. Print.

La Spina, Silvana. *La mafia spiegata ai miei figli (e anche ai figli degli altri)*. Milano: Bompiani, 2006. Print.

Laurino, Maria. "Bensonhurst." Laurino, *Were* 121–55.

———. "Italians on TV: From the Fonz to *The Sopranos*, Not Much Evolution." *Miscellanea Rubrica d'Attualità*. Miscellanea, 24 Dec. 2000. Web. 23 June 2003.

———. *Were You Always an Italian? Ancestors and Other Icons of Italian America*. New York: Norton, 2000. Print.

Lavery, David, ed. *Reading the Sopranos: Hit TV from HBO*. New York: Palgrave, 2006. Print.

———, ed. *This Thing of Ours: Investigating* The Sopranos. New York: Columbia UP, 2002. Print.

Lawton, Benjamin. "America through Italian/American Eyes: Dream or Nightmare?" Tamburri, Giordano, Gardaphe 397–429.

———. "Giuseppe Giacosa and Giacomo Puccini." *Abroad in America: Visitors to a New Nation: 1776–1914*. Reading: Smithsonian Inst., 1976. 247–59. Print.

———. "*Taxi Driver*: 'New Hybrid Film' or 'Liberated Cinema'?" *Italian Americana* 5.2 (1979): 238–48. Print.

———. "What Is 'ItalianAmerican' Cinema?" *VIA: Voices in Italian Americana* 6.1 (1995): 27–51. Print.

Leed, Eric. *The Mind of the Traveller: From Gilgamesh to Global Tourism*. Boulder: Perseus, 1992. Print.

———. *Shores of Discovery: How Expeditionaries Have Constructed the World*. New York: Basic, 1995. Print.

Lent, John A. "Television." LaGumina, Cavaioli, Primeggia, and Varacalli 625–28.

Lentricchia, Frank. *The Edge of Night: A Confession*. New York: Random, 1994. Print.

———, ed. *Introducing Don DeLillo*. Durham: Duke UP, 1991. Print.

Lichter, Robert, and Linda Lichter. *Italian American Characters in Television Entertainment*. West Hempstead: Order Sons of Italy in Amer., 1982. Print.

Lionnet, Françoise. "Transnationalism, Postcolonialism or Transcolonialism? Reflections on Los Angeles, Geography, and the Uses of Theory." *Emergences* 10.1 (2000): 25–35. Print.

Lipari, Loryn. "Cracked." DeSalvo and Giunta 123–30.

Lippi-Green, Rosina. *English with an Accent: Language, Ideology, and Discrimination in the United States*. London: Routledge, 1997. Print.

Lloyd, Susan Caperna. *No Pictures in My Grave: A Spiritual Journey in Sicily*. San Francisco: Mercury, 1992. Print.

Lomas, Clara. "Transborder Discourse: The Articulation of Gender in the Borderlands in the Early Twentieth Century." *Frontiers* 24.2-3 (2003): 51–74. Print.

Lombardi, Anna. Interview by Daniela Petruzzella. Spring 2003.

Long, Clair. Message to Marisa Trubiano. 29 Nov. 2004. E-mail.

Lourdeaux, Lee. *Italian and Irish Filmmakers in America: Ford, Capra, Coppola, and Scorsese*. Philadelphia: Temple UP, 1990. Print.

Lowe, Lisa. *Immigrant Acts: On Asian American Cultural Politics.* Durham: Duke UP, 1996. Print.

Lowe, Sarah. *Tina Modotti: Photographs.* New York: Abrams, 1998. Print.

Lummis, Trevor. "Structure and Validity in Oral History." Perks and Thomson, *Oral History Reader* 273–83.

Macari, Anne Marie. *Gloryland.* Farmington: James, 2005. Print.

———. *Ivory Cradle: Poems.* Philadelphia: Amer. Poetry Rev., 2000. Print.

Macrorie, Ken. *Searching Writing.* Rochelle Park: Hayden, 1980. Print.

Maffi, Mario. *Nel mosaico della città: Differenze etniche e nuove culture in un quartiere di New York.* Milano: Feltrinelli, 1992. Print.

Maggio, Theresa. *Mattanza: Love and Death in the Sea of Sicily.* Cambridge: Perseus, 2000. Print.

———. *The Stone Boudoir: Travels through the Hidden Villages of Sicily.* Cambridge: Perseus, 2002. Print.

Magliocco, Sabina. "Imagining the *Strega*: Folklore Reclamation and the Construction of Italian American Witchcraft." *Italian American Review* 8.2 (2001): 57–81. Print.

Maisel, Eric. *Fearless Creating.* New York: Putman, 1995. Print.

Malanga, Gerard. *No Respect: New and Selected Poems, 1964–2000.* Santa Rosa: Black Sparrow, 2001. Print.

Mandelbaum, Allen, trans. *The* Aeneid *of Virgil: A Verse Translation.* Berkeley: U of California P, 1981. Print.

———, trans. *The Divine Comedy.* By Dante. New York: Random, 1995. Print.

Mangione, Jerre. *Mount Allegro: A Memoir of Italian American Life.* 1942. Syracuse: Syracuse UP, 1998. Print.

———. *A Passion for Sicilians: The World around Danilo Dolci.* 1968. New Brunswick: Transaction, 1985. Print.

———. *Reunion in Sicily.* 1950. New York: Columbia UP, 1984. Print.

———. *The Ship and the Flame.* New York: Wyn, 1948. Print.

Mangione, Jerre, and Ben Morreale. *La Storia: Five Centuries of the Italian American Experience.* New York: Harper, 1992. Print.

Manguso, Sarah. *The Captain Lands in Paradise.* Farmington: James, 2002. Print.

———. *Siste Viator.* New York: Four Way, 2006. Print.

Mannino, Mary Ann. *Revisionary Identities: Strategies of Empowerment in the Writings of Italian/American Women.* New York: Lang, 2000. Print.

Mannino, Mary Ann, and Justin Vitiello, eds. *Breaking Open: Reflections on Italian American Women's Writing.* West Lafayette: Purdue UP, 2003. Print.

Maraschio, Nicoletta. "L'italiano del doppiaggio." *La lingua italiana in movimento.* Firenze: Acad. della Crusca, 1982. 137–58. Print.

Marazzi, Martino. *Little America: Gli Stati Uniti e gli scrittori italiani del Novecento.* Milano: Marcos, 1997. Print.

———. *Misteri di Little Italy: Storie e testi della letteratura italoamericana.* Milan: Angeli, 2001. Print.

———. *Voices of Italian America: A History of Early Italian American Literature with a Critical Anthology.* Trans. Ann Goldstein. Madison: Fairleigh Dickinson UP, 2004. Print.

Marchand, Jean-Jacques, ed. *La letteratura dell'emigrazione. Gli scrittori di lingua italiana nel mondo.* Torino: Fondazione Giovanni Agnelli, 1991. Print. Popolazioni e culture italiane nel mondo.

Mariani, Paul. *The Great Wheel.* New York: Penguin, 1996. Print.

Marotta, Kenny. *A Piece of Earth.* New York: Morrow, 1985. Print.

Martelli, Sebastiano. "Letteratura ed emigrazione: Congedo provvisorio." *Il sogno italo-americano. Realtà e immaginario dell'emigrazione negli Stati Uniti.* Ed. Martelli. Naples: Cuen, 1998. 405–43. Print.

Masini, Donna. *That Kind of Danger.* Boston: Beacon, 1994. Print.

———. *Turning to Fiction: Poems.* New York: Norton, 2004. Print.

Maso, Carole. *AVA.* Normal: Dalkey Archive, 1993. Print.

———. "From *The Bay of Angels.*" *Tasting Life Twice: Literary Lesbian Fiction by New American Writers.* Ed. E. J. Levy. New York: Avon, 1995. 320–337. Print.

———. *Ghost Dance.* Hopewell: Ecco, 1995. Print.

———. "Interview with Nicole Cooley." *American Poetry Review* 24.2 (1995): 32–35. Print.

———. *The Room Lit by Roses: A Journal of Pregnancy and Birth.* Washington: Counterpoint, 2000. Print.

Massara, Giuseppe. *Americani.* Palermo: Sellerio, 1984. Print.

Massimilla, Stephen. *Forty Floors from Yesterday/Quaranta piani da ieri.* Trans. Luigi Bonaffini. Boca Raton: Bordighera, 2002. Print.

Mathias, Elizabeth, and Richard Raspa. *Italian Folktales in America: The Verbal Art of an Immigrant Woman.* 1985. Detroit: Wayne State UP, 1988. Print.

Mayes, Frances. *Under the Tuscan Sun: At Home in Italy.* New York: Bantam, 1997. Print.

Mazza, Cris. *Indigenous: Growing Up Californian.* San Francisco: City Lights, 2003. Print.

Mazzucco, Melania G. *Vita.* Milano: Rizzoli, 2003. Print.

McCarthy, William Bernard. "Using Oral Tradition in a Composition Classroom." Foley 436–44.

McDonnell, Jane Taylor. *Living to Tell the Tale: A Guide to Writing Memoir.* New York: Penguin, 1998. Print.

Mecca, Tommi Avicolli, and Anthony Julian Tamburri. *Fuori: Essays by Italian/ American Lesbians and Gays.* West Lafayette: Bordighera, 1996. Print.

Merithew, Caroline Waldron. "Making the Italian Other: Blacks, Whites, and the Inbetween in the 1895 Spring Valley, Illinois, Race Riot." Guglielmo and Salerno, *Are* 79–97.

Messenger, Chris. The Godfather *and American Culture: How the Corleones Became "Our Gang."* Albany: State U of New York P, 2002. Print.

Messina, Elizabeth, ed. *In Our Own Voices: Multidisciplinary Perspectives on Italian and Italian American Women.* West Lafayette: Bordighera, 2003. Print.

———. "Stereotyping of Italian Americans: Reflections on the History of Racism in the History of Psychology toward Italian Americans." Italians in the Americas. John D. Calandra Italian American Institute Conference. Queens Coll., New York. 25 Apr. 2008. Address.

Messina, Maria. "American 1911" ["La Merica"]. M. Messina, *Behind* 32–47.

———. *Behind Closed Doors: Her Father's House and Other Stories of Sicily.* Trans. Elise Magistro. Introd. and afterword by Magistro. Pref. Fred Gardaphé. New York: Feminist, 2007. Print.

Miller, Randall M., ed. *Ethnic Images in American Film and Television.* Philadelphia: Balch Inst., 1978. Print.

———, ed. *The Kaleidoscopic Lens: How Hollywood Views Ethnic Groups.* Englewood: Ozer, 1980. Print.

Mirabal, Nancy Raquel. "'No Country but the One We Must Fight For': The Emergence of an Antillean Nation and Community in New York City, 1860–1901." *Mambo Montage: The Latinization of New York.* Ed. Augustín Laó-Montes and Arlene Dávila. New York: Columbia UP, 2001. 57–72. Print.

Mohanty, Chandra Talpade. "Introduction: Cartographies of Struggle: Third World Women and the Politics of Feminism." *Third World Women and the Politics of Feminism.* Ed. Mohanty, Ann Russo, and Lourdes Torres. Bloomington: Indiana UP, 1991. 1–47. Print.

Monga, Luigi. "Travel and Travel Writing: An Historical Review of Hodeoporics." *Annali d'Italianistica* 14 (1996): 6–54. Print.

———. "The Unavoidable 'Snare of Narrative': Fiction and Creativity in Odeoporics." *Annali d'Italianistica* 21 (2003): 7–45. Print.

Montclair Forum. "Montclair Civil Rights Audit, 1947." *Applied Social Science Research.* Montclair State U, 25 July 2002. Web. 15 Apr. 2008.

Monte, Joseph L. "Correcting the Image of the Italian in American Film and Television." Miller, *Ethnic Images* 109–10.

Moreau, Michael, ed. *Fante/Mencken: A Personal Correspondence, 1930–1952.* Santa Rosa: Black Sparrow, 1989. Print.

"Murder in Brooklyn: Teen Dies Because He Is Black." Editorial. *New York Times* 28 Aug. 1989, late ed.: A10. Print.

Muscio, Giuliana. *Piccole Italie, grandi schermi. Scambi cinematografici tra Italia e gli Stati Uniti, 1895–1945.* Rome: Bulzoni, 2004. Print.

Nachmanovitch, Stephen. *Free Play: Improvisation in Life and Art.* New York: Tarcher-Putnam, 1990. Print.

Napolitano, Louise. *An American Story: Pietro di Donato's* Christ in Concrete. New York: Lang, 1993. Print.

Nardini, Gloria. "Is It True Love? or Not? Patterns of Ethnicity and Gender in Nancy Savoca." *VIA: Voices in Italian Americana* 2.1 (1991): 9–17. Print.

Newman, Louise Michele. *White Women's Rights: The Racial Origins of Feminism in the United States.* New York: Oxford UP, 1999. Print.

"Northcliffe Fears Aliens' Influence." *New York Times* 7 Nov. 1909, late ed., sec. 13: 3. Print.

Olsen, Tillie. *Silences.* New York: Feminist, 2003. Print.

Orleck, Annelise. *Common Sense and a Little Fire: Women and Working-Class Politics in the United States, 1905–1965.* Chapel Hill: U of North Carolina P, 1995. Print.

Orsi, Robert. *The Madonna of 115th Street: Faith and Community in Italian Harlem, 1880–1950.* 2nd ed. New Haven: Yale UP, 2002. Print.

Ossip, Kathleen. *The Search Engine*. Philadelphia: Amer. Poetry Rev., 2002. Print.

Osteen, Mark. *American Magic and Dread: Don DeLillo's Dialogue with Culture*. Philadelphia: U of Pennsylvania P, 2000. Print.

Palmer, Michael. *The Lion Bridge: Selected Poems, 1972–1995*. New York: New Directions, 1998. Print.

Panetta, George. *We Ride a White Donkey*. New York: Harcourt, 1944. Print.

Panunzio, Constantine. *The Soul of an Immigrant*. New York: Macmillan, 1921. Print.

Paoletti, Gianni. *John Fante: Storia di un italoamericano*. Perugia: Foligno, 2005. Print.

Paolicelli, Paul. *Dances with Luigi: A Grandson's Search for His Italian Roots*. New York: Dunne, 2000. Print.

———. *Under the Southern Sun: Stories of the Real Italy and the Americans It Created*. New York: Dunne, 2003. Print.

Papaleo, Joseph. "Ethnic Pictures and Ethnic Fate: The Media Image of Italian-Americans." Miller, *Ethnic Images* 93–97.

Parati, Graziella. *Mediterranean Crossroads: Migration Literature in Italy*. Madison: Fairleigh Dickinson UP, 1999. Print.

———. *Migration Italy: The Art of Talking Back in a Destination Culture*. Toronto: U of Toronto P, 2005. Print.

Parenti, Michael. "The Italian-American and the Mass Media." Miller, *Ethnic Images* 105–07.

Parini, Jay. "Amalfi Days." Ciongoli and Parini 107–13.

Pattie, David. "Mobbed Up: The Sopranos and the Modern Gangster Film." Lavery, *This Thing* 135–45.

Pellegrini, Angelo. *Immigrant's Return*. New York: Macmillan, 1951. Print.

Peragallo, Olga. *Italian American Authors and Their Contribution to American Literature*. New York: Vanni, 1949. Print.

Perella, Nicolas J. *Midday in Italian Literature: Variations on an Archetypal Theme*. Princeton: Princeton UP, 1979. Print.

Perez, Hiram. "If You White, You Write: Teaching Race-Consciousness." *Transformations: The Journal of Inclusive Scholarship and Pedagogy* 16.1 (2005): 83–102. Print.

Perillo, Lucia. *Luck Is Luck: Poems*. New York: Random, 2005. Print.

———. *The Oldest Map with the Name America: New and Selected Poems*. Random, 1999. Print.

Perks, Robert, and Alistair Thomson. "Critical Developments: Introduction." Perks and Thomson, *Oral History Reader* 1–8.

———. "Interpreting Memories: Introduction." Perks and Thomson, *Oral History Reader* 269–72.

———, eds. *The Oral History Reader*. London: Routledge, 1998. Print.

Perrotta, Tom. *Election*. New York: Penguin, 1998. Print.

Picano, Felice. *The Lure*. New York: Delacorte, 1979. Print.

Piovene, Guido. *De America*. Milano: Garzanti, 1962. Print.

Pola, Antonia. *Who Can Buy the Stars?* New York: Vantage, 1957. Print.

Portelli, Alessandro. *L'ordine è già stato eseguito: Roma, le Fosse Ardeatine, la memoria*. Rome: Donzelli, 2001. Print. Trans. as *The Order Has Been Carried*

Out: History, Memory, and Meaning of a Nazi Massacre in Rome. New York: Palgrave, 2003.

Pratt, Mary Louise. *Imperial Eyes: Travel Writing and Transculturation*. New York: Routledge, 1992. Print.

Prezzolini, Giuseppe. *America in pantofole*. Firenze: Vallecchi, 2002. Print.

——. *I trapiantati*. Milano: Longanesi, 1963. Print.

——. *Tutta l'America*. Firenze: Vallecchi, 1958. Print.

Pucelli, Rodolfo, ed. *Anthology of Italian and Italo-American Poetry*. New York: Humphries, 1955. Print.

Puleo, Stephen. *Dark Tide: The Great Boston Molasses Flood of 1919*. Boston: Beacon, 2003. Print.

Puzo, Mario. *The Fortunate Pilgrim*. New York: Atheneum, 1964. Print.

——. *The Godfather*. New York: Putnam, 1969. Print.

——. *The Godfather Papers and Other Confessions*. New York: Fawcett, 1972. Print.

Quigley, Margaret. "The Roots of the I.Q. Debate: Eugenics and Social Control." *Eyes Right! Challenging the Right Wing Backlash*. Ed. Chip Berlet. Boston: South End, 1995. 210–22. Print.

Quinn, Roseanne Giannini. "'We Were Working on an Erotic Song Cycle': Reading Carole Maso's *AVA* as the Poetics of Female Italian-American Cultural and Sexual Identity." *MELUS* 25.3-4 (2001): 91–113. Print.

Rabasca, Rosemarie. Message to Marisa Trubiano. 29 Nov. 2004. E-mail.

Raffaelli, Sergio. "Il dialetto del cinema in Italia (1896–1983)." *Rivista italiana di dialettologia* 7.1 (1983): 13–96. Print.

Ragusa, Kym. "Baked Ziti." DeSalvo and Giunta 276–82.

——. *La pelle che ci separa*. Trans. Clara Antonucci and Caterina Romeo. Afterword by Romeo. Roma: Nutrimenti, 2008. Print.

——. *The Skin between Us: A Memoir of Race, Beauty, and Belonging*. New York: Norton, 2006. Print.

Ravo, Nick. "Marchers and Brooklyn Youths Trade Racial Jeers." *New York Times* 27 Aug. 1989, late ed., sec. 1: 32. Print.

——. "Two Hundred Fifty Whites Jeer Marchers in Brooklyn Youth's Death." *New York Times* 28 Aug. 1989, late ed.: B3. Print.

Reich, Jacqueline. "Godfathers, Goodfellas and Madonnas: A Pedagogical Approach to the Representation of Italian Americans in Recent American Cinema." *VIA: Voices in Italian Americana* 4.1 (1993): 45–64. Print.

Repetto, Vittoria. *Not Just a Personal Ad*. Toronto: Guernica, 2006. Print.

Reville, Luigia. "Ai rivoluzionarii, in nome del gruppo 'L'azione femminile' di Parigi." *La questione sociale* 5 May 1900: n. pag. Print.

Ricciardi, Guglielmo. *Ricciardiana: Raccolta di scritti, racconti, memorie, ecc. del veterano attore e scrittore Guglielmo Ricciardi*. New York: Eloquent, 1955. Print.

Richards, David A. J. *Italian American: The Racializing of an Ethnic Identity*. New York: New York UP, 1999. Print.

Riis, Jacob A. *How the Other Half Lives*. 1890. Boston: Bedford, 1996. Print.

Rimanelli, Giose. *Benedetta in Guysterland*. Toronto: Guernica, 1993. Print.

Rimbaud, Arthur. A Season in Hell *and* Illuminations. Trans. Mark Treharne. London: Dent, 1998. Print.

Rinaldi, Tiziana Castro. *Il lungo ritorno.* Rome: E/O, 2000. Print.

Ritchie, Donald. *Doing Oral History.* New York: Twayne, 1995. Print.

Rizzardi, Alfredo, ed. *Conference Proceedings, October 5–7, 1983: Italy and Italians in America.* Issue of *RSA Journal–Rivista di Studi Nord Americani* 3.4-5 (1984–85): 1–569. Print.

Roach, Joseph. *Cities of the Dead: Circum-Atlantic Performance.* New York: Columbia UP, 1996. Print.

Rocchietti, Giuseppe. *Ifigenia tragedia.* New York: Lockwood, 1842. Print.

———. *Lorenzo and Oonalaska.* Albright and Di Fabio 43–218.

Rodriguez, Richard. *Hunger of Memory: The Education of Richard Rodriguez.* New York: Bantam, 1982. Print.

Roediger, David R. *Towards the Abolition of Whiteness: Essays on Race, Politics, and Working-Class History.* New York: Verso, 1994. Print.

———. *Working toward Whiteness: How America's Immigrants Became White: The Strange Journey from Ellis Island to the Suburbs.* New York: Basic, 2005. Print.

Romano, Rose. "Dago Street." *The Wop Factor.* Brooklyn: Malafemmina, 1994. 19–23. Print.

Romeo, Caterina. *Narrative tra due sponde: Memoir di italiane d'America.* Rome: Carocci, 2005. Print.

Rossi, Adolfo. *Nel paese dei dollari. Tre anni a New York.* Milan: Kantorowics, 1893. Print.

Rossi, Agnes. *Gonna a spacco.* Milan: Mondadori, 1995. Print. Trans. of *Split Skirt.*

Rotella, Mark. *Stolen Figs: And Other Adventures in Calabria.* New York: North Point, 2003. Print.

Roth, Henry. *Call It Sleep.* New York: Ballou, 1934. Print.

Rowbotham, Sheila. *Hidden from History: Three Hundred Years of Women's Oppression and the Fight against It.* London: Pluto, 1973. Print.

Rucker, Allen, and Michele Scicolone. *The Sopranos Family Cookbook: As Compiled by Artie Bucco.* New York: Warner, 2002. Print.

Rushdie, Salman. "Imaginary Homelands." *Imaginary Homelands: Essays and Criticism, 1981–1991.* New York: Granta, 1991. 9–21. Print.

Russell, Francis. *Sacco and Vanzetti: The Case Resolved.* New York: Harper, 1986. Print.

Russo, John Paul. "The Choice of Gilbert Sorrentino." Tamburri, Giordano, and Gardaphé 338–56.

———. "From Italophilia to Italophobia: Representations of Italian Americans in the Early Gilded Age." *Differentia* 6.7 (1994): 45–76. Print.

———. "The Hidden Godfather: Plenitude and Absence in Francis Ford Coppola's *Godfather I* and *II.*" Tropea, Miller, and Beattie-Repetti 255–81.

———. "An Unacknowledged Masterpiece: Capra's Italian-American Film." LaGumina, Cavaioli, Primeggia, and Varacalli 225–32.

Sacco, Nicola, and Bartolomeo Vanzetti. *The Letters of Sacco and Vanzetti.* 1928. New York: Penguin, 2007. Print.

Salerno, Salvatore. "'I Delitti della Razza Bianca' (Crimes of the White Race): Italian Anarchists' Racial Discourse as Crime." Guglielmo and Salerno, *Are* 111–23.

Sánchez-Gonzalez, Lisa. *Boricua Literature: A Literary History of the Puerto Rican Diaspora.* New York: New York UP, 2001. Print.

Saracino, Mary. *Finding Grace.* Duluth: Spinsters Ink, 1999. Print.

———. *Voices of the Soft-Bellied Warrior: A Memoir.* Denver: Spinsters Ink, 2001. Print.

Savarese, Julia. *The Weak and the Strong.* New York: Putnam, 1952. Print.

Scalapino, Leslie. *It's Go in Horizontal: Selected Poems, 1974–2006.* Berkeley: U of California P, 2008. Print.

Scapp, Ron, and Anthony Julian Tamburri, eds. Spec. issue of *Differentia: Review of Italian Thought* 6-7 (1994): 1–379. Print.

Scappettone, Jennifer. "Sonnet Macronic." *Boston Review* Oct.-Nov. 2001: n. pag. Web. 27 Apr. 2008.

Scarpaci, Vincenza. *The Journey of the Italians in America.* Gretna: Pelican, 2008. Print.

Schiavelli, Vincent. *Bruculino, America: Remembrance of Sicilian-American Brooklyn, Told in Stories and Recipes.* Boston: Houghton, 1998. Print.

Schneider, Anthony. *Tony Soprano on Management: Leadership Lessons Inspired by America's Favorite Mobster.* New York: Berkley, 2004. Print.

Schneider, Jane. "Neo-Orientalism in Italy (1848–1995)." Introduction. *Italy's "Southern Question": Orientalism in One Country.* New York: Oxford, 1998. 1–24. Print.

———, ed. *Italy's "Southern Question": Orientalism in One Country.* New York: Berg, 1998. Print.

Sciorra, Joseph. "'Italians against Racism': The Murder of Yusuf Hawkins (R.I.P.) and My March on Bensonhurst." Guglielmo and Salerno, *Are* 192–209.

———. "The Language of Rap Italiano." *Italian Rap.* Sciorra, 4 Apr. 2008. Web. 30 Apr. 2008.

Scott, Joan W. "Experience." *Women, Autobiography, Theory: A Reader.* Ed. Sidonie Smith and Julia Watson. Madison: U of Wisconsin P, 1998. 57–71. Print.

Scotto, Assunta. Message to Marisa Trubiano. 11 Apr. 2008. E-mail.

Scriboni, Mirella. "Il viaggio al femminile in Oriente nell'Ottocento: La Principessa di Belgioioso, Amalia Nizzoli e Carla Serena." *Annali d'Italianistica* 14 (1996): 304–26. Print.

Segale, Blandina. *At the End of the Santa Fe Trail.* 1932. Albuquerque: U of New Mexico P, 1999. Print.

———. *Suor Blandina: Una suora italiana nel West.* Vicenza: Neri Pozza, 1996. Print.

Seller, Maxine. "Antonietta Pisanelli Alessandro and the Italian Theatre of San Francisco: Entertainment, Education, and Americanization." *Educational Theatre Journal* 28.2 (1976): 206–19. Print.

Severgnini, Beppe. *Ciao, America! An Italian Discovers the US.* New York: Broadway, 2002. Print.

Shakur, Tupac. "Me and My Girlfriend." *Don Killuminati: The 7 Day Theory.* Interscope, 1996. CD.

Shell, Marc, ed. *American Babel: Literatures of the United States from Abnaki to Zuni.* Cambridge: Harvard UP, 2002. Print.

Shell, Marc, and Werner Sollors, eds. *The Multilingual Anthology of American Literature: A Reader of Original Texts with English Translations.* New York: New York UP, 2000. Print.

Shengold, David. "A Young Man's Confusion." *Gay City News* 14 Oct. 2004: n. pag. Web. 20 Feb. 2009.

Shreve, Susan Richards, ed. *Dream Me Home Safely: Writers on Growing Up in America.* Boston: Houghton, 2003. Print.

Simeti, Mary Taylor. *On Persephone's Island: A Sicilian Journal.* New York: Vintage, 1995. Print.

Simmons, Marc. Foreword. Segale, *At the End* xiii–xxii.

Smith, Denis Mack. *Mazzini.* New Haven: Yale UP, 1994. Print.

Smith, Lawrence R. *The New Italian Poetry, 1945 to the Present: A Bilingual Anthology.* Berkeley: U of California P, 1981. Print.

Smith, Sidonie, and Julia Watson. "Situating Subjectivity in Women's Autobiographical Practices." Introduction. Smith and Watson, *Women* 3–57.

———, eds. *Women, Autobiography, Theory: A Reader.* Madison: U of Wisconsin P, 1998. Print.

Soldati, Mario. *America, primo amore.* Palermo: Sellerio, 2003. Print.

Soliday, Mary. "Translating Self and Difference through Literacy Narratives." *College English* 56.5 (1994): 511–26. Print.

Sollors, Werner, ed. *The Invention of Ethnicity.* New York: Oxford UP, 1989. Print.

———, ed. *Multilingual America: Transnationalism, Ethnicity, and the Languages of American Literature.* New York: New York UP, 1998. Print.

The Sopranos: The Book. New York: Time, 2007. Print.

Sorrentino, Gilbert. "Gilbert Sorrentino: A Writer's Writer Returns." Interview by Joseph Barbato. *Publishers Weekly* 27 May 2002: 30. Print.

———. *Little Casino.* Minneapolis: Coffee House, 2002. Print.

———. *New and Selected Poems: 1958–1998.* Los Angeles: Green Integer, 2004. Print.

———. *Selected Poems, 1958–1980.* Santa Barbara: Black Sparrow, 1981. Print.

Southern, Eileen. *Readings in Black American Music.* 1971. New York: Norton, 1983. Print.

Soyer, Daniel, ed. *A Coat of Many Colors: Immigration, Globalization, and Reform in New York City's Garment Industry.* New York: Fordham UP, 2005. Print.

Spickard, Paul. *Almost All Aliens: Immigration, Race, and Colonialism in American History and Identity.* New York: Routledge, 2007. Print.

Stefanile, Felix. *The Country of Absence: Poems and an Essay.* West Lafayette: Bordighera, 1999. Print.

———. *The Dance at St. Gabriel's.* Brownsville: Story Line, 1995. Print.

Stein, Leon. *The Triangle Fire.* 1962. Introd. William Greider. Ithaca: Cornell UP, 2001. Print.

Steinbeck, John. *The Grapes of Wrath.* Viking, 1939. Print.

Steiner, George. "De Mortuis." Rev. of *The Hour of Our Death,* by Philippe Ariès. *New Yorker* 22 June 1981: 112–14. Print.

Stella, Gian Antonio. Introduction. Guglielmo and Salerno, *Gli italiani* 11–15.

———. *L'orda: Quando gli albanesi eravamo noi.* Milan: Rizzoli, 2002. Print.

Stoeltje, Beverly J., and Nancy Worthington. "Multiculturalism and Oral Traditions." Foley 423–35.

Una Storia Segreta: When Italian-Americans Were "Enemy Aliens." Amer. Italian Hist. Assn., 2003. Web. 27 Mar. 2009.

Stroffolino, Chris. *Stealer's Wheel.* West Stockbridge: Hard, 1999. Print.

Szczepanski, Karen. "The Scalding Pot: Stereotyping of Italian American Males in Hollywood Films." *Italian Americana* 5.2 (1979): 196–205. Print.

Talese, Gay. *Unto the Sons.* New York: Knopf, 1992. Print.

———. "Where Are the Italian-American Novelists?" *New York Times Book Review* 14 Mar. 1993: 1+. Print.

Tamburri, Anthony Julian. "Beyond 'Pizza' and 'Nonna'! or, What's Bad about Italian/American Criticism." *MELUS* 28.3 (2003): 149–74. Print.

———. "Italian/American Briefs: Re-visiting the Short Subject." *Revisiting Italian Americana: Specificities and Generalities on Literature and Film.* New York: Bordighera, forthcoming.

———. *Italian/American Short Films and Videos: A Semiotic Reading.* West Lafayette: Purdue UP, 2002. Print.

———. "Poetry." LaGumina, Cavaioli, Primeggia, and Varacalli 475–80.

———. *A Semiotic of Ethnicity: In (Re)Cognition of the Italian/American Writer.* Albany: State U of New York P, 1998. Print.

———. "Spectacular Imagery in Italian/American Short Films: Race as Stage-Display Pageantry." Camaiti Hostert and Tamburri, *Screening* 321–38.

———. *To Hyphenate or Not to Hyphenate? The Italian/American Writer as Other American.* Montreal: Guernica, 1991. Print.

Tamburri, Anthony Julian, Paolo A. Giordano, and Fred L. Gardaphé, eds. *From the Margin: Writings in Italian Americana.* 1991. 2nd ed. West Lafayette: Purdue UP, 2000. Print.

Tassi, Jane. *And Songsonglsonglessness / E nonuncantononuncantouncanto.* Trans. Ned Condini. Lafayette: Bordighera, 2004. Print.

Taviano, Stefania. "*Over There*: Rediscovering Sicily through Theater." *Borderlines: Migrazioni e identità nel Novecento.* Ed. Jennifer Burns and Loredana Polezzi. Isernia: Iannone, 2003. 261–64. Print.

Taylor, David A., and John Alexander Williams, eds. *Old Ties, New Attachments: Italian-American Folklife in the West.* Washington: Lib. of Cong., 1992. Print.

Tedesco, Cynthia. *Letters Found After.* Santa Fe: Sesquin, 1997. Print.

"The Test of Literacy." *New York Times* 30 Jan. 1907, late ed., sec. 8: 3. Print.

Timpanelli, Gioia. *De anima sicula.* Palermo: Flaccovio, 2004. Print. Trans. of *Sometimes the Soul: Two Novellas of Sicily.*

Tirabassi, Maddalena. *Itinera: Paradigmi delle migrazioni italiane.* Turin: Fondazione Giovanni Agnelli, 2005. Print.

————. Preface. Tirabassi, *Ripensare* 14–15.

————, ed. *Ripensare la patria grande. Gli scritti di Amy Allemande Bernardy sulle migrazioni italiane (1900–1930)*. Isernia: Iannone, 2005. Print.

Tocci, Carrie Anne. "Counting on Rising." *First Intensity* 17 (2002): 18. Print.

————. "Dividing Dorothy by Days." *Barrow Street* 1.1 (1998): 85–87. Print.

————. "Farewell to May." *First Intensity* 17 (2002): 18. Print.

————. "May's Anatomy." *First Intensity* 17 (2002): 180–85. Print.

Tomasi, Mari. *Like Lesser Gods*. 1949. Shelburne: New England, 1988. Print.

Tonelli, Bill, ed. *The Italian American Reader: A Collection of Outstanding Fiction, Memoirs, Journalism, Essays, and Poetry*. New York: Morrow, 2003. Print.

Torgovnick, Marianna De Marco. *Crossing Ocean Parkway: Readings by an Italian American Daughter*. Chicago: U of Chicago P, 1994. Print.

————. "On Being White, Female, and Born in Bensonhurst." Torgovnick, *Crossing* 3–18.

Torrielli, Andrew. *Italian Opinion on America as Revealed by Italian Travelers, 1850–1900*. Cambridge: Harvard UP, 1964. Print.

Treleven, Dale. "Caught on Tape: Voices from UCLA's Past." Interview by Amy Ko. *UCLA Today* 9 Nov. 1999. Web. 30 Apr. 2008.

The Triangle Fire: A Documentary Film. Triangle Project, 2007. Web. 4 Mar. 2009.

Tropea, Joseph L., James Edward Miller, and Cheryl Beattie-Repetti, eds. *Support and Struggle: Italians and Italian Americans in a Comparative Perspective*. Staten Island: Amer. Italian Hist. Assn., 1986. Print.

Truesdell, Barbara. "Oral History Techniques: How to Organize and Conduct Oral History Interviews." *Center for the Study of History and Memory*. Indiana U, n.d. Web. 30 Apr. 2008.

Turco, Lewis. *A Book of Fears / Un libro di fobbie*. West Lafayette: Bordighera, 1999. Print.

————. *Fearful Pleasures: The Complete Poems, 1959–2007*. Scottsdale: Cloudbank, 2007. Print.

————. *The Shifting Web: New and Selected Poems*. Fayetteville: U of Arkansas P, 1989. Print.

Tusiani, Joseph. *Ethnicity: Selected Poems*. Ed. Paolo Giordano. West Lafayette: Bordighera, 2000. Print.

————, trans. *Jerusalem Delivered, Torquato Tasso*. Rutherford: Fairleigh Dickinson UP, 1970. Print.

————. *Rind and All: Fifty Poems*. New York: Monastine, 1962. Print.

Twain, Mark. *The Innocents Abroad; or, The New Pilgrims' Progress*. New York: Oxford UP, 1996. Print.

2005–2007 American Community Survey 3-Year Estimates. U.S. Census Bureau. US Census Bureau, 2008. Web. 14 July 2009.

United States Immigration Commission. *Reports of the Immigration Commission*. Vol. 7. Washington: GPO, 1911. Print. 42 vols.

"Unread Immigrants." *New York Times* 7 Dec. 1910, late ed., sec. 12: 4. Print.

Untermayer, Louis, ed. *Modern American Poetry: An Introduction*. New York: Harcourt, 1919. Print.

Valesio, Paolo. "The Writer between Two Worlds: The Italian Writer in the United States." *Differentia* 3-4 (1989): 259–76. Print.

Vangelisti, Paul. *Days Shadows Pass.* Los Angeles: Green Integer, 2007. Print.

———. *War Variations: Amelia Rosselli.* Los Angeles: Green Integer, 2005. Print.

Vansina, Jan. *Oral Tradition as History.* Madison: U of Wisconsin P, 1985. Print.

Vecchio, Diane C. *Merchants, Midwives, Laboring Women: Italian Migrants in Urban America.* Urbana: U of Illinois P, 2006. Print.

Vecoli, Rudolph J. "The Making and Un-making of an Italian Working Class in the United States, 1915–1945." Cannistraro and Meyer 51–76.

Ventura, Luigi D. *Peppino.* New York: Jenkins, 1885. Print.

Verdicchio, Pasquale. *Bound by Distance: Rethinking Nationalism through the Italian Diaspora.* Madison: Fairleigh Dickinson UP, 1997. Print.

———. Introduction. Gramsci 7–26.

Verga, Angelo. *A Hurricane Is.* New York: Jane Street, 2002. Print.

Verga, Giovanni. *The House by the Medlar Tree.* Trans. Maria A. Craig. Whitefish: Kessinger, 2005. Print.

———. *I malavoglia.* Ed. Piero Nardi. Milan: Mondadori, 1964. Print.

Vettori, Alessandro. "L'America . . . questa musa ispiratrice: L'esperienza di Emanuel Carnevali, poeta espatriato." Carrera and Vettori 391–97.

Violi, Paul. *Breakers: Selected Poems.* Saint Paul: Coffee House, 2000. Print.

Viscusi, Robert. *Astoria.* 1998. Toronto: Guernica, 2004. Print.

———. "Breaking the Silence: Strategic Imperatives for Italian American Culture." *VIA: Voices in Italian Americana* 1.1 (1990): 1–13. Print.

———. *Buried Caesars and Other Secrets of Italian American Writing.* Albany: State U of New York P, 2006. Print.

———. "*Il Caso della Casa*: Stories of Houses in Italian America." Juliani 1–9.

———. "*De Vulgari Eloquentia*: An Approach to the Language of Italian American Fiction." *Yale Italian Studies* 1.3 (1981): 21–38. Print.

———. *An Oration upon the Most Recent Death of Christopher Columbus.* West Lafayette: Bordighera, 1993. Print.

———. "The Semiology of Semen: Questioning the Father." Caporale 185–96.

Von Drehle, Dave. *Triangle: The Fire That Changed America.* New York: Atlantic Monthly, 2003. Print.

Waldo, Octavia. *A Cup of the Sun.* New York: Harcourt, 1961. Print.

Walker, Nancy. "Stepping Out: Writing Women's Travel." *Annali d'Italianistica* 14 (1996): 145–51. Print.

Watson, Patrick. *Fasanella's City.* New York: Knopf, 1973. Print.

Wesley, Marilyn. *Secret Journeys: The Trope of Women's Travel in American Literature.* Albany: State U of New York P, 1999. Print.

Williams, Miller, ed. *A Roman Collection.* Columbia: U of Missouri P, 1980. Print.

Williams, Raymond. *The Long Revolution.* New York: Columbia UP, 1961. Print.

———. *Marxism and Literature.* Oxford: Oxford UP, 1977. Print.

Woll, Allen L., and Randell M. Miller. "The Italians." *Ethnic and Racial Images in American Film and Television: Historical Essays and Bibliography.* New York: Garland, 1987. 275–307. Print.

Woolf, Virginia. *A Room of One's Own.* San Diego: Harcourt, 1989. Print.

Wycoff, Joyce. *Mindmapping.* New York: Berkley, 1991. Print.

Yacowar, Maurice. *The Sopranos on the Couch: Analyzing Television's Greatest Series.* New York: Continuum, 2003. Print.

Yans-McLaughlin, Virginia. *Family and Community: Italian Immigrants in Buffalo, 1880–1930.* Ithaca: Cornell UP, 1977. Print.

Yung, Judy. "The Social Awakening of Chinese American Women as Reported in *Chung Sai yat Po,* 1900–1911." *Unequal Sisters.* Ed. Ellen Carol DuBois and Vicki Ruiz. New York: Routledge, 1990. 195–207. Print.

Zandy, Janet. "Fire Poetry on the Triangle Shirtwaist Company Fire of March 25, 1911." *College Literature* 24.3 (1997): 33–54. Print.

———. Introduction. *Calling Home: Working-Class Women's Writings: An Anthology.* Ed. Zandy. New Brunswick: Rutgers UP, 1990. 1–13. Print.

Film and Television

Aladdin. Dir. Ron Clements. Disney, 1992. Film.

"All the Way." *Happy Days: The Complete First Season.* Created by Gary Marshall. Perf. Henry Winkler and Ron Howard. ABC. 15 Jan. 1974. Paramount, 17 Aug. 2004. DVD.

Among Women. Dir. Renata Gangemi. Third World Newsreel, 1996. Film.

At the Altar. Dir. D. W. Griffith. American Mutoscope and Biograph, 1909. Film.

The Avenging Conscience; or, "Thou Shalt Not Kill." Dir. D. W. Griffith. Majestic, 1914. Film.

The Baggage. Dir. and prod. Susan Caperna Lloyd. 2001. Film.

Baretta. Perf. Robert Blake. Huggins–Public Arts. 1975–78. Television.

Beauty and the Beast. Dir. Gary Trousdale Kirk Wise. Disney, 1991. Film.

Un bellissimo ricordo / A Beautiful Memory: A Mother and Her Sons against the Mafia. Dir. and prod. Anthony Fragola. 2008. Film.

Big. Dir. Penny Marshall. Gracie, 1988. Film.

The Bigamist. Dir. Ida Lupino. Filmmakers, 1953. Film.

Big Night. Dir. Stanley Tucci and Campbell Scott. Rysher, 1996. Film.

The Blinking Madonna. Dir., writ., and prod. Beth Harrington. New Video Documentaries, 1995. Film.

Bonino. Perf. Ezio Pinza. NBC. 1953. Television.

A Bronx Tale. Dir. Robert De Niro. Price, 1993. Film.

The Bullwinkle Show. Dir. Gerald Baldwin and Frank Braxton. Gamma. 1961–73. Television.

Carrie. Dir. Brian De Palma. Redbank, 1976. Film.

Celtic Pride. Dir. Tom DeCerchio. Caravan, 1996. Film.

Che bella famiglia. Dir. Diane Frederick. Diane Frederick, 1993. Film.

Christ in Concrete. Dir. Edward Dmytryk. Eagle-Lion; General Film Distributors; Plantagenet, 1949. Image Entertainment, 2003. DVD.

"Christopher." *The Sopranos.* Dir. Timothy Van Patten. Writ. David Chase and Michael Imperioli. HBO. 29 Sept. 2002. Television. Season 4, episode 3.

Cobra. Dir. Joseph Henabery. Ritz-Carlton, 1925. Film.

Columbo. Perf. Peter Falk. Universal. 1971–990. Television.

"Commendatori." *The Sopranos.* Dir. Timothy Van Patten. Writ. David Chase. HBO. 6 Feb. 2000. Television. Season 2, episode 4.

I compagni [*The Organizer*]. Dir. Mario Monicelli. Avalia Film, 1963. Film.

The Continental. Perf. Renzo Cesana. CBS. 1952–53. Television.

The Conversation. Dir. Francis Ford Coppola. American Zoetrope, 1974. Film.

Daytrippers. Dir. Greg Mottola. Alliance Communications, 1996. Film.

The Dean Martin Show. Perf. Dean Martin. Garrison. 1965–74. Television.

The Deer Hunter. Dir. Michael Cimino. EMI, 1978. Film.

Election. Dir. Alexander Payne. Paramount, 1999. Film.

"Eloise." *The Sopranos.* Dir. David Chase. Perf. James Gandolfini, Tony Sirico, Steve Van Zandt, and Michael Imperioli. HBO Home Video, 2003. DVD. Season 4, episode 12.

The Fallen Sparrow. Dir. Richard Wallace. Perf. William Edmunds. RKO, 1943. Film.

The Family Caring. Dir. Michael Angelo DiLauro. MichaelAngelo, 1986. Film.

Federal Hill. Dir. Michael Corrente. Eagle Beach, 1994. Film.

The Florentine. Dir. Nick Stagliano. American Zoetrope, 1999. Film.

"Fonzie Loves Pinky (1–2)." *Happy Days.* Created by Gary Marshall. ABC. 21 Sept. 1976. TV Land, June 2003. Videocassette recording. Episodes 64–65.

"Fonzie Loves Pinky (3)." *Happy Days.* Created by Gary Marshall. ABC. 28 Sept. 1976. TV Land, June 2003. Videocassette recording. Episode 66.

"Forty-Six Long." *The Sopranos.* Dir. Daniel Attias. Writ. David Chase. HBO. 17 Jan. 1999. Television. Season 1, episode 2.

The Frank Sinatra Show. Perf. Frank Sinatra. CBS. 1950–52; 1957–58; 1959–60. Television.

Fuori/Outside. Dir. Kym Ragusa. Ibla Productions, 1997. Film.

The Gangster Chronicles. Perf. Michael Mouri, Louis Giambalvo, and Richard Castellano. Universal. 1981. Television.

Gardenia, Vincent. Interview by Emelise Aleandri. *Italics: The Italian-American Magazine.* CUNY-TV, New York. Sept. 1989. Television.

Garrison's Gorillas. Perf. Cesare Danova. Selmur. 1967–68. Television.

The Godfather [*Il Padrino*]. Dir. Francis Ford Coppola. Paramount, 1972. Film.

The Godfather: Part III [*Il Padrino: Parte III*]. Dir. Francis Ford Coppola. Paramount, 1990. Film.

The Godfather: Part II [*Il Padrino: Parte II*]. Dir. Francis Ford Coppola. Paramount, 1974. Film.

Golden Boy. Dir. Rouben Mamoulian. Columbia, 1939. Film.

The Golden Door. Dir. Emanuele Crialese. Rai Cinemafiction, 2006. Film.

Goodfellas. Dir. Martin Scorsese. Warner Brothers, 1990. Film.

Happy Days. Perf. Henry Winkler. ABC. 1974–84. Television.

Heaven Touches Brooklyn in July. Dir. Tony DeNonno. DeNonno, 2004. Film.

Hidden Island/L'isola sommersa. Dir. Mariarosy Calleri. Marden, 1998. Film.

Hill Street Blues. Perf. Daniel Travanti and Veronica Hamel. MTM. 1981–87. Television.

A Hole in the Head. Dir. Frank Capra. Sincap Productions, 1959. Film.

Household Saints. Dir. Nancy Savoca. Columbia TriStar, 1993. Film.

"I Dream of Jeannie Cusamano." *The Sopranos.* Dir. David Chase. Perf. James Gandolfini, Tony Sirico, Steve Van Zandt, and Michael Imperioli. HBO Home Video, 2000. DVD. Season 1, episode 13.

The Italian. Dir. Thomas Ince and Reginald Baker. Perf. George Beban. Paramount, 1915. Film.

Italianamerican. Dir. Martin Scorsese. Natl. Communications Foundation, 1974. Film.

Italian American Presence(s). Dir. Luisa Pretolani. Pahni, 1996. Film.

It Happened in Brooklyn. Dir. Richard Whorf. Perf. Jimmy Durante. MGM, 1947. Film.

"It's My Life." Dir. David La Chapelle. Perf. No Doubt. Interscope, 2003. Music video.

The Jimmy Durante Show. Perf. Jimmy Durante. NBC. 1954–57. Television.

Joe and Sons. Perf. Richard Castellano. CBS. 1975–76. Television.

Kiss of Death. Dir. Henry Hathaway. Twentieth Century Fox, 1947. Film.

Laverne and Shirley. Perf. Penny Marshall. Miller-Milkis. 1976–83. Television.

A League of Their Own. Dir. Penny Marshall. Columbia, 1992. Film.

Lena's Spaghetti. Dir. Joseph Greco. Florida State U, 1994. Film.

Life with Luigi. Perf. Alan Reed. CBS. 1952–53. Television.

Little Caesar. Dir. Mervyn LeRoy. Perf. Edward G. Robinson. First Natl., 1930. Film.

Little Kings. Dir. Marylou Tibaldo-Bongiorno. Bongiorno, 2003. Film.

Love with the Proper Stranger. Dir. Robert Mulligan. Pakula-Mulligan, 1963. Film.

Marty. Dir. Delbert Mann. Hill-Hecht-Lancaster, 1955. Film.

Mean Streets. Dir. Martin Scorsese. Taplin-Perry-Scorsese, 1973. Film.

Midnight Cowboy [Un uomo da marciapiede]. Dir. John Schlesinger. MGM/UA, 1969. Film.

Moonstruck. Dir. Norman Jewison. MGM, 1987. Film.

The Mothers-in-Law. Perf. Kaye Ballard. Arnaz. 1967–69. Television.

Mother-Tongue: Italian American Sons and Mothers. Dir. Marylou Tibaldo-Bongiorno. Bongiorno, 1999. Film.

Mr. Deeds Goes to Town. Dir. Frank Capra. Columbia, 1936. Film.

My Fair Lady. Dir. George Cukor. Warner Bros., 1964. Film.

My Sacred Island. Dir. Gia Marie Amella. Insekt Multimedia, 2000. Film.

The Nanny. Writ. Peter Marc Jacobson and Fran Drescher. CBS. 1993–99. Television.

Not Wanted. Dir. Ida Lupino. Emerald, 1949. Film.

Nunzio's Second Cousin. Dir. Rachel Amodeo. Crossroad, 1994. Film.

One Day at a Time. Perf. Bonnie Franklin. Allwhit. 1975–84. Television.

The Origin of Gangsta. Def Jam Presents. Universal, 2003. DVD.

Outrage. Dir. Ida Lupino. Filmmakers, 1950. Film.

Paradise Alley. Dir. Sylvester Stallone. Image Ten, 1978. Film.
Part of Your Loving. Dir. Tony DeNonno. DeNonno, 1977. Film.
Passing. Dir. Kym Ragusa. 1996. Film.
"Paulie Walnuts." *The Sopranos. HBO.* HBO, 2009. Web. 20 Feb. 2009.
The Perry Como Show. Perf. Perry Como. Roncom. 1948–63. Television.
Petrocelli. Perf. Barry Newman. Miller-Milkis. 1974–76. Television.
"Pine Barrens." *The Sopranos.* Dir. David Chase. HBO Home Video, 2002. DVD. Season 3, episode 11.
Pinocchio. Dir. Hamilton Luske and Ben Sharpsteen. Disney, 1940. Film.
Prisoners among Us: Italian-American Identity and World War II. Dir. Michael Angelo DiLauro. MichaelAngelo, 2003. Film.
Processione: A Sicilian Easter. Dir. and prod. Susan Caperna Lloyd. 1989. Film.
The Purple Heart. Dir. Lewis Milestone. Perf. Richard Conte. Twentieth Century-Fox, 1944. Film.
Raging Bull. Dir. Martin Scorsese. Chartoff-Winkler, 1980. Film.
Riding in Cars with Boys. Dir. Penny Marshall. Gracie Films, 2001. Film.
Rocky. Dir. John G. Avildsen. Chartoff-Winkler, 1976. Film.
Rocky II. Dir. Sylvester Stallone. Chartoff-Winkler, 1979. Film.
Rocky III. Dir. Sylvester Stallone. Chartoff-Winkler, 1983. Film.
Rocky IV. Dir. Sylvester Stallone. Chartoff-Winkler, 1985. Film.
Rocky V. Dir. John G. Avildsen. Chartoff-Winkler, 1990. Film.
The Rose Tattoo. Dir. Daniel Mann. Paramount, 1955. Film.
Sacco and Vanzetti. Dir. Giuliano Montaldo. Jolly Film–Unidis, 1971. Ripley's Home Video, 2002. DVD.
Saturday Night Fever. Dir. John Badham. Paramount, 1977. Film.
Scarface. Dir. Brian De Palma. Perf. Al Pacino. Universal, 1983. Film.
Scarface. Dir. Howard Hawks. Perf. Paul Muni and Ann Dvorak. Universal, 1932. Film.
Serving with Dignity. Dir. Gia Marie Amella. Femmina, 1996. Film.
The Sheik. Dir. George Melford. Perf. Rudolph Valentino. Paramount, 1921. Film.
Simply Slow Food. Dir. Gia Marie Amella. Insekt Multimedia, 2005. Film.
Somebody Up There Likes Me. Dir. Robert Wise. MGM, 1956. Film.
The Sonny and Cher Comedy Hour. Perf. Sonny Bono and Cher. Blye-Beard. 1971–74. Television.
Son of the Sheik. Dir. George Fitzmaurice. Perf. Rudolph Valentino. Feature, 1926. Film.
The Sopranos. Exec. prod. David Chase. HBO with Brillstein Grey Entertainment. 1999–2007. Television.
Talking Back. Dir. Renata Gangemi. Third World Newsreel, 1992. Film.
Tarantella. Dir. Helen De Michiel. Independent Television, 1995. Film.
Taxi Driver. Dir. Martin Scorsese. Columbia Pictures, 1976. Film.
Teatro: The Legacy of Italian-American Theatre. Dir. and prod. Emelise Aleandri. 1995. Videocassette.
Things I Take. Dir. Luisa Pretolani. Pahni, 1997. Film.
Toma. Perf. Tony Musante. Huggins–Public Arts. 1973–74. Television.

Touch. Dir. Dina Ciraulo. San Francisco State U, 1995. Film.

True Love. Dir. Nancy Savoca. Forward, 1989. Film.

Truth or Dare. Dir. Alex Keshishian. Perf. Madonna. Live Home Video, 1991. Videocassette recording.

The 24th Day. Dir. Tony Piccirillo. Nazz, 2004. Film.

Uncovering. Dir. Mariarosy Calleri. Marden, 1996. Film.

The Untouchables. Desilu. 1959–63. Television.

Vendetta. Dir. Nicholas Meyer. HBO, 1999. Television.

"Wanksta." Dir. Jessy Terrero. Perf. 50 Cent. BET, 2002. Music video.

What about Me. Dir. Rachel Amodeo. Eclectic, 1993. Film.

"A Woman Not under the Influence." *Happy Days.* Created by Gary Marshall. ABC. 28 Sept. 1982. TV Land, June 2003. Videocassette recording.

Year of the Dragon. Dir. Michael Cimino. De Laurentiis, 1985. Film.

Index

Modern Language Association of America
Options for Teaching

Teaching Italian American Literature, Film, and Popular Culture. Ed. Edvige Giunta and Kathleen Zamboni McCormick. 2010.

Teaching the Graphic Novel. Ed. Stephen E. Tabachnick. 2009.

Teaching Literature and Language Online. Ed. Ian Lancashire. 2009.

Teaching the African Novel. Ed. Gaurav Desai. 2009.

Teaching World Literature. Ed. David Damrosch. 2009.

Teaching North American Environmental Literature. Ed. Laird Christensen, Mark C. Long, and Fred Waage. 2008.

Teaching Life Writing Texts. Ed. Miriam Fuchs and Craig Howes. 2007.

Teaching Nineteenth-Century American Poetry. Ed. Paula Bernat Bennett, Karen L. Kilcup, and Philipp Schweighauser. 2007.

Teaching Representations of the Spanish Civil War. Ed. Noël Valis. 2006.

Teaching the Representation of the Holocaust. Ed. Marianne Hirsch and Irene Kacandes. 2004.

Teaching Tudor and Stuart Women Writers. Ed. Susanne Woods and Margaret P. Hannay. 2000.

Teaching Literature and Medicine. Ed. Anne Hunsaker Hawkins and Marilyn Chandler McEntyre. 1999.

Teaching the Literatures of Early America. Ed. Carla Mulford. 1999.

Teaching Shakespeare through Performance. Ed. Milla C. Riggio. 1999.

Teaching Oral Traditions. Ed. John Miles Foley. 1998.

Teaching Contemporary Theory to Undergraduates. Ed. Dianne F. Sadoff and William E. Cain. 1994.

Teaching Children's Literature: Issues, Pedagogy, Resources. Ed. Glenn Edward Sadler. 1992.

Teaching Literature and Other Arts. Ed. Jean-Pierre Barricelli, Joseph Gibaldi, and Estella Lauter. 1990.

New Methods in College Writing Programs: Theories in Practice. Ed. Paul Connolly and Teresa Vilardi. 1986.

School-College Collaborative Programs in English. Ed. Ron Fortune. 1986.

Teaching Environmental Literature: Materials, Methods, Resources. Ed. Frederick O. Waage. 1985.

Part-Time Academic Employment in the Humanities: A Sourcebook for Just Policy. Ed. Elizabeth M. Wallace. 1984.

Film Study in the Undergraduate Curriculum. Ed. Barry K. Grant. 1983.

The Teaching Apprentice Program in Language and Literature. Ed. Joseph Gibaldi and James V. Mirollo. 1981.

Options for Undergraduate Foreign Language Programs: Four-Year and Two-Year Colleges. Ed. Renate A. Schulz. 1979.

Options for the Teaching of English: Freshman Composition. Ed. Jasper P. Neel. 1978.

Options for the Teaching of English: The Undergraduate Curriculum. Ed. Elizabeth Wooten Cowan. 1975.